14-99

PREMODERN SEXUALITIES

edited by

Louise Fradenburg and Carla Freccero

with the assistance of Kathy Lavezzo

ROUTLEDGE

New York and London

Published in 1996 by

Routledge
29 West 35th Street
New York, NY 10001

Published in Great Britain in 1996 by

Routledge
11 New Fetter Lane
London EC4P 4EE

Printed in the United States of America
Design: Jack Donner

Library of Congress Cataloging-in-Publication Data

Premodern sexualities / edited by Louise Fradenburg and Carla Freccero.
     p.   cm.
  Includes bibliographical reference and index.
  ISBN 0–415–91257–1 (HB)   ISBN 0–415–91258–X (PB)
  1. Sex—History. 2. Sex customs—History. 3. Homosexuality in literature—
  History. 4. Sex in literature—History.
  I. Fradenburg, Louise Olga, 1953– .   II. Freccero, Carla, 1956– .
HQ12.P74 1995
306.7—dc20   95–30227
                                                           CIP

Contents

Preface

Louise Fradenburg and Carla Freccero

Premodern Sexualities addresses the interest in sexuality, sexual practices, identities, and communities that is explored in queer theory and in work on the history of sexuality, particularly that work inspired by the writings of Michel Foucault. Most of this work has focused on the nineteenth century, because Foucault regarded this period as the moment when modern sexual "identities" were decisively organized. But various debates have also been launched that speak to the "time before" modernity, as part of an attempt to construct a richer genealogy for the history of sexuality. In particular, scholars have argued hotly about whether the cultures of premodern Europe emphasized sexual acts rather than identities in their understanding of the body. Prior to the nineteenth century's organization of sexuality into medicalized categories of deviant identity—hysterics, onanists, homosexuals—did sexuality instead take the ethico-juridical form of permitted and prohibited acts? What might such a change, if indeed it occurred, have meant for the ways in which bodies have been disciplined and pleasures enjoyed?

The study of premodern sexualities has taught us that, to comprehend what it means to "have" a sexuality, we need to know how understandings of bodies, pleasures, and desires have changed over time as well as from place to place. The many scholars and thinkers who, in addition to Foucault, have inspired this volume—John Boswell, Judith Butler, Carolyn Dinshaw, Jonathan Dollimore, Jonathan Goldberg, David Halperin, Teresa de Lauretis, Gayle Rubin, Eve Kosofsky Sedgwick, to name just a few—have all tried, from divergent theoretical perspectives, to make sure we do not forget that sex has a history. The chief purpose of this volume is to help us think further about what we mean when we say that sex has a history and that we need to know more about about it.

There are some stark reasons to take a hortatory tone about the importance of remembering the history of sexuality. The cultural treatment of AIDS has been a shattering reminder of the ethical significance of historical knowledge. That the plagues of the later Middle Ages were associated with sodomites and Jews is crucial knowledge for AIDS activists, because it shows that the repetitions of trauma, far from being the signs of something sub- or ahistorical, are part of the changing work of history. Reproductive technologies and their investments in property rights, the meaning of family, and biosocial population management have suggested as well that the sexualities we practice now are part of a history of "discipline and punishment," of "social control," of the ways communities construct people's bodies and touch them in rage or in welcome. We have learned that the meaning and performance of sexuality can and will change. But we have also learned that our sexualities have a past that forms and informs them as they are today.

Rage and welcome barely begin to cover the ways in which our bodies have been touched by the communities that make us. If, as Slavoj Žižek writes, "what really bothers us about the 'other' is the peculiar way it [s/he] organizes its [his/her] enjoyment," it is also true that what motivates this "bother" is precisely the community's own fragile stakes in enjoyment (1990, 54). Scholars and activists have reminded us not only that sex has a history, but also that history has its pleasures. Queer theory, the history of sexuality, and gay and lesbian studies pursue a fraught but ebullient rethinking of the ethics of pleasure. While recent studies in sexuality make clear that we ought to know the past, they also affirm that we want to. It is true, of course, that after Freud—and Foucault—"wanting" will never be the same. But one of the most productive paradoxes of contemporary work in sexuality is that, while it does not take pleasure at face value, it also does not take it for granted. Pleasure can be doubted, scrutinized, politicized, historicized, debated—and enjoyed.

We do not, then, pursue the history of sexuality just because we think we must; we study it because we know that what we must or ought to do is intimately related to what we want to do. And we want history; the joy of finding counterparts in the past, for example, problematic though it may be, is not simply to be dismissed as anachronism. While we do not want to talk naïvely about fore-queers or fore-mothers, any more than we want to talk about forefathers, we also need to recognize how our scruples about doing so might function as disciplinary. After all, similar historical scruples have been hard at work for a long time in driving wedges between popular and academic history, between the histories we "love"—Roman love-slaves, Viking warriors, Joan of Arc—and books like *The Decline and Fall of the Roman Empire* and *Anglo-Saxon England*. History—and not just family history—is an erogenous zone, and knowing this helps us understand sexuality itself a lot better. It might also help us better understand the kinds of ethical structures at stake in historical thinking. For example, the argument that modern desires and perspectives can and must be set aside if we are to read the past properly is itself revealing, for it suggests that historical knowledge is often founded on the renunciation, the *ascesis*, of "self." And to the degree that this renunciation tries to hide its own narcissistic investments, it begs for queer scrutiny.

The essays collected here represent a wide range of queer readings in premodern studies. They draw on several different disciplines, including the history of science and of law; Romance Studies; Spanish, French, English, and comparative literary studies. At stake in their very diversity, however, is a shared commitment to enriching and complicating our assumptions about the ways in which sexuality is historical, and history sexual.

Part One, "The Erotics of Conquest," examines emergent nationalisms in Europe and North Africa and encounters between the "old," European world and the Americas. These essays are linked by their awareness of the power of legend—the vanishing Indian, the black stud, Don Juan, Henry V—in the making and remaking of history. Jonathan Goldberg, José Piedra, María Carrión, and Richard Corum all take up the question of how cultures shape and signify sexuality in the construction of their most charged historical narratives.

Jonathan Goldberg's "The History that Will Be" powerfully argues that the interweaving of past, present, and future is crucial to the memorialization and reproduction of bonds between men. In reading colonialist narratives—such as Thomas Harriot's account of the Roanoke Algonkians—Goldberg reexamines contemporary formulations of kinship, alliance, and the law (by Lévi-Strauss, Derrida, Foucault, Sedgwick, and Butler). He argues that the colonialist fantasy of a power that can transform and extinguish the filiations of native flesh is one that denies the law's vulnerability and incompleteness. This fantasy promises that genocide finishes things off (the indigenous cultures of the Americas and their histories); but "the history that will be," the resurgence of indigenous movements in contemporary politics, suggests that the law can never completely determine bodies and their temporal relationships.

José Piedra, in "In Search of the Black Stud," traces the trajectory of a still-current myth, that of the black man's superior erotic powers, through the translation of empires from Islam to Spain to the New World. In a series of readings of Arabic and Spanish texts, he explores the dialectical relation between colonial conquest and figures of (symbolic) erotic power, showing how the longstanding ideological purchase of the myth of the black stud has been secured precisely through its translatability. María Carrión, in "The Queen's Too Bawdies: *El burlador de Sevilla* and the Teasing of Historicity," reads the mythic sexuality of Don Juan in tandem with his philological tradition. She shows how Don Juan figures the changing historical meanings of honor in early modern Spain, and how his philological tradition has been shaped by its anxious reception of Don Juan's dishonorable performances. Richard Corum's "Henry's Desires" focuses on a nation in the making through a reading of Henry V's performative—and perhaps failed—homosocial self-construction in Shakespeare's *The Life of King Henry the Fifth*. Through an examination of Henry's attempts to construct his own history and reception, Corum also explores the homosocial/sodomitical divide that organizes early modern English masculinities.

If the essays in Part One of this collection study, in Žižek's terms, "the way subjects of a given ethnic community organize their enjoyment through national myths," the essays in Part Two, "Medicine and Law," focus closely on intimate regulations of enjoyment in premodern European culture (1990, 53). Through readings of fourteenth-century English court cases, of medical texts on the secrets of women's bodies and of legal and medical discussions of hermaphroditism, Part Two explores the making of medical and legal knowledges and the roles played by these knowledges in the shaping of communities' intimacies with the bodies of subjects.

David Boyd and Ruth Karras, in "'*Ut cum muliere*': A Male Transvestite Prostitute in Fourteenth-Century London," translate a unique record of a case involving a male transvestite prostitute, John Rykener. Their careful analysis of the language used in the record to define the nature of Rykener's transgression complicates our notion of how "acts" determined premodern sexual criminality. They argue that Rykener's case reveals the definitive importance of gendered categories in late medieval interpretations of sexual practices. In "The Hermaphrodite and the Orders of Nature: Sexual Ambiguity in Early Modern France," Lorraine Daston and Katharine Park examine a shift in early modern French medical and philosophical constructions of hermaphroditism. Through their study of the early modern fortunes of two competing medical traditions—the Hippocratic and the Galenic—they argue that a newly intense fascination with the figure of the hermaphrodite betrays exacerbated cultural anxieties about the uncertain boundaries of sexual difference. Karma Lochrie's "Don't Ask, Don't Tell: Murderous Plots and Medieval Secrets" also emphasizes the importance of gender categories to premodern understandings of sexuality. She argues that late medieval medical writing about the "secrets" of women's bodies constructs the will and capacity to "know" those secrets as masculine, and the incapacity to know them as feminine. The "regime of secrecy" thus produced bears an important resemblance, Lochrie contends, to what Sedgwick describes as the contemporary "epistemology of the closet," and to the regulation of knowledge currently governing gays in the military. Lochrie thus explores how powerfully the figure of (secret) knowledge can work across as well as through specific cultural formations of the body.

Part Three of *Premodern Sexualities*, "Sexuality and Sanctity," addresses perhaps the most prominent arena of discussions of sexuality in premodern times, the religious, and examines it in a new and queerly inflected way. Essays by Simon Gaunt and Kathy Lavezzo examine the copresence of sexuality and sanctity; the identifications and desires at work in the production of charismatic sanctity and stardom; and the importance of sanctity for the formation of the community's enjoyment. By exploring the dialectic between "the sacred" and "the profane," their work complicates any easy distinctions we might be tempted to make between a religious later Middle Ages and a secular Renaissance or modernity; communal pleasure proves to be at stake in the most otherworldly of discourses.

Simon Gaunt's "Straight Minds/'Queer' Wishes in Old French Hagiography: *La Vie de Sainte Euphrosine*" reads the tradition of vernacular hagiography in France, discovering queerness in the tale of a female transvestite saint and the desires "s/he" incites in a community of monks and also, potentially, in readers of the tale. Through his analysis of these desires, Gaunt shows how the ambience of queer eroticism could fuel the power of the saint as a central cultural symbol of personhood and hence as an example for others to follow and admire. Kathy Lavezzo's "Sobs and Sighs Between Women: The

Homoerotics of Compassion in *The Book of Margery Kempe*" finds in Kempe's extravagant performative weeping over the body of Christ a mediated circulation of desire among women, provocatively suggesting that premodern female devotional practices may have had queerish aims. Lavezzo's work also suggests that the late medieval emphasis on lay piety in general, and on female lay piety in particular, may have proceeded partly through the solicitation and management of such desires.

While all of the essays in *Premodern Sexualities* attend closely to questions of textuality and representation, the essays in Part Four, "Rhetoric and Poetics," offer particularly intense scrutiny of the ways in which premodern European cultures eroticized reading and writing. These essays examine how literary language figures desire and subjectivity, and how it disrupts and deploys heteronormativity. They suggest that premodern representations of textual production and reception were inseparable from premodern understandings of generation, reproduction, inheritance; they also examine the complex histories of these very understandings.

Patricia Parker's "Virile Style" studies the history, from Ancient Rome through early modern France and England, of the notion that authors should cultivate a masculine style. Emphasizing rhetorical and scientific texts, Parker teases out the anxieties about masculinity in early modernity's imagining of the relation between gender and "style." She suggests that something queer inhabits the linguistic play between virility and effeminacy that governs the rules of rhetoric, and demonstrates that concerns about gender performativity and the linguistic power to personify have preoccupied discussions of language and rhetoric for a very long time. Elizabeth Pittenger's "Explicit Ink" focuses on Alain de Lille's *De planctu Naturae*—a text which could stand as the epitome of medieval neo-Platonism's apotheosis of the creativity of divine Authorship—and its denunciation of human perversity. But Pittenger's analysis of pedagogical and scribal transmission, both in and of the *De planctu Naturae*, reveals pederastic desires and incitements at work in the discourse of grammar. In thus queering one of the most authoritative medieval discussions of the value of philology, Pittenger's work encourages us to revalue the erotic materiality of our own philological practices.

Bruce Holsinger's "Sodomy and Resurrection: The Homoerotic Subject of the *Divine Comedy*" similarly offers a pathbreaking reading of one of the most privileged literary and philosophical texts of the Middle Ages. The *Divine Comedy* has long been regarded as a superlatively seminal representation of the transcendent generativity of centuries of masculine authorship. Holsinger instead asks us to read the trajectory of the *Divine Comedy* as an inscription of a specifically homoerotic and homoerotically valorized religious subjectivity forged in the pilgrimage from Hell to Paradise. And he argues that premodern sexualities be theorized in terms of subjectivity rather than identity. The question of whether the distinction between sexual acts and identities can be used to divide premodernity from the modern is an issue to which we will return in our Introduction, "Caxton, Foucault, and the Pleasures of History." There we will pursue in greater detail some of the theoretical concerns that urged us to edit a collection foregrounding these meeting places of queer theory and historicism.

This project began as a special issue of *GLQ: A Journal of Lesbian and Gay Studies* 1.4 (1995), entitled *Premodern Sexualities in Europe*. Early versions of the essays by Boyd and Karras, Daston and Park, Goldberg, Gaunt, Lochrie, and of our Introduction originally appeared there. We thank the editors of *GLQ*, Carolyn Dinshaw and David Halperin, for permission to reprint revised versions of these essays. José Piedra's essay previously appeared in *Callaloo* 16.4 (1993) as "The Black Stud's Spanish Birth." We are grateful for permission to republish the essay.

The editors wish to thank the contributors for their careful and thoughtful readings and revisions. We wish to extend special thanks also to Robert Miotke and Dana Blumrosen for their research assistance for the Introduction; to Rachel Borup and Madelyn Detloff, who provided editorial assistance early on; to Carolyn Dinshaw and Jody Greene for their help with the original journal project; and to the editors at Routledge for their encouragement and patience in seeing *Premodern Sexualities* through to completion. Financial support for the project was provided by the Interdisciplinary Humanities Research Center at the University of California at Santa Barbara, the Center for Cultural Studies at the University of California at Santa Cruz, and the University of California, Santa Cruz Committee on Research of the Academic Senate.

Premodern Sexualities could not have been completed without Liddy Detar and the editorial assistance of Kathy Lavezzo, and we thank them here for the many ways they contributed to the realization of this collection.

WORKS CITED

Žižek, Slavoj. 1990. "Eastern Europe's Republics of Gilead." *New Left Review* 183: 50–62.

Introduction

Caxton, Foucault, and the Pleasures of History

Louise Fradenburg and Carla Freccero

In the "Prohemye" ("Proem") to his 1482 edition of the *Policronicon*, a history of Britain, William Caxton, England's first printer, remarks that:

> For certayne [history] ... is a greet beneurte unto a man that can be reformed by other and strange mennes hurtes and scathes/and by the same to knowe/what is requysyte and prouffytable for hys lyf. ... Therefore the counseylls of auncyent & whyte heeryd men in whome olde age hath engendryd wysedom been gretely praysed of yonge men/And yet hystoryes soo moche more excelle them/as the dyuturnyte or length of tyme includeth moo ensamples of thynges & laudable actes than thage of one man may suffyse to see (Caxton 1928, 64–65).

> (For certainly [history] ... is a great blessedness to a man who can be reformed by other and strange men's hurts and injuries, and by the same [injuries] to know what is necessary and beneficial for his life. ... Therefore the counsels of ancient and white-haired men in whom old age has engendered wisdom are greatly praised by young men. And yet histories so much more excel [those counsels], since the long duration and length of time includes more examples of things, and praiseworthy acts, than the age of one man will suffice to see.)

History, for Caxton, is a site of intersection and mutual transformation between suffering ("hurts and injuries") and life, and between the wound that is alterity ("other and strange men's hurts") and "a man" himself. History enables relations of power and knowledge between death and life, "a man" and his others ("strange" because they are of another place or time, or are simply unfamiliar). History is how the living know the dead, how the familiar know the unfamiliar; it is how the dead and the strange instruct the living, how life and death, the knowable and the unknowable, become mutually intelligible. As such it is salvific, providing what Caxton calls "beneurte" ("blessedness"). And history in Caxton's account is salvific partly because it incites men to glory, to sacrifice. Histories cause young men "more valyantly to entre in Ieopardyes of batayles for the defence & tuicion of their countrey and publyke wele" (Caxton 1928, 65 "more valiantly to enter into the jeopardies of battles for the defense and protection of the country and the public weal"). Through the knowledge history makes about life and death, young men will be more likely to risk their lives for the common good. Caxton thus posits and legitimizes the lethal productivity of history: jeopardy redemptively produces the defense of countries and "public weal"; and records of "other and strange men's hurts" teach us, again, how to live. That is, if "we" are good fighting men.

History's production of glory through loss, however, has entailed not only praiseful images of sacrifice, but the definition of practices and identities unfit to serve, or to serve openly, "country and public weal."[1] The production of glorious loss for some kinds of persons and not for others—of "bodies that matter" and those that do not—extends also to individualized and privatized categories of persons, such as the genius or the criminal.[2] The discourses of history continue to produce knowledges of "life"—including knowledge of who or what is most alive and vital, who or what makes the most life for the "country" or is useless or dangerous to the country. The question of how our histories become "beneficial" to us is an urgent one precisely because historical discourse has for so long been central to the cultural uses of life and death that have defined and persecuted—and sometimes defended—"lethal" sexualities and erotic practices. Thus one of the most important questions that students of the history of sexuality are asking themselves is: What does it mean to practice a discipline whose designs on the life and death, pleasure and suffering of the body have, however often effaced or repressed, nonetheless been a central part of its cultural work?

And how has this cultural work proceeded? For Caxton, the salvific project of history works through exemplarity—through the fact that "a man" can be reformed by "other and strange men's hurts and injuries." At the heart of the exemplary power of history is the power of time—"old age"—to engender wisdom in "ancient and white-haired men," whose "counsels" will be "greatly praised by young men." Homosociality appears here as a generative phenomenon, working through time as well as through the living to make networks of power, knowledge, and pleasure. Caxton's work thus suggests that the interweaving of past, present, and future is crucial to the memorialization and reproduction of bonds between men. And this homosocial relationality across time is secured through the power of examples; the discourse of history, and its technologies of speaking, writing and (now) print, are for Caxton organized affectively and ethically through processes of identification. Indeed, these discursive technologies are designed to magnify and exacerbate such processes.

Caxton sees history as a communicative technology whose purpose is to develop the homosocial (and national) bonds made possible by the sacrificial sufferings of masculinity. The first English printer announces his technological project *as* a historiographical project whose purpose is to forge likenesses and relations among men of different generations in order to produce subjects who will sacrifice for their "nation." A masculinist technology of generation (which confers upon history generative powers of life and death) triumphs over material practices of reproduction, or the biosocial production of life. But in pursuing its aims, this technology exposes what is queer about the homosocial, even as it restages the very heteronormative reproductivity of history itself.[3] The historiographic intentionality Caxton describes includes the erotic practices of desire, identification, and reproduction, yet it also tries to efface the risks and plea-sures of mortal embodiment. Can, and should, we name as "premodern" these complex ways of designing as well as repudiating the transient body?

Recent historicisms have been inspired by a diverse range of ideological imperatives. Empiricism and positivism continue to ensure the prestige of the archives and of old and new philologies. Feminist, race, postcolonial, and queer theories remain largely committed to the concept of historical specificity, because it seems to guarantee the primacy of culture in the construction of gender, ethnicity and sexuality. Poststructuralism struggles over the (im)possibility of various *grands récits*, among them Marxist historical narrative.[4] Diverse as such projects may be, many of them share, to borrow Suleri's term (1992, 12), an "alteritism"—a belief in the absoluteness of cultural and/or historical difference—that has, for many students of modernity, come to signify the essence of our contemporaneity. We are modern insofar as we know that we are incommensurably different from our past and from other cultures. A culture that can think its radical difference, eschewing providential, universalist, or evolutionary narra-tives of human time—this is modernity.

But what does this formulation of modernity imply for our understanding of premodern eras? Caxton's historicism may, at first, seem medieval because of the nakedness of its didacticism. For Caxton, history is a discursive means of generating, as well as detecting, a salvific unity of time and place in the form of the "country and public weal"—a version, perhaps, of Homi K. Bhabha's "pedagogical" narration of the nation (1990). But is Caxton's thinking about history and the national good in fact radi-cally distinct from that of modernity? What might we learn about the history of bodies and pleasures from an engagement with his work?

For Caxton, the value of history is actually inseparable from otherness, from the power of alterity to produce knowledge requisite for the fostering of "life." When a man can be reformed by "other and strange men's hurts and injuries," he can learn how to survive (to do what is "requisite" for his life) and how to live well (to do what is "beneficial"). Caxton reminds us that alteritism often proceeds in a dialectical relation to concepts of sameness or universality; for Caxton, countries are generated through the perpetual transformation of and identification with otherness. The production of homosociality cannot take for granted sameness between men; this sameness must be created, and it is created out of men's very strangeness to each other. Caxton's formula-tion thus urges the salience of concepts of alterity and identity—and their intimate interrelation—to the structuring of ideas about history, sexuality, and erotic practices.

The concept of difference—difference of past from present, of one culture from another—has come to have an epistemological privilege in a number of branches of historical and cultural studies today; it is primarily by appealing to this concept that we have assessed the limits and nature of our fragile, relativized knowledges. But how, for example, does difference or specificity, when invoked in the context of postcolonial theory, compare with its use in analyses of heteronormativity? Such analyses continue to foreground the *de*normativizing of difference; the normativity of sexual difference remains explicitly what is in question. Here we might suggest a locus for the mutual interrogation of queer theory and history. To reformulate, in the terms of cultural historicism, the debate about the (hetero)normative "split" between identification and desire (that they are, and must be, mutually exclusive), we might ask: how does the "same"—even, or especially, a constructed, adopted, performed "same"—in the figure of "same-sex" love and in related modes of analysis, align itself with respect to the deep reserve about the construction of sameness operative elsewhere in cultural studies?[5]

If it appears to us that sameness can have oppositional force in some discursive contexts, though not in others—if there are no guarantees about the political effects of producing sexual, cultural, or temporal identities—such a perception may itself mark our modernity, insofar as resistance to the universalization of political and discursive strategies can be understood as modern.[6] Yet again, such pliancies are legible in premodern texts. If Caxton registers the intimacy between homosociality and historical discourse, he also registers the instability of these formations. It is clear that, for Caxton, history is a non-"natural" production of identities and identifications; the modes of discourse that give homosociality its temporal dimension and reach appropriate, and also exceed, heterosexual generation. The historian does not so much retrace the past as magnify our power to see it; history is not pure repetition, because its very pursuit of sameness (in the form of accurate representation) requires a technology of transformation. As such, history is riddled by the paradoxes of identification: by the impossible pleasures and obligations of imitating the past. Caxton again points us to the question of how processes of identification—in which resemblance, however powerfully sought, can never be perfect—are at work in current historicisms.

Of particular importance in this respect is Foucault's disruption of "continuist" historiography—history-writing whose purpose is chiefly to assert the continuity over time of valued historical protagonists like "the French nation" or "democracy." Foucault (1970) argued instead for the possibility of radical discontinuities between epochs or "epistemes." Foucault's accompanying destabilization of "truth"—his contention that truth is always an effect of particular relations of power—means, of course, that historiography can never tell a truth that is not contingent. Foucault's work disturbs the very normativity of historical narrative that Caxton's "Proem" might at first glance seem to exemplify: history is not a record of "reproduction" for Foucault, but of the multiple, often divergent contingencies of power.

One of the assumptions of contemporary historicism might be that "medieval" or "premodern" understandings of history are complicit with archaic sovereignal, universalizing forms of power (monarchies, universal churches, organicist social theories) to a degree that modernity is not (Foucault 1978, 81–89). But, to echo Bruno Latour and (in this volume) Jonathan Goldberg: Have we ever been modern? As we continue to think through the association of sovereignal or universalizing forms of power with the premodern, we might also consider those current and influential histories of modernity and postmodernity that continue to universalize power in juridico-monarchic ways—through, for example, neo-Hegelian notions of "the end of history" or "the new world order." Furthermore, the reception of Foucault, as Sedgwick notes, has too often taken place in an atmosphere of epistemological certitude, and, we would add, historiographical conservatism (Sedgwick 1992, 285). Thus, precisely if we are to honor Foucault's insistence on the unpredictability of political strategies, we should not discount the oppositional potential even of grand narratives and continuist histories.[7]

It is impossible to overemphasize the importance of the concept of historicity to queer theory and other critical enterprises devoted to dismantling the universals, essences and natures that have for centuries been used to define and persecute "others," including those others understood by dominant ideologies to be excessively fond of the pleasures of sameness. The oppositional edge of historicity is at work in this volume; but the historiography of sexuality could, we believe, go further in its project of dislodging and indeed queering the truth-effects of certain historicist practices. Especially in question are those historicist practices that repudiate the roles of fantasy and pleasure in the production of historiography—roles alluded to by Caxton's figure of praiseful young men, in which we might read historiography's own "queer wishes" (see Gaunt in this volume).

Historiographic repudiations of pleasure and fantasy have a long and complex history. The literature of the later Middle Ages and the Renaissance often describes historical process as a conflict between something like Caxton's "public weal" and the partial or particular interests which must be sacrificed in the service of it (Fradenburg forthcoming a). The discourse of masculine friendship has also been structured, at least since Cicero, by this conflict, and has helped to produce the uneasy relations between masculine homosociality and homosexuality that characterize current military culture and, in some accounts, modernity.[8] It can be argued that the ideological function of such sacrificial narratives (recounted for the benefit of the sovereign or the state) is to efface pleasure. Caxton's rhetoric, for example, does not urge close scrutiny of the pleasures taken by young men in their older counsellors, nor of the role such pleasures might play in militant heroism. But, as we have noted, if the queer implications of these pleasures are obscured, they are nonetheless legible.

One way that current historicisms might seem to differ from their predecessors is by their very habit of analyzing the pleasurable and/or political investments in the production of truth-effects; as we have already suggested, the foregrounding of problems of historical understanding might itself serve to distinguish our contemporaneity from its past. Again, however, the fact that the pleasure we take in historical identifications has been put on the table for discussion does not mean that it has ceased to operate. Far from it; and would such a development even be desirable? For it seems that one of the central challenges queer perspectives offer to historicist practice is their insistence that the purpose of recognizing pleasure's role in the production of historical discourse is not necessarily to launch yet another renunciation of such pleasure. We take queer theory to be a pleasure-positive discourse, despite the fact that its own discussions of pleasure and aversion have been at times quite compli- cated and heated; and one of the most important analytical challenges offered today by queer positionalities is their reconsideration of the very stances of epistemological certitude that have played so large a role in the definition and proscription of danger- ous pleasures, indeed of pleasure *as* dangerous.[9] At the same time, while queer theory has sought to undo the proscription of pleasure as such, it also recognizes that plea- sures can be used to endanger, disempower, and manage people. Coarticulations of feminist and queer theories, such as those explored in this collection, have been particularly important in mediating between the ethical imperatives of queer studies and its revaluation of pleasure. In order to further this mediation, we must also understand as fully as possible the role that territorial identifications with particular periods or epochs may be playing in the writing of the history of sexuality and erotic practices.[10]

At least since Joan Kelly doubted that women had a Renaissance, we have had at our disposal the resonant notion that the history of the "premodern" (and thus of the "modern") might, when viewed from the standpoints of the "othered," take on some uncanny shapes. Recent histories of sexuality have vigorously questioned the bound- aries between the premodern and the modern; but some oppositions require continu- ing scrutiny. The contrast between acts and identities sometimes serves to distinguish a corporate medieval subjectivity from a more individuated successor; the contrast between canonists' and theologians' fulminations against sodomy, on the one hand, and secular prosecution on the other is sometimes used to distinguish a religious Middle Ages from the more secular Renaissance. Scholarly arguments that cross such divides—John Boswell's, for example—are sometimes critiqued for offering a "trans- historical" viewpoint and, as a corollary, for being caught up in fantastic identifica- tions with the eroticisms of the past (see Gaunt in this volume; Boswell 1991; Halperin 1991; Padgug 1991).

Desire, however, is at work in alteritist understandings of the past as well as in transhistorical ones, while approaches to history that recognize how the past can interrupt and inform the present have also produced important knowledges. And, in struggling against cultural demonizations of certain kinds of sameness, queer perspec- tives can usefully call into question the historiographical status of concepts of alterity and sameness. One of the richest controversies in queer theory has concerned the question of the dangers and pleasures of identification; whether and how, for example, gay and lesbian performances of gendered roles and images associated with heterosex- uality are transgressive. In returning us to the centrality of questions of identification in political deployments of sexuality, such controversies can speak to the construction of identifications with the past, with earlier communities and sexualities. Might such endeavors constitute the historiographical equivalent of subversive reinscription? One might also think here of the pleasures of historical costume, and of the ebullient roles historical scenes and figures enjoy in erotic practices and fantasies.

Let us be clear: we do not urge a return to transhistoricist nostalgia. We urge instead continuing attention to the role played by desires, residues, and repetitions in the historical construction of sexuality, and in particular to the fantasmatic figure of a modernity symmetrically and absolutely opposed to premodernity. Desire sustains the fantasy of such a borderline, just as much as it urges its crossing. But if we queer the tendency of historical discourse to repudiate the aims of pleasure, does this imperil the power of oppositional history to critique the fantasies of hegemony? If critique becomes simply a matter of warring fantasies, what happens to activist politics? This apparent analytical impasse—that in order to reveal truth-effects as truth-*effects*, the authority of the positions from which such revelations emanate will also have to be in perpetual question—in fact enables an intellectual/political praxis open to contest and accommodation among differing, and mutually transforming, positions of power, pleasure, and knowledge. Such a formulation does not undo the epistemological and political force of oppositional critique, particularly since "fantasies" themselves have historical agency.[11] What seems crucial to a queering of historiography is not the rejection of truth for pleasure—which would only repeat the myth of their opposition—but rather the recognition of their intimacy.

One challenge is thus to recognize and confront Foucault's notion of a "pleasure of analysis," a "pleasure in the truth of pleasure" (Foucault 1978, 71). Another is to recognize and confront the pleasure we take in renouncing pleasure for the stern alterities of history. The opposition between transhistoricist perspectives which seek, in the past, the allure of the mirror image, and historicist perspectives that "accept" the difference of past from present, is itself highly ideological. What has to be asked is whether the observation of similarities or even continuities between past and present inevitably produces an ahistoricist or universalizing effect. Do long histories—Marxist ones, for example, or the analyses of colonialism pursued by Said (1994, 3–61)—mean no history? If long histories were to mean no history, how would we write the history of the way the past works so hard to define its future—in some cases, grimly hard, as in the sedimentation of negative stereotypes? For that matter, how would we write the history of the ways in which the past is *in* us, our identities being perhaps as temporally unstable as they are in other ways?[12] If the practice of queer theory has taught us that neither alterity nor similarity is an inevitable conceptual guarantor of oppositional political force, that the construction of desirous identifications can be potentially destabilizing as well as totalizing, then we must see that positing the power of the past to disrupt and remake the present is not necessarily to adopt a naïve continuism. Is it not indeed possible that alterism at times functions precisely to stabilize the identity of "the modern"?

In part because of its subtle treatment of questions of alterity and identity, queer theory can make an important contribution to the discussion of historiographical concepts like sedimentation (Jameson 1981; Butler 1993), and in general to the notion that, in studying the specificity of a particular "moment," it might, precisely, be more pleasurable *and* ethically resonant with our experience of the instabilities of identity-formation to figure that "moment" as itself fractured, layered, indeed, historical. It seems symptomatic of how alterity is too often now used to stabilize periods or epistemes that the academic reception of Foucault has tended to emphasize the radical difference of one episteme from another and to de-emphasize those aspects of Foucauldian thought engaged with multiple time lines. In contrast, we might point to Foucault's own emphasis, however ambivalent, on the ways in which the "confessional regimes" he traces to early Christian forms of truth-telling and expiation continue to operate in modern institutions of power-knowledge such as medicine, therapy, and education; consider also the popular arenas of personal advertisements and talk shows.

The contributors to this volume all take a fresh look at some of the concepts structuring the recent historiography of sexuality. One question this volume wishes to further with respect to the distinction between acts and identities is, simply, what is the salience of the distinction? Given, again, that identities can at least potentially be as productive of pleasure and oppositional power as they can be disciplinary, and given that identities can be said to be made *by* acts (Dinshaw 1989; Butler 1990, 1993), exactly what differences are at stake when acts, rather than identities, are targeted for cultural attention? Would the demonization of acts, for example, necessarily be less destructive to "persons" if it meant that *all* persons were potentially liable with respect to unspeakable pleasures? Can we be confident that a regime of acts is not more psychoticizing in its effects, *because* of its intermittence and instability, than a regime of persons/identities, particularly when we consider how the tension between these regimes operates in the discourses and deployments of AIDS?[13] Might there, as well, be other ways of theorizing sexuality less dependent on schematic uses of this distinction? We are thinking here, for example, of Jonathan Dollimore's use of the term perversion, which, since at least Augustine's *Confessions,* suggests the category of deviant desire, and thus of internally divided subjectivities as well (Dollimore 1991, also de Lauretis 1994). Our purpose is not to deny the interest of distinctions like that between acts and identities, but rather to keep the distinction in question open, and to foster new thinking about its precise implications and effects.

It seems crucial, as well, that we consider how ongoing constructions of the difference between the "Middle Ages" and the "early modern period" that rely on concepts of creativity and/or reproductive accuracy (print, humanist philology, and so on) benefit from scrutiny from the standpoint of queer studies. It is, after all, in part the promise of a newly technically powerful homosociality that inspires the Renaissance's way of admiring its "self" through communication with the beautiful antique dead.[14] To what extent are current histories of sexuality participating in discourses of "enlightenment"—of which the notion of the Renaissance is itself an instance—that have sought, at various moments, to distinguish a darker, blinded, "other" past from a more clear-sighted and splendid present? What kinds of queer wishes or phobic scaffoldings might be at work in premodern technologies of memorialization like scribal reproduction and humanist editing, and, more recently, in new historicisms and the new philology?

It should be clear from the preceding remarks that we hope this volume of essays will be useful to people working on modern as well as premodern constructions of sexuality and erotic practices, and not only because we believe that modernity and premodernity are mutually constructed. We hope to show both that contemporary thinking has enormous relevance to the study of past pleasures, and that study of past pleasures can in some cases powerfully address or reframe contemporary practices and problems. Thus we have urged continued exploration of the role of periodization in the study of sexuality for a number of reasons. While we need to continue exploring "sodomy" and its relation to the emergence of the figures of the "homosexual" and the "lesbian," we also need to query these terms and the ideological work they perform in current scholarship (Goldberg 1994). What images of premodern culture(s)—their greater harmoniousness, or ease, or primitiveness, or lack of "development" of administrative styles of discipline—might be at work in narratives about the differences between sodomy and homosexuality? In turn, what fictions about sexuality are at work in our conventional periodizations? Moreover, in part because of the very range of premodern definitions of sodomy, the term's imprecision with respect to gender can too easily efface the erotic practices of women (Traub 1992, 1995). How does the current tension between queer theory and feminism on the mutual implications and exclusions of sexuality and gender function ideologically with respect to the practice of history? (Dinshaw 1994; Butler 1994).

The past may not *be* the present, but it is sometimes *in* the present, haunting, even if only through our uncertain knowledges of it, our hopes of surviving and living well. The questions we are raising about the practice of history may help us understand better the living and dying of twentieth-century bodies and pleasures. And we hope that consideration of the ways in which historicisms are currently questioning sexuality, and sex studies questioning historicism, will work to affirm the pleasures of mortal creatures.

NOTES

1. Several medievalists have recently explored the connections between history and memory, loss and violence. (See Le Goff 1992; Carruthers 1992; Enders 1996; Fradenburg, forthcoming b.) In our discussion of loss and sacrifice, we do not intend to oppose pain to pleasure; rather, we mean to emphasize the ways in which ideological structures, such as those of the (military) state, are able to make use of pleasure, pain, and the intricacy of their relation to one another.

2. (See Fradenburg 1992) on the heroization of suffering in chivalric culture; and Schiesari, on the construction of the male melancholic as artistic and heroic genius (1992, 255–56) for the link between "the melancholic genius" and the "historical sensibility of modern subjectivity." Stephanie Jed analyzes early modern gestures of castigation foundational to historiography and the construction of gender; Freccero's work on early modern masculine subjectivity (1993, 107–123; 1994, 73–84) explores identificatory pleasures and their foreclosure in relations of cultural alterity. See also Butler (1993), and Silverman (1992), on (the occlusion of) pleasure in the discourse of masculine suffering.

3. See Sofia (1984), and Haraway (1991), among others, for feminist analyses of discourses on reproduction. Generative practices that seek to exceed biosocial reproduction can have both oppressive and oppositional effects. Goldberg (1992) has argued that nonbiosocial forms of reproduction—"simulations"—can work to disrupt heteronormative naturalizations of reproduction. As nonbiosocial reproduction, history is already "queer"; but insofar as a history is masculinist or homosocial or

antimaterial (i.e., wishes to be disembodied and without sex) it might be "queer" in a way not necessarily friendly to the goals of feminist politics.

4. On the "new philology," see Nichols (1990), and Middleton (1992); and also Fradenburg, forthcoming b.

5. Our purpose is not to reify the distinction between sameness and alterity, but to suggest their interrelatedness and discursive power. The relationships between sameness and difference within queer theory are extensively nuanced. Queer theory's reception of psychoanalysis, for example, produces alterities from (apparent) samenesses in order to analyze "sameness"—i.e., in formulations of such concepts or issues as the split subject, the parental binary, identification versus desire, etc. (Sue-Ellen Case (1991) discusses "the paradox of identification"). Moreover, the use of concepts of sameness and difference to theorize sexuality has been complicated by analyses of the potential gender asymmetry of categories of sameness deployed, since Freud, to understand sexual desire—for example, by Luce Irigaray's critique of the notion of sexual difference (1985); by de Lauretis's "paradox of sexual (in)difference" (1991); and by subsequent revisionist efforts by Sedgwick (1985, 1990), Dollimore (1991), Butler (1990b, 1993) and de Lauretis herself (1994) to distinguish (male) homosociality from (male) homosexuality, and "sexual difference" from the specificities of female heterosexual and lesbian desire (de Lauretis [1994, 3–9] discusses Irigaray and her own thinking on this subject).

6. See Wendy Brown (1991, 1993). Several analyses of nationalism have stressed the political indeterminacy of identities; the subject is explored extensively in Parker 1992.

7. Jameson's *The Political Unconscious* (1981) remains one of the most challenging attempts to date to rethink Marxist historical narrative; see also Deleuze and Guattari (1987), for a striking combination of historical schemes and "rhizomatic" multiplicities. Dinshaw's "Getting Medieval" (forthcoming) is an excellent analysis of Foucault's *History of Sexuality: Volume I* and its construction of the Middle Ages.

8. Derrida (1988) discusses the history of discourses on masculine friendship, which produce an antagonistic relation between the public good and the private, particular interests of friendship. See Freccero (1994) on Derrida and the erotics of male friendship in Montaigne. For the distinction between homosexuality and homosociality in the modern period see Sedgwick (1985).

9. On pleasure and aversion, see Sedgwick (1992, 288–91); Bersani (1987); and Crimp (1987, 3–16). See also (Dean 1993).

10. Butler (1994) discusses the problem of constituting a "proper object" for a field of study, specifically with regard to current relations between queer or gay/lesbian theory and feminism.

11. The ontological status of "fantasy" as empty illusion—a status challenged by psychoanalytic understandings of fantasy—is a prime suspect in that long history of the privileging of presence and Being analyzed by Derrida. On the reality of fantasy in psychoanalysis, see Laplanche (1976). For a psychoanalytically-informed critique of the fantasmatic production of the real, see Butler (1990a). On contestation and identity politics, see Laclau and Mouffe (1985); Brown (1991); and Sandoval (1991).

12. See Silverman's chapter on "Historical Trauma and Male Subjectivity" (1992); Bhabha (1990) and Kristeva (1993) on history and the uncanny; de Certeau (1988); and Fradenburg, (forthcoming b).

13. In this connection one might ask about the ethical consequences of a too-rigorous insistence on distinctions between acts and identities, as is suggested by the difficulty of current activist efforts to (re)define HIV infection in terms of an acts-based rather than an identity-based discourse.

14. See Jackson (1994), on the sexual politics of the Renaissance reimagining of antiquity.

WORKS CITED

Baudrillard, Jean. 1987. *Forget Foucault.* New York: Semiotext(e).

Bersani, Leo. 1987. "Is the Rectum a Grave?" *October* 43: 197–222.

Bhabha, Homi K. 1990. "DissemiNation: Time, Narrative, and the Margins of the Modern Nation." *Narrating the Nation.* New York: Routledge. 291–322.

Boswell, John. 1980. *Christianity, Social Tolerance, and Homosexuality: Gay People in Western Europe from the Beginning of the Christian Era to the Fourteenth Century.* Chicago: University of Chicago Press.

———. 1991. "Revolutions, Universals, and Sexual Categories," in Duberman *et al., Hidden from History.* 17–36.

Brown, Wendy. 1991. "Feminist Hesitations, Postmodern Exposures." *differences* 3.1: 63–84.

———. 1993. "Wounded Attachments." *Political Theory* 21: 390–410.

Butler, Judith. 1990a. "The Force of Fantasy: Feminism, Mapplethorpe, and Discursive Excess." *differences* 2.2: 105–25.

———. 1990b. *Gender Trouble: Feminism and the Subversion of Identity.* New York: Routledge.

———. 1993. *Bodies That Matter: On the Discursive Limits of "Sex."* New York: Routledge.

———. 1994. "Introduction: Against Proper Objects." *differences* 6.2: 1–26.

Carruthers, Mary. 1992. *The Book of Memory: A Study of Memory in Medieval Culture.* 2nd ed. Cambridge: Cambridge University Press.

Case, Sue-Ellen, ed. 1991. *Performing Feminisms: Feminist Critical Theory and Theatre.* Baltimore: Johns Hopkins University Press.

Caxton, William. 1928. *The Prologues and Epilogues of William Caxton,* ed. W. J. B. Crotch. Early English Text Society. e.s. 176. London: Oxford University Press.

Crimp, Douglas, ed. 1987. *AIDS: Cultural Analysis, Cultural Activism.* Special issue of *October* 43.

de Certeau, Michel. 1988. *The Writing of History,* trans. Tom Conley. New York: Columbia University Press.

de Lauretis, Teresa. 1991. "Sexual Indifference and Lesbian Representation," in Case, *Performing Feminisms.* 17–39.

———. 1994. *The Practice of Love: Lesbian Sexuality and Perverse Desire.* Bloomington: Indiana University Press.

Dean, Tim. 1993. "The Psychoanalysis of AIDS." *October* 63: 83–116.

Deleuze, Gilles, and Felix Guattari. 1987. *A Thousand Plateaus: Capitalism and Schizophrenia,* trans. Brian Massumi. Minneapolis: University of Minnesota Press.

Derrida, Jacques. 1988. "The Politics of Friendship." *The Journal of Philosophy* 85: 632–644.

Dinshaw, Carolyn. 1989. *Chaucer's Sexual Poetics.* Madison, WI: University of Wisconsin Press.

———. 1994. "Queer Speculations." Society for Medieval Feminists, Medieval Institute International Congress on Medieval Studies, Kalamazoo, MI, May 6.

———. Forthcoming. "Getting Medieval: *Pulp Fiction,* Gawain, Foucault" in *The Book and the Body: Material and Textual Corporeality in Medieval Reading,* ed. Dolores Frese and Katherine O'Brien O'Keeffe. University of Notre Dame.

Dollimore, Jonathan. 1991. *Sexual Dissidence: Augustine to Wilde, Freud to Foucault.* Oxford: Clarendon Press.

Duberman, Martin, Martha Vicinus and George Chauncey, eds. 1991. *Hidden from History: Reclaiming the Gay and Lesbian Past.* New York: Penguin.

Enders, Jody. 1996. "Rhetoric, Coercion and the Memory of Violence," in *Criticism and Dissent in the Middle Ages,* ed. Rita Copeland. Cambridge: Cambridge University Press. 24–55.

Foucault, Michel. 1970. *The Order of Things: an Archaeology of the Human Sciences.* New York: Vintage.

———. 1978. *The History of Sexuality, Volume I: An Introduction,* trans. Robert Hurley. New York: Random House.

Fradenburg, Louise. 1992. "'Our owen wo to drynke': Loss, Gender and Chivalry in *Troilus and Criseyde,*" in *Chaucer's* Troilus and Criseyde: *"Subgit to alle Poesye": Essays in Criticism,* ed. R. A. Shoaf. Binghamton, NY: Medieval & Renaissance Texts and Studies. 88–106.

———. Forthcoming a. "Troubled Times: Margaret Tudor and the Historians," in *The Thistle and the Rose: Essays on the Cultural History of Late Medieval and Renaissance Scotland,* ed. Sally Mapstone and Juliette Wood. Edinburgh: Canongate Academic.

———. Forthcoming b. "'So that we may speak of them': Appropriation, Mourning, and the New Philology," in *Medieval Cultural Studies,* ed. D. Vance Smith and Michael Uebel.

Freccero, Carla. 1993. "Practicing Queer Philology with Marguerite de Navarre: Nationalism and the Castigation of Desire," in *Queering the Renaissance,* ed. Jonathan Goldberg. Durham: Duke University Press. 107–23.

———. 1994. "Cannibalism, Homophobia, Women: Montaigne's 'Des Cannibales' and 'De L'amitié,'" in *Women,*

"Race" and Writing in the Early Modern Period, ed. Margo Hendricks and Patricia Parker. London and New York: Routledge. 73–84.

Fukuyama, Francis. 1992. *The End of History and the Last Man.* New York: Free Press.

Goldberg, Jonathan. 1992. "Recalling Totalities: The Mirrored Stages of Arnold Schwarzenegger." *differences* 4.1: 172–204.

———, ed. 1994. *Reclaiming Sodom.* London and New York: Routledge.

Greenblatt, Stephen and Giles Gunn, eds. 1992. *Redrawing the Boundaries: The Transformation of English and American Studies.* New York: Modern Language Association.

Halperin, David M. 1990. *One Hundred Years of Homosexuality and Other Essays on Greek Love.* New York: Routledge.

———. 1991. "Sex Before Sexuality: Pederasty, Politics and Power in Classical Athens," in Duberman *et al., Hidden from History.* 37–53.

Haraway, Donna. 1991. *Simians, Cyborgs, and Women: The Reinvention of Nature.* New York: Routledge.

Irigaray, Luce. 1985. *This Sex Which Is Not One,* trans. Catherine Porter. Ithaca: Cornell University Press.

Jackson, Earl, Jr. 1994. *Strategies of Deviance: Studies in Gay Male Representation.* Bloomington: Indiana University Press.

Jameson, Fredric. 1981. *The Political Unconscious: Narrative as a Socially Symbolic Act.* Ithaca: Cornell University Press.

Jed, Stephanie. 1989. *Chaste Thinking: The Rape of Lucretia and the Birth of Humanism.* Bloomington: Indiana University Press.

Kelly, Joan. 1984. "Did Women Have a Renaissance?" *Women, History, and Theory: The Essays of Joan Kelly.* Chicago: University of Chicago Press. 19–50.

Kristeva, Julia. 1993. *Nations Without Nationalism,* trans. Leon S. Roudiez. New York: Columbia University Press.

Laclau, Ernesto, and Chantal Mouffe. 1985. *Hegemony and Socialist Strategy: Towards a Radical Democratic Politics,* trans. Winston Moore and Paul Cammack. London: Verso.

Laplanche, Jean. 1976. *Life and Death in Psychoanalysis,* trans. Jeffrey Mehlman. Baltimore: Johns Hopkins University Press.

Latour, Bruno. 1993. *We Have Never Been Modern,* trans. Catherine Porter. Cambridge, MA: Harvard University Press.

Le Goff, Jacques. 1992. *History and Memory,* trans. Steven Rendall and Elizabeth Claman. New York: Columbia University Press.

Middleton, Anne. 1992. "Medieval Studies," in Greenblatt and Gunn, *Redrawing the Boundaries.* 12–40.

Nichols, Stephen G. 1990. "Introduction: Philology in a Manuscript Culture." *The New Philology.* Special issue of *Speculum 65:* 1–10.

Padgug, Robert. 1991. "Sexual Matters: Rethinking Sexuality in History," in Duberman *et al., Hidden from History.* 54–64.

Parker, Andrew, *et al.,* eds. 1992. *Nationalisms and Sexualities.* New York: Routledge.

Said, Edward. 1994. *Culture and Imperialism.* New York: Vintage.

Sandoval, Chela. 1991. "U.S. Third World Feminism: The Theory and Method of Oppositional Consciousness in the Postmodern World." *Genders* 10: 1–24.

Schiesari, Juliana. 1992. *The Gendering of Melancholia: Feminism, Psychoanalysis, and the Symbolics of Loss in Renaissance Literature.* Ithaca: Cornell University Press.

Sedgwick, Eve Kosofsky. 1985. *Between Men: English Literature and Male Homosocial Desire.* New York: Columbia University Press.

———. 1990. *Epistemology of the Closet.* Berkeley: University of California Press.

———. 1992. "Gender Criticism," in Greenblatt and Gunn, *Redrawing the Boundaries.* 271–302.

Silverman, Kaja. 1992. *Male Subjectivity at the Margins.* New York: Routledge.

Sofia, Zoe. 1984. "Exterminating Fetuses: Abortion, Disarmament, and the Sexo-Semiotics of Extraterrestrialism." *Diacritics: A Review of Contemporary Criticism* 14: 47–59.

Suleri, Sara. 1992. *The Rhetoric of English India.* Chicago: University of Chicago Press.

Traub, Valerie. 1992, repr. 1994. "The (In)Significance of 'Lesbian' Desire in Early Moden England," in *Queering the Renaissance,* ed. Jonathan Goldberg. Durham: Duke University Press. 62–83.

Part One

THE EROTICS
OF CONQUEST

The History that Will Be

Jonathan Goldberg

I take my title from an episode in the first volume of Eduardo Galeano's brilliant trilogy, *Memory of Fire*.[1] In it, for once in these narratives of the European invasion of the Americas, the Spaniards find themselves surrounded by natives, forced to drink urine since their water supplies have been exhausted, dependent upon the arrows shot into their fortress for firewood. The Araucanian chief approaches, addressing the Spanish captain, telling him to assess his situation and to surrender before his fortress is burned and all inside are killed. The Spaniard refuses:

> "Then you'll die!"
> "So we die," says Bernal, and yells: "But in the long run we'll win the war! There'll be more and more of us!"
> The Indian replies with a chuckle.
> "How? With what women?" he asks.
> "If there are no Spanish ones, we'll have yours," says the captain slowly, savoring the words, and adds: "*And we'll make children on them who'll be your masters!*" (1985, 138).

This episode sets the terms for my concerns in this essay. The Spaniard speaks of the future with absolute certainty. If his words seem authoritative, it is because of the hindsight we bring to them; their truth would seem to be guaranteed by history, by the facts of conquest that have determined that the so-called Americas were founded in the massive destructiveness of European incursion. The Spaniard speaks, that is, with a foresight that accounts of the history of the Western hemisphere would seem to confirm.

The response of the Indian chief, his chuckle, points, however, to an impossibility that he sees in the Spaniard's prediction. Unless the population of Europe were to be transferred to the New World, he implies, the Spaniards must reproduce, and lacking women, that would seem to set a limit upon the Spaniard's prediction that there will be "more and more of us." The ironies that attend this moment are legible through narratives that Galeano mobilizes elsewhere in his book. On the one hand, the New World *will* be populated massively, with the refuse of Europe, castoffs as well as those who inhabit a futurity unavailable in the Old World—soldiers, criminals, missionaries, merchants—even the conquistadors were men on the make with dim prospects in their feudal homeland. Further, the trade in African slaves will forever alter the demography of the Americas. On the other hand, the Spaniard's assurance that the subjugation, rape, and enslavement of native women will produce a population of half-breeds true to their fathers—men who will continue these initial acts of rapine until the entire land is devastated, women who will remain serviceable to their masters—opens itself to another reading. Nothing guarantees, in the long run, that history will confirm the Spaniard's prophecy.[2] Indeed, given the impure origins of a "mestizo America," an America that is characterized by contingent and shifting relations between and among cultures, the future cannot rest securely on the stratified and hier-archized power relations between Europeans and indigenes, between men and women, that the Spaniard assumes to be forever in place.[3]

Galeano's narrative depends upon, even as it undermines, the assurance of the Spanish version of truth and history; it disturbs the implicit analogy between Indians and women, Spaniards and men, the inevitability that heterosexual relations are a means solely of reproducing the values of the father. In short, Galeano locates his ironies in this episode within the assumption that only through sexual reproduction is social reproduction possible; while the Spaniard depends upon this belief, his all-but-defeated status, his sexual rapacity at the point of death, undermine the security of his final taunt. The episode closes, that is, by opening a space for a rejoinder; it implies that there might be something uncontrollable in sexual/social reproduction. This episode resonates with others in *Memory of Fire*, as even the title of the book means to imply, since it suggests that the holocaustal destructiveness of the invasion of the New World also inspires, burns in, memories that prove to be indelible loci of resistance. Therefore the episode also has an irony directed against the biologism voiced by the Indian chief, for cultural transmission and reproduction do not simply take place biologically; claims of descent or racial affiliation can hardly be reduced to determinations of genetic quantification.[4] For Galeano, one site (somewhat idealistically) for these possibilities lies in the scenes of writing and reading in his book, the way, for instance, this episode positions a reader's identification with the Araucanian chief against the Spaniard's deterministic view and self-satisfied assurance. To see that in this moment the history that will be is an open question, not the one foreclosed by the Spaniard and by those who have written as if he spoke with the voice of history, is to become engaged in a scene of revisionary reading made possible not simply by Galeano's text, but by its full imbrication in the multiples of history that enabled him to write in the first place. Any number of voices, now, could find themselves in the open space of implicit rejoinder.

The themes, then, that I wish to pursue here are centered on the relation between the writing of history as prediction and as retrospection. The history that will be is, after all, as much how we recount what happened as how we project a future; the history that will be is, inevitably, a history of the present, that divided site that must look both ways at once. The loci for my speculations in what follows are those suggested by Galeano: relations between colonial narratives and modes of cultural transmission that exceed the assumption that historical reproduction is tied to heteronormativity.

It would be possible to recast the reading of Galeano that I have offered into a more explicit theoretical register. This would involve, for instance, translating "the history that will be" into the Derridean idiom and tense of the future anterior: the history that will have been. That is, to oppose the truth of the Spaniard's vision, the truth assumed in books with titles like *The Conquest of America* (Todorov 1984), I seek to open the historical text to its multiples, to what Derrida describes in *Of Grammatology* (1974–1976) as a root system that remains unrooted, to a play of *différance* that does not mean to ignore the devastations wrought in the New World, but that also seeks to keep open the alternatives that remain, the reserves and resources not entirely effaced in the so-called conquest of America.[5] "A text always has several epochs and reading must resign itself to that fact," Derrida writes (1974–1976, 102). In suggesting that I pursue a Derridean protocol of reading here, I must add several caveats. First, that the historical impact of colonialism is effaced in *Of Grammatology*, particularly in Derrida's treatment of Lévi-Strauss, where colonial violence appears as a merely empirical and entirely contingent local instance of the more universal problematic of the violence of the letter (Goldberg 1990, 3–6, 15–18). Moreover, as I will suggest, when one moves from this central chapter in *Of Grammatology* to Derrida's reading of Rousseau, the syntax of the scandal of writing is located within a frame of unquestioned heteronormativity. This is so, I would argue, because the chapter on Lévi-Strauss provides a colonialist hinge to Derrida's text that permits a certain anthropological stance that remains to be read through the chapters on Rousseau, especially as they are organized by the scandalous equation of writing and masturbation. Whether or not this colonialist trajectory from Lévi-Strauss to Rousseau is essential to the Derridean argument, it is also the case that Derridean protocols of reading can be unhinged from their roots. To locate a blind spot in the Derridean account need not mean to inhabit it in this attempt to mobilize Derridean habits of reading to an argument that may not seem ultimately very Derridean at all.

Derrida's argument with Lévi-Strauss, as is well known, is in large measure methodological. The anthropologist is valued insofar as his work broaches Derrida's own deconstructive project by failing to deliver a term that would effectively divide nature from culture or, to translate these anthropological terms into their Derridean equivalents, that would divide voice from writing. He is critiqued for the failure in rigor that leads Lévi-Strauss to construct his narrative of the relations between European and indigene as an encounter between a corrupt and literate society and an innocent unlettered one. What is endorsed, then, is the foundational move by which Lévi-Strauss installs the incest taboo as at once natural and cultural. How fundamental this paradigm is to the Derridean project is suggested by the epigraph from Rousseau's *Confessions* that stands at the head of the second part of *Grammatology*: "I felt as if I had committed incest." How troubling this endorsement is has been more than demonstrated by feminist and especially lesbian-feminist critiques of Lévi-Strauss. The incest taboo installs the traffic in women as the essential trait of sociocultural institutions, and retrospectively guarantees that foundational moment as also, at the same time, natural. The law of culture is also the law of nature, and it mandates heterosexual relations. The responses to this scenario have sought to unpack the consequences of the incest taboo, and therefore valuably contest the foundational moment in Lévi-Strauss that Derrida embraces. Gayle Rubin (1975) troubles this foundational narrative in "The Traffic in Women," insisting that before the incest taboo that supposedly founds and mandates heterosexuality there must have been an earlier prohibition against same-sex relations, indeed a time before the law that failed to mark gender at all. Monique Wittig's separatist response takes this foundational moment as propounding a gender difference that renders impossible same-sex desire as fitting within this social bond: thus, for her, a lesbian cannot be a woman since "woman" is that which is traded between men (1992, 20). Luce Irigaray's critique even more radically locates woman as an imaginary term in this scenario, not merely barring relations between women, but also making the sociocultural a sphere of entirely male relations, woman being only a ruse and a projection (1985, 170–97). Judith Butler's reading entertains Rubin's scenario of a time before the law only, finally, to insist that the law is a regulatory device that installs compulsory heterosexuality only through its compulsion to repeat: thus every performance of the social bond is necessarily subject to failure since the need for repetition is the sign of incompletion and imperfection (1990, 72–78).[6]

To read Derrida's acceptance of Lévi-Straussian anthropology within these critiques is, of course, to subject his text to a subsequent epoch of reading that exposes how Derrida's position participates in a normativizing view of the sex/gender system. This anthropological inheritance is particularly salient in Derrida's analysis of the Rousseau who felt "as if" he had committed incest.

"As if" because, in the imaginary moment of a nature before culture, there could be no incest, because there would have been no law prohibiting it; because after the foundation of society there would be no incest because it is forbidden ("before the prohibition, it is not incest; forbidden, it cannot become incest except through the recognition of the prohibition" [Derrida 1974–1976, 267]). Butler has remarked on how Lévi-Strauss is so entranced by his narrative of prohibition that he overtly declares that incest has never occurred; Derrida's more oblique statement distances himself from Lévi-Strauss only insofar as he refuses the empirical as a terrain for theoretical operations, that is, because his formulation deals at the level of the law (of the incest taboo) rather than in terms of its operation. Incest can only be an "as if."

What follows from this? In Derrida's account, writing, which retranslates the originary natural/social problematic, is a male activity; the single time that Derrida calls up a scene of a woman writing in Rousseau's text—the scene of the "magic wand" with which the beloved traces her lover's face—it is to put the pen (the penis) in her hand, and then to elide it with the finger of God, the writer. These interpretive moves—while they may well describe the working of gender in Rousseau's text—are not unpacked with an aim of providing a critical distance from the gendered relations they describe. Rather, for Derrida, as for Rousseau, the problem of intersubjective relations must inhabit spheres of male-male relations, because woman is that which is written upon or one whose writing can only be a male projection and simulation. The subjective position of autoaffection is male territory. But further: this means that masturbation must be imagined solely as male masturbation in which a fantasmatic woman—Rousseau conveniently calls her mamma—divides the male subject: between his hand and his penis is this image of self-division.

This not only consigns women to the sphere of the imaginary; it also provides a syntax of a compulsory heteronormativity. Derrida reads the scene of writing in Rousseau as one in which the auto of autoeroticism, autoaffection and, by extension, the locus of subjectivity and consciousness, is split by a hetero whose otherness is marked by gender and by the failure of access to activity and subjectivity except in the instance of a simulated writing: "between auto-eroticism and hetero-eroticism, there is not a frontier but an economic distribution" (Derrida 1974–1976, 155). But that economy is, as in Lévi-Strauss, one that depends upon the traffic in women; the other that is requisite to the self, even as it splits the self, is marked as female. To go back from this to our initial colonial instance: Derrida's scene of writing—as cultural transmission, as foundationally human—depends upon the elisions of nature and culture in the foundational move of Lévi-Straussian anthropology. Heteronormativity assumes a foundational position.

If what remains valuable in the Derridean critique is its potential for troubling any account of origins, what remains disturbing are the reinscriptions I have been outlining here. But these too haunt, as if insuperable, the feminist critiques I summarized before, which nonetheless enable a reading of Derrida's complicities with a foundational plot of heteronormativity. However different the writings of Rubin, Irigaray, Wittig, and Butler are, they all seek to dismantle the force of the supposedly foundational law that installs heterosexual desire and gender division as at one and the same time natural and culturally mandated. Nonetheless, while these critiques dispute the truth and value of the law, and seek in multiple ways to establish terrains for female subjectivity or for nonheterosexual relations, these are imagined as having to take place through the evasion, undermining or dismantling of the law. Moreover, in attempting to theorize massive and undeniable gender inequalities, the critiques run the risk of universalization and dehistoricization.

Butler's work, for instance, most energetically disputes a time before the law, and insists on the performativity of the law, but it nonetheless cannot do without the category of the law. And these problems become all the more acute when the energies of such critiques are lodged within the psychoanalytic paradigm that is the counterpart of the anthropological narrative, since, of course, on the level of the individual, the story Lévi-Strauss tells is called the Oedipus complex, or, in Lacanian terms, the Symbolic and the Law of the Father. To get beyond this impasse of being locked into a narrative that one seeks nonetheless to dismantle, it seems necessary to me (as it does to Butler too) to turn to Foucault.[7] Here I want to recall some arguments from the introductory volume of his *History of Sexuality* (1978), and not least because they permit a valuable lesson in the ways in which both the anthropological thesis and its feminist critiques participate in the history of sexuality as Foucault outlines its formations.

Foucault's complex and compressed genealogical account has many aims: to explain how the modern subject has been formed around the secret of sexuality; to explain how the narrative of repression covers for and nonetheless serves as an incitement to discourses that mark modernity; to explore the institutional sites that characterize modernity and that function within, and as the conveyers of, these incitements. Foucault traces a number of different narratives with different historical reaches, some stretching back through Christian rituals of penance and confession (this is the longest narrative offered), others arising in the seventeenth and later centuries around the discourses of pedagogy and the figure of the masturbating child, the family, eugenics, population control, medicine, and psychiatry. These multiple histories cannot easily be reduced to a singularity. One overarching organization, however, is the shift from social formations dominated by notions of alliance (family and property ties secured through the institution of marriage) to the modern deployment of sexuality—a sphere of management and incitement that knows no limits, and whose focus is less on the hetero couple than on all the deviations from the norm. Alliance is the domain of the law. Stunningly, sexuality is moved from the center upon which juridical apparatuses concentrated (in the regimes that took the ties of alliance as socially foundational) to the workings of power that fasten on and produce bodies and desires—sexual identities, in fact—not reducible to a world secured through reproduction. Foucault writes:

> This power had neither the form of the law, nor the effects of the taboo. On the contrary, it acted by multiplication of singular sexualities. It did not set boundaries for sexuality; it extended the various forms of sexuality, pursuing them according to lines of indefinite penetration. It did not exclude sexuality, but included it in the body as a mode of specification of individuals (1978, 47).

Foucault's account of the modern regimes of sexuality, as I have outlined it, would seem to balk at the foundational scene of a regulatory heteronormativity which deforms the anthropology I have been discussing, much as it would seem to position itself against later feminist accounts that take the law as the insuperable problem to be worked through or evaded. In part, this is certainly the case, and there are striking passages throughout *The History of Sexuality* directed against the explanatory force of the law as well as "recent analyses concerning the relationships of power to sex" (90). The strategy of attempting to imagine desire "before the law," whether by that phrase one means to constitute desire as prior to the law or as inevitably subject to it, is explicitly declared "beside the point." "It is this image," Foucault concludes,

> that we must break free of, that is, of the theoretical privilege of law and sovereignty, if we wish to analyze power within the concrete and historical framework of its operation. We must construct an analytics of power that no longer takes law as a model and a code. (90)

Nonetheless, this argument is only part of the thesis that Foucault argues, and the situation is more complex, not simply to be reduced to an exposure of the poverty of the law. For Foucault does not trace the replacement of alliance with sexuality; rather he insists on their ultimate imbrication by the end of the nineteenth century. The vast epistemic shift that ushers in modernity does not, in this instance, represent an effacement of previous regimes so much as their relocation and redescription. Indeed, it is precisely that redeployment that enables the modern discourse of repression, of the law of desire, and of widespread anthropologies to occur, making possible the homologism between social and individual origins in the incest taboo, the mirroring of anthropology and Freudian and Lacanian psychoanalytic theory, and the installment of a foundational law of compulsory heterosexuality. As Foucault explains it, the notion of the law is one that makes acceptable the workings of modern power, which, rather than flowing from the sovereign down (whether by the sovereign one has in mind the political apparatus or the Law of the Father), operates from everywhere, in every relationship in which there is a perceived power differential (which is to say, in every relationship). This vision of sovereignty is acceptable, Foucault argues, because it appears to allow for a space of evasion (or of acceptance) as a sphere of individual liberty and choice, whether that entails lifting the forces of repression that work upon one's desires, or finding a site of freedom, presumably in private, interpersonal relations, supposedly sheltered from public scrutiny.

In the stunning pages in which he lays out the "domain" of his researches, the family becomes the anchoring point in which alliance and sexuality interpenetrate, as the locus for the incitement and control of sexuality. It is through this crossbreeding—indeed through this retroactive mobilization of the claims of a law that no longer in fact dominates the social, but is, rather the relay point for the vast mechanisms of modern surveillance, those capillary actions of power without limit (the condition, in short, of late capitalism)—that incest is lodged "at the heart of this sexuality" (113), as foundational for the subject and for the social. In discovering the supposedly "universal" law of incest as foundational, the law is resecured, and modern power thereby made acceptable. "If one considers the threshold of all culture to be prohibited incest," Foucault writes,

> then sexuality has been, from the dawn of time, under the sway of law and right. By devoting so much effort to an endless reworking of the transcultural theory of the incest taboo, anthropology has proved worthy of the whole modern deployment of sexuality and the theoretical discourses it generates (110).

So much, implicitly, for Lévi-Strauss; and, in terms of our investigation here, so much for the retroactive working of the modern regimes of sexuality as a transhistorical, foundational truth. In the "endless reworking of the transcultural theory of the incest taboo," the history that will be is cast back as the originary moment for culture and, of course, for the individual. This move bolsters the failing family, and hides the workings of power beneath the register of the sovereign, the father in all his guises.

Foucault's point is not some weak version of constructionism, a mere nominalism, nor the revelation that social construction is simply a cover to be seen through. Rather, this situation is lived, and it has real effects: of sociosexual inequality between genders, of dominations and exclusions along axes of sexual choice and racial difference. Nonetheless, what is crucial to remark, as Foucault does, is that the discourses that have effectively produced the repressive hypothesis, a vision of identity, and a notion of the acceptable limits of power are part of an ideological construct—a lived ideology, to be sure—at odds with (because it denies its relation to) the productive mechanisms of modernity, which, rather than impeding desire, has incited it, productively multiplying it, rather than regulating, cancelling, silencing, and making it disappear. Modern sexuality is not produced solely under the regime of the law of desire, not limited to a compulsory heterosexuality, not centered on the requirements of reproduction. To quote Foucault:

> There is no single, all-encompassing strategy, valid for all of society and uniformly bearing on all the manifestations of sex.... The idea that there have been repeated attempts ... to reduce all of sex to its reproductive function, its heterosexual and adult form, and its matrimonial legitimacy fails to take into account the manifold objectives aimed for, the manifold means employed in the different sexual politics concerned with the two sexes, the different age groups and social classes (103).

Foucault's arguments go some way towards opening the field that Eve Kosofsky Sedgwick's recent work furthers by probing questions about how the multiplicity of nineteenth-century sexualities got reduced to the spuriously symmetrical homo/heterosexual duo; his compressed account suggests some of the apparatuses—psychoanalysis, anthropological and cultural theory—that were involved in the installment of heterosexual reproduction (regulated by the laws of alliance) as the newfound, normative, and profoundly *desexualized* heterosexuality whose other name, as Sedgwick remarks, is History.[8] Moreover, what these disciplines enforced—retroactively—were narratives of origin, projecting late nineteenth-century compulsory heterosexuality onto the beginnings of culture and the "natural" origin of the human subject. Here it seems crucial to make the distinction between gender and sexuality that Rubin (1984) argues for in "Thinking Sex": the traffic in women or the family and its production of gendered difference make use of the biology of reproduction to install gender relations that are always at the same time entailments that concern property and power; they do not legislate sexualities. This point, in fact, calls into question Rubin's earlier effort to theorize a prohibition on homosexual relations as antecedent to the incest taboo, for such a narrative of a time before the law assumes that the disciplinary apparatuses that characterize the modern regimes of sexuality—the supposed mutual exclusivity of homosexuality and heterosexuality—are transhistorical formations, that legislation installing one must proscribe the other. It is only the retroactive pronouncements of the discourse that Rubin seeks to expose that impose this assumption and make it seem logical. This opens, therefore, another path to take, one that can indeed register the force of compulsory heterosexuality on the twentieth-century subject, but that can also—following upon the crucial work of the feminist critics I have cited, or the recent contribution represented by Lee Edelman's *Homographesis* (1993)—further the work of dismantling the hetero/homo binarism, and extend the ongoing constructivist disengagement of the spheres of biological reproduction from essentializing notions of gender and the naturalization of heterosexual relations. Such analyses provide us with a vantage point, moreover, to project back to regimes not organized by the homo/heterosexual divide, and to reread stories of beginnings written under that aegis. To look forward to the history that will be, one must look at and retell the history that has been told.

To return now to my starting point, I want to focus on one piece of the story of the imbrication of colonialism with sexuality, in theory as well as in historical accounts, as it is made available by an episode whose familiarity is assured thanks to its analysis in Stephen Greenblatt's best-known essay (1981; 1985; 1988). The text I want to consider is Thomas Harriot's *New Found Land of Virginia*, and particularly the episode of "invisible bullets" that gives Greenblatt's essay its title. My aim here is to explore the trope of "invisible bullets" as a metaphor for historicity, a future projection. The metaphor is offered in the series of explanations that Harriot records in which the North Carolina Algonkians attempt to understand why, with the arrival of the English, they died in such unprecedented numbers:[9]

> Some therefore were of opinion that wee were not borne of women, and therefore not mortall, but that wee were men of an old generation many yeeres past then risen againe to immortalitie.
>
> Some would likewise seeme to prophesie that there were more of our generation yet to come, to kill theirs and take their places, as some thought the purpose was by that which was already done.
>
> Those that were immediately to come after us they imagined to be in the aire, yet invisible & without bodies, & that they by our intreaty & for the love of us did make the people to die in that sort as they did by shooting invisible bullets into them (Harriot 1972, 29).

Greenblatt finds the metaphor of "invisible bullets" striking for its "eerily prescient" articulation of the future consequences of what he terms "unintended biological warfare," and further remarkable for "a conception of the disease that in some features resembles our own" notions of germ theory. The native explanation is a future talk that would, he writes, "ultimately triumph" (1988, 36). Metaphorically, it is not merely prescient, it is science. A modern discourse also assures Indian extermination; the ultimate triumph of Old World disease and Old World invaders is twinned.

Historians have, for many years now, been arguing for the cataclysmic role played by epidemics in the New World, how the importation of European diseases like smallpox, influenza, measles, decimated (literally, reduced to one tenth) native populations that had never been exposed to these diseases before.[10] The attractiveness of this hypothesis is obvious. It further nullifies the kind of moral/providential narrative that motivates Harriot when he opines that only Indians who resisted the English were struck down by disease, as well as numerous seventeenth-century New England writers, who similarly proclaimed that God was on the side of the English.[11] Moreover, it counters the secularized version of this narrative, in which primitivism is rescued (at however great a cost) by being introduced to civilization, or the version of this narrative that attributes European success to technological superiority, whether of firearms or, as in the case of Todorov, advanced communication skills.

If these are reasons for subscribing to the thesis about disease, there are also reasons to pause. Greenblatt is not alone when he characterizes epidemics as "unintended biological warfare"; Henry Dobyns, a major demographic historian, describes the Europeans' destruction of what he calls a native "paradise" as happening "not intentionally, but simply because they carried Old World disease agents" (1976, 1), while Alfred Crosby, the most notable ecological historian, echoes him: "It was their germs, not these imperialists themselves, for all their brutality and callousness, that were chiefly responsible" (1986, 196). The epidemic narrative does not merely remove the moralizing explanation that attributed success to some aspect of the supposed superiority of European culture, it removes moral explanation entirely, replacing it with a supposedly neutral, natural—indeed, biological—explanation. Epidemics were mistakes; no European could have known that lethal pathogens were being unleashed on the natives, and no European was in control of that onslaught. The decimation of America was simply an accident for which the Europeans were not responsible. Thus, Dobyns (1976) takes to task P. M. Ashburn's early medical history, which argues for the disease theory and uses "military campaign terms" (Ashburn 1974, 25), including chapters with titles like "Shock Troops: Eruptive Fevers" or "Total War: Malaria," for its metaphorical suggestion of a relationship between the invaders and their unsuspected pathogen allies, though it has to be remarked that such metaphors do not fail to appear in Crosby's *Ecological Imperialism*. He writes, for instance, about pathogens as "unprecedented invaders" (1986, 199). Crosby's broad historical account posits a common European heritage for both Old and New World populations—the inhabitants of the New World were the first to arrive in the Western hemisphere; they became separated from their Old World relatives and lingered in earlier stages of the Paleolithic Revolution while the Old World moved at greater speed towards modernity—and for this already-invidious historicizing account, Crosby describes the original inhabitants of the New World as the "shock troops" preceding the sixteenth-century European invaders (285). A moral economy is restored here, and with a vengeance; the "shock troops" are already an invading force, and the later invasion simply completes their design. With one and the same stroke, the later arrivals rejoin their long-separated advance guard even as one stock replaces the other. The errors and divisions of history are overcome: Old World and New can now march in step.

If, in Crosby's terms, these "servant and parasite organisms" were as unknown to the Europeans as they were to the indigenes (104), if they were, to quote P. M. Ashburn, who seems uncannily to be quoting Harriot's Algonkians, "pallid, patient specters" following the Europeans (1947, 56), these "unintended" allies cannot simply be regarded as unrelated to the violence through which the Europeans realized their intentions. It is a simple point, but one often overlooked in these explanations: these particular epidemics would not have occurred had the Europeans not been there. Moreover, the explanation that gives such force to the agents of disease underplays all of the cofactors involved, the sheer brutality that so often characterized the forces of invasion. "Not only European diseases killed Roanoke Indians during the first year that the colony existed," Russell Thornton comments, "the colonists also killed them" (1987, 67).[12]

Harriot, mathematical genius, exemplary scientist, reputed freethinker, sympathetic recorder of the Algonkians, knower of their language, has often been treated as a benign voice among the invaders, and his text taken as a guarantee of a degree of humanity unusual among those who came over.[13] Yet there is nothing to suggest that he was far removed from the brutality of Ralph Lane, who governed the first Roanoke colonists, one of whose first actions upon landing was to destroy an entire village to punish Indians supposed to have stolen a silver cup from the English (Quinn 1955, 1–191). Only a few sentences down from Harriot's recording of the belief in "invisible bullets" is his admission that "towardes the ende of the yeare" some of the English "shewed themselves too fierce, in slaying some [natives] . . . upon causes that . . . might easily enough have been borne withall," immediately making it clear, however, that "it was on their [i.e., the Indians'] part justly deserved" (1972, 30). The overuse of force is morally defended; Harriot only hesitates because excessive ferocity is strategically suspect as a means of winning over the natives, though he immediately overcomes even that hesitation. As natives come to see the justice of their punishment, they will undoubtedly come to value the English, Harriot concludes. So doing, he points to what disease battened on: violence to bodies and to beliefs. By itself, disease might not have decimated native populations. It is a consoling and self-justifying history that believes otherwise.

By writing an account that attributes force to invisible agents, visible agents are made invisible and the relationship between visible bullets and invisible ones is effaced. More than that: suddenly, Europeans who suffered scurvy on ship, plagues at home, and appalling mortality rates are treated as if they were disease-free. This is, of course, what Harriot claims, and historians have followed in his path. And to maintain the natives in an entirely vulnerable position, it is also necessary that each contact with natives be treated as a first encounter, something palpably not the case on Roanoke, when the English colonists brought back with them two Indians taken on the previous expedition to North Carolina. Manteo and Wanchese had spent a year in England, learning English and, for whatever reason, had not succumbed to Old World pathogens, which must have been even more present there than in the New World. Nor should one forget that the Roanoke Algonkians had also had contact with the Spanish before the English ever arrived.

Colonial suppositions remain fully at work in scientific accounts; in, for instance, Crosby's long-spanning history that ensures that native culture represents a past for

Western civilization, one, predictably enough, characterized as a disease-free paradise.[14] One might be reading Lévi-Strauss or, for that matter, Harriot, especially the 1590 printing of his text that includes John White's illustrations, in which natives hold up a mirror of Edenic practices, and are pictured alongside native Picts, ancient Britons who also collate New World invasions with British expansionism, notably in Ireland (the training ground for Ralph Lane and for Harriot as well). And, to bring gendered suppositions back into focus, we should note that the term historians use for these histories of pathogens gone wild is "virgin soil epidemics," a locution which, like the Spanish projection with which I began, conflates the rape of native women with the ravaging of the land, and makes the European triumph tantamount to a plot advancing heterosexual relations, in which natives once again stand in for subordinated women.[15]

This plot is equally implicit in the ways in which demographic historians chart the resurgence of native populations in recent years, as if the story to be told were simply that of natives finally acquiring the immune defenses to begin the work of reproduction. As if, that is, the story is simply one rooted in biology. And here we might note, too, that these histories of decimation by disease batten on suspect biological/racial categories; the "disappearance" of tribes, for instance, often depending on the extinction of "purebred" Indians, or the mistaking of migration, whether indigenous patterns of movement or enforced regroupings, for the disappearance of tribes, many of which, it must also be added, only came into existence as strategic units formed to defend against white incursions.[16] Commentators seem unable to resist the pathos of the so-called "Lost Colony," the next group of English to arrive at Roanoke, only to be abandoned; but the Roanoke Indians are not described as "lost." They are, instead, "extinct," despite the fact that at least one early eighteenth-century traveler recorded the presence of Indians on Roanoke who claimed descent from the Indians Harriot encountered, and today the Lumbee tribe in North Carolina claims descent from the Roanoke Indians as well as the "Lost Colony."[17] That the Lumbee do not speak any language other than English, that they have no native customs, that they are said to look more Black than Indian, poses a problem to those who would deny their claims; but the problem has to do with wanting natives to remain "pure" natives, untouched by history; to consign them not merely to a past, but to a past that is absolutely irrecoverable, cut off from the present. Should one, for instance, recall, as David Beers Quinn does in his volumes of documents and accounts of the Roanoke voyages, that when Sir Francis Drake arrived at Roanoke, he had on board some three hundred South American Indians as well as one hundred Black slaves? What happened to them after Drake took the Roanoke colonists back to England? "The Indians and negroes," Quinn writes, "may well be a 'lost colony'" (1955, 1–255). Anglos can claim descent from the Mayflower without pausing for a moment to consider how unrecognizable these forebears might be were one to encounter them today; but natives must be like the ones drawn by John White if they are to claim descent.[18]

All of which is to say, along with Bruno Latour (1993), that one must suspect the narratives that seek to cordon off "hard science" from the social, and must recognize that modernity is precisely that regime intent upon these separations. The discourse of a dispassionate and simply true science might usefully be placed beside the regulatory apparatuses of the disciplines that Foucault describes. Effectively, the truth of "hard" science need not be questioned; no more the law that goes under the name of the Father or the Phallus. And, to return to Harriot, and to the reading of "invisible bullets" that sees the term metaphorically anticipating modernity, and to the range of explanations I have been discussing implicit in such a reading, one must ultimately ask how it is that the Indians know so well what modern Westerners will think. Is it, perhaps, because what is being recorded as if spoken by the natives may well be in part a European fantasy, one, moreover, that would, by making the natives "prescient," establish a connection rather than a disconnection between the premodern and the modern, and would thereby call into question scientific truth and the unmetaphoricity of fact? Need it be remarked that the move from metaphor to knowledge is Rousseau's story about language? That it repeats the nature/culture divide, the projection onto primitives of a kind of categorical confusion relieved by modern separations and clarifications? Is there not legible, in this reading of "invisible bullets," all the assurance of modern enlightenment and a making-acceptable of the Algonkians as our ancestors, as those who testify to their own disappearance and replacement by us?

I do not mean to silence native voices in asking these questions, only to suggest the multivocality of Harriot's account. The record that Harriot's text offers must be one of complicities, accommodations, projections, mistranslations, a hybrid text that will not settle the issue into a single historical trajectory. If one tries to note the place within Harriot's text of this native vision of the future, it is not with the aim of producing a monological text. Rather, it is to suggest the multiple and conflicting openings towards a future that Harriot's text cannot control. For if we ask, since Harriot could not have known about germs—even as he is providing a discursive structure which can come to be read as anticipatory of germ theory—what this metaphor of "invisible bullets" is doing in his text, the answer might be that it is a trope implicated throughout his account. As much as the natives, Harriot is projecting a future, seeking to silence the naysayers and skeptics, to advance the project of colonization. While many pages of his tract merely look like a list of the resources of the newfound land, it is less a catalogue of what *is* there as what may be there once English agricultural habits are transported, English plants are planted, European animals are foraging. There will be "marchantable commodities" once "art" is "added" (7), flax and hemp, once they are planted (8), grapes for wine, "when they are planted and husbanded as they ought" (9), oil, "when there are milles" (9). The rife and "full" lists that cover page after page of his text are projections onto a landscape that as often as not, seems to be empty: Virginia offers "ground enough" for these projected plantings and manufactures (11); natives have no advanced skills, the land lies before the English to be planted. Replacement and making-disappear are implied throughout the report.

Moreover, on numerous occasions, accounts of planting report failures, produce claimed to have been brought back is instead lost at sea, gums "now lost," pearls swallowed in storms (11). This text has nothing to show for itself except the words on the page, the illusion of reference. Those black marks on the page are the bullets Harriot shoots into the future, and which he seeks to make invisible precisely because the aim of his text is also to deny the materiality of its practices, to treat its words as if they were transparently referential rather than fantasmatically projective. Thus natives are scoffed at when they take the Bible as an object of magical powers, when it is the word, the spirit, Harriot affirms, that is powerful. Yet what Harriot attempts to dazzle the natives with are technological instruments, including writing. The text dissimulates the materiality of the text; it makes its bullets invisible. It dreams a technological dream of transportation without loss, of the simple replanting of the English across the Atlantic, of the word producing the referent.

To do this, it must suppress the fact that the English depended for their sustenance on natives, who may not have known how to plant European-style, but did know how to feed themselves and to manipulate food supplies for the English; Harriot records the "good taste" of their "pottage" (14), the abundance of their produce, the "sucking" of tobacco (16), and the fact that the Indians supplied game (19). Harriot's account keeps indicating that, with penetration of the interior, greater resources will appear, but his projections beyond the seacoast depend upon natives pointing the English in that direction. To treat these as merely indexicals congruent with his listing, Harriot eschews the narrativizing of an account like Ralph Lane's about his inland adventures: attacks, imprisonments, ambushes, hostility, and starvation from which the English were only too glad to escape when Drake arrived with his rescue ships (only Harriot's allusion to the "experiment" of eating dog tallies with the record in Lane [20]). "I might have said more," writes Harriot in closing his account of marketable commodities (12), ending his book by "referring my relation to your favourable constructions" (33), for what he has to offer is "not yet seene" (31). The measure of Harriot's future projection lies in our taking his words as inevitably leading to English success, and White's pictures of North Carolina Algonkians as recording those who no longer exist.

"Invisible bullets" might be the name for these mystifying, textualizing practices, and for the fully conflictual site that they open as they attempt to foreclose and dematerialize their operations and their limits. My point here is not, as others have done, to invite a sympathetic reading of the pathos of the failed attempts at colonization on Roanoke Island. It is rather to point to the irreducibility of this trope to a singular historical trajectory. The sign of such irreducibility is the ontological confusion that characterizes this future vision, in which the English are assumed to be "risen againe," having exceeded the boundaries of life and death, that the "more to come," the future generation, are disembodied, in the air, responding to the English desire for the future by accommodatingly shooting their "invisible bullets" with their anything-but-immaterial effects (29). Yet the agents of the future are curiously will-less, responding to the call of the present. In the earlier versions of Greenblatt's essay (1981, 50; 1985, 26), this vision is termed an "Algonkian 'Night of the Living Dead,'" and the comparison is apt; the agents of futurity have all the uncanniness of the shuffling and insatiable zombies in Romero's film.[19] The comparison suggests, once again, that this vision cannot be solely a product of native society, that it may offer a version of Western horror even as it asks the natives to articulate it.

The Algonkians propose their account of the English and the possibility that they will replace the native inhabitants by pondering precisely the mystery that provoked the chuckle of the Araucanian chief whose encounter with the Spanish opened this paper. "They noted . . . that we had no women amongst us, neither that we did care for any of theirs" (29). How is replacement to take place outside reproduction? How, but by these succubi and demonic forces? How, but by a kind of strange lovemaking between future and past Englishmen, whose reproduction is hardly to be credited to the workings of heterosexual reproduction? If these English are not born of women, as the natives opine, they reproduce themselves into the future on the force of desire. "By our intreaty & for the love of us," the future shoots back and ahead (29). Harriot tells us of his "special familiarity" with the priests (26), and his account of the future is everywhere belied by this "familiarity." For the vision of this commingling of bodies, this strange love between men, might, in other contexts, be called sodomy; as here the relationship between English futurity and the spread of pestilence and plague are utterly confused, crossing the boundaries between acceptable and unacceptable male-male relations. Among these ghastly lovers, in this scene of male-male sex, in this autoerotic scene of conjuring up the desired future, is the body of the Indian, a strange specular double for these English shooters.

Reading this passage from the present prospect, it is hard to resist seeing this scene of transmission as anticipating the discourse that surrounds AIDS, and not least if we follow Alfred Crosby, who entertains the thesis "that native American virgin soil epidemics have been especially lethal to young adults" (1976, 294; cf. 1986, 199). The possibility of such a reading lies precisely in the ways in which supposedly superseded narratives of the kind embedded in Harriot, in which cataclysms like plagues are seen as having been *caused* by social dissidents (heretics, natives, atheists, sodomites), have once again been mobilized in discourses around AIDS, in which the syndrome is attributed to Africans, African-Americans, prostitutes and homosexuals.[20] The possibility that such accounts cannot be consigned to the past adds to the poignancy that Judith Butler has recently remarked upon, reading the final chapter of Foucault's *History of Sexuality*, with its almost utopian vision of modernity as a time no longer subject to the plagues and famine marking premodernity—sentences written by someone already HIV-positive and taken by an unforeseeable, entirely accidental plague that disrupts the confidence with which one can speak of modernity, the surety that scientific knowledge will explain what has occurred and will govern what will be (Butler 1992). We have never been modern, Bruno Latour contends, and our world is not the site of absolute separations, but of relays and networks that pass through and that are founded upon hybrids and instabilities. Microbes do not have an existence of their own, but are part of the social. The late nineteenth-century discoveries—so-called—attributed to Pasteur cannot be thought of, Latour says, without their complicities with electricity, gymnastics, colonization, the telephone, radio, X-rays, and psychoanalysis (1988, 40). So, too, Harriot's "invisible bullets" are complicit with the technologies of overcoming distance, of transportations that always involve accidents and unprecedented couplings. The radical ontological insecurity of Harriot's trope is what we must fasten upon to think the history that will be.

NOTES

1. The episode, set in Chile in 1563, is recounted in *Memory of Fire: Genesis*. Galeano's trilogy encompasses the history of Latin America from the conquest to the twentieth century; his vignettes draw upon history and myth, citation from source materials (indicated by the use of italics) and imaginative reconstruction.

2. These relations continue; at the time of writing of this essay (January 1994), "rebels" in Chiapas (Mexico) composed of "peasants" and "Indians" were combatting not only the government but, U.S. news reported, "mestizos" who chose government loyalty rather than class and racial ties to the "rebels."

3. The phrase "our *mestizo* America" was coined by José Martí, and is invoked by Roberto Fernández Retamar (1989, 4).

4. On the limits of biologism as a means of determining descent, see Appiah (1986, 26).

5. For a recent attempt to articulate Derridean *différance* as a historical concept compatible with a Marxist dialectic, see Terdiman (1993, 57–71).

6. Irigaray's nonceword "hommosexualité," coined to describe the male structures of domination, needs to be discriminated into the homosocial/homosexual/homophobic matrix mobilized in Sedgwick's rethinking of the paradigm of the traffic in women (1985), a critique made forcefully by Owens (1987, 219–32), who also usefully calls up an alternative anthropological model that *includes* male-male relations within the primary family unit (the privileged tutelage relationship between the mother's brother and her son).

7. To anticipate the argument that follows, and to clarify my point here, I would note the following: Butler's turn to Foucault parallels the move I make, as when, in *Gender Trouble*, addressing the problem of the law in all its guises, she writes: "Here it seems wise to reinvoke Foucault who, in claiming that sexuality and power are coextensive, implicitly refutes the postulation of a subversive or emancipatory sexuality which could be free of the law" (1990, 29). But note here that the "law" is preserved, while in sentences following this one "power" replaces it (just as it does in the index to *Gender Trouble*, where under "law" the reader is referred to "power"), or, as in this sentence, law and power are treated as the same notions. In "Sexual Inversions," Butler argues persuasively against the law/power distinction by pointing to the fact that the law is not solely repressive and prohibitory—it is also necessarily productive (of troubled gender differences, of incoherently differentiated prescribed and proscribed sexual relations) (1992). On this basis, Butler seeks to dismantle Foucault's law/power distinction as well as his historical narrative of the divide that modernity represents. Again, I am quite sympathetic to this move, since, as I seek to argue in this essay, historic possibilities must depend upon mobilizations that would be unthinkable if history was segmented across uncrossable divides. Nonetheless, what I am also trying to argue here supports differences between law and power, between historical regimes, insofar as the objects and persons on which they focus (which they produce) are not transhistorically identical, not always located in the same way *vis-à-vis* institutions (like marriage, say) which are themselves not invariably fixed in the same sociopolitical terrains.

8. See Sedgwick (1992): "making heterosexuality historically visible is difficult because, under its institutional pseudonyms such as Inheritance, Marriage, Dynasty, Domesticity, and Population, heterosexuality has been permitted to masquerade so fully as History

itself—when it has not been busy impersonating Romance" (293). See also "Jane Austen and the Masturbating Girls" (Sedgwick 1993; 1990).

9.   Citations are from the Dover facsimile of the 1590 De Bry edition of *A Briefe and True Report of the New Found Land of Virginia*. The rare 1588 edition is reprinted in Quinn 1955, which collates it with the 1590 as well as the 1589 reprint in Hakluyt, which can be found reprinted in Quinn and Quinn 1982. It should be remarked that Harriot is not the only one to record this "native" belief; Ralph Lane, who commanded the colonists on this venture to Roanoke, records their belief "that they have bene in the night, being 100. myles from any of us in the ayre shot at, and stroken by men of ours, that by sicknesse had dyed among them: and many of them hold opinion, that wee be dead men returned into the worlde againe, and that we doe not remayne dead but for a certaine time, and that then we returne againe" (Quinn, 1955 1:278).

10. Studies of epidemics have usually proceeded in tandem with demographic studies seeking to establish the population of native inhabitants upon European arrival. Some prominent accounts include Cook (1981), Crosby (1972), Dobyns (1983).

11. Sir Francis Drake, for instance, records that "the wilde people at first comminge of our men died verie fast and said amongest themselves, It was the Inglishe God that made them die so faste" (cited in Quinn 1955, 1:306).

12. For an account of the first Roanoke expeditions that treats the events as holocaustal without ever mentioning disease, see Turner (1983, 171–99).

13. For this view, see, e.g., Shirley (1983).

14. For the persistence of this trope of historical distance in anthropology, see Fabian (1983).

15. See Crosby (1976). Crosby here indulges in an account of Indians with "no previous contact" with Westerners (289), which was not the case in Roanoke, and he charts the disappearance of "pure Indians and Eskimos" (289), an unthought racialism that also characterizes his account in *Imperialism* (1986, 98), of the Guanches, natives of the Canary Islands, whom the Spanish enslaved (these islands were for Spain what Ireland was for the English, a training ground for New World encounters); Crosby writes of the Guanches that "they died without reproducing, or they scattered their seed in alien wombs or gave birth to strangers"; hence "pure Guanches" disappeared. In his essay, Crosby also entertains the possibility that "genetic weakness" accounts for a lack of native resistance to Old World pathogens (1976, 292).

16. For a brief but incisive account of native history that supports these arguments, see Brasser (1971).

17. "Extinct" is Hutton's term in his Introduction to the Dover reprint of the 1590 Harriot (1972, xiii); for John Lawson's 1709 account, see Swanton (1946, 137); for a good discussion of the Lumbee, see Blu (1980).

18. For the persistence of such suppositions, see Berkhofer (1978, 28–29), *et passim* on the thematics of the inevitable disappearance of natives.

19. For an account of George Romero's trilogy and its uncanny audience relations, see Shaviro (1993, chap. 2), where one emphasis is on the mimetology of infection. It is worth noting that Lane's report of transmission—by the dead/infected/revived bodies of the English (Quinn 1955, 1:278) is even closer to the scenario. It almost allows for contact between English and Algonkian bodies; it might be mentioned that if the disease in question was, as has been supposed, typhus, it is transmitted through feces; see Cook and Lovell (1991, 226).

20. For considerations of remobilizations of this kind see, for instance, the essays in Fee and Fox (1988), as well as the initial group of essays joined under the rubric "History Teaches: What Have We Learned?" in Klusacek and Morrison (1992). Crosby's contribution to this section, "New Diseases," correlates Renaissance epidemics with AIDS; but varying his argument about one-way transmission in *Ecological Imperialism*, he stresses the highly ques-

tionable thesis that Europeans acquired syphilis from the New World, and then likens AIDS to these sexual ravages; thus rather than the parallel between European invasion and native decimation, Crosby draws a parallel between native infection and European debility, a narrative reproduced in AIDS discourses that see a "general population" invaded by African drug-abusing/homosexual/prostitute disease, and in which the disease becomes a metonym for the populations thought to be responsible.

WORKS CITED

Appiah, Anthony. 1986. "The Uncompleted Argument: DuBois and the Illusion of Race," in *"Race," Writing, and Difference*, ed. Henry Louis Gates, Jr. Chicago: University of Chicago Press. 21–37.

Ashburn, P. M. 1947. *The Ranks of Death: A Medical History of the Conquest of America*. New York: Coward-McCann.

Berkhofer, Robert F., Jr. 1978. *The White Man's Indian*. New York: Vintage.

Blu, Karen I. 1980. *The Lumbee Problem: The Making of an American Indian People*. Cambridge: Cambridge University Press.

Brasser, T. J. C. 1971. "The Coastal Algonkians: People of the First Frontiers," in *North American Indians in Historical Perspective*, ed. Eleanor Burke Leacock and Nancy Oestreich Lurie. New York: Random House.

Butler, Judith. 1990. *Gender Trouble*. New York: Routledge.

———. 1992. "Sexual Inversions," in *Discourses of Sexuality*, ed. Domna C. Stanton. Ann Arbor: University of Michigan Press. 344–61.

Cook, Noble David. 1981. *Demographic Collapse: Indian Peru, 1520–1620*. Cambridge: Cambridge University Press.

Cook, Noble David and W. George Lovell. 1991. *"Secret Judgments of God."* Norman: University of Oklahoma Press.

Crosby, Alfred. 1972. *The Columbian Exchange: Biological and Cultural Consequences of 1492*. Westport, CT: Greenwood.

———. 1976. "Virgin Soil Epidemics as a Factor in the Aboriginal Depopulation in America." *William and Mary Quarterly* 33: 289–99.

———. 1986. *Ecological Imperialism*. Cambridge: Cambridge University Press.

———. 1992. "New Diseases," in *A Leap in the Dark*, ed. Allan Klusacek and Ken Morrison. Montreal: Vehicule. 10–15.

Derrida, Jacques. 1974–1976. *Of Grammatology*, trans. Gayatri Chakravorty Spivak. Baltimore: Johns Hopkins University Press.

Dobyns, Henry F. 1976. *Native American Historical Demography*. Bloomington: Indiana University Press.

———. 1983. *Their Number Become Thinned*. Knoxville: University of Tennessee Press.

Edelman, Lee. 1993. *Homographesis*. New York: Routledge.

Fabian, Johannes. 1983. *Time and the Other*. New York: Columbia University Press.

Fee, Elizabeth and Daniel M. Fox. 1988. *AIDS: The Burdens of History*. Berkeley: University of California Press.

Foucault, Michel. 1978. *The History of Sexuality: An Introduction*, trans. Robert Hurley. New York: Pantheon.

Galeano, Eduardo. 1985. *Memory of Fire: Genesis*, trans. Cedric Belfrage. New York: Pantheon.

Goldberg, Jonathan. 1990. *Writing Matter: From the Hands of the English Renaissance*. Stanford: Stanford University Press.

Greenblatt, Stephen. 1981. "Invisible Bullets: Renaissance Authority and Its Subversion." *Glyph* 8: 40–61.

———. 1985. "Invisible Bullets: Renaissance Authority and Its Subversion, *Henry IV* and *Henry V*," in *Political Shakespeare*, ed. Jonathan Dollimore and Alan Sinfield. Ithaca: Cornell University Press. 18–47.

———. 1988. *Shakespearean Negotiations*. Berkeley: University of California Press.

Harriot, Thomas. 1972. *A Briefe and True Report of the New Found Land of Virginia*, intro. Paul Hutton. New York: Dover.

Irigaray, Luce. 1985. *This Sex Which Is Not One*, trans. Catherine Porter. Ithaca: Cornell University Press.

Klusacek, Allan and Ken Morrison. 1992. *A Leap in the Dark*. Montreal: Vehicule.

Latour, Bruno. 1988. *The Pasteurization of France*, trans. Alan Sheridan and John Law. Cambridge, MA: Harvard University Press.

———. 1993. *We Have Never Been Modern*, trans. Catherine Porter. Cambridge, MA.: Harvard University Press.

Owens, Craig. 1987. "Outlaws: Gay Men in Feminism," in *Men in Feminism*, ed. Alice Jardine and Paul Smith. New York: Methuen.

Quinn, David Beers. 1955. *The Roanoke Voyages, 1584–1590*. London: Hakluyt Society.

Quinn, David Beers and Alison M. Quinn. 1982. *The First Colonists*. Raleigh: North Carolina Department of Cultural Resources.

Retamar, Roberto Fernández. 1989. *Caliban and Other Essays*, trans. Edward Baker. Minneapolis: University of Minnesota Press.

Rubin, Gayle. 1975. "The Traffic in Women: Notes on the 'Political Economy' of Sex," in *Toward an Anthropology of Women*, ed. Rayna R. Reiter. New York: Monthly Review. 157–210.

———. 1984. "Thinking Sex: Notes for a Radical Theory of the Politics of Sexuality," in *Pleasure and Danger*, ed. Carole S. Vance. Boston: Routledge and Kegan Paul. 267–319.

Sedgwick, Eve Kosofsky. 1985. *Between Men: English Literature and Male Homosocial Desire*. New York: Columbia University Press.

———. 1990. *Epistemology of the Closet*. Berkeley: University of California Press.

———. 1992. "Gender Criticism," in *Redrawing the Boundaries*, ed. Stephen Greenblatt and Giles Gunn. New York: Modern Language Association.

———. 1993. *Tendencies*. Durham: Duke University Press.

Shaviro, Steven. 1993. *The Cinematic Body*. Minneapolis: University of Minnesota Press.

Shirley, John W. 1983. *Thomas Harriot: A Biography*. Oxford: Clarendon.

Swanton, John R. 1946. *The Indians of the Southeastern United States*. Washington, DC: United States Government Printing Office.

Terdiman, Richard. 1993. *Present Past: Modernity and the Memory Crisis*. Ithaca: Cornell University Press.

Thornton, Russell. 1987. *American Indian Holocaust and Survival*. Norman: University of Oklahoma Press.

Todorov, Tzvetan. 1984. *The Conquest of America*, trans. Richard Howard. New York: Harper & Row.

Turner, Frederick. 1983. *Beyond Geography*. New Brunswick, NJ: Rutgers University Press.

Wittig, Monique. 1992. *The Straight Mind*. Boston: Beacon.

In Search

of the Black Stud

2

José Piedra

Then they all paired off, each with each: but the Queen, who was left alone, presently cried out in a loud voice, "Here to me, O my Lord Saeed!" and then sprang with a drop-leaf from one of the trees a big slobbering blackamoor with rolling eyes which showed the whites, a truly hideous sight. He walked boldly up to her and threw his arms round her neck while she embraced him as warmly; then he bussed her and winding his legs round hers, as a button-loop clasps a button, he threw her and enjoyed her. On like wise did the other slaves with the girls till all had satisfied their passions, and they ceased not from kissing and clipping, coupling and carousing till day began to wane; when the Mamelukes [light-pigmented slaves] rose from the damsels' bosoms and the blackamoor slave dismounted from the Queen's breast; the men resumed their disguises and all, except for the negro who swarmed up the tree, entered the palace and closed the postern-door as before.

—Burton's translation of the frame tale of the anonymous Arabic text better known as *The Book of the Thousand Nights and a Night.*

1. TALL, DARK, AND HANDSOME

Throughout Euro-centered history self-serving schemes based on racial polarization inform the balance between political power and sexual prowess. That is, power is to the "colorless" as prowess is to those "of color." A tall, dark, and handsome being might exert a hold over a slight, light, and wishful-thinking one. But what sort of strings are attached to such a hold? And, what happens to those who do not live in a black or white world?

The powerful might appear to be sharing the power-podium with lesser beings by paternalistically and cunningly "empowering" them with sexual prowess. In fact, those who propose this precariously balanced form of sharing gear it toward remedial intervention. Civilized love and, worse yet, savage sex, beg control. From the perspective of the powers that be, the powerless should accept their assigned places in the realm of sexual prowess as opportunities for second-hand and second-rate empowerment.

Whatever excesses of prowess the powerful assign away, whatever benefits they receive from such projections, the process remains under control. Deviations from a pre-established norm are readily corrected by acts of chastisement that include political subjugation. Those in charge construe their remedial actions not only as a fitting antidote to their charges' erotic performance, but also as a guilt-redemptive reaction against libidinal provocation. Like Adam towards Eve, or Othello towards Desdemona, sin-sensitive traditions prescribe checking out the genitally-obsessed dependant for any purportedly independent display of the libido.

Whether indeed sexual provocation remains a mere excuse for political subjugation or is able to transcend such confines remains to be seen. The two possible outcomes inform my study of premodern sexual politics, a field constantly reassessing prejudices deriving from the status quo claimed by white leading European males at a time, or concerning a time, in which few arbitrarily and/or genetically darkened and feminized Others could be heard. I am speaking of attitudes emerging during the preamble of modern times, as signaled in Spain by the emerging nation's evolution from a trans-mediterranean occupied land to a transatlantic occupier. As Spain comes of age as a modern nation, the dark sister of Europe ceases to be an Afro-Arab domain to become a singular upholder of whiteness for a whole dark continent taken over together under the name of America.

Taking into consideration the efforts Spain had to make to evolve at once from an occupied territory of premodern times to an occupying power of modern times, I gather that this nation was apt to understand full well the notion of rainbow coalitions and widespread compromises: racial, ethnic, religious, social, and libidinal. I surmise that the forging of Spain's national character had very much to do with its relative attitude toward "conquest," understood in its full range of interpretations and mostly leading toward a policy of unification, consolidation, and integration. From such a perspective I shall consider how a nation controlled by ostensibly white and straight males came to rely literarily and literally on the import and export business of black studs capable of serving as the ruling Spaniards' tall, dark, and handsome alter egos.

If by compensatory genitalizing of their physical and physiological attributes darker men became ad hoc models of white desire, lighter males assumed being able to emulate and/or control them and their activities. Keep in mind that, while lighter men viewed themselves as capable of allowing and/or managing black-assigned prowess, they ostensibly never succumbed to a black man's desire. Instead, women of all colors became vulnerable to the sexual subjection of tall, dark, and handsome intruders, and of Spaniards impersonating them. Furthermore, among women, the darker ones emerged as more sexually offensive, while the lighter ones remained more sexually defensive. In fact, white women, and a few recorded instances of light, lady-like men, provided the prime targets of black male subjection and provoked white male suppression.

From premodern and prenational Spain onward, that is within the Afro-Hispano-Arabic period that precedes the American encounter, the black stud becomes a troublesome icon of conquest. Beyond the dubious, polarized cliché of light victim and dark victor of prowess and power, stands a wide range of potential mediators and mediations. Indeed, situations allowing for fluid definitions of ethnicity, gender, and sexuality might allow a core group of otherwise disenfranchised citizens to translate sexual differences into political advantages. I intend to explore such a situation in Spain by summarily considering the period from the eighth to the fifteenth century, which seals the literary fate of the black male, and more rarely female, stud.

The premise for my study places the perception of racial differences above gender definition and sexual preference in the establishment of the rules of "conquest." Racial constructs, particularly as applied to the vagaries of conquest, are capable of blurring the boundaries between male and female, or straight and gay behavior. For instance, whereas the tendency of Afro-Hispano-Arabic societies is to identify white and straight masculinity with domination, in these same societies some dark women emerge as dominatrixes and some light men are, in turn, enslaved—if nothing else than for the sake of sexual power play. Likewise, some women—whether light or dark—become strategically dependent on, or captured in, traps set up in the name of love. Meanwhile some men—whether racially dark, or not—gain both a totemic and taboo status for being "tall, dark, and handsome" conqueror-types.

2. HANDS-ON EXPERIENCE

Late in my search for significant literary models defining the status quo of the black stud, I found a singular partner in Richard F. Burton, whose erotically-stressed translation of the *Arabian Nights* (1885) underscores a full array of prejudices in Arab portrayals and treatment of their darker siblings, particularly Berbers and sub-Saharan Africans. Moreover, in whatever form the tales reached first North Africa and then Spain, they likely influenced the perceptions of blackness in that area and time. In hindsight I can anticipate in Burton's *Arabian Nights* just about every shade of treatment of black prowess and power I have ascertained in the Arab context of the formative period of the Spanish nation.

Early on in his tales, Burton's translation underlines an icon of conquest which he considers both appealing and appalling. From the "frame tale" of the *Thousand Nights* emerges a "hideous sight" that sets the tone of the entire translation. Even if relegated to a note, it is still rare for a Victorian traveller like Burton to indulge in explaining why Arab characters, and subliminally himself, readily succumb to the lure of black sexual prowess. To put it succinctly, Burton pinpoints

> debauched women [who] prefer negroes on account of the size of their parts. I measured one man in Somali-land who, when quiescent, numbered nearly six inches. This is a characteristic of the negro race and of African animals: e.g. the horse (6).

Burton then proceeds to explain the effect of the long conduit of desire on the postponement of ejaculation, which "adds greatly to the woman's enjoyment." (6) As he had not given his readers enough justification for indulging in the reverie of the sexuality of the dark other, his introduction encroaches negatively upon my home territory. The actual lack of local excitement only serves to enhance the literary memory of the darkest of his hands-on experiences:

> During my long years of official banishment to the luxuriant and deadly deserts of Western African, and to the dull and dreary half-clearings of South America, [the original of the *Arabian Nights*] proved itself a charm, a talisman against ennui and despondency (xxiv).

A reading of Burton's translation and editorial apparatus of the frame tale would bring to mind elements common to different formative stages in Spain's perception of blackness. I am referring to the presumptive incidence of:

1) a moral dilemma in the partnership between black men and white women. The overwhelming sexual prowess and matching weakness in the nature and actions of the former engage the moral weakness and sexual appetite of the latter. The situation demands the martyr-like witnessing and judgmental heroics of elite light men;

2) a military dilemma of white men facing up to invading black soldiers and of white women enthralled and/or enslaved by these soldiers' naïvely perverse sexual militancy. As a consequence, civilized interpreters of savagery experience a paradoxical desire to turn the outsider into an insider, harnessing aggression into cooperation, and transforming the outrageous into an outstanding member of the society he recklessly assailed;

3) a religious dilemma brought about by the treatment of the black body as sexual fetish. Whereas whites metaphysically, and even physically, portray sin as a "black stain" and the devil as the "forces of darkness," the same people would likely admit that a black man has the right to fight for redemption. Some might even argue, as was common in medieval Spain, that God himself chose a dark man as his envoy.[1] In the worst of cases, the black man would have to fight twice as hard as the white in order to reach such a redemption, never mind women's awesome disadvantages.

In seeking redemption, black sinners would at once prove to be more in tune with the mysteries and foibles of human nature in need of remedial exploration and action—be it moral, military, or religious. In the long run, by virtue of his effort if for nothing else, the dark sinner's redemptive abilities invest him, and his female equivalent, with alternative powers which are no less real or valuable because they tend to be associated with the controlled exercise of the libido.

All together, the different aspects of the dark character in question enlighten the perception of the black unknown in one's own self, midst, memory, voyages, and fantasies. The many facets of Burton's approach to the black intruder in *Thousand Nights* illustrate the stages of Spain's perception of blackness, each cumulative step roughly datable to a particular historical period. These stages can be summarized as follows:

1) seventh to tenth century, in which the fear and awe of the savage black dovetails with that of a monstrously beguiling stud putting into question Spain's moral responsibility to process him;

2) eleventh to thirteenth century, in which the black stud becomes an intuitive messenger of the unknown as well as a well-trained soldier ready—by force and/or by love—to stay and to be part of Spain;

3) fourteenth and fifteenth century, in which Spain's black prodigal son sheds the "racial" stain of original sin in order to become a messenger of God, following whichever Messiah—Moses, Mohammed, or Christ.

3. EROTIC MILITANCY

From the seventh to the tenth century, the fantasy of black militant forces began to claim a rhetorical space within Islamic culture. Toward the end of this period, as Islamicized African soldiers prepared to invade the Spanish territory *en masse,* texts from both sides of the Strait of Gibraltar ceased to treat blacks as largely silent voices and conquerable targets and increasingly portrayed the conquering qualities of their bodies and minds. At the time in question, texts written in Islamic territory on both sides of the Strait of Gibraltar problematically considered the blurring of the boundaries between the bodily and soulful features of the black stud and, consequently, between the carnal service and intellectual knowledge he provides. In this section I will concentrate on the North African side of the Strait of Gibraltar, leaving the "Spanish" side for the next.

In North Africa, lighter-skinned peoples subjected their recently converted darker siblings to a wide repertoire of inferiorities, dependencies, and control measures. This treatment did not impede the enrolling of darker into the army, either as cause or effect of their being adjudicated a daredevil reputation in the erotic as well as the heroic fields. Keep in mind that it must have been both religiously and politically expedient to relegate sexual feelings and fighting chores to the lesser members of society. The double arming, libidinal and military, of the darker citizens might have actually brought about the lighter rulers' perceived need for tighter restrictions.

A few lines by Nusayb the Younger, the eighth-century black poet, illustrate the problematic consequences of Islam's libidinal empowerment of black citizens:

> Black man, what have you to do with love?
> Give over chasing white girls if you have any sense!
> An Ethiop black like you can have no way to reach them (Lewis 1990, 30).

Nusayb pronounces on the fantasy that casts black citizens in the role of sexual objects, rather than subjects of love. The poet warns his racial, religious, and ethnic brothers against thinking in terms of love in regards to white women. Even the possibility of mere sex is curtailed as well for, as the poet suggestively denounces, an "Ethiop black like you can have no way to reach them." While Nusayb does not actually mention what is the object of his black brother's shortcomings, prejudices behind the scene would assure any black man the attribution of large penis size. As the poet would have it, even if this were quantitatively true, the quality of the genital outreach would not actually guarantee the intended goal—be it conquering the heart of a light-colored woman or obtaining the trust of the light-colored man.

Certain contemporaries of Nusayb the Younger tend to be more direct in addressing the fine line between actual and fantasized attributes of blackness or, for that matter, between such attributes and their social function and guarantee of acceptance. Some, like Nusayb ibn Rabah, feistily defend the deep-seated worth of blackness beyond its superficial attributes and circumstantial conditions. The black poet even rises above the negative side-effects of defining oneself according to notions of race that lie beyond his control:

> Blackness does not diminish me, as long
> as I have this tongue and a stout heart,
> [If] some have been raised up by their lineage,
> the verses of my poems are my lineage.
> How much better is a black, eloquent and keen-minded,
> than a mute white (Lewis 1990, 28).

Ibn Rabah treats the social perception of blackness not so much as a virtue or a curse, but as a quality that, like his "heart," he can manipulate rhetorically in his intellectual and emotional self-defense. Through the cunning manipulation of poetic licence, ibn Rabah is capable of turning upside down traditional prejudices against blackness which taint the libido and stain language. This poet's "black" eloquence stands defiant and virtually on its own against a background of white noise or blank silence. Indeed Nusayb ibn Rabah's cautious and cautionary tongue is a fair match for the warning signs Nusayb the Younger attaches to a black man's genital instrument of white outreach.

For better or for worse, I view verbal gutsiness not just as an alternative to erotic prowess, but also as relative compensation for a lack of political power. It is no surprise that the act of verbal and genital self-assertion unifies blacks, women, and gays. Self-effacement and self-containment—not to mention silence and penis-lessness—, barely guarantee the oppressed a conditional space and dependent identity. Yet from the perspective of the oppressor, assertion is perceived as aggression. At the very least, claims of identity bring about in the oppressed the label of self-indulgence.

Some Arab poets protest the predicament in which their culture places a black poet who dares speak up. For instance, Kuthayyir comments on ibn Rabah's persona: "even if he be oppressed, he has the dark face of an oppressor" (Lewis 1990, 29). The notion of blackness as an inherently "aggressive" quality, reaches here ridiculous proportions. The prevailing powers treat not just verbal and libidinal provocation, but the mere display or expression of equality or difference, as tongue-lashings and phallic challenges deserving retaliation.

If, at least rhetorically, all of the above-mentioned writers are caught between proclaiming the difference that blackness makes and the equality it deserves in relation to whiteness, no poet is as ready to explore its paradoxical conclusions as Huhaym:

> My blackness does not harm my habit, for I am like musk;
> who tastes it does not forget it.
> I am covered with a black garment, but under it there is a
> lustrous garment with white skirts (Lewis 1990, 28–29).

Huhaym distills poetic justice from what others might perceive as a prejudice or handicap. He metaphorizes his appreciation of blackness as an unforgettable and winning characteristic; that is, as an inherent scent which is capable of distilling black identity into a habit-forming essence. The true nature of this sensitive stud's musk breathes through the coverup of "white skirts"—that is it surfaces from beneath the "feminized" layers of programmatic subservience.

4. LOVING SOLDIERS

On the other side of the Strait of Gibraltar, there are contemporary Spanish echoes of the uneasy parallels between blackness and erotic militancy. However, in the case of the emerging European nation, there is no doubt that its citizens have become the unwilling recipients of the erotic militancy of soldiers of war and love. Indeed, participation in military occupation intensifies the paradoxical treatment of black prowess as a conditional and dependent form of power. On the African side of the Strait of Gibraltar Islam's religious principles would give special consideration to the sexual freedom of blacks while proselytizing its redemption. On the European side, black Muslims earn a place in society by championing the just war of expansion. Once across, the other two religious cultures of Spain, that of Christians and Jews, take a similar if more dramatic look at the channeling of blackness.

At least two important proto-Spanish, pre-Islamic, writers writing in Latin already consider the pros and cons of what they view as inherent black aggression. For instance, Saint Isidore of Seville identifies West Africans as satyrs and Aegypans, while the Beatus of Liébana portrays one of the traditional horsemen of the Apocalypse as a riderless black horse.[2] And yet for both Saint Isidore and the Beatus, the arrival of blackness into the Spanish conscience remains under divine control. That is, the black (militant and military, erotic and heroic) forces shall irremediably lead to the end of the world as Europeans know it. Yet, Europeans also view this dramatic ending as part of God's plan leading to the metaphysical renewal of sin-ridden human souls, and even the physical uplifting of fallen bodies. If the darker the body the darker the soul, all are nevertheless inherently redeemable. According to the religious hegemonies converging in Spain, race might condemn, but faith shall tame, humankind's wildest beasts, including the scourge of being black or assailed by the black stud.

In his words and, above all, in his illustrations, the Beatus fetishizes evil as a black man who tempts the world with his naked body—iconographically represented as an approximate combination of a curled-up phallus and a question mark (Devisse 1979, 64–65). By extension, black tongues—daringly/mockingly phallic in their depiction—become predominant features in the Beatus's messianic imagery. Arguments about the tentative nature of black "knowledge" begin to feed the early Christian debate as to whether blacks were "contrary" or "contrary to *known* nature."[3]

Spain's pre-Islamic iconic treatment of blackness only intensifies after the Muslim arrival. Inserted in Muhammad al-Himyari's geographic survey of the Islamic territories on the Iberian Peninsula, we find a moral tale in Arabic about Mauaz, a black man who defies Muslim Spanish society and defines himself from his singular viewpoint on "knowledge" (Lévi-Provençal 1938, 82). The tale itself appears in this geographic treatise as a long-winded explanation of the Arabic genesis for (re)naming a natural feature of Spanish soil. Through his manipulation of knowledge Mauaz, today a largely forgotten character, proposed to become a permanent fixture of Muslim thought and of the Spanish territory.

The tale, roughly, has Mauaz climbing the lady-like curves of Mount Galtara on a daily pilgrimage, at the end of which he crouches on all fours to gaze over the edge of the precipice. He does this while exposing his bare bottom and holding onto a mulberry bush for safety. From there he cries out three times, elliptically exhorting or warning the people below: "O, people of the Rambla [Torrent]" (82)! The population at large one day decides they have had enough and cut the tree, making sure that it nevertheless appears to be intact. Mauaz falls for the trick and tumbles to his death.

What is the meaning, if any, of Mauaz's ritual mounting of Galtara; of his peering down at his lighter neighbors living below in the Torrent; of his elliptical message and showing off his buttocks; of his falling for the treacherously cut bush? Is Mauaz simply the victim of his lighter neighbors' jealousy or fear? Do we have here the people's triumph over Mauaz's anally daring/endearing exhibitionism? Or are both sexist heterosexuality and sodomitic homosexuality being at once condemned and banished with the sacrifice of Mauaz?

Through a daily dosage of four-legged postures and three ritual calls, Mauaz makes both infra-human and supernatural attempts to draw oral (should we say hysterical?) and genital (should we say anal?) attention to his ambivalent position as a human being, a mixture of devout believer and seductive sinner. "Mauaz's Precipice" thus becomes a geographic entry in al-Himyari's literary geography (82). Mauaz's daring, gender-bending and sexually provocative ritual gesture and ensuing private call and public outcry attempt to change the face of Spain, genitally and libidinally, linguistically and geographically. If history has not openly and officially recognized Mauaz's impact, literature and convention subliminally have.

5. VISIONARY GUTS

From the eleventh to the thirteenth century the transformation of the stud into an exceptionally intuitive messenger of the unknown also marks him as a forced member of the Afro-Hispano-Arabic culture. I will focus in this section on the Hispanicization of the black stud as both erotic vision and heroic visionary on both sides of the Strait of Gibraltar, and in the next section on his impact on the forging of the multiracial conscience of the Spanish nation under Muslim occupation.

Medieval texts in Spanish and Arabic which allude to the (un)natural worth and problematic beauty of the black body also suggest an attraction toward the enigma of the black mind. This enigma consists of the ability to fantasize and dream, combined with a keen sense of intuition, magic, divination, witchcraft, and "mythological powers that parallel the genital prowess of black bodies."[4] In short, whatever the self-proclaimed white Spaniards and Arabs do not see fit to imagine, they shall project unto their less fortunate darker brothers, and to a lesser extent on their sisters, light or dark.

Special bodily as well as intellectual (perhaps merely oral) gifts could transform a black slave into a lord—as suggested by the following lines from Ar-Ramadi's tenth-century Andalusian gay prison poem dedicated to a "black" youth:

> I talk to him so that he will answer me, but I
> Do so on purpose to hear him scatter pearls:
> I am his slave, he is the lord....[5]

The "white" master poet who shares a cell with the black slave summarily transforms the black youth he covets into not just his sexual but his intellectual better. We are dealing here with a poetic service no less demeaning than the stud one. In other words, just as the black libido serves to project white desires, so do the black "pearls of wisdom" speak for a love that, in "white" terms, does not dare, as the phrase goes, "speak its [sexual] name" or necessarily guarantee the black, pearl-festooned, wise object of desire speaking for himself. However, the sexual attraction of a lower class youthful black stud justifies the manifest desire of an upper class older white poet to succumb.

Ar-Ramadi makes an effort, askew and demeaning as it may be, to come to terms with his sexy black object, and wise silent subject, of desire. Spanish contemporaries echo the ultimate consequences of such a paradoxical partnership. I am thinking in particular of the anonymous dramatic fragment *Auto de los Reyes Magos*, likely the first play in Castilian, and the Galician-Portuguese *Cantigas de Santa María*, which were written, collected, and/or edited by Alfonso X, the Wise (Pidal 1900).

The *Auto de los Reyes Magos* presents blackness through the mysterious ability of certain people to read into "dark" enigmas, as well as the ensuing (phallic) gutsiness to stand by such readings. This is manifested in a play undoubtedly composed to proselytize Christianity beyond the walls of the official building and word of the Church to what undoubtedly was a heterogeneous population of the lower economic strata.

Although by this time tradition dictated that one of the three Christ-signifying kings was black, at the time this text was written the choice of which one was, at best, tentative. The openness of the identification may have had a favorable impact on the public of the time; or perhaps the racial clue was left up to the casting of citizens in the different roles. Most likely, readers of the fragmentary drama guess that one of the characters is black by a comparative analysis of the attitudes each magus manifests toward his knowledge of the Messiah's arrival. Thus, I choose Balthasar as the black African magus because he knows how to read the holy omen in the stars:

> CASPAR TO BALTHASAR: God save you, Lord, are you a star-reader [*estrelero*] ?
> Tell me the truth, I want to know it from you.
> Can you see the marvel?
> A star is born.
>
> BALTHASAR: Our Creator has been born,
> who is the lord of the people;
> I shall go to adore him (Pidal 1900, 11).

This exchange comes in the text after each of the three magi has a soliloquy in which it becomes apparent that, even though they all witness the star, only Balthasar is willing to ascertain its signaling the birth of Christ. Balthasar is also alone in admitting that he cannot explain what the phenomenon actually means—"in real terms," that is. Thus, in pushing the boundaries of the phenomenon the black magus appears to be giving a supernatural interpretation of a natural phenomenon. For this he relies on his naïve instinct, his unique faith, and/or his extraordinary, if dark, powers of perception. Perhaps the clue to the nature of his seemingly unnatural gift is given to us by Caspar calling Balthasar an *estrelero:* a word that could mean "star-man" or "star-gazer," but also "star-reader" or a student of astronomy—and more specifically of Venus, the "sexy" star.

Nowhere is the black potential to exemplify the full range of knowledge—from the carnal to the sublime—more apparent than in the illustrations accompanying the encyclopedic materials compiled by Alfonso the Wise. In his *Lapidario*, a black man is iconized as a four-legged monster with a hint of elephantine skin and proboscis, and portrayed in phallicized naked poses; while in his *Chessbook* Alfonso shows black players challenging white ones or at least becoming equal partners in this game of strategy.[6]

For my present purposes the most singular historical evolution in the perception of blackness among the works attributed to the learned King appears in "Of How the Virgin Mary Liberated a Woman from the Fire," which is number 186 of the *Cantigas de Santa María*. In it a black man is in the role of *agent provocateur* and scapegoat. Although we have reviewed a similar double role in the tale of Mauaz, not to mention *Thousand Nights*, in these examples a black man provides a daredevil form of erotic provocation while receiving blame without actual retribution. Instead the *Cantiga* casts the black co-protagonist as a man "used" and "martyrized" for a sinful copulation in which he is barely a "tool."

In summary, the tale centers on a woman who loves her husband very much and the Virgin Mary even more. The protagonist's mother-in-law decides to test the limits of the protagonist's virtue. During her son's absence, his mother leads a blackamoor into her daughter-in-law's bedroom. Upon return, the husband finds the wife in bed with a man, presumably the "heaven-sent" stud service. According to custom, justice condemns the young woman to be burned along with the black man, even though the former is relatively innocent of a sin she did not premeditate or promote, and the latter is relatively innocent because of the untamed savagery of his libido. However the moralistic tale delivers a subtextual variation:

> They took the woman to a large square, and the moor with her, who was quite black, like a fish. And the people came over ... running and setting the two of them in the greatest circle of fire you have ever seen, and the falsely treacherous moor burned, while the woman did not feel a thing, as if she had been in her own home (209).

The moor's dark skin signals his having been physically and/or metaphysically tainted from birth by the *macula* of sin. He also bears the Christian mark of the fish for which he is condemned to death. After all he, like Christ, is born to die for sins he did not actually commit. The twice-burned martyr points out society's bad conscience and humanity's unavoidable original sin and potential for a final redemption. If only "verbally," the apocalyptic "greatest circle of fire" exonerates the blackamoor, who is declared "*falsely* treacherous." In turn, the white woman escapes punishment by remaining as cool amidst the flames as in her own home. Her coolness might suggest that she has remained more chaste than appearances make us suspect; indeed she joins the black man in suffering for superficial appearances. Meanwhile, the certainly righteous and plotting mother-in-law and the likely aloof and misreading husband await the readers' metatextual retribution.

If to be black is to be sinful, every repentant Christian can empathize. If to be a woman is to be susceptible to conquest, everyone in occupied Spain can empathize. Alfonso's encyclopedic efforts might not give blackness equal opportunity, but it accepts black citizens as a variation of the norm—at least in the realms of carnal and divine love. It is difficult to ascertain whether, in the balance, the *Cantigas* are fair or unfair about Spain's black citizens, but Afro-Hispanic differences match the fate of other lesser members of societies—such as women—who fight for a place within the self-appointed white and male established order. In occupied Spain, Alfonso's position is not only strategically important, but a move in the right direction.

6. NATIONAL SEEDLINGS

As already established, not all blacks arrived in Spain as Islam's inducted soldiers or slaves; many were ordinary or extraordinary citizens who came of their own free will. However, as the group in question seeks and finds its own space within the emerging nation under siege, most have to fight a prejudiced background that attaches blackness to libidinous savagery in need of channeling. Both the channeling of the libido as a conquering force and the fueling of national pride from visionary qualities, gain Afro-Hispano-Arabs a singular beach head in the forging of the nation.

Take, for instance, the processing of Africa in Spain's national epic *Mio Cid*, an eleventh-century event that takes definitive textual shape in the thirteenth (Pidal 1945). I will concentrate on the epic's best-known episode, "La Afrenta de Corpes" ("The Corpes Affront").

After being ashamed by their own show of cowardice toward a pussycat of a lion on the loose, the Infantes de Carrión kidnap their own brides, after accepting as an engagement gift two swords from their father-in-law, Rodrigo Díaz de Vivar, alias El Cid (Hispano-Arabic for "The Lord"). The swords in question are Colada and Tizón, roughly translatable as "Distilled" or "Sneaky One," and "Scourge" or "Burning Ember." These are the swords that El Cid captured from Islamicized Africans, light and dark—"*las gané a guisa de varón*" (roughly, "I earned them playing the macho role," Canto 124, verse 2576; 242). The swords signal the twin phallic instruments of power borrowed from the light (Arab) and dark (Berber and Sub-Saharan) invading forces. On the one hand we have a civilized, white, superficial cutting instrument and, on the other hand, its barbaric, black and deep-burning partner.

Demeaned men (by a lion and other "lionizing" forces) are imbued with a false sense of phallic and royal prowess—through "paternal" swords and brides. They take revenge against the very daughters of the Spanish Lord they swore to serve. The final push for their crime is actually provided by a seemingly unnatural pocket of nature, "*Montes Claros*" ("Clear Thickets") the no-man's land of Spanish territory where they "*aguijan a espolón,*" ("prick away with their spurs") (Canto 128, verse 2693; 248). The Infantes also prick the innocence of their virgin brides and that of a divided nation. Perhaps the motivation for the paradoxically poetic and savage rendering of a very real rape remains encapsulated in the name and history of the place in which it occurred.

According to Ramón Pidal's recognized linguistic authority, "*Montes Claros*" was the term applied to the Atlas Mountains of North Africa and, by extension, to sub-Saharan or Black Africa (1945, 764–65). When they first appear in the text—in the episode of the lion's defeat of the Infantes—the Montes Claros are placed outside and then, during the rape scene, inside Spain. The evolution of the notion of this space of licentiousness suggests the nominal and geographical Iberian incorporation of a Black African space of rampant libido.

As previously reviewed, the officializing self matches the spirit of conquest and the libido of an other, casting them as black and female "parts" that fight and lose the phallic challenge. It is no surprise that the picture is completed by a sexual interpretation of the Infantes' demeaning encounter with the lion, from which they emerge with a wounded masculinity against models of straight macho pride. However, Spain's others and overwhelming otherness exploit the after-effects of a scene ripe with wounded pride, lawlessness, and forced invasion. A deeper African analysis of the Montes Claros than suggested by Pidal advances such an interpretation.

I suggest, for example, that the use of Montes Claros as an African space derives from the introduction of the Bantu notion of *muntu*, or "community," into the language of *Mio Cid* and indeed, into Spanish ever since. The Bantu interpretation of the word *muntu* as a place where the community gathers, traditionally a clearing in the forest, has practically taken over the Spanish *monte*, whose Latin root suggests "mount." The etymology of the Spanish word is further enriched by cross-references to the verb *montar*, Spanish for "to mount" in its many interpretations, from riding an animal to overcoming someone sexually or otherwise. The Spanish evolution parallels the Bantu one, and eventually transforms a public space into a pubic one: the "*Monte de Venus*," or "Thicket of Venus." Thus linguistically and erotically, this African space marked for the coming-to-conscience and the ensuring of a biological and cultural heritage, transplants a piece of the imaginary, unknown, dark, and conveniently feminized—implying conquerable—continent within the Spanish landscape. The effect is at best problematic for women, the forced keepers of the flame.

The phallocentric plot continues to thicken. Internalized in the language of the episode and the geography of the country, the epic transforms a tortuous white show of truant male hypersexuality and violence against women, into a national/ist agenda built on an imported patch of savage blackness. The father of the two rape victims is inspired to unify (if not necessarily to whiten or dephallicize) the territory while realizing that his enemies are not necessarily the Arabs, or for that matter the Jews or the sub-Saharan Africans, but rather the dark forces within the Spanish soul and land, erotically misappropriated by unruly Spaniards.

7. NAKED IDEALS

In the fourteenth and fifteenth century the black stud, so far a mediating agent, becomes an icon of power rising beyond the carnal and divine knowledge he invariably exploits or, more likely, for which he is exploited. As such, he continues to be both revered and feared, sometimes both at once. Ibn Hazm, the eleventh-century Afro-Hispano-Arabic writer, gives us an early example of what is to become, three to four centuries later, a central issue in the Spanish perception of blackness:

> Even if you were king of all the Muslims you should know that the king
> of the Sudan, a wretched black man with bare genitals, and ignorant,
> has a kingdom bigger than yours (Lewis 1990, 116 n.35).

The features of this poem to keep in mind are the combination of the denigration and the exultation of a "wretched black man," whose "bare genitals" and "ignorant" views do not prevent him from being, as it were, a powerful lord or, in other instances, an abused slave. Thus, it is not always sexual prowess or extraordinary knowledge that empowers the black Afro-Hispano-Arab. In this section, I will review cases in which black power transcends the domain of prowess; in the next, cases in which black prowess leads to virtual powerlessness.

During the period in question the key texts in Spanish dealing with black empowerment beyond prowess are Don Juan Manuel's *El conde Lucanor et Patronio* ("The Count Lucanor and Patronio") and the anonymous *Semeiança del Mundo* (Bleuca 1971; Bull and Williams 1989). The black characters in both of these works appear to be, at least in principle, supervised by, or subservient to, characters and authors who do not identify themselves by race (a propensity of those who attribute the norm to themselves). However, black characterization does evolve. The advantage over portrayals from previous centuries, such as in *Auto de los Reyes Magos*, the *Cantigas* and *Mio Cid*, concerns visibility and specificity. For instance, whereas in the three works mentioned we know, by inference, that a behind-the-scenes character, quality and/or space are gifted with a black sixth sense, in later texts the action centers on the skill of a black character or characteristic. Needless to say, the more visible and specific the more controversial blackness becomes: he who was once an overt savage has developed occult powers of observation that put him at the forefront of discovery. A lingering sense of sexual prowess taints every gain in empowerment.

In one of the vignettes from *El conde Lucanor* (Bleuca 1971), Don Juan Manuel has the count's servant Patronio bring up as a judge of human nature, a sensible and sensitive black man. The vignette in question is a singular version of the European tradition of tales that has come to be known as "the emperor's new clothes." In this case it is the black man who acknowledges the emperor's nakedness in spite of the fact that this appears to negate the emperor's illusion that he is wearing "new clothes." One can read this variant of the tradition in at least four different ways:

1) the black character is the only one with enough common sense to tell the truth, for he acknowledges nakedness as a legitimate option, if not necessarily through a process of open and unbiased selection;
2) he is incapable of lying in spite of the potential retributions, because he is morally superior to the rest of the citizens;
3) he takes a slight chance in stating the obvious because of his educated guess that the emperor is actually testing the reliability of his subjects;
4) only he is capable of facing up to the naked truth or the truth about nakedness.

Whatever your choice, you probably recognize society's delegation of responsibility to an outsider's ability to appreciate nakedness, a quality associated with those used to dealing with erotically compromising situations. However, nakedness emerges here as a clue to powers of perception beyond the erotic—furthering the tradition previously announced by the Arabic treatment of a naked Mauaz.

About the same time as Don Juan Manuel, the anonymous author of *Semeiança del Mundo* (Bull and Williams 1989) generalizes as "extraordinary" the African's knowledge in both the cutting-edge sensual and scientific worlds. The assumption throughout this text is that Africans are so intrinsically attached to nature in a primitive, primordial, or primary fashion, that they are likely (under the right circumstances) to systematize that knowledge. Since *Semeiança del Mundo*, as its name, *Facsimile of the World*, indicates, is an attempt at an encyclopedic gathering of information, whereby the authors and readers transform knowledge into ownership, the worth of Africans as sages of a sort might entice explorers and colonizers to exploit their abilities, even if it required enslavement. *Semeiança* furthers a tradition of trapped black knowledge already announced by the lessons taught by a martyr-like black, like the allegedly sexual servitude of the co-protagonist of the previously studied *Cantiga*.

8. OVERLY SATED

At approximately the same time as the previous explorations of black raw power, we encounter texts lashing out against Afro-Hispano-Arabic citizens with a dark skin, penis, and skills. It might not surprise us that it is precisely these texts that feature black women, whose presence I construe as more problematic from the perspective of the straight, white, male writer. And yet, even though to be a woman, more than to be black, impairs the writer's perception of the other as an erotic and heroic challenger, such controversial texts end up facing up to the real problem of "sharing" power. The issue at hand is what I have come to know as the *phallic fallacy*: leading males are willing to amass power by joining their penises to those with more quantity and less quality, as long as they top the civilized pyramid and retain the savage reins of conquest.

I have found not only support for, but an ironic representation of, the phallic fallacy in *La carajicomedia* (*The Prick-a-comedy*) (Varo 1981). This neglected humorous epic depicts Spain as a plural society largely made up of a motley diversity of peoples headed by a pompous elite that views itself as a macho conquering unit. In two crucial episodes it is women, one white and one black, whose stud-like stance mocks the prowess and power of the presumably white, upright establishment.

The first episode stars a nameless white street woman who, upon being accosted by a pair of low-ranking soldiers, assumes the stance of "a great lady [who] started to attack them verbally," protesting being taken for a whore. The scene culminates in an orgy in which a whole regiment, representing the male members of society at large, all of them "well-endowed" ("*bien apercibidos*"), "proceeded to transform her cunt into a lake of sperm" ("*le hicieron todo el coño lagunajo de esperma,*" 193–94). The denouement of the scene offers a near *da capo* of sorts: the arrival of a pair of "black horsemen" ("*negros caval-lerizos*") to whom she refuses entry (194).

The cacophony of double meanings dooms everyone in this episode to erotically demeaning caricatures: the two low-ranking soldiers take pleasure in thinking they are raping a lady; the lady is presumed to be so because she screams a theatrical "no"; subsequently every man takes pride in his genital and ejaculatory abilities to conquer the whore, who remains very much in command by rejecting two "*negros cavallerizos,*" either because of their horse-like size or because of their being penniless.

The second episode stars Mari López, a black whore otherwise known as *La Malmaridada*, "The Badly-married (or unmatched) woman," who flashes an impressive, street-wise *curriculum vitae,* including having a mouth of troglodytic proportions ("*tragonita*"), a "speedy cunt" ("*de coño veloce*"), extraordinary in "thrust and climax" ("*fuerças y cuño*") (185). Her appearance does not stop her professional advancement. In spite of her bulky and ugly body, "as an Ethiopian, she is cute enough to support herself" ("*assí etiope, es algo graciosa, la qual la sostiene*") (185). I suspect that the author is playing here with the words that the *Song of Songs* places in the mouth of the Queen of Sheba: "I am black, but beautiful" (1: 4–5). Mari López's sexual abilities might appear demeaning to most, but they earn her a living from deceiving appearances, playing the exotic part, and faking extreme pleasure.

In general the plot presents the world genitalized and commercialized as a whorehouse of epic proportions. The limits of that erotic space are guarded by black horsemen and women of whatever race who pretend to succumb complacently only to white men of horse-like proportions. The epic space shares important aspects with the "Clear Thicket" from *Mio Cid*, particularly in so far as both free-zones serve as controversial testing grounds for a nation's view of unity, ranging from copulation to consolidation. Both epics disseminate to the entire nation the character and responsibility of the space in question and the characteristics and actions of the cast of characters there assembled. Ultimately the issue is the politics of conquest, and in both texts the tension is not so much between black and white, as between male and female.

The anonymous text bears, as its title suggests in Spanish, the fallacious sign of the phallus which, black or white, is the ultimate bittersweet target for *Prick-a-comedy's* subliminal feminist polemic. After the author declares the work finished, "the text" itself goes on to recount the death of the author's head/prick in a battle between the brigades of light pricks and dark cunts over the hegemony of the Spanish territory. After the decisive battle of orgasms is won by the cunts, their strategy becomes evident: as soon as "the cunts would have solicited the treacherous entry; the hard pricks would have denied an exit" ("la pérfida entrada los coños querían, la dura salida las pixas negavan"), until they were too depleted to fight back (230).

9. MODEL BLACKNESS

The last period covered by my study coincides with Spain's final steps into nationhood, territorial control, modern times, and the launching of its imperial career. These activities assumed a slow-brewing "purifying" effort, including the well-known inquisitorial pontification on the validity of a citizen's commitment to the principles upheld by a precariously positioned Church and State. And, as these two institutions consolidated, punishment and banishment were accorded to those who did not comply.

The very notion of religious and political purity is somewhat absurd for an occupied territory. During the period in question there is an intense review of what it means to be Spanish, which certainly includes the cultural impact from at least three sources, Arabic, Jewish, and Christian, and a highly bureaucratized and controlled process of internalization and hybridization. To my surprise, such a process is known to star a black character capable of giving witness to the complexity of the Spanish world and worlds beyond. The *Poema de José* (Johnson 1974) is a case in point. It is an *aljamiada* masterpiece (a "foreign" or "barbarous" tradition, as the Arabic origin of the word indicates). Whereas the term for this literary tradition derives from an Arabic word rendered in Spanish and pointing to this barbarity, by contrast, the texts themselves approximate the Spanish language in Arabic signs.

The plot of the *Poema de José* is modeled on chapter XII of the Qur'an and the biblical story of Joseph in Genesis 39. I find great difficulty in differentiating the Muslim from the Jewish and Christian elements in the plot of the *Poema*, for the theme serves as messianic sign for the three cultures of Spain, already presented from an elliptically black perspective in the *Auto de los Reyes Magos* (Pidal 1900). All of these sources make a contribution to the *Poema*'s erotic syncretization, starring a José who is under the expert guidance of a black teacher. José, like his counterparts, the Biblical and Qur'anic Josephs, dreams up his religious "illumination" by focusing on the reading of a star, and armed with such a knowledge embarks on a bumpy road of temptations.

The *Poema*'s key secular variation from the divine theme occurs during José's encounter with Zalifa. This encounter, according to the traditional explanation by Baidawi, is the culmination of *wa'ilman*, "'knowledge' of the interpretation of dreams," and of *hukman*, "'wisdom,' which is knowledge backed up by action; or 'authority' among men" (Beeston 1963, 14). In spite of Baidawi's exhaustive—and exhausting—catalogue of ways in which females can share this male prerogative, there is little solace for feminist—or for that matter erotic—interpretation of such prerogatives. The *Poema*, however, bridges the gap with ease and portrays José as enjoying a near-complete erotic practice based on the godly gift of knowledge to the phallically-endowed believer.

The *Poema* (Johnson 1974) centers on the secular application of this divine theory of mankind coming into maturity. In this Spanish literary example, José's nameless black teacher serves to put into erotic practice the adolescent's theoretical reading of the stars and attempts to turn the young adult into a virtual porn star of wanderlust. José's training begins in a geographically unplaceable "*monte*" (34–35)—which resonates with *Mio Cid*'s *Montes Claros*. At that point in the text, José's older brothers having virtually buried him in a hole, they return to the site to make sure of his fate. The brothers' latent facsimile of sexual burial, by way of an innocent man's hopeless and deadly abandonment in a hole, is now revisited through some sort of necrophilic castration plot. José's antagonistic siblings attempt to "*esmemb(e)rar*" him (that is, "to dismember" or to "exhume" the hopeless boy or the dead body; 36).

But the black merchant finds José before his fatal date with destiny and as he lifts him from the depth of the hole, in which he has been left for dead, the protagonist begins his hormonal journey into manhood—"*sallia el bella barba*," that is, "he grew a nice beard" (39). Manhood and mankind's enlightenment go hand in hand, as the dark teacher promises to take his light student to the Holy Land—presumably leading the way for the tribes of Israel to reach a safe haven.

Upon facing an ominous tempest in the journey, the two men begin to identify with each other. Joseph's help and consolation bring about his being called "oh brother, oh friend, deserving one" ("*ay ermano, ay amigo, g(a)ranado*"; 46). However, José is less a student than merchandise which the merchant must deliver to his ultimate destiny. To such an end, the black man dresses up José as an angel, equally capable of standing above all other men and of succumbing to the temptation of women. However, in more practical terms, José is wrapped in appropriate finery to be sold as a slave.

The merchant accomplishes José's investment in spite of his own intentions and condition: "*maguer que yera oscuro, el bien lo b(a)lanquiaba*" ("in spite of being black, he was able to whiten him"; 47). Whatever interpretation we may give to this transformation, it depends on a balancing of sin and redemption, blackness and whiteness, which supposes the identification between a more than ordinary merchant and a less than divine messenger of God.

At the end of their journey, the team stirs up passion and compassion, not to mention securing a great price upon delivery. The local Caliph buys José to serve as the son the old man could not give her. Presumably Zalifa expects much more, and so do we the readers, for José has been exposed to the black teacher's lessons in the art of love—"*doze mulleres que tengo con amor*," or "I have made twelve women fall in love" (51). But José is either a slow learner or has a more sublime notion of love than a sportsman's display of sexual promiscuity. After attempting to seduce him by various means, Zalifa opts to assert her right to offer herself to him as sexual merchandise: "*yo faré al materia que se venga a vuest(o)ro leijo*" ("I shall provide the 'matter' [means] to get to your bed"; 54). Zalifa here uses the sort of market strategy which she might assume José has learned from his merchant teacher—to no avail.

Zalifa goes overboard: she orders an all-white palace to be built, on whose walls she and José are painted as succumbing to each other. Once the painted palace has been finished, she summons him to it. He is so reluctant to enter that she: "*t(a)rabolo de la falda, levolo do jazia*" ("wrapped him into her skirt and pulled him down"; 55). The text insists twice on the failed attempt to entrap José; the third time, as the husband is watching, her skirt tears at the seams (56). Is this a sign that she has symbolically lost her virginity, her willpower, or her battle of love, fought with the husband's tacit approval? The fact is that José feels compromised by guilt: "*su corazón negro, por miedo de pecado*"—("his heart black, fearful of sin"; 56). Whether José and Zalifa did it or not we shall never know. In spite of the tailor-made white palace of porn and the light-skinned heavy seductress with the theatrical loss of virginity, and under the powerful master of ceremonies' watchful eye, the situation only succeeds in revealing the blackness of José's heart.

The *Poema* ends with the suggestion of a crazed, sadomasochistic lesbian orgy. A chorus of women throw themselves into a passionate bloodletting fantasy inspired by the figure of the black-trained angelic stud:

> The women, the minute they saw him, lost their sanity,
> So dashing and of such a good looking figure was he,
> They thought he was an angel, and this drove them wild.
> They cut their hands and that which does not heal (Johnson 1974, 58; my translation).

The open ending leaves to each reader the interpretation of the fantasy of what it is that does not heal. The Qur'an does refer to women cutting themselves because of communal guilt. However, Baidawi's respected interpretation of the passage suggests the first menstrual flow—as if coming face to face with José would have brought about these women's coming of age. In a more suggestive mood, Baidawi views the women's reaction as a mirror of their mistress' finding love, that is their choral response to the acknowledgment that "he [Joseph] has pierced the *shaghaf* of the heart, which is its membrane, until he has penetrated to her [Zalifa's] inmost heart with love" (Beeston 1963, 17).

In Afro-Hispano-Arabic literature up to this point and beyond, black men, white women, and those who follow their footsteps, continue to share the treacherous lesson that sexual prowess does not equal military, moral, religious or, for that matter, any other form of power. There are serious retaliations for every moment in which slaves become masters; their erotic and heroic deeds become acts of martyrdom. Such acts might, in fact, lead to the hybridization of Spanish culture, but at what a tremendous price!

10. CODA

"How many people there must be in the world who flee from others because they cannot see themselves" (Frauca 1554/1926, 84). This assertion, from the mouth of the protagonist of *Lazarillo de Tormes*, Spain's anonymous sixteenth-century proto-novel, refers to his biracial half brother's hysterical rejection of his own black step-father. The line also applies to Lazarillo's own place in society and Spain's place in the world. After all, Lazarillo, like most of Spain, has hardly been recognized as the member of an elite. On the contrary, the text's protagonist is a Spanish nobody, born and bred, the bastard product of hybridization. The situation undoubtedly reflects that of the author, likely a crypto-Jewish writer who was interested in exploring and surviving the emerging nation's coming into the modern age and a conquering power struggling with its precarious international launching. At least in hindsight, this paradoxical double goal must have demanded breaking through the rhetorical weave of artificial differences, hypothetical appearances, and at least seven centuries of multicultural "occupation."

The tendency of the text of *Lazarillo*, that of the protagonist, the author, and the Spanish nation is to place on the shoulders of a known intruder the responsibility for the trials and tribulations of prowess and power. This intruder is Zaide, the servile black "horseman" who "services" his mother's needs, his own, and those of his family after Lazarillo's true father has been sent to prison and from there to fight for Spain and the church against the Moors. Oftentimes unnatural step-figures exercise their assigned prowess in an intrusive fashion that rivals and challenges the paternalistic powermongering of natural father figures. For instance, Lazarillo, like the formative journey of Spanish culture, grows up under many masters and master plans, studded with literary figures like Zaide, the mother-servicing black stallion, the brother's rejected father, and the picaresque hero's phallic bread and butter. Lazarillo's heritage, knowledge, identity, survival, success, and above all, life of compromise, depend on the good heart as much as on the sexual desire of his mother's black stud. The lesson is well-taken; Spanish upstarts, like those in Lazarillo's family, learn to live under the shadow of the black conqueror/conquered like their predecessors did during the Afro-Islamic period.

Upon reviewing the birth of the Spanish nation from three faiths and cultures of occupation—Christian, Muslim, and Jewish—it would seem that the highly mixed peoples living such an experience attempted to meet each other on some common symbolic ground that would be less problematic than the disputed territory they realistically could not share as equals. Some aspects of sub-Saharan black culture, organized around the figure of black eroticism, provide an unfortunate but crucial pretext for unification. The black slave and citizen, mediator, provider, and teacher of love and lust, arguably also the most other of Spanish others, found a place of dubious honor at the head of a foreign legion of leading phalluses. The protomacho effigy also gets the honor and the blame for his perceived manipulation of erotic encounters that unavoidably lead to the miscegenation of peoples and cultures prevented by their own strictures from fantasizing on their own and writing about it directly.

NOTES

1. The phrase *"negro como un pez,"* "black like a fish," abounds in medieval Spanish literature, oftentimes in reference to Christ, who is both a "black fish" and the redemptory "fisherman of sins." For an example see section 5 of this paper.

2. Illustrations published in Devisse (1979, 53, 64–65, 67).

3. Rabanus Maurus, quoted by Devisse (1979, 58).

4. For a brief analysis of the magical quality of blackness in Patristic Literature, see Courtés (1979, 18–22); and for its "animalistic" excesses in the Hispano-Arabic context, see Lewis (1990).

5. Ar-Ramadi is also known as Abu 'Omar (wrongly Abu 'Amr) Yusuf ib Harun al-Kindi al-Qurtubi. Nykl (1946, 59).

6. For illustrations, see Devisse (1979, 88–96).

WORKS CITED

Alfonso X, el Sabio. 1986. *Cantigas de Santa María*, ed. Walter Mettmann. Madrid: Castalia.

Beatus of Liebana. 1915. *A New Text of the Apocalypse from Spain. Extracted and Translated from the Latin Text of the Morgan Manuscript of the Eighth Century* [Pierpoint Library m644]. New York: n.p.

Beeston, A. F. L., ed. 1963. *Baidawi's Commentary on Surah 12 of the Qur'an* (with an interpretive rendering and notes). Reprint 1978. Oxford: Clarendon.

Blecua, José Manuel, ed. 1971. *Libro de los enxiemplos del conde Lucanor et de Patronio.* 2nd ed. Madrid: Castalia.

Bull, William E. and Harry F. Williams, eds. 1989. *Semeiança del Mundo: A Medieval Description of the World.* Berkeley and Los Angeles: University of California.

Burton, Richard F., trans. 1885. *A Plain and Literal Translation of the Arabian Nights' Entertainments, Now Entitled the Book of the Thousand Nights and a Night* (with introduction, explanatory notes on the manners and customs of Moslem men and a terminal essay upon the history of *The Nights*). Vol. I. London.

Courtes, Jean Marie. 1979. "The Theme of 'Ethiopia' and 'Ethiopians' in Patristic Literature," in *The Image of the Black in Western Art*, ed. Devisse. 9–32.

Devisse, Jean, ed. 1979. *The Image of the Black in Western Art*, trans. William Granger Ryan. New York: William Morrow.

Frauca, Julio Cejador y, ed. 1554/1926. *La vida de Lazarillo de Tormes. Y de sus fortunas y adversidades.* Madrid: Ediciones "La Lectura."

Johnson, William Weisiger, ed. 1974. *Poema de José: A Transcription and Comparison of the Extant Manuscripts.* Valencia: University of Mississippi.

Lévi-Provençal, E. 1938. *La Péninsule Ibérique au Moyen-Age.* Leiden: E. G. Brill.

Lewis, Bernard. 1990. *Race and Slavery in the Middle East.* New York and Oxford: Oxford University Press.

Lindsay, W. M., ed. 1911. *Isidori hispalensis episcopi etymologiarum sive originum.* Oxford: Clarendon.

Nykl, A.R. 1946. *Hispano-Arabic Poetry and its Relations with the Old Provençal Troubadours.* Reprint 1986. Baltimore: J. H. Furst Company.

Pidal, Ramón Menéndez, ed. 1900. *Disputa del Alma y el Cuerpo y Auto de los Reyes Magos.* Madrid: Revista de Archivos, Bibliotecas y Museos.

———, ed. 1945. *Cantar del mio Cid: Texto, gramática y vocabulario.* Vol. 2: *Vocabulario.* Madrid: Espasa Calpe.

———, ed. 1944. *Poema del mio Cid.* Madrid: Espasa Calpe.

Piedra, José. 1991. "Literary Whiteness and the Afro-Hispanic Difference," in *The Bounds of Race*, ed. LaCapra. 278–310.

Varo, Carlos, ed. 1981. *Carajicomedia.* Madrid: Editorial Playor.

The Queen's Too Bawdies   **3**

El burlador de Sevilla and the Teasing of Historicity

María M. Carrión

"Truth, whose mother is history, rival of time, depository of deeds, witness of the past, exemplar and adviser to the present, and the future's counselor." History, the *mother* of truth: the idea is astounding. Menard, a contemporary of William James, does not define history as an inquiry into reality but as its origin.

—Jorge Luis Borges, "Pierre Menard, Author of the *Quixote*"

For David Carrión Fuentes. *In memoriam*

THE QUEEN'S TOO BAWDIES

In the year of 1957, Ernst Kantorowicz set in motion the idea of "the king's two bodies," a concept that explained the complexities the figure of a monarch confronted in the political, religious, and human arenas during the Middle Ages in Europe. This theory proposed that there were subtle lines that divided the "private" and "public" in this multiple yet organic entity, which made the crown a set of irreconcilable parts that had to be coordinated in order for the king to rule properly over all other bodies under him.[1] Kantorowicz's principles seem to apply perfectly to the representation of kingly figures in the seventeenth-century Spanish play *El burlador de Sevilla y convida do de piedra* (Casalduero 1987) (translated as *The Trickster of Seville and the Stone Guest* [Edwards 1986]): the two kings who appear struggle to keep law and order under control by enforcing cultural and political codes that are expected to help maintain social harmony.[2] The first one, the King of Naples (nameless in the play, but associated with Roberto of Naples, whose government extended from 1309 to 1343), briefly rules on the disaster of the Duchess Isabela having being dishonored on his own palatial grounds: he asks the lady a few questions, puts both the apprehended subjects and the matter itself in the hands of his best man for the job, Don Pedro Tenorio, and turns "his royal eyes elsewhere" (I: 29–35). When briefed about the amazing escape of the suspect, he learns that the reason why Isabela screamed for help was that her fiancé, the Duke Octavio, had just seduced her. Seeing his greatest of fears come true, he mumbles: "[Ap.] ¡Ah, pobre honor! Si eres alma / del hombre ¿por qué te dejan en la mujer inconstante, / si es la misma ligereza?" ([Aside] Oh, fragile honor, source and very essence / of man's existence, yet your pure wholeness / relies entirely on fickle woman, / herself the very image of inconstancy"; EI: 153–56).[3] He puts a price on Octavio's head, and makes a final token appearance as the judge of Isabela, ordering her to be silent, for "no word" of hers can mend the attack she has inflicted upon his royal persona through a series of secret and illicit encounters with her fiancé which violate openly the palatial protocol. He carries out his duty to sentence her by committing her to a tower, the ultimate space for women's stillness and quiet in medieval life and letters. When she begs him not to turn his back on her, he categorically answers: *"Ofensa a mi espalda hecha / es justicia y es razón / castigalla a espaldas vueltas"* ("Since the offence took place behind my back, / the punishment's appropriate and just; / my back is turned towards the one who's guilty"; EI: 184–86).

The King of Naples is related to the second king, the King of Castile, both by plot and structure: the supposed Roberto knows only part of the truth, and he acts upon that. But Alfonso, the King of Castile (historically, Alphonse the Eleventh), learns nothing but the truth from his High Chamberlain Don Diego Tenorio, who at the beginning of the second act receives a letter from his brother Don Pedro with information about the trick of a deceitful seduction Don Juan Tenorio has perpetrated upon Doña Isabela in Neapolitan territory. Alfonso decides that he ought to fix up this mess, and hence he decides to straighten out the story and tell his fellow king Roberto the truth, so he can free the innocent Octavio and make Don Juan Tenorio, son of Diego and nephew of Pedro, marry Isabela, thus restoring her honor.[4] As in practically every other Spanish drama from the seventeenth century, these two royal figures play a significant role in the texture of El burlador.[5] They represent the top layer of hierarchical political power, but in this particular case they also represent an emblem of the blindness and the absurdity that royalty had achieved because of its incompetence as a class of rulers. The fact that the text plays with issues of historical identification is one of the many ways in which the neat scheme of the "king's two bodies" is parodied: Roberto and Alfonso correspond to figures of the Spanish past, but their dramatic rendition brings forth a number of issues at stake in the formation of new masculine identities, and in the formation of new national and political identities as well. Furthermore, the relationship between the two kings and their best men, emblematic of the *valido* system that characterized the exercise of monarchy for most of the seventeenth century in Spain, suggests a network of references that complicates even further the possible historical allusions, and yet enhances the plasticity of the text of El burlador when read in tandem with Kantorowicz's theory.

For instance, among the many historical models proposed by scholars for characters in El burlador, the Duke of Osuna stands out, since he was, in 1620, the High Chamberlain to the king (Philip III) and, hence, in charge of His Majesty's personal care and the ceremonial events celebrated on palatial grounds. In principle this figure seems to correspond well, as Edwards has pointed out, to the bearded and honorable father of the *burlador,* Don Diego (EI: 571n.), whose name in the twin variant of *El burlador*—entitled *Tan largo me lo fiáis* (*Trust me a while longer*)—is Don Juan Tenorio the Old, and not Don Diego Tenorio, as he is named in *El burlador;* a fact that supports the "nameless" trait of his son in this manuscript: *"yo soy un hombre sin nombre"* ("I am a nameless man"; I: 15).[6] If not by Don Diego-Don Juan, Osuna could perhaps be better represented in both manuscripts by Don Gonzalo de Ulloa, Doña Ana's father and future Stone Guest. However, the fact that the historical character of Osuna is not merely a decent and honorable man in power, but a myriad of contradictory traits, offers possible identifications with more than one male character in the play. In a gross simplification, we can describe this historical persona in two ways, both of which have been capitalized on by history books. First and foremost, the Duke is Don Pedro Téllez de Girón, Marquis of Peñafiel, later to become the Duke of Osuna, whom Blanca de los Ríos has argued might be Tirso de Molina's possible half brother.[7] On the other hand, much has been written about the influential political figure that he turned out to be, most of it agreeing that he was one of the most—if not the most—successful of Philip III's Italian viceroys, stationed in Naples, and the one who firmly maintained Spain's authority over the Mediterranean with his energetic actions.[8] What survives of all this in the play, ironically enough, does not point in the direction of any of the above-mentioned men; instead what survives takes the form of Don Juan's trait of adaptation to change, a trait required in order to be in tune with the changes in manners, values, and ideologies of the time. Osuna, the Count Duke of Olivares and Don Juan, Jr. share the power that emanates from arresting images, typical of historical characters, a power that leads to readers' identification with their characters despite the fact that they were morally unacceptable, or in the best of cases, politically ambiguous.[9]

These dynamics of shift in power and identification find correspondences in numerous social and literary instances. At the highest level of political hierarchies, government began to favor the delegation of duties, and by the beginning of the seventeenth century the king was able to enjoy life and the arts privately, while the plotting and actual ruling took place from the desk of the *validos.*[10] Philip IV, counting on a much stronger *valido,* Olivares, attempted to train himself to be a king by reading history, writing his own under the form of the *autosemblanza* and, more than anything else, trying to balance the fact that, as a child, "he had spent more time on pursuits that had given him pleasure than on ones which would be useful to him in later life."[11] With such inspiration from the top players in government, supposed models of citizenship, Don Juan plays onstage differently from a mere exception to heroic codes or an irreverent heir of higher-styled traditions of literature. One among many bodies under the rulership of such a decomposed exercise of monarchic power, Don Juan represents a case study of what Anthony Cascardi calls the "subject of control," that individual whose different agencies were intimately related to the fact that his or her life was highly regulated, which made a great part of his or her actions reactions to the demands of courtly dictations.[12]

The fact that the "king's bodies" were not just two anymore, but multiple, since the royal power circulated from hand to hand, led to the grand cultural motif of this period, the *desengaño,* or disillusionment, which all of Don Juan's victims experience first-hand as a result of his obsessive characteristic trait of *burlar.* Indeed, the quasi-gestalt of *desengaño* acquires a different value when seen within the context of an unsustainable—and, I might add, unbearable—behavioral code of honor.[13] Hence Don Juan's inquiry into the nature of disillusionment and perversity is not so much an *essai* on the decep-tion of women, as it is a way to create and resolve the problem of desire, but not in a univocal way. The promise of creating a narrative, a *copula,* is endlessly delivered, and yet it remains unfulfilled, as it is not the actual consummation of heterosexual inter-course that is at stake, but the control and management of desire, carnal and otherwise, as prescribed during the Council of Trent.[14] Instead of representing a faithful applica-tion of the principles of "the king's two bodies," what *El burlador* brings forth is a disorga-nization of this concept, or what I call "the queen's too bawdies," a queer rendition of the displacement of the power of the royal persona onto a subject of control, Don Juan, who evades punishment with his fantastic tricks, and finds a way out in a nonorthodox management of sexuality and death.

One of the impulses behind this disorganization is a questioning of the validity of post-Tridentine legislations on sexual matters, from the nakedness of the human body to coital issues, and the representation of these ideas in the arts. First, and possibly fore-most is the way in which the regulation of human behavior and sexual, political, and national identities tried to recover the hegemony of the imperial era, that moment of the genesis of the Spanish imperial dream that alluded to the literary topos of grammar and empire going hand in hand. This was set in stone when Antonio de Nebrija estab-lished that the organicity and order of grammar was what José Piedra labels "the core of a citizen's apprenticeship," which "guided the recording and making of history and, hence, the official channel of spreading the truth."[15] The grammarians, then, became symbolic warriors of empire, a sociocultural class in charge of defending the correspon-dence between national identity and the historical enterprise, which Nebrija laid out in the prologue of his *Grammar* (Muñoz and Romero 1946). This might help explain what Nancy Struever calls the "fashionableness and self-confidence of the Humanists" rooted in rhetorical and grammatical skills, and the "depth of their scholarly commitment," a trait among the guards of the imperial tradition that, in Spain, linked certain castigating philological uses with the production of history.[16] The "cause" of this defense of gram-mar was to benefit from the power to conquer that could be derived from a systemati-zation of the Spanish language, which yoked it to the imperial enterprises of the present and the past. This enterprise conveniently incorporated the two favorite semantic fields of men of arms and letters: love and war. And it is this power to use the language in his own systematized way that has made Don Juan historically a man of good standing, and hence worthy of the favor of kings, *validos,* and even many readers, despite the blatancy of his abuse. His most memorable trait is, then, not the favor—just or unjust, deserved or not—from the king, but his totalitarian exercise of will, even if it means falling out of grace or out of the categories expected from a man of his kind.

As a woman reading a seducer in order to disengage from the trick that would "leave me without honor," I propose an alternative to unilateral readings and writings of this character. The character of Don Juan is, above all, about seduction, and thus about the performance not only of great macho tricks, but also of the pleasure of rereading the history of staging different masculinities, such as the king, the hero, or the lover. Regardless of how much the character exploits ethical codes, issues of intentionality and inequality or disproportionate power in human relations, the authorial figure of *El burlador* brings forth hidden transcripts of human behavior, and articulates a literary experiment on the application of the arts of domination and resistance to the areas of power and sexuality (Scott 1990). This dramatic rendition is a disorganized entity, one that moves not primarily to consum(mat)e coital heterosexual anxieties, but to stimulate new renditions of a language of relations between the sexes/genders. Don Juan's "promises" to marry are promises to continue to promise and nothing else, rather than simple transgressions of matrimonial rites. For what defines him, what the readers can understand as his identity, is not his sexual attraction to women, but to the act of promising and making people react to the act of breaking promises.[17] Hence, his eternal bond to the Stone Guest can be read as an emblem of the bond between different male characters, a union between two struggling heroes at a time when heroic codes were up for grabs.

The rehearsal for the third seduction, which never takes place but which results in the death of the woman's father is a case in point. After the Marquis of Mota's lusty speech on his desire to win the beauty and virtues of his cousin Doña Ana de Ulloa, Catalinón warns him "[*Ap.*] *No prosigas, que te engaña | el gran burlador de España*" ("[*Aside*] Say no more, for you are being fooled / by the great trickster of Spain"; II: 1279–80). The *gracioso*'s rhetorical gesture of complicity is embodied by the rhyme "*engaña-España,*" emblematic sign of Don Juan's many operational fields. The first part of this couplet places Mota on the same level of passivity as the trickster's four conquests, given that he is as deceived as are the four women. The second line of the couplet acknowledges his superiority over the gentlemen Octavio, Don Diego, Don Gonzalo, the king, and even his own rival trickster, Mota. But the couplet finds references outside of the text as well, as the ambiguous "*de España*" suggests (both "from" and "of" Spain). The Trickster of Seville is fully conscious, as is his native land (because it "speaks" in the text), that besides being a great lover and charmer, Don Juan is a *burlador*, a man who has the supreme ability to perform tricks on others. In effect, as Mota exits the stage, Don Juan plans and savors his future victory over both Doña Ana and the Marquis with a boasting confirmation that "*Sevilla a voces me llama | el Burlador, y el mayor | gusto que en mí puede haber | es burlar a una mujer | y dejalla sin honor*" ("*Seville shouts my name, | the Trickster, and the greatest | pleasure that there can be in me | is to deceive a woman, | and to leave her without honor*"; II: 1313–17).[18] This reference directly alludes to Don Juan's triumphs over women. But, what is more significant, it represents the reification and subordination of the term "mujer," and it proposes a critique of the notion that the intrinsic value of honor—a sociocultural asset still very much alive today as an essential trait of "Spanish" character—is ultimately reserved for the male counterpart of the woman, be he the father, lover, brother, husband, or fiancé, even though its specific locus is the body of the woman and its lack of sexual activity.[19]

Thus Doña Ana de Ulloa, exemplary instance of a body that matters both for its femaleness and for its compliance with the concept of "femininity," represents a token of the "currency" within the economy of *El burlador*'s differential production of the heroic character's glory through loss.[20] Don Juan's anticipated delight represents a desire to consummate one more act of villainy, the "tricking of a woman" (*"burlar a una mujer"*). From this specific point of view, he is adhering *ad literam* to Covarrubias' definition: "a lying deceiver, one who damages others" and who "has little *valor* (value, courage) and *asiento* (balance)," for his *burlas "se contraponen a veras"* ("are contrary to truth").[21] But he is indirectly—if powerfully—moved as well by an irresistible temptation to "dump her and dispossess her of her honor" (*"dejalla sin honor"*), that valuable token of responsibility and good citizenship that sets in motion the majority of social and dramatic conflicts in Golden Age Spain. Taking Doña Ana's honor involves the mechanical repetition of a trick: lying, entering her private space, and publicizing a supposed act of possession of her body.[22] But even though Don Juan acknowledges in public that he derives his pleasure from the combination of *"burlar"* and *"dejar sin honor,"* the transgression is not directly related to the sexed aspect of this female body, at least not literally, in the case of Doña Ana. Her silence makes Don Juan's third *burla*, more than any other one perpetrated in the text, primarily affect those who can effectively restore the offense and thus are the ultimate receptacles of the precious social commodity of honor: Don Gonzalo, her father; Mota, the suitor; and Octavio, Doña Ana's fiancé by royal order in that moment in the development of the play. Her figure is simply the currency for a series of transactions of power. Among all the women in the play, her social status makes her the best candidate for what conduct manuals such as that of Luis de León called a "perfect wife." But the talk about her beauty and virtuosity provokes the desire of both tricksters, Don Juan and Mota, making her a pretextual "angel" for nineteenth-century characters such as Zorrilla's Inés or, in a different vein, Laclos' Tourvel in *Les Liaisons Dangereuses*. Doña Ana is such an asset that even the king uses her to play politics, by appeasing first Don Juan's father, and then the offended Duke Octavio, with the promise of her hand to whoever needs a trophy. Meanwhile, Mota praises her by saying that *"Veréis la mayor belleza / que los ojos del rey ven"* ("You will see the greatest beauty / that the king has ever laid eyes on"; II: 1273–74). And yet, despite all this value—or perhaps precisely as representative "divinity" in the midst of all this male gazing—her body never appears onstage. The audience only hears her offstage voice, uttering four caricaturized slogans of the code of honor: two lines unmasking Don Juan, *"¡Falso!, no eres el marqués, / que me has engañado. . . . ¡Fiero enemigo, / mientes, mientes!"* ("Traitor!, you are not the Marquis, / you have deceived me. . . . Fierce enemy, / you liar, you liar!"; II: 1557–60), and two more acknowledging the tragedy of her *deshonra* and begging for its only remedy, *"¿No hay quien mate este traidor, / homicida de mi honor? . . . Matalde"* ("Is there no one who will kill this traitor, / assassin of my honor? . . .

Kill him"; II: 1562–68). Doña Ana's physical absence from this scenario can be read as a commentary on the abuse of the female figure as a token of exchange between men, currency without which the kings, the gentlemen and even the trickster himself could not survive in the textual economy of El burlador.[23] This dependence on the sacrificial rite of a woman's body is what has, in turn, survived of the character of Don Juan beyond the production of El burlador de Sevilla.

EL BURLADOR DE SEVILLA **AND THE TEASING OF HISTORICITY**

In Spanish the term "donjuan" touches upon a whole range of myths of masculinity. The term has been used, for instance, as the starting point for certain universal myths of male hegemony, in an effort to justify the power of "man" over "woman," or the "naturally understandable" triumph of man's will or skill over those of woman. These myths, in turn, are linked to the foundation of cultures of *machismo*, which revolve around the idea that men, as a sex, are superior to women. The competent exercise of *donjuanismo* is the central axis of a successful representation of a man in a *machista* environment. On a more specific level, the *Diccionario de la Lengua Española* defines a "donjuan" as a *"tenorio,"* an allusion to the central character of *El burlador de Sevilla* (548). A "donjuan," continues the *Diccionario*, is a *"galanteador audaz y pendenciero,"* "a man who engages in bold and challenging gallant behavior," "gallant" being the adjective that refers to acts of flirting and courtship in order to seduce a woman (1390). These acts of *donjuanismo* are still essential for the definition of certain masculine identities: blatant lies, relentless stalking, possession of a female body by tricking her into consent, and bragging about it all regardless of whether any of it happened or not. These acts of abuse are rooted in a mythical—for some even archetypical—figure who granted pleasure a position of priority in his life, and who derived his pleasure from performing sexual tricks. But these misreadings of the precursor have not turned out to be mere poetic instances. These ritual practices are convenient partial readings of Don Juan Tenorio that lead to a reduction of the central character of *El burlador* to an immoral, inhuman, or satanic entity who only laughs when he destroys dumb women, and whose point in life is merely to defy the laws of man and God. They bypass other traits of the character of Don Juan, such as his tremendous erotic quality, or his skillful teasing of the process of becoming a historical artifact. Rather, the history of the reception of the character of Don Juan has been an alternating sequence of praise and blame that tells us more about the respective readers than about this landmark of Spanish literary history itself.[24]

The process of transformation of the legendary character of Don Juan into an emblem of male superiority has been made possible in part through a reductive understanding of the role the *"pendenciero"* plays in the configuration of a *"tenorio."* One reading of the "challenging" aspect of this gallant persona freezes the masculine qualities of his character in a unilateral, aggressive rite of defending his power as a heroic figure. And Don Juan performs a number of these defensive swerves in *El burlador*. However, *"pendenciero"* also refers to a figure—literary and otherwise—who, reacting to a threat, can play the jousting game not merely with aggressions but with shifts in positions, with playfulness, in an elusive or unexpected manner more than in a static or prefor-mulated way.[25] Within this context, the figure of Don Juan can be read as an *agon* of medieval epic heroes or polished Renaissance gentlemanly courtiers; he can, in other words, also be understood as an antagonist of these molds that predetermine and put severe limits to his commitment to pleasure. As a teaser of these precursors, Don Juan performs routines, gestures, and situations that correspond to the changing historical meanings of honor and masculinity in early modern Spain.

The historical narratives about the beginning of this literary tradition in Europe have, not surprisingly, many traits in common with the character of Tenorio: they are usually perceived as ambivalent phenomena with difficult, artificial, or excessive styles. One of these master historical narratives is that of Américo Castro who, searching for answers in the areas of heroicity, religiosity, and the code of honor within the history of poetic and cultural diction in Spain, finds new interpretations of these values by dwelling on the text of *El burlador*.[26] Castro's lifelong commitment to the reading of this play leads him to understand that, by the beginning of the seventeenth century, Spanish literature and society no longer valued the anthropomorphic Renaissance ideal of *dignitas hominis*, a programmatic centering of the male figure as the referential axis for cultural and social production. The abandonment of this sense of decorum is partially due to the fact that what was "appropriate" in Renaissance terms was a luxury that Spain could not afford anymore, literally and figuratively.[27] Hence, the way in which the authorial hands bring the character of Don Juan to life is radically different from the way in which Renaissance humanists recovered the classics.[28] The Stone Guest, for instance, represents "petrified" ideas of heroicity, typical of epic narratives, and not merely a literal monument to the grandeur of things past. At the same time, Don Juan's evasiveness in relation to both marriage and death are reiterative critiques of dramatic and social "realities" built upon the principle that only through these two conventions would life, narrative, and drama come to a closure, to a sense of fulfill-ment that would coincide in a satisfactory manner with "The End." The fact that the Statue asks Don Juan for his hand fuses the management of death and marriage in a parodic gesture, opening new grounds for dramatic and historical character. The author restores Renaissance ideals of a harmonious society when he—in an almost apocryphal manner—adds the classic ritual of marital matches approved by the king to the fatal union of Don Juan and the Stone Guest. Alfonso adds his royal signature to this level of "reality" in the appendix to the play, by ordering the immediate transfer of the cadaver of the Stone Guest from this unbearable space of his union with Don Juan to a memorable landmark, the pantheon of San Francisco, a hermitage that was turned into a church in the fifteenth century (III: 983–1068). This double ritual of the wedding scene and the monumental funeral rites can, of course, be read as a clear condemnation of Don Juan's immoral fiber; but it is also an "illogical" about-face to the feast of devil-ish food and the hand-holding of the two prominent male characters, thus establishing textual grounds for different and even contradictory interpretations of *El burlador*.

One of the textual instances of this representation of contradictory myths of masculinity in *El burlador* can be seen in Don Juan Tenorio's second performance. Just arrived from Naples, where he has dishonored Isabela, Don Juan survives a shipwreck. After trying to save his soul mate, Catalinón, Don Juan faints, and then Catalinón drags him ashore. Miraculously recovered from his near-death experience, he engages in gallant behavior with his female rescuer, the fisherwoman Tisbea: *"Don Juan: Muerto soy. Tisbea: ¿Cómo, si andáis? | Don Juan: Ando en pena, como veis. | Tisbea: Mucho habláis. Don Juan: Mucho entendéis. | Tisbea: ¡Plega a Dios que no mintáis!* ("Don Juan: I'm dead. Tisbea: How come? You are still walking. / Don Juan: Dragging my feet with sorrow, as you can see. / Tisbea: You talk too much. Don Juan: You understand too much. / Tisbea: For the love of God I hope you are not lying!"; I: 693–96). The supposed heartache that afflicts Tenorio directly contradicts his active plotting in the preceding verses, making his alleged death a joke consistent with his bragging refusal to confront death, which he repeats so routinely throughout the play that it becomes his most famous verbal trait: *"tan largo me lo fiáis* (trust me a while longer)." Each charms the other, and they both leave the stage on a promising note. This scene is linked in structure and content to the one that will eventually follow between Tenorio and the shepherd, Aminta: in both scenes the act of seduction takes place onstage for the most part. Unlike the other women in the play, Tisbea gets a chance to expose who she is, a unique and independent woman, the keeper of her honor: *"Mi honor conservo en pajas, | como fruta sabrosa, | vidrio guardado en ellas | para que no se rompa"* ("But that straw protects my virtue, / a perfect fruit without the slightest blemish, / a piece of glass packed with the utmost care / to avoid the risk of damage on the journey"; EI, 423–26). Her life is the sea, and fishing is what she wants to go back to once she is done with her soliloquy: *"Pero [amor], necio discurso | que mi ejercicio estorbas, | en él no me diviertas | en cosa que no me importa. | Quiero entregar la caña | al viento, y a la boca | del pececillo el cebo"* ("But that's enough of all this foolish [love] talk! / It's only interfering with my fishing; / and what's the point of squandering my time / on something that's not worth a second thought? / I'll cast out my line, see how far the wind / carries it out to sea, so that the fish / into its eager mouth will take my bait"; EI: 475–81). The shipwreck interrupts her, and she makes the mistake of looking at the sea one second too long, discovering the two manly figures that are delivered to her by the waters. Don Juan immediately begins his wordplay as soon as Tisbea brings him back from the dead, going straight for her jugular: *"vivo en vos, si en el mar muero | . . . pues veis que hay de amar a mar | una letra solamente"* ("I can live in you, if I die in the sea / . . . for you see, [in Spanish] only a letter separates / the ocean from love"; I: 584, 595–96). Tisbea's cool response is like "burning snow" in the trickster's eyes, while she perceives Don Juan as "ice with fire" (I: 631–35). Don Juan's act as a nameless man leads Tisbea into a sexual discourse unheard of by her, a teasing of words and worlds which drives her away from her lone ranger character. Her looks win over Don Juan, they both succumb to the flirting, and then exit.

Don Juan is not the only teaser, however; for the text of *El burlador* does not close this dramatic technique of a gap between the tease and the actual seduction with a delivery of the promised account of the consummation of the expected trick. Instead of a wrap to their flirt, what follows the exit of the supposed lovers from the scene is an uncanny appearance onstage of Don Gonzalo de Ulloa, hitherto unknown to the audience, along with the king Don Alonso of Castile.[29] They do not talk about Don Juan and the conflict he has stirred up in Naples, but about the diplomatic mission to Lisboa from which Don Gonzalo has just returned. They briefly exchange impressions on warships, the king's cousin Juan, and epic glory; but what develops as the center of their conversation are the wonders of the prominent lusitanian urban space.[30] The royal mess Don Juan has left behind him in Italy, which his uncle tries to rectify for him in order to preserve the good name of the Tenorio family, is nothing compared to the mess Don Gonzalo's excursus on Lisboa (I: 721–857) represents for the reading and staging of this play. For what is a boldly historical *ricorso*, such as the glorious depiction of a foreign city where the king has sent an ambassador, doing in the middle of a dramatic seduction scene? What has "love"—or the promise of a nasty seduction—got to do with all the convents of this city, its valleys and mountains, its ships and palaces, its castles and neighbors? Unless it is read as a foreground for Tisbea's capitulation, or as an excuse to cool down the rampant eroticism of the previous scene between her and the trickster, the accounts of the beauties of this urban landscape might throw audiences and readerships overboard.[31]

The answers to these questions about the role of the *ricorso,* which is present not only in *El burlador de Sevilla* but in many other instances of Spanish Golden Age art and literature, belong to a tradition of stagings of memorable national moments framed within literary and artistic production of seventeenth-century Spain that has been associated with propaganda, but that is firmly rooted in aesthetics as well.[32] Having had a tradition of historiographers who were primarily writers, illustrators, or designers of emblems, the monarchy moves during the sixteen hundreds from a rhetorical and emblematic stance to a more plastic practice of history that prefers media as disparate as painting, tapestry, and drama. This leads to the incursion of historical information in layered instances of artistic references such as this private screening of Lisboa done by Don Gonzalo for his one spectator, the king.[33] Thus the emplotment of historicity within a dramatic frame tries to devalue the rhetorical and stylistic supremacy of sacrificial gestures, and attempts to restore the feeling of pleasure in accounts of the past, for the sake of establishing a commentary on the present and the uncertain—and for many, dreadful—future. In other words, the report about Don Gonzalo's accomplished mission in Lisboa does not target a *"verosimil"* representation of his voyage into a foreign land, but an account of marvelous possessions of the crown abroad that fits the frame of a fairy tale better than that of a monumental description of reality, past or present. The apparition of Lisboa, then, as out-of-context and as meaningless as it might seem at first glance, has a *raison d'être* within the context of teasing historicity, of promising the formulation of an historical discourse without, nevertheless, delivering it thoroughly. The foundational narrative of Lisboa goes back to the classical tradition of epic heroes, one that returns over and over again in *El burlador*. Ulises leads to Ulisiboa, and from there the guided tour continues through different kinds of valuable urban possessions until it hits the centerpiece, the *"pedestal de las llagas / que en la batalla sangrienta / al rey don Alfonso Enríquez / dio la Majestad inmensa"* ("pedestal of the wounds / that in the bloody battle / granted King Don Alfonso / the immense Majesty"; I: 822–25). The description of Don Gonzalo's discovery of Lisboa reveals itself as a parodic allusion to historical narratives, to what Louise Fradenburg and Carla Freccero call, in the introduction to this volume, a "production of glory through loss," through images of the sacrifice of bodies that matter (xiv). In the specific case of *El burlador,* these bodies are not just Don Juan's victims on stage, male and female, but also the readers of the text, of which such victims of the trickster are the perfect emblems. For Don Juan does not only deceive his fellow (male and female) characters in *El burlador*; his tricks can also be seen at work in the sexual myths produced by the philological tradition and by elements of the reception of his character, both of which are highly relevant for the reading of the text and its mysterious authorial figure.

The history of the manuscript of *El burlador,* considered by some scholars as a mere variant of *Tan largo,* brings forth the same issue that its contents raise; that is, the interplay between an arresting image and its "victims," between the character who can perform any role he wants in order to trick whomever he pleases, and those whom he literally seduces and deceives both within the plot and also outside it. The "victims" would be those readers, inside and outside the play, whom Carla Freccero associates with "the humanist philological impulse to contaminate and violate in order, subsequently, to castigate and purge" (1994, 108). This multilayered exercise has focused, in the case of these two manuscripts (*El burlador* and *Tan largo*), on assigning more importance to one while devaluing the other. The two manuscripts, like the central male figure of the play, have been submitted to threats of punishment as a result of what Judith Butler calls "the symbolic demand that institutes 'sex'" (1993, 46). The reception of these two manuscripts and of their central male figure—the grand history of "the king's two bodies"—then, responds largely to the anxiety of having to live with the consequences of a dishonorable performance, one of them being the fear of castration "motivating the assumption of the feminine" both in the manuscripts and in the character: my story of "the queen's too bawdies," for instance. The limiting force of the threat of constant "punishment" translates into the perpetration of the emblematic trick that *El burlador* inflicts upon women and men inside and outside the play, responding, in turn, to an anxiety on Don Juan's part—and, by extension, on the part of *El burlador*—not to fall into the category of either of the two "inarticulate" figures of abject homosexuality (for which there is no room either in *El burlador*'s stagings of aggressive masculinities, or in the code of honor): the "feminized fag" and the "phallicized dyke."[34] In the same way, the terror of considering either one of the manuscripts a "hybrid" with respect to the other, which in literary terms would place it in a position of "submission," is a terrible thought to bear for some readers. The sexed position of both Don Juan and *El burlador* has sprung, therefore, not so much from the character and/or the text, but from the abuse of a scenario that implicitly promises the punishment of castration for those who do not perform their reading of the text in a sufficiently "aggressive" or "incisive" manner. This threat of punishment, which would result in "debilitation" and/or "weakness," has, when applied to the play, predetermined and limited a number of possible interpretations of the text.[35]

For instance, in *Tan largo me lo fiáis* the Lisboa scene is substituted by Tenorio's Sevillian welcoming reception for the Duke Octavio. This textual variant has puzzled many scholars who have labored to explain which one of the two versions should be considered the "original," or source of "truth" about the life of the text, and the other, the "copy," or receptacle of its true spirit. The Lisboa/Sevilla scene is one of great importance for such discussions. María Rosa Lida de Malkiel, for example, favors the text of *Tan largo* over *El burlador*, arguing that the first is more historically accurate than the second.[36] For her, *Tan largo* refers to the conquest of Ceuta (1415) and Tanger (1471) in a manner chronologically coherent with the presence onstage of King Alfonso, which makes *El burlador*'s inclusion of the conquest of Goa, dated in history books as a sixteenth-century event, anachronistic and, therefore, a "feeble" textual instance of historicity. Furthermore, Lida de Malkiel argues, Don Juan, a native Sevillian and Octavio's rival, shows the city to the newcomer *caballero* in *Tan largo* in a much more "natural" fashion within the drama than occurs in *El burlador*, while in *El burlador* Don Gonzalo supposedly so annoys the king with his descriptions of Lisboa that the supreme figure is compelled to beg for a chair in a decidedly indecorous manner that lacks all historiographic proportion and dignity. In sum, the *El burlador* version appears, for Lida de Malkiel, to be a careless abbreviation of a much better, original dramatic piece, *Tan largo*, composed more in agreement with the fabric of Don Juan's character, to please the people's taste.

But ironically enough, Lida de Malkiel's condemning conclusions get closer to the vital center of *El burlador* than many celebratory remarks made *a propos* of this play, even when she prefers the text of *Tan largo*. For when she refers to the identification of the latter with "seriousness" and other qualities that in principle agree with the paradigm of great historical and literary enterprises, she argues that *El burlador* is flawed because of its interpolation of sources, textual inferiority, and historical errors, and its insertion of the description of Lisboa, among other factors. Yet these same elements have elevated Don Juan to the status of an international tradition. Granted, in principle the report narrated by the successful ambassador of *El burlador* might seem superfluous and gratuitous. But his self-gratification is only apparent, and the author furnishes a logical explanation for his insertion: once the report is done, King Alfonso finds Don Gonzalo's pseudohistorical account—as flawed as it is in its lack of accuracy when it comes to dates and places—so praiseworthy that he rewards him with a "perfect" match for Don Gonzalo's highly desirable daughter. The scene is ironic, for not only is the "flawed" historical account blatantly out of context and style, it serves the key function of revealing yet again Alfonso's monarchic ineptitude, as he makes a futile attempt to stop Don Juan from running around looking for trouble. In this ironic reading of the scene, Doña Ana performs the role of the castrating instrument used by "respectable" figures, the king and his associates; she is the tool that is designed to stop Don Juan's search for pleasure.

The textual insertion of Don Gonzalo's excursus on Lisboa in *El burlador* allows the audience to imagine a continuation of the seducer's offstage scene with Tisbea. This cannot happen in *Tan largo* because Don Juan is present onstage with Octavio. Thus *El burlador* highlights the "escape motif" that is quintessential to Don Juan's character. Indeed, this motif, like Don Juan's anxiety—and anxieties about Don Juan—can thus be read as a resistance to earlier representations of obsolete, yet deeply admired and revered, historical and epic figures in the literature and the society of seventeenth-century Spain.[37] Rather than a "flawed" historical account that merely represents an inaccurate view of the past, the Lisboa scene in *El burlador* can be read as one way in which the obsolescent model of historical narratives is questioned, and a new model is proposed; a look into the present moment—the seduction scene happening offstage—links that very past of the trip to Lisboa to the future: the conclusion of the seduction. The text of *El burlador* poses, then, some fundamental questions about the process of becoming a historical artifact, and of assuming an image with tremendous power to elicit identifications, whose precise forms will also be shaped by ideological or political enterprises. But we must still ask what the significance is of these elements and scenes for the reading of the two plays and for their location within the frame of historical development in the first turbulent three decades of seventeenth-century Spain.

This is one among many instances in which "teasing" becomes the operative term for historicity in *El burlador*: there is a promise of identification with historical units, agents, characters, and themes that is not totally fulfilled. For instance, the play is not to be considered a "historical" play, a dramatic text that versifies a historical plot or theme in the same way that a number of other plays of this period do, such as Luis Vélez de Guevara's *Más pesa el rey que la sangre* (1979).[38] On the other hand, the incorporation of historical material into the texture of *El burlador* is essential to the development of the play, even if the inscription of historical details is not *"verosimil"* or "accurate": thus, for instance, the function—or delectable dysfunction—of the kingly figures, which is a *sine qua non* for the reading of the piece, regardless of whether or not the second king is Alfonso XI.[39] *El burlador*, in fact, fights the traditional movement of Spanish letters, in which the hero of the epic tradition goes from an emphasis on personal issues such as love, loyalty and friendship, in the *Poema de mio Cid* for instance (Lacarra 1983), to a more military-oriented trend of representation in historical chronicles such as the *Crónica de veinte reyes* (Alonso et al. 1991). Despite all this transformation, the historical crystallization of this character in the chronicle preserves intact the vocabulary and the grammar of the character's anatomy, with the heart (representing the hero's emotions), the hand (signifying humility, allegiance or petition), and the beard (the most memorable feature of the Cid, sign of his virility and authority) being the three signifying features most commonly used both in the epic *Poema* and the historical *Crónica*. But in terms of the role that the epic hero plays, the first feature to be omitted in the historical version is the ironic dimension of El Cid's character, replaced by that of a happy warrior whose individuality and heroic persona are simplified, thus making his behavior more dull and predictable. A second feature that was suppressed for historicizing purposes is the Cid's family, only mentioned because of its prominence in the story, but mentioned as little as possible in the *Crónica*, as are the Moors, while the Cid's friend and enemies stay.[40]

The author-figure of *El burlador* reverses this movement in the character of Don Juan in an effort to resuscitate some of the strengths of the epic character that were rendered opaque by the historical writings.[41] In a way, what the play appropriates from the Cid is the aspect of the legend, what de Certeau calls an arrangement of "'curiosities' in an order in which they *must be read*."[42] That part of the Cid that the character of Don Juan recovers is the one that fuses the past and the present in such a way as to propose imaginary masculine identities for the future. The relationship between Rodrigo Díaz de Vivar and his hands, beard, wife, daughters, sword, and bravery were already organized and mediated for the composition of the *Poema*. *El burlador* inscribes some of these traits of the legendary aspect of El Cid Campeador, and disfigures them even more, making them at times almost unrecognizable. For example, the beard and sword of the Comendador/Stone Guest, all present in different instances of the play, represent the process of petrification of this epic tradition in the final scene of the play. This is a process that, again, can be read as a denunciation of the stiffness of historical and epic characters, but that can be reactivated as well within the context of Don Juan, the new heroic material boy, holding hands with the ghost of traditions that preceded him, in much the same way as Don Quixote meets with himself and the ghost of the chivalric world in the oneiric scene of the cave of Montesinos.

But the Cid is not the only classical epic hero to undergo a transformation in *El burlador*. Besides Ulysses, who is brought up because of his etymological relationship to the name of the city of Lisboa, Hector and Aeneas are also remembered in the play. Their token appearances do not evoke their many victories in the battlefield, nor the war wounds they bore on their bodies as signatures of their virtue and promise of *klaîos*, the eternal warrior's glory. Instead, they are mentioned for being simply young, crazy, and tricky. Don Juan is called *"el Héctor de Sevilla, porque ha hecho mocedades"* ("the Hector of Seville, for having done / so many and strange deeds, worthy of a young hero"; II: 1086). Aeneas, founder of Rome and protagonist of one of the most prestigious monuments of European poetics, is rescued from oblivion with a memorable *"lo mismo hizo Eneas / con la reina de Cartago"* ("Aeneas did the same / to the queen of Carthage"; I: 899–900), referring the audience to the fact that Virgil's character deceived his queen, too.[43] Don Juan, the inverted heroic subject, is referred to by Tisbea as a "Greek horse" (I: 613), alluding to the fact that, in spite of his self-assurance, he is a figure as prominent as the wooden horse, but also as vulnerable. The Trojan War, subject of *The Iliad* and poetic impulse for *The Odyssey*, resurfaces in *El burlador* when Tisbea shouts *"Mi pobre edificio queda / hecho otra Troya en las llamas; / que después que faltan Troyas / quiere amor quemar cabañas"* ("My poor edifice has been reduced / to another Troy in the fire / for love, having no Troys left, / turns to burning humble huts"; I: 989–92). The crucial role played by the literary *topos* of the journey in the foundational discourses of the epic tradition is revised every time Don

Juan abuses the hospitality of his hosts, that sacred bond between noble warriors that guarantees that they will be as safe in their host's house as they would be in their own home.[44] In *El burlador*, the violation of this sacred bond of hospitality is not exclusively directed against the fellow hero, the host, but instead it appears to be sustained by a rite of initiation into masculinity, which requires the sacrifice of the body of a woman and a shattering of both her trust and that of the man who represents her and validates her persona in society.

This fundamental violation of trust is perhaps the most blatant of all tricks practiced by *El burlador*. It is an act that has enormous, if different, repercussions for men and for women; but these differences are only apparent, for, gender connotations aside, men and women alike fall for Don Juan's promises. Don Juan Tenorio deceives four women in all, but consummating the deception is not the main focus of his acts of treachery. The textual economy of *El burlador* reveals a much greater investment of space in the areas of planning, escaping, and bragging than in the execution of the sexual acts *per se*, which by default become dramatic gaps. In his reencounter with his trickster soul mate, the Marquis of Mota, Don Juan inscribes the tradition of the *rodomontada*, or *catalogue raisonnée* of women a hero has had.[45] In this parodic instance, he does not mention the two foolish kingly figures or the gentlemen—fathers, uncles, suitors, chamberlains—who have been caught in these acts of deception, whose congregation stands as a ghostly parallel to the list of ladies, women, and prostitutes whom Don Juan publicly claims to have tricked and possessed. Don Juan's fellow male characters try to catch up with him, but they can barely keep up with his pace.

For although the two kings attempt to manage the disorder created by Don Juan's wrongdoings, they do not succeed in that enterprise. Alfonso of Castile goes so far as to try to match him with different wives, in order to make Tenorio settle down and, therefore, to restore social harmony. His Majesty even offers to accommodate Tenorio's social standing to the stratum of the woman in question: *"Conde será hoy don Juan Tenorio / de Lebrija; él la mande y la posea, / que si Isabela a un duque corresponde, / ya que ha perdido un duque, gane un conde"* ("Starting today, Don Juan Tenorio will be Count / of Lebrija; may he be her master, and possess her, / for if Isabela is good enough for a duke, / since she's lost one, may she win a count"; III: 700–703); an absurd gesture on the part of this king which, again, since Don Juan refuses to engage in marital rites, leaves him looking more incompetent than divinely inspired. Don Pedro, too, makes a point of picking up the pieces by helping Don Juan flee from Naples when his nephew reminds him that he, also, was once young and crazy, and that they are bound by kinship (I: 53–120); but his unfortunate way of patching up is to arrest Octavio, and thus his character is stained by this act of corruption and blatant nepotism (I: 250–374). Don Juan's own father, Don Diego, tries at first to stop the duel between Octavio and Don Juan by convincing the King of Castile that it is a matter of "father's honor" (II: 45–46), but the only way he finds out of this conflict is to exile his son by royal command, and to agree to Don Juan's marriage with the Duchess Isabela against his son's will (III: 688–733). When the Duke Octavio begs the king for a duel, Don Diego defies the king by responding to Octavio before the royal voice can make a pronouncement. His argument is that Don Juan's blood is noble, and that he will defend it himself to the death (III: 755–71). But in the end he capitulates too, under the pressure of those people who have been deceived by his son, asking the king to "honor" him: *"en premio de mis servicios | haz que le prendan y pague | sus culpas, poque del cielo | rayos contra mí no bajen, | si es mi hijo tan malo"* ("by punishing this son | of mine, for then perhaps the Heavens will spare | a poor father, forgive him for the birth | of such a worthless child"; EIII: 1024–27). Doña Ana's father, Don Gonzalo, also tries to control Don Juan, but the enterprise literally takes his life. Don Juan's rivals, Octavio, Mota, and Anfriso, see themselves deceived and put in a position of having been tricked, just like all the other "victims" of the *burlador*. Don Gonzalo, the apparently petrified version of heroicity and gentlemanship in his Stone Guest appearance, is the only one who can manage to freeze Don Juan and immortalize him by asking him for his hand, and then by holding it.

This final bond between Don Juan and the Stone Guest, an unexpected fusion of the fields of sexuality and death in one gesture, is a dramatic rendition of what Wayne Koestenbaum has called "double talk," an expression of homosexual desire "which, far from reinforcing patriarchy, undermines it, and offers a way out (1989, 3)." Although both aggressors surrender their physical life, they go on to inhabit a dimension of remembrance, a "way out" that permits rereadings of some aspects of the play and its contexts. This way out begins with an understanding that, instead of assigning "priority" to either character, traditional trait, or version of the play, the pleasures of history in *El burlador* can begin to be activated with an acknowledgment of the erotics of male collaboration exemplified, for instance, by the double talk of Tirso and Claramonte, which is emblematized by Don Juan and the Stone Guest or by Don Juan and Catalinón. Rodríguez López-Vázquez's recent critical tale of this philological crypt offers one version of this collaboration: "either Claramonte knew all this because he had the *comedia* attributed to Tirso in his hands, or they both, Tirso and Claramonte, used the same sources with a surprising unity of aim, or perhaps the author of both [*El burlador* and *Tan largo*] is one and the same person, that is to say, Claramonte" (1987, 4; my translation). This view, instead of exposing one cultural artifact and deeming it superior to the other, acknowledges the common ground and the depth both of the character and of the two versions, which in the end are able finally to escape petrified formulations of masculinity and of philology.

We can thereafter understand the "two lines of linguistic inquiry" that Mandrell finds in *El burlador*: one, Don Juan's relationship with female characters, "associated with the seductions proper and serving to reveal Don Juan as an actor;" and the other, his relationships with male characters, "deriving from Don Juan's dealing with figures of worldly authority." According to Mandrell, they all "converge and come into focus in Don Juan's encounter with the sepulchral Statue of the Comendador" (1993, 74). The Statue, a substitute father figure, shares two crucial moments with Don Juan—the food and the holding of hands—in both invitations to dinner. Both motifs are leftovers from the epic tradition, but inverted. The second invitation extended to Don Juan by the Stone Guest requires that Tenorio lift a tombstone, which Don Juan does without hesitation, adding to his willingness the bragging statement that, if needed, he can *"levantar esos pilares"* ("lift those pillars"; III: 2698); a gesture that brings Sampson's phenomenal strength on stage with Don Juan's fabulous narcissism. Once he has impressed the Stone Guest, who is now the host, the meal begins. Every dish is a different representation of infernal tortures, so Don Juan, in a very ladylike manner, alleges that he has eaten already when the *"guisadillo de uñas"* ("little nails stew"; III: 2738–40) arrives on the table, the last entree on a menu of scorpions, vipers, and blood to drink. Immediately after he has seen this, Don Gonzalo commands Tenorio to give him his hand, in a blatant parody of an indecent marriage proposal. This is a hand that, when Don Juan accepts it, burns with the same fire that burned Tisbea, the other character of the play whose gender is unaligned. Don Gonzalo, however, does not respond to Don Juan's performance—radically different from the others—with teasing games, as did the fisherwoman. Don Gonzalo, instead, goes back to his old Comendador ego, the enforcer of patriarchy, and starts the litany of Don Juan's many sins. Tenorio, in turn, loses all perspective and attempts to kill the ghostly Don Gonzalo *"con la daga"* ("with the dagger"; III: 2754), but gets tired of the knife falling "on empty air." He alleges that he did not offend Doña Ana, a fact that is corroborated soon thereafter by other "witnesses," but the father figure is determined to collect the debt and give Don Juan what he deserves: his death.

Don Juan's blatant challenge to death, his characteristic slogan that gives the twin manuscript its title, *"tan largo me lo fiáis"* ("trust me a while longer"), finds a temporary substitute when faced with the imminence of death. Instead of defying the future, Don Juan acknowledges his loss of control, and begins a different recitation, which is dangerously close to that of his "victims": the sequence progresses from *"¡Que me abraso! ¡No me abrases con tu fuego!"* ("I am burning up! Don't burn me up with your flames!"; III: 2743–44) to *"¡Que me abraso! ¡No me aprietes!"* ("I am burning up! Don't squeeze me!"; III: 2753) to a final scream of *"¡Que me quemo! ¡Que me abraso!"* ("I am burning up! I am burning up!"; III: 2763), uttered right before repeating his staple phrase with which he used to announce a seduction, this time literally and truthfully pronounced as he collapses, dead, onstage: *"Muerto soy"* ("I am dead"; III: 2764). In the end, Don Juan is forced to surrender his body, his locus and primordial tool of identification with masculinity. His sin, to have informed this staging of masculinity above all with a desire to write it, direct it, and perform it himself, meets the unbearable touch of the vengeful fatherly embrace. This is the punishing father, the one who insists on castigating and punishing him for all the violations that he has committed. The expectations of marriage, the social order, and obedience to preformulated "imaginary" and "real" laws imposed on each of the characters can thus only lay the ground for their communication—inside the textual space and outside—as a crippling exercise; lifting these expectations, as I have tried to suggest, can set these bodies—bawdies—in motion with life, energy, and vibrant desire. The ghost, justifying his condemnation of the figure of Don Juan with a *"quien tal hace, que tal pague"* ("you reap what you sow"; EIII: 2768), a remark that supposedly comes straight from God's mouth, can be read as a spokesman of Don Juan's condemnatory fan club. But he might also be understood to be performing a critique of that particular condemnatory voice, in another instance of the teasing of historicity in *El burlador de Sevilla*, or of the (ghostly) echo of the "queen," also bawdying.

Notes

I am grateful to the Spanish Department of Columbia University for a leave for the year 1993–1994, during which time I wrote a first version of this article, and to the Literature Humanities Program at Columbia for a Chamberlain Fellowship. Also, to Carla Freccero and Louise Fradenburg for their faith, patience, and wisdom, and to Emily Honig, Hugo Rodríguez-Vecchini, and Dara Goldman for their inspiration and solidarity. To Gus Puleo and Ben Sifuentes-Jáuregui, thanks for listening to my endless utterances of this project; and to Ruth Hill, Carla, and Louise, great editors, thanks for your voices and advice.

1. See Kantorowicz (1957). Carol Kirby, applying this formulaic invention of historicity to the play *El rey don Pedro en Madrid*, views it as a political-theological doctrine "according to which a monarch possesses both a finite, human essence which linked him to his fellow men in sinfulness and physical corruptibility (the body personal), and a spiritual nature (the body mystical) through which God invested in him the office of the monarchy as a continuing social institution. The ideal ruler, in theory, harmoniously incorporated both bodies" (1981, 149).

2. The translations that refer to the Casalduero edition are mine and, hence, offer my own vision of the reading. Act and verse numbers from this edition are indicated in parentheses.

3. Edwards (1986) offers adequate translations for some difficult passages and, hence, I quote his version directly. Act and verse numbers from this particular translation will be indicated in parentheses, preceded by the letter E.

4. Gustavo Correa's (1958) study is the best introduction to the subject of honor in the context of Spanish Golden-Age drama. Jones (1958), and McKendrick (1984) offer the most convincing arguments of the complex, symbiotic relationship between this code in society and its dramatic renditions.

5. The representation of kingly figures has a whole discursive tradition in Golden-Age drama. Fox (1986) sees it specifically in the case of Calderón's political issues, but there are other playwrights and perspectives that justify the overpopulation of royal figures on the stage.

6. Sloman (1965, 33) establishes the basic, textual problem: "*¿Tan largo me lo fiáis?* and *El burlador de Sevilla* are different versions of the play, and that of *Tan largo* is the earlier. Both versions survive in texts that are defective." Defective, meaning that one manuscript, that of *El burlador*, is more suggestive for its deficiencies than a polished literary text (with less *lacunae*, both in thematic and stylistic terms), while the other is more finished but with a central character that has not been appealing to readers interested in *El burlador*'s fabulous (ab)uses of dramatic techniques such as, for instance, gapping or irony. Wade (1969) has proposed models from that period to identify the character of Don Juan, and posed some preliminary questions of authorship that led critics to consider seriously what possible roles Claramonte might have played in this historical puzzle. See also Fernández (1981).

7. Edwards remembers this character of Spanish history as a possible source for the play: "In his own lifetime (1579–1624) Don Pedro's adventures were indeed scandalous. During his teenage years, his father found it impossible to control him, he married early but continued to indulge in numerous affairs, he frequently broke his word, lied, obtained money under false pretences, and even killed a man in a brawl" (1986, xxi). The more literally

"historical" play about the Duke, though, is *Las mocedades del Duque de Osuna*, by Cristóbal Monroy y Silva, no doubt a parody of Antonio Vélez de Guevara's *Las mocedades del Cid* and its model, the *Poema de mio Cid*.

8. Like his fellow viceroys, the Duke of Osuna was closer to Olivares in what John H. Elliott calls his "militant and aggressive policy" than to his predecessor, Lerma, in that he refused to "reconcile himself to the humiliating pacifism of Philip III's government." Elliott's description of the character of Olivares, in turn, can be associated as well with Don Juan: "A restless figure, never fully at ease with others or with himself, Olivares was less one personality than a whole succession of personalities, co-existing, competing, and conflicting within a single frame. By turns ebullient and dejected, humble and arrogant, shrewd and gullible, impetuous and cautious, he dazzled contemporaries with the versatility of his performance and bewildered them with his chameleon changes of mood" (1963, 324–25).

9. This ambiguity might be understood within the context of a symbolic change that had started to take place during this period in Spanish history: a shift in what Elliott has called "the imperial tradition," from an established system of imagery of masculine power (whose pinnacle was Saint James symbolizing the warrior-saint, hope and savior of the nation) to the emergence of a feminine partner (Saint Teresa, canonized at the beginning of the century and responsible for a new injection of faith and strength in the exhausted arks of the national imaginary). This tradition, argues Elliott, "believed firmly in the rightness, and indeed the inevitability of Spanish, and specifically Castilian, hegemony over the world. Under the government of Lerma this tradition had been muted in the capital of the Monarchy, where the eclipse of the crusading tradition had been curiously symbolized by the displacement in 1617 of St. James from his position as sole partner in Spain. In future the warrior saint was to have a feminine partner in the person of a highly idealized St. Teresa" (1963, 324).

10. Elliott acknowledges the two sides of this highly significant coin: on the one hand, this all came about because the kings, were all "men who lacked both the ability and the diligence to govern by themselves." At the same time, and on the other hand, this was also a reflection of "the growing complexity of government, which made it increasingly necessary to have an omni-competent minister, capable of extracting some decision from the mountain of *consultas* which piled up on the royal desk" (1963, 301).

11. Quoted in Brown and Elliott (1980, 41).

12. Cascardi understands Don Juan as an attempt "to answer the Counter-Reformation's moralizing threats of impending spiritual doom with a Baroque extension of time, brought about by means of repeated appeals to the will: "Trust me a while longer!" ("*¡Tan largo me lo fiáis!*") (1992, 246).

13. Cascardi argues that "a more appropriate model for the psychology of Don Juan would be one in which the moral problem of desire is both *created* and *resolved* by modes of persuasion available to subjects of the Baroque" (1992, 246; my italics).

14. Ruano de la Haza acknowledges the fact that these *alcaldes* "could be considered as the presence of central power in the administration of Madrid" (1988, 68). These Mayor figures, representatives of the king in the happening of the dramatic event, were the physical enforcers of this complex, almost maddening set of post-Tridentine regulations. Ruano de la Haza's document retraces some of the legal principles that regulated the life of popular theatrical space, among which the prohibition of any form of decoration onstage can be found. This responds not to a stoic principle of theatrical practices, but more than anything else to a need on the part of the government to restrict whatever might fire imaginations, and hence damage the *decorum* or what was proper or appropriate in social interactions. The *decorum* in the case of the actresses or *comediantas*, for example, began with the fact that in order for them to be legal citizens, they ought to be married.

And the women who attended the stagings of *comedias* in the *corrales* or playhouses built around inner courtyards of apartment houses, no matter what they did, were perceived as loose characters with little social value in the stock market of the patriarchal economy; in other words, their standing as wifely materials was, by default, low, simply because they dared attend these social events. See some examples of this concept in Díaz Borque (1990, 224–26).

15. The racial implications of this network of language, memory, and power in this period of vogue of regulations—political, cultural, economic, and otherwise—has been analyzed by Piedra (1986–87, 303–332).

16. "It is one thing to see rhetoric as a useful embellishment and to regard one's trade as rhetoric; it is another to confront all the linguistic *aporia* of the classical period using rhetorical terms and maxims as your fundamental categories" (Struever 1970, 107).

17. This *"scandale du corps parlant,"* to use Shoshana Felman's expression, is related to a practice of promising which, rooted not only in reality but in functions of language such as "performance" or "abuse," was as well part of this imperial design. Don Juan's good standing is not just "between men," but also within the context of an idea of empire that, at this time, was clearly doomed, and hence, a promising act that was bound to deceive its subjects. This combination of knowledge and pleasure, as Felman sees it, has seduced thinkers and artists, forming a tradition in European literature: "The *Don Juan* effect is, pragmatically, that of confusion between meaning and reference, and, theoretically, that of problematization, of subversion of the dichotomy between self-referentiality and linguistic referentiality" (Felman 1983, 81). James Mandrell has seen this specifically in the text of *El burlador*—differently from Felman, who reads Molière and Mozart: "When Don Juan swears to fulfill his promise his intention is completely otherwise. Don Juan's sins against society are not so much sins of carnality as they are sins of linguistic perversion" (Mandrell 1993, 76).

18. Curiously enough, in *Tan largo* it is not "Seville" who shouts the epithet, but the entire nation of Spain (II: 1390). See Rodríguez López-Vázquez (1990).

19. El Saffar has seen this double-edged sword in the context of the formation of "a new man" in seventeenth-century Spain: "When Cervantes struggles with the literary problem posed by courtly love, he is also struggling with the dominant consciousness of his day. And when he finally reaches a point in his fiction when the undesirable or off-limits woman becomes the object of the hero's desire, he will impose on that hero travails that will undercut every assumption he holds dear" (1984, 14).

20. Sebastián de Covarrubias Orozco (1943), does not include the term "femininity" which, in time, would be coined by the Royal Academy of Language as a twofold version of what a woman is: either a biological receptacle, inseminable territory, or the owner of rights to inheritance or *mayorazgo* in the event of the absence of a male heir to an estate. They are differentiated by one letter: "feminidad" and "femineidad." The term "mujer" does have a definition, and it is almost exclusively identified with the notions of disgrace, transgression, and negation (fol. 117r). Butler wraps up this all too common historical movement with her notion of the theatricality of gender, within which femininity is "not the product of a choice, but the forcible citation of a norm, one whose complex historicity is indissociable from relations of discipline, regulation, punishment" (1993, 232).

21. Covarrubias (1979, fols. 159v–160r). The term *burla* derives either from the dress made of the fabric, *buriel*, "vile and cheap" that led to *burrhiel*, "object of little value, a toyish thing," or from the French term *bourde*, "joking lie" (159v).

22. Joaquín Casalduero (1987, 13) establishes the anatomy of the trickster as a threefold game of motifs: Don Juan deceives his victims, then possesses them, and then escapes from them.

23. Sedgwick (1985) lays the foundations of this set of transactions of homoerotic desire and their relationship to patriarchal establishments.

24. Miguel de Unamuno labels him a "stupid braggart, a complete idiot" (1945, 118–26). In the blaming instances, curiously enough, the attack on the character has been directed largely towards his lack of masculine "strength" or "potency," and explained by "the mother complex," in order to justify his egoism. Gregorio Marañón, biologist and psychiatrist, reads Don Juan's character as a "latent homosexual," an "aberration" which in his view had to do with Tenorio's doubtful virility and disproportionate degree of effeminacy, when he compares Don Juan to the "perfect" man, the *varón castellano* (1937, 38; c.1960, 81–82, 87–89, 109–110). Leo Weinstein considers Marañón's views as "negative" remarks about Don Juan's virility, and reads the character not as a "persona" or a "figura," but as a simple myth (1959, 3). See a review of all these different readings of Don Juan's sexuality in Wade (1969, 17–27). Ortega y Gasset (1966, 58–59), on the other hand, positions his reading in a romantic angle: he finds Don Juan an admirable character for rebelling against morality in his search of a "vital plenitude." And Oscar Mandel aligns his reading with Ortega's celebratory remarks. He focuses on Don Juan as a representation of the "triumph of sensuality," and calls the text of *El burlador* a "spirited though crude and faulty piece of entertainment ... an excellent romp, a tough morality play, more play than morality," if "not really erotic" (1963, 44–45).

25. Wade reads this aspect of the character of Don Juan as inscribed both in the trait of the *burlador* and in its possible translation into English, the literary, folkloric, and mythical tradition of The Trickster: a "creator and destroyer, affirmer and negator at one and the same time, he finally transforms himself through his activities into a being approximating that of man" (1969, 45).

26. Johnson (1976, 193–220) points out the fact that for more than two decades the theme of Don Juan has been the analytical centerpiece in Castro's academic career. But even after 1950, Castro makes his interpretation of this "conflictive age," as he labeled it, revolve around *El burlador*.

27. Beverly (1992, 224) sees this as a "relative liberalization of literary policy," an attempt not to return to purely feudal seigneural authority, but to "recuperate" and "mobilize" literature banned by the Inquisition in order to serve Church and state imperial designs.

28. Cascardi (1988, 156) argues that Don Juan in *El burlador* exercises discursive practices that can be identified with "modern" desires. This effect is achieved, according to Cascardi, through a movement toward a form of stillness of character and, ultimately, a partial identification with the tragic hero because of the death of both the Comendador and Don Juan, and by the repression or "management" of this desire through the wedding scene as apparent closure of the text, a dramatic convention associated with comedy.

29. It can be argued that Don Juan's tease of Tisbea is the larger frame for this, since the conversation between Don Gonzalo and the king is embedded within the lovers' tale. However, the dramatic gap here serves not just the purpose of increasing the erotic level of the scene between a doomed heterosexual couple, but also to highlight alternative gender practices: the homoerotic bond between different male characters, and the claudication of the most "unfeminine" female character of the play.

30. The point here is that this centerpiece of historical representation is another instance of anachronism, one more reason for true philologists to discard *El burlador* as an "inferior" manuscript. See Wade's review of the implications of this insert (1969, 184–89).

31. For Casalduero, the scene first and foremost "cuts the blinding erotic frenzy with the serenity and age of the two respectable characters—both for their age and status; second it shifts the sensuousness of man in the painting of Lisboa from the carnal attraction to abundance and opulent splendor of Nature and human creation; a heightening sensuousness, glory of divine manifestation, in contrast with the fury of sin and the degrading sexuality of the Sevillian *barrio* named Lisboa ..." (1987, 18).

32. Beverly (1992, 224–25) qualifies this as a "profoundly historicist cultural form," with great problematic dimensions.

33. Brown and Elliott argue that for the Olivares-Philip IV team "history-painting as much as history-writing was to be a device for projecting the triumphs of king and minister" (1980, 164). It is not a coincidence that, in the sixteenth and seventeenth century, the genre of *semblanzas* (portraits) becomes so popular, and that it has turned out to be an invaluable archive for the reading and writing of the history of this period in Spain.

34. Butler links this anxiety to the position of a subject within language: "The Lacanian scheme presumes that the terror over occupying either of these positions is what compels the assumption of a sexed position within language, a sexed position that is sexed by virtue of its heterosexual positioning, and that is assumed through a move that excludes and abjects gay and lesbian possibilities" (1993, 96).

35. Although the *"mujer varonil"* was a favorite character among theatergoers and playwrights of this time, the effeminate male character was not more than an insult and a threat. Legal discourse plays as crucial a role as that of the Law of the Father (in the Lacanian sense), since the staging of an act of sodomy or any other "unnatural crime," or even its mere suggestion, represented a legal problem that in the case of these subjects, from playwright to readers, including actors and directors, was a matter of life or death. Mary Elizabeth Perry gives an overview of what she calls "sexual rebels," exceptional cases of people in sixteenth-century Seville who were committed to "agrammatical" lifestyles (1990, 118–36). She quotes as well the article of Louis Crompton (1981), still unsurpassed as introductory reading on this subject.

36. Lida de Malkiel (1962, 283n.) thus sides with the 1952 editor of *¿Tan largo?*, Blanca de los Ríos Lampérez (1946–1958). So does Michael McGaha (1977).

37. El Saffar offers one of the most important reasons for this paradoxical stance: "The balance of masculine and feminine energies that was the dream of so many Renaissance thinkers from Ficino to Bruno gave way in the period we have come to call the Baroque to visions instead of separation, suppression and dominance. The unconscious fears that Shakespeare and Cervantes tapped of the female virago were outpictured collectively in the seventeenth century in the witch mania that swept most of the countries of Europe" (1988, 7).

38. This literal notion of historicity finds a strong tradition in the *Comedia* or seventeenth-century Spanish theatre, which in turn has elicited a whole critical school that has set the standard for historical representation in dramatic texts of this period; a fact that has been greatly significant for the way in which *El burlador* has been read. See, as one example among many, Carvalho (1988).

39. An idea that might help reconcile the discourses of "history" and "literature" (or fiction) that are at the core of the dramatic conflict in *El burlador* is Beverly's argument that, in general, it would be more appropriate to see the representations of the state in the Spanish Baroque culture as "an *imaginary*—in the Lacanian sense of a projection of desire that systematically misconstrues the reality of absolutism than as an expression of its actual coherence and authority" (1992, 224).

40. Powell (1983) traces in detail the development of this movement. In the thirteenth century, the founding stone of literary history in Spain as understood until very recently, the *Poema*, was turned into prose for the purpose of being incorporated as historical material in the national history project sponsored by Alfonso the Tenth, the *Estoria de España*. But the historical project as conceived by the wise king was never completed, and the *Poema* did not form part of a definitive historical text approved by Alfonso. The prose version of the *Poema*, though, under the form of a compilation of different materials in principle collected for the *Estoria*, went on to become part of the *Crónica* and, for the period after the year 900, it became representative of what the *Estoria* would most likely have

been, if it had ever been completed. Later on, the chroniclers of the *Crónica* crystallized the trend by preserving materials from the poem that were "mainly of military and political interest, while reducing or removing material from the original which was irrelevant to or unsuitable for their purposes. This means, for example, a much smaller role for Jimena and her daughters in the *Crónica* than in the *Cid*." The chroniclers then went on to alter, and in many cases to omit, targets such as the "ungentlemanly behaviour of characters" (Powell 1983, 102).

41.   Fox establishes the importance of this particular instance for seventeenth-century drama in Spain: "Hegel sees the Cid, the medieval Spanish hero, in the same sort of prelegal independent personal and social situation. Shakespeare's recourse to medieval chronicles and romances as the sources of tragedies can be attributed to the fact that in the early days, unencumbered by social restrictions, true heroism could exist.... In contrast to Shakespearean drama, however, Spanish Golden-Age *comedias* set in the Middle Ages supply the aggrieved protagonist with an accessible higher authority, so that the freedom Hegel describes should not be expected to apply here" (1991, 4).

42.   This trait of the legendary character translates, within the context of what de Certeau understands as the labor of production of historical texts, into an aspect of this writing which "provides the imaginary dimension that we need so that the elsewhere can reiterate the very here and now" (1988, 287).

43.   Castro (1956) pointed out the evocation of the Roman hero.

44.   Daniel Rogers convincingly argues that Don Juan breaks this guest-host relationship in all four instances of seduction. I agree with Rogers that the play's questioning of authority is not simply directed toward the aesthetic principles of the epic tradition, but also to the "social, and more especially, moral, responsibility; the necessity of facing the social and moral consequences of one's actions (*no hay deuda que no se pague*), and the impossibility of postponing this indefinitely (*no hay plazo que no llegue*)" (1964, 150).

45.   The favorite topics in this genre, part of the epic tradition that linked physical with verbal skills, were the hero's bravery, valor, and his success with women. Denah Lida (1970, 555–57) sees this point in *El burlador* as one among many parodies of the epic hero. I thank Diane Marting for bringing this reference to my attention.

WORKS CITED

Alonso, César Hernández, et al, eds. 1991. *Crónica de veinte reyes.* Burgos: Excelentísimo Ayuntamiento de Burgos.

Beverly, John. 1992. "On the Concept of the Spanish Literary Baroque," in *Culture and Control in Counter-Reformation Spain,* ed. Anne J. Cruz and Elizabeth Perry. Minneapolis: University of Minnesota Press. 216–30.

Brown, Jonathan, and John H. Elliott. 1980. *A Palace for a King: The Buen Retiro and the Court of Philip IV.* New Haven: Yale University Press.

Butler, Judith. 1993. *Bodies That Matter: On the Discursive Limits of "Sex."* New York: Routledge.

Carvalho, Susan de. 1988. "The Legend of *The Siete Infantes de Lara* and Its Theatrical Representation by Cueva and Lope." *Bulletin of the Comediantes* 40 (1): 85–102.

Casalduero, Joaquín, ed. 1987. Maestro Tirso de Molina, *El burlador de Sevilla y convidodo de piedra.* Mardrid: Cátedra.

Cascardi, Anthony. 1988. "Don Juan and the Discourse of Modernism," in *Tirso's Don Juan. The Metamorphosis of a Theme.* ed. Josep M. Solá-Solé and George Gingras. Washington, DC: The Catholic University of America Press. 151–63.

————. 1992. "The Subject of Control," in *Culture and Control in Counter-Reformation Spain.* ed. Anne J. Cruz and Elizabeth Perry. Minneapolis: University of Minnesota Press, 231–54.

Castro, Américo. 1956. "El Don Juan de Tirso y el Eneas de Virgilio," in *Semblanzas y estudios españoles*. Princeton: Insula. 397–401.

Correa, Gustavo. "El doble aspecto de la honra en el teatro del Siglo XVII," *Hispanic Review* XXVI (1958): 99–107.

Covarrubias Orozco, Sebastián. 1943. *Tesoro de la lengua castellana o española*. Barcelona: Horta.

Crompton, Louis. 1981. "The Myth of Lesbian Impunity: Capital Law from 1270 to 1791," in *Historical Perspectives on Homosexuality*. ed. Salvatore Licata and Robert Petersen. New York: Haworth Press; Stein and Day. 11–25.

de Certeau, Michel. 1988. *The Writing of History*, trans. Tom Conley. New York: Columbia University Press.

de los Ríos, Blanca, ed. 1946–1958. Tirso de Molina. *Obras dramáticas completas*. 3 vols. Madrid: Aguilar.

Díaz Borque, José María. 1990. *La vida española en el Siglo de Oro según los extranjeros*. Barcelona: Ediciones de Serbal.

Diccionario de la Lengua Española. 1992. Madrid: Real Academia Española.

Edwards, Gwynne, trans. 1986. *The Trickster of Seville and the Stone Guest*. Warminstire, Wilshire: Aris and Phillips.

El Saffar, Ruth. 1984. *Beyond Fiction. The Recovery of the Feminine in the Novels of Cervantes*. Berkeley: University of California Press.

———. 1988. "Literary Reflections on the 'New Man:' Changes in Consciousness in Early Modern Europe." *Revista de Estudios Hispánicos* 22 (2): 3–17.

Elliott, John H. 1963. *Imperial Spain 1469–1716*. London: Penguin Books.

Felman, Shoshana. 1983. *The Literary Speech Act. Don Juan with J. L. Austin, or Seduction in Two Languages*, trans. Catherine Porter, Ithaca: Cornell University Press.

Fernández, Xavier. 1981. "Precisiones diferenciales entre El burlador y Tan largo," in *Homenaje a Tirso*. Madrid: Revista Estudios. 39–46.

Fox, Dian. 1986. *Kings in Calderón: A Study in Characterization and Political Theory*. London: Tamesis.

———. 1991. *Refiguring the Hero: From Peasant to Noble in Lope de Vega and Calderón*. University Park: The Pennsylvania State University Press.

Fradenburg, Louise and Carla Freccero. 1996. "Caxton, Foucault, and The Pleasures of History," in *Premodern Sexualities*, ed. Carla Freccero and Louise Fradenburg. New York: Routledge.

Freccero, Carla. 1994. "Practicing Queer Philology With Marguerite de Navarre: Nationalism and the Castigation of Desire," in *Queering the Renaissance*, ed. Jonathan Goldberg. Durham, NC: Duke University Press. 107–23.

Hunt, Lynn. 1993. *The Invention of Pornography: Obscenity and the Origins of Modernity, 1500-1800*. New York: Zone Books.

Johnson, Carroll B. 1976. "The Classical Theater and its Reflection of Life," in *Américo Castro and the Meaning of Spanish Civilization*, ed. José Rubia Barcia. Berkeley: California University Press. 193–220.

Jones, C. A. 1958. "*Honor* in Spanish Golden-Age Drama: Its Relationship to Real Life and Morals." *Bulletin of Hispanic Studies* XXXV: 199–210.

Kantorowicz, Ernst. 1957. *The King's Two Bodies*. Princeton: Princeton University Press.

Kirby, Carol. 1981. "Theater and the Quest for Anointment in El rey Don Pedro en Madrid." *Bulletin of the Comediantes* 33(2): 149–59.

Koestenbaum, Wayne. 1989. *Double Talk: The Erotics of Male Literary Collaboration*. New York: Routledge.

Laccara, María Eugenia, ed. 1983. *Poema de mio Cid*. Madrid: Taurus.

Lida de Malkiel, María Rosa. 1962. "Sobre la prioridad de ¿Tan largo me lo fiáis? Notas al Isidro y a El burlador de Sevilla." *Hispanic Review* 30: 275–95.

Lida, Denah. 1970. "El 'catálogo' de Don Giovanni y el de Don Juan Tenorio," in *Actas del Tercer Congreso Internacional de Hispanistas*, ed. Carlos Magis. México: El Colegio de México. 555–57.

Mandel, Oscar. 1963. *The Theatre of Don Juan: A Collection of Plays and Views.* Lincoln, Nebraska: University of Nebraska Press.

Mandrell, James. 1993. *Don Juan and the Point of Honor: Seduction, Patriarchy, and Literary Theory.* University Park: The Pennsylvania State University Press.

McGaha, Michael. 1977. "In Defense of *¿Tan largo me lo fiáis?*" *Bulletin of the Comediantes* 29: 75–86.

McKendrick, Melveena. 1984. "Honour/Vengeance in the Spanish *Comedia*: A Case of Mimetic Transference?" *Modern Language Review* 79(2): 313–35.

Nebrija, Antonio de. 1946. *Gramática castellana*, ed. Pascual Galindo Romero and Luis Ortiz Muñoz. Madrid: Edición de la Junta del Centenario.

Ortega y Gasset, José. 1966. "El tema de nuestro tiempo," in *Revista de Occidente. Edición especial para la Universidad de Puerto Rico.* Madrid. 58–59.

Perry, Mary Elizabeth. 1990. *Gender and Disorder in Early Modern Seville.* Princeton: Princeton University Press.

Piedra, José. 1986–1987. "Literary Whiteness and Afro-Hispanic Difference." *New Literary History* 18: 303–32.

Powell, Brian. 1983. *Epic and Chronicle. The* Poema de mio Cid *and the* Crónica de veinte reyes. London: The Modern Humanities Research Association.

Rogers, Daniel. 1964. "Fearful Symmetry: The Ending of *El burlador de Sevilla.*" *Bulletin of Hispanic Studies* XLI: 141–59.

Ruano de la Haza, José. 1988. "Noticias para el gobierno de la Sala de Alcaldes de Casa y Corte." *Bulletin of the Comediantes* (40)1: 67–74.

Scott, James C. 1990. *Domination and the Arts of Resistance. Hidden Transcripts.* New Haven: Yale University Press.

Sedgwick, Eve K. 1985. *Between Men: English Literature and Male Homosocial Desire.* New York: Columbia University Press.

Sloman, Albert. 1965. "The Two Versions of *El burlador de Sevilla.*" *Bulletin of Hispanic Studies* XLII: 18–33.

Struever, Nancy. 1970. *The Language of History in the Renaissance. Rhetoric and Historical Consciousness in Florentine Humanism.* Princeton: Princeton University Press.

Tirso de Molina, Maestro. 1987. *El burlador de Sevilla y convidado de piedra*, ed. Joaquín Casalduero. Madrid: Cátedra.

———. 1986. *The Trickster of Seville and the Stone Guest*, trans. Gwynne Edwards. Aris & Phillips.

Unamuno, Miguel de. 1945. *Perplexities and Paradoxes*, trans. Stuart Gross. New York: Philosophical Library.

Wade, Gerald, ed. 1969. *El burlador de Sevilla y convidado de piedra.* New York: Scribner's Sons.

Henry's Desires   4

Richard Corum

... not the physical past whose existence is abolished, nor the epic past as it has become perfected
in the work of memory, nor the historic past in which man finds the guarantor of his future, but
the past which reveals itself reversed in repetition.

—Jacques Lacan

Let me begin with a brief account of the materials on one's desk when one sits down to
work on Shakespeare's *The Life of King Henry the Fifth*. First, the figure Henry. Too visible
after the fact, and altogether unrecoverable as a fact, Henry, "like himself," is by 1415
already a legendary figure inherently vulnerable and inescapably defensive, a vanishing
point in the real not to be separated from the imaginary/symbolic orders which
constructed him nor to be untangled from those imaginary and symbolic orders which
unfold from him.[1] Then, the various pre-Shakespearean, post-Henrician textualiza-
tions of this figure: chronicle histories, earlier plays, poems.[2] Despite destabilizing
genealogical differences, these texts construct Henry as a miraculously reformed
Prince "applyed ... unto all vyce and insolency [who became] a majestie ... that both
lived & died a paterne in prince-hood, a lode-starre in honour, and mirrour of magnifi-
cence." As an object of government control, censorship, containment, Henry's life is a
site for the production of an official history that registers and adjudicates competing
points of view in order to speak with "full mouth" of the figure it holds up as a
"paterne" for, and of, those who wield power.[3] In the face of this official historiographical project, another group of representations/valuations comes quickly to mind: those
dissenting knowledges and voices that this official, totalizing, and territorializing
narrative of perfection was constructed to make illegitimate and inaudible; subversive
points of view and antithetical judgments of Henry, that is, which, despite state power
"descending to the most recalcitrant fibers of society," have nevertheless been to a
degree recovered—"nomadic" valuations (to use Deleuze and Guattari's term) which
neither idealize Henry, nor praise him (Foucault 1982, 795; Deleuze and Guattari 1987).[4]

When we place Shakespeare's play(s)—three quartos and a folio; Globe and
Jacobean Court performances—in the context of this official history/unofficial histories binary, we realize that for a common actor-playwright to write and produce, not
just *a* life, but *The Life of King Henry the Fifth* in early modern England was a risky under-

taking to the extent that his *Life* did not reproduce the official version. So it is (and long has been) of considerable interest, reading the folio and the sources, to see that although the play gives us the official life, it also supplements this life with extensive additions, changes and omissions. What can be said with complete confidence about this Folio text is that there is nothing in it (given the dangers, there could be nothing in it) that can conclusively prove that Shakespeare was not wholly committed to the official version of Henry's life, and much to suggest that he was. On the other hand, there is also nothing in this text which conclusively proves that Shakespeare was committed to this official version, and much to suggest that he was not. If in dramatizing the official version Shakespeare added a parallel, unofficial and destabilizing version/valuation of Henry's life and actions, this version, by the logic of censorship, would have had to be officially invisible, however unofficially accessible.[5]

When we turn to the extensive critical/performative materials surrounding Shakespeare's play, it is not surprising to discover that, apart from those who found the play a disappointment, critics and producers have been sharply divided into three principal groups: first, those who read the sources, the stage tradition and the play, and see no significant difference between the official Henry and Shakespeare's Henry except that the latter serves the state as a more powerful ideological vehicle than the chronicles or the earlier dramatizations; second, those who read the sources and the play and perceive a profound difference between the official representation of Henry as ideal and the play's ironic rerepresentation of Henry as a manipulative, conscienceless autocrat who masked his will to power and consequent predations under a carefully constructed "godlie" image. For this group, Shakespeare's semiotic excess, voicing subversive knowledge and transgressive values, radically negates the official version of Henry's sovereign ideality which of necessity it must also articulate. Thus Shakespeare stands, not as a self-effacing handmaid of the state, but as a powerfully articulate subversive who brought text/performance critically to bear against a dominant formation of power, its construction of identity and subjectivity, its apparatuses of representation and dissemination, its appropriations of theatre and so on. In brief, a second Henry, a second Shakespeare and a second logic: not the official logic of sovereign ideality supplemented by Shakespeare's dramatic genius, but an unofficial, deconstructive logic of Shakespearean supplementarity identifying a fissure between dominant myth and historical fact.[6] Finally, there are those who argue, in an attempt to mediate this longstanding controversy, that Shakespeare's text gives us both an eagle Henry *and* a hyena Henry because, as Kantorowicz argued, kings have two bodies (1957). The text, Norman Rabkin asserted, is indeterminate, and although there are those who will insist on determining it one way or another, the wiser critic will step back and see that the play gives both views of Henry in tension, and that Shakepeare's text, far from taking one or the other side of this difference, is caught up, as Shakespeare and his culture were caught up, in what Anthony Brennan and Graham Bradshaw term the "complex multiplicity" of sovereignty itself.[7]

What general observation can we make about this controversy, and what role can we say postmodern theory, particularly queer theory, plays when it enters the space of this debate? The *Henry V* controversy has not been primarily about Shakespeare's Henry. Instead Henry has long functioned as a particularly charged archaeological site where English-speaking cultures have recorded, layer upon layer, their deeply contestatory attitudes towards one or another manifestation of masculine aggressive sovereignty. As Rabkin (1981) implicitly understood, the controversy has always had a powerful displacement effect. When Henry ceased being useful as an object for Tudor and pre-Tudor discussions of monarchical sovereignty itself, he became a site for discussions of the value of human (as opposed to divine) monarchical sovereignty in a Protestant state; then, with the decline of monarchy, the value of bourgeois England's nationalistic opportunisms in, and imperial aggressions against a radically expanding Third World; and, more recently, after the partial decline of two English-speaking empires, the value of masculine authority in a variety of domestic spheres, particularly, on this side of the Atlantic, patriarchal institutions (Congress, the Supreme Court, the military, the family, marriage) and professions, including, of course, the profession of English itself.[8] From 1415 to the present, the debate about Henry has been a debate about the *value* of various forms of masculine sovereignty and has been fueled in part by the need to enlist the foremost literary genius of the culture on one or the other side of one of the most important issues of the last several hundred years: absolute patriarchal sovereignty and its monopolizations of identity, rule, aggressivity, logic, and representationality.

When postmodern theorists entered this deeply layered and massively contested field, they did so, in the main, to further destabilize dominant masculine sovereignties as well as the subjectivities and memory constructs (the "histories") such dominance has produced. Postmodern theorists engaged in this analytical/deconstructive enterprise work to prevent the return of such sovereignties and their sociopolitical consequences, and to understand and represent (as well as legislate against) the culture's long attraction to, its dependencies on, its identifications with, and its endless imitations of patrilogosovereignties. One could say, in brief, that postmodern theories are the most recent powerfully articulate return of those intellectual/cultural activities that absolute patriarchal sovereignties have long repressed. Thus, whereas among other things, new historicists and cultural materialists decenter "Shakespeare" as an effect of cultural appropriation in order to reposition a rehistoricized Shakespeare on the subversive/transgressive margins of Elizabethan/Jacobean culture, and whereas deconstructionists and feminists decenter Henry as an effect of essentialist and misogynistic cultural formations, queer and psychoanalytic theorists decenter Henry as an effect of desire and the unconscious, political or otherwise.[9]

As a general theorization of sexuality and the cultural production and use of sexualities, queer theory makes visible the private parts, so to speak, of the language that constitutes a textual/theatrical phenomenon like *Henry V*. Queer theory interrogates Henry's, Shakespeare's, critics', directors', editors', and audiences' sexualities—their libidinal, erotic investments, their desires and pleasures—as a function of their knowledge/power/unconscious and its production of actions, texts, performances, critical representations, cultural constructions, and pedagogical interventions. For example, Jonathan Goldberg's "Desiring Hal" section of *Sodometries* addresses (among numerous other issues) a question raised a century and a half ago by Hazlitt: "How then do we like [Hal]?"[10] Working from the rich resources of postmodern queer theory (particularly the work of Foucault, Bray, and Sedgwick) as well as alongside Lacan's mirror stage and aggressivity papers, Goldberg's answer is that those critics and audiences who like Hal do so (to put a complex argument very briefly) because they desire Hal, identify with him, and construct themselves after his "paterne" in order to manifest his ideal Christian, heterosexual image while acting out the homophobic, misogynistic repressions this image necessitates and disguises. That is, dazzled by an "imaginary ... identification" with Henry "that founds the ego in its desire for sovereignty," those who endorse Hal "as the very locus of [their] identity" do so to *be* Hal, and to blind themselves, as Hal does, to the homonarcissistic foundations of this identification (Goldberg 1992, 147).

In this paper, queer theory is again brought to bear on *Henry V*, but the question I address concerns Henry's desires as these desires are articulated by the language of the play. My argument assumes that Shakespeare's theatrical resources are not limited to an official historicization of Henry's life and actions as a public figure; rather, *Henry V* is seen as a particularly brilliant historicization of a subjectivity whose "deep truth" (to use Foucault's phrase) is its sexuality.[11]

To plot the actions by which Henry traverses homosocial space is not to repeat the history *Henry V* is ostensibly telling us; rather, it is to articulate an alternative history that Shakespeare's text is showing us. This unofficial history (to borrow a sentence from Harry Berger, Jr.'s discussion of *Lear*) is not the history Henry prefers to hear about himself, but an account of his life, as I read it, "which strikes closer to home and which [Henry] would find harder to bear," though how hard will not become fully clear until the third section of this paper (Erickson and Kahn 1985, 210–29).[12]

Having lingered outside homosocial space (as we know from *2 Henry IV*, if not from the chronicles) as an associate of prostitutes, thieves and a dissolute, ex-homosocial man, Falstaff, in whose company he has been addicted "to courses vain," Henry has lost phallic stature except in name.[13] In this exterior space he has become, in effect, penile, and, content to be little more than penile, he has enjoyed the sodomitical pleasures afforded by the penis.[14] Thus his position at the death of his father (that is, at the end of *2 Henry IV*) is a precarious one. Neither his homosocial God—the Phallus—nor his homosocial lords can be pleased with his performance, though his defeat of Hotspur at Shrewsbury (in *2 Henry IV*) proved an exception to his dissoluteness. Thus, at the beginning of *Henry V*, most of Henry's lords do not respect or fear him. Probably none of them love him, and several love his cousin, Mortimer, a man who has a better claim to the throne than Henry. No doubt others also desire to take his place. In this position Henry has options. He can stay "outside" and die, since if he does not come in, one of his

cousins—Mortimer, Cambridge or York—will take his place and he will be too dangerous to be allowed to live. Or he can "come in." But because there are doubts ("Can I/he
possibly be/come phallic?"), and because there are desires ("I/he can be/come phallic"),
Henry must quickly and thoroughly phallicize himself if he is to survive and rule.

How does Henry do this? First, at the end of *2 Henry IV*, he reestablishes homosocial
space by re-drawing its boundary with "himself" inside. In Holinshed's account, he
banishes his "misrulie mates of dissolute order and life ... from his presence ... inhibit-
ing them upon a great paine, not once to approoch, lodge, or sojourne within ten miles
of his court or presence" (280). For Henry to have brought any of these sodomitical
outsiders inside would have violated a fundamental rule of homosocial space and would
have destroyed him as surely as such behavior destroyed Edward II and Richard II.

Once back inside (and prior to the beginning of *Henry V*), Henry labors to purge
himself of his penile habits, desires, pastimes, vices. To quote Canterbury's account of
this "mortification," this "scouring [of] faults," we are to understand that:

> Consideration like an angel came
> And whipped th'offending Adam out of him,
> Leaving his body as a paradise
> T'envelop and contain celestial spirits (1: 2, 28–31).

Rather than an "offending" sodomitical vessel containing mortal spirits (sperm/alco-
hol/money), Henry's body, given a clean new mythic interiority, is reimagined as an
Edenic "paradise," a granary, to be filled only with celestial, phallic seed.

Thus, having emptied himself of "th'offending Adam," Henry must now fill his
paradisical body with celestial spirits, and he must prove to his homosocial God that it
is so filled, so that this God will embrace, love, empower, and protect him. Of the available technologies for interiorizing the phallus—cannibalism, necrophagy, positive and
negative predation, inheritance, self-sacramentalization, education—it seems, from
Ely's account (1:1, 38ff.), that Henry's first attempt is to fill himself with knowledge.[15]
This gives him some phallic status ("when he speaks, / The air, a chartered libertine, is
still, / And the mute wonder lurketh in men's ears / To steal his sweet and honeyed
sentences"), but not enough to suffice. In *2 Henry IV* Henry had also turned to positive
predation, trading some of his dark, wet, penile stains for Hotspur's hot and dry phallic
fame and glory; but clearly, only limited resources of this sort are available to him in
England. Nor is reliance on his inheritance a sure solution, since his father was a
usurper and a murderer, and one of his cousins has a better claim to his throne than he
does. Given these obstacles, Henry must go to war. Aggressivity, in the ancient form of
trial by combat/trial by ordeal, is the only viable way Henry can weed out his rivals,
regain his legacy in France, and achieve phallic dominance.

Henry's next problem is how he is going to persuade his lords to follow him into
battle. It does not seem likely that homosocial men will be eager to wage war under the
direction of a young man who has been lingering outside, who lacks the phallus, and

whom, as a consequence, they cannot fear, respect or love. Clearly, Henry will have to manipulate them into making him wage war. But how will he do this? From what the first two scenes of the play give us, we can infer (if we have not been blinded by official representations of Henry as ideal, "godlie" sovereign) that before the action of the play begins, Henry has sent ambassadors to France insultingly and arrogantly demanding his properties there, and that he has also reintroduced a bill from his father's reign, which, if passed, would empty half of the church's coffers and massively reduce its power and influence. With this threat in his hands, we can also infer that Henry then lets it be known to Canterbury that if he does not produce a compelling argument to accomplish Henry's desire, Henry will prosecute this bill. Henry waits to convene council until the French reply to his demand is in his anteroom. Then, in council (as the second scene of *Henry V* documents), Henry, presenting himself as a pious young king facing a difficult crisis, first humbly and dutifully seeks the advice of his spiritual lord by asking Canterbury, on the life of Canterbury's soul, what he should do about the French matter, as if this matter had just come to his attention, and then summons the French ambassadors so his temporal lords may hear their reply, knowing that the insults and arrogance he sent to France will have provoked sufficient insults and arrogance in turn to provoke his temporal lords. In response to the urgings of these lords, Henry declares his intention of going to war if his property in France is not returned immediately, a demand he knows will be refused. Thus, although Henry seems to follow textbook protocol (faced with a difficult problem, a young king requests, listens to, and accepts sage advice), Henry is in fact manipulating his lords into creating the political fiction and the war it entails that he needs if he is to phallicize himself.

Having declared war, Henry must figure out how to win it, and the solution he adopts is (to use Lacan's phrase) to make his desire the desire of the phallic Other, by constructing the war he is about to wage not as his war, but as his God's war. And since this intolerant phallic God wants a pure and unified homosocial England, one with an unstained, phallic identity (just as he wants Henry to have a pure, unstained, phallic identity), Henry will use war as a way of doing to England and France what he is doing to himself. As God's angel, Henry will whip "th'offending Adam" out of the body of England (a body symbolized by his army), making England a "paradise/ T'envelop and contain celestial spirits." He will also use war to whip "th'offending Adam" out of England's other "garden," France, making it, too, a paradise to envelop and contain his celestial spirit.

Who are these offending Adams whom Henry must whip out if he is to rewrite England as a perfect homosocial paradise? Needless to say, they are the French, who wrongfully penetrated and sodomitically fill what was once England's "paradise" with thousands of offending, penile Adams, and, among these thousands, most particularly a Dauphin who loves, who writes sodomitical verses to, a horse that is his "mistress" (3:7, 42). Needless to say, too, they are also the Eastcheap occupants: Falstaff, Bardolph, Pistol, Nym and Mistress Quickly, those very uncelestial spirits fouling the interiority of England. And, among others, they are Cambridge, Scroop, and Gray, traitors to Henry and to homosociality itself.

If in personal terms, then, war allows Henry to invert his status as sodomitical object of homosocial law into scouring agent of such law, and if in narrative terms the plot of the play is Henry be(com)ing the chosen, only begotten, phallic son whose homosocial identity is no longer obnubliated by any sodomitical stain whatsoever, the other plot of this play is the construction of England as a pure homosocial space. The objective of Henry's weeding, pruning, limbing, lancing, and burning is not to steal or destroy France, but to create for England a *national* homosocial identity, and thus the kind of unity, purity, maturity, and completeness which will enable Henry and England not only to be "the mirror of all Christian kings" and all Christian states, but also to be the mirror in which Henry's God will see nothing but his own "ideal image." The objective here is not just that Henry, having rid his God's England of penile, sodomitical difference, will surely be chosen and blessed by this God; it is also that Henry's kingship will be a sacrificial ritual of purification: those homosocial men who survive Agincourt will have proved themselves to be the celestial spirits who alone will be enveloped and contained by the English paradise Henry's God is creating through the instrumentality of Henry's acts. And this is the tableau we witness at the play's end: a happy band of celestial brothers occupying a homosocial Christian paradise, with Henry the most celestial, the most phallic, the most homosocial, standing on top of an enormous pile of dead sodomites who had to be pruned from the sacred tree in order for Henry and England to blossom. In short, Henry "like himself" is one of the chief architects, if not the chief architect, of that reactionary rise of intolerance which radically reshaped English homosociality in early modern England.[16]

We are now in a position to analyze specific aspects of Henry's reactionary homosocialization and homonationalization of himself and England as these are illuminated by the play. Of the numerous scenes, episodes and passages about which questions have been asked and answers given, there is space here to look at only three: why Henry takes only one quarter of his army to France, why he orders his soldiers to kill their prisoners at Agincourt, and why he hangs Bardolph. These scenes are important to address because they typify the textual detail which tends to be ignored or simplified in modernist discussions and productions of this play, erasures that have the effect of deleting Henry's subjectivity/sexuality from the play's historiographical project.

The official explanation for the first of these is that Henry must leave three quarters of his army in England to deal with the unruly Scots: "We must not only arm t'invade the French, / But lay down our proportions to defend / Against the Scot...." (1: 2, 136–37). The way "proportion" is argued in council makes it seem that Henry is doing what he can under the circumstances: he would take a larger proportion if he could. From the perspective of homosociality, however, we realize that Henry's purpose for taking only one quarter of his army is that Henry *chooses* to reduce the size of his army, despite the fact that if a military leader is facing two opponents one of which is three times larger than the other, he ought to put one quarter against the lesser threat, Scotland, the rest against the greater, France, other things being equal. Henry, a man schooled in military strategy, knows this, yet he does exactly the opposite. What, then, is Henry's strategy, if this action seems calculated to lose the very war he must win? The answer is that the war Henry must win is not the war we see him fighting on the ground. Henry has to find out if and prove that his God is on his side, and the only way he knows to do this—the only way he knows to make his God reveal his choice—is to make his English army so small that it cannot possibly win without his God's blessing and help. In short, Henry takes one quarter of his army to effect a religious miracle. If he wins with an army too small to have a chance of winning in its own right, he will know beyond doubt that his God has forgiven him. War is his God's instrument of judgment, and Henry is determined to prove himself "straight" in its crucible: "be he ne'er so vile [Agincourt] shall gentle his condition" (4:3, 62–63). Knowing that "the man whose mind is backward" will perish in war (4:3, 72), Henry has good reason to insist that the victory at Agincourt is "none but [God's]": "be it death proclaimed through our host / To boast of this [victory], or take that praise from God / Which is his only" (4:8, 109–111). A victory that is not God's would be useless to him because it would not prove what Henry must prove, namely, that he is no longer a sodomite. Agincourt, that is, is Henry's way of writing himself as exemplary, and France is the fatted calf Henry's God slaughters to honor his rephallicized prodigal.

Of course, there is also a practical, manipulative side to this matter of proportions. What Henry needs to produce is a victory he can retroactively represent as (and, to the extent he can dominate representation, *will* be read as) a divine blessing/gift. So Henry studies history, not the myths of England's legendary past, but the practical military history of numbers, positions, probabilities: how Edward III won at Crécy. So Henry learns exactly how many men he will need, exactly where to put his archers, exactly how far his lines will have to be from the French (and how muddy it will have to be) to slow the French advance to an exhausted crawl, and exactly how much to reduce his own army to get it stuck in just a tight enough corner to insure that his soldiers will fight in phallic fashion or die. But this manipulative aspect of Henry's behavior should come as no surprise. Henry at war, like Henry in the council scene, is staging a theatrical show, *The Miracle of Agincourt*. Playwright, producer, set designer, chief actor—what role is Henry not performing? And although the "new man" whom this victorious war produces has seemed to many to be a complete transformation of Henry's prodigal adolescence into solid Christian/homosocial maturity, it is necessary to recognize that this war, this victory, this new man are no less theatrical productions than the prodigal Hal we saw in Eastcheap, except that here Henry, not Falstaff, is writing the script, and that here the script Henry writes is a homosocial masque, not the antihomosocial anti-masque Falstaff wrote in the past. To set aside childish things for adult things is, for Henry, setting aside apprenticeship in one kind of transgressive theatricality for a sovereign appropriation of theatricality itself. And though the official view is that this appropriation produces a noble, mature, complete Henry as Henry's aggressive, manipulative performance plays itself out in the real, it would be more accurate to say that Henry assumes (and has been contained by) the despotic structure of power that he and Falstaff had previously mimically subverted.

Critics have long been troubled by Henry's reasons for ordering his soldiers to cut their prisoners' throats.[17] The official version, worked out in the chronicles and in modernist criticism/performances against doubts about the morality of such an action, is that Henry gives this order either because a fresh attack by the French would overwhelm an English army heavily burdened with prisoners, or because Henry's rage requires revenge for the slaughter of his baggage boys. From a homosocial perspective, however, what Henry sees as playwright and director when he looks over his battlefield is that men like Pistol are contemplating how rich they will become when their prisoners are ransomed. The only way Henry can put an end to this theft of his inheritance ("France is mine," he is saying to himself, "and it is not penile money; it is my phallic wealth/inheritance"), the only way he can keep penile men like Pistol from getting rich at his expense, and prevent them from penilizing his war, is to force them to kill their prisoners. To phallicize his men rather than merely enrich them—to get the phallus inside them rather than French gold in their pockets—Henry orders this castration of the penile, sodomitical other. What this act also means, of course, is that if the English are captured they will be killed, not ransomed. So, by forcing his men to kill their prisoners, Henry powerful induces them to stop thinking about making money and to start turning themselves into aggressive, celestial spirits capable of whipping the French.

A third incident queer theory is in a position to illuminate is Bardolph's execution (3.6). In defiance of Henry's edict against plunder, Bardolph has stolen a pax from a French church. He is tried, found guilty, and hanged. Why does Henry not pardon his old friend? One pro-Henry answer is that Henry needs to send a strong message to his soldiers or run the risk of having his decrees trifled with in a situation where trifling could destroy his chance of victory, and what stronger message could Henry send than the one being sent by the execution of Bardolph? From a homosocial perspective, however, Bardolph, a man with no phallic essence, is penile, and, worse, a man immune to phallic penetration: his ears do not take in Henry's edict against plundering. What Bardolph perceives as stealing a piece of gold from a French altar in order to enrich himself in a base, material, nonhomosocial manner is in fact a blasphemous misperception of a synecdochical piece of the phallus as a source of monetary profit. Moreover, since this small piece of France is part of Henry's phallic inheritance, Bardolph is stealing Henry's legacy in order to engross himself financially outside, and at the expense of, an economy of homosocial aggressivity. This mistake is, of course, the same mistake Bardolph and his associates made in the past with respect to Hal. They took the prince to be a means of profit and were unable to perceive that, despite his stains, Hal was part of the phallus. Hanging Bardolph restores this theft, revenges this misrecognition, reconstructs this eroded difference, and thus marks Henry as an extension of the omnipotent Phallus.

Hanging Bardolph also functions in another register of Henry's imaginary. To prove that he has moved from outside to inside, from prodigal son to phallic leader of the chosen people, Henry must consistently produce greater and greater differences between the past and the present—differences he can then record as history, differences which he can use official "history" to reify as fact. In the present theatre of Agincourt, he needs a band of happy brothers, whereas in the past theatre of Eastcheap, he needed a ragtag, stained band of happy rogues. Thus, given his needs at Agincourt, he cannot allow a homosocial army to plunder the countryside in the manner his Eastcheap's army had plundered Gadshill in the past. To allow such a sameness would be to let his stained past stain his present, collapsing the boundary between outside and inside, past and present, and thereby to destroy the binary differences (phallus/penis) he has worked hard to construct. To execute Bardolph, then, is to execute the past, construct a difference, and transform a former penile "love" into a phallic/aggressive love. It would be a mistake, however, not to see that, both at Gadshill and at Agincourt, Henry's script satisfies the same will to power in the same theatrical fashion. The reason Henry must compulsively enforce with repetitive acts of violence the difference he is trying to construct is that the difference between these two wills to power inevitably keeps collapsing into a terrifying sameness: his repetitively repressed sodomitical stains keep returning no matter how many times he whites them out. Thus, no matter how many times he whips those offending Adams out of his domains, they have an uncanny way of returning, a return (a sameness) against which Henry defends by writing a history of his life and actions in which a deeply wished-for perfection fictively triumphs over the real.

In much the same way that Troilus' Cressida "is, and is not Cressida," Shakespeare's *Henry V* is, and is not a homosocial history, because it records not only the phallic, but also the penile, truth of Henry's life. And (if I may state my thesis before presenting supporting documentation) the penile truth about Henry's life is not just that Henry was an adolescent sodomite in his "bed-pressing" moments with Falstaff and others outside homosocial space, but that, as England's sovereign, he remains a sodomite *inside* this space. Fueling Henry's actions is the fact that although Henry presents himself (and must present himself) as a person who is free of the offending Adam, he knows this whipping has failed in one fundamental respect: his body is still full of sodomitical desires. The "barbarous license" (1: 2, 272) rumored about his past and officially declared to be a thing of a juvenile past is not just a thing of the past. And though everything Henry does in public appears to validate the claim that his desire has been entirely subjected to the desire of his phallic Christian God, in fact Henry's desire is not, and cannot be, the desire of this Other. He cannot scour this stain from his homosocial identity because it *is* his identity. As a result, he is no doubt terrified. He knows that (like Pistol) "he is not the man that he would gladly make show to the [w]orld he is" (3: 6, 81–82). He knows homosocial law condemns him. He knows that to *be* a sodomite (as Goldberg writes with respect to Edward II and Piers Gaveston) is "to be damned, a being without being." But "it is just such 'being' that [Henry] has" (Goldberg 1992, 121–22). Sodomy, in short, is Henry's treasonous subjectivity. To be Henry "like himself" is to be his God's and culture's worst traitor.[18]

As the French Ambassador's initial speech makes clear, the French know this to be the case:

> ... the prince our master
> Says that you savor too much of your youth,
> And bids you be advised: There's naught in France
> That can be with a nimble galliard won;
> You cannot revel into dukedoms there.
> He therefore sends you, meeter for your spirit,
> This tun of treasure....
> KING: What treasure, uncle?
> EXETER: Tennis balls, my liege (1: 2, 250–56, 259).

Tennis balls are "meeter for [Henry's] spirit" because, as the Dauphin's tun insinuates, Henry's body is gendered (in homosocial terms), not with lethal, phallic "gun stone" testicles, but with sodomitical "tennis balls": "You, Henry, are this tun, and what is inside this tun is, symbolically speaking, inside you; thus we present you with the truth of your sexuality in the form of tennis balls, and we do so as a mockery of your present homosocial, phallic pretensions." In short, a tun of French treasure has the effect of outing Henry not just as a former sodomite, but also as a present one, and does so in front of Henry's entire homosocial court.[19]

Henry tries to "wash [this sodomitical] mote out of his conscience" (4: 1, 169–70) by, for example, fighting and killing Hotspur. By rooting a too-hot political spur out of the body of England, Henry can be seen as trying, in displaced fashion, to root a too-hot libidinal spur out of his own body. Likewise, one could argue that, taken in and by itself, the fact that Henry digs up Richard II's body and reinters it in Westminster Abbey need suggest nothing more than guilt with respect to his father's usurpation, anxiety about his legitimacy, and a penitential effort to put things as right as he can; but in conjunction with a second curious fact, that Henry brings Richard II's body to Westminster and reinters it there with the body of Richard's wife, Anne, does suggest an attempt not only to compel Richard to assume his proper heteronormative identity after the fact, but to map onto Richard's royal body the same reheterosexualization that Henry must enact on his own.

But the task proves impossible. To Henry's despair, his homosocial desire to destroy his sodomitical desire fails. So, filled with fear, guilt, anxiety, he must have told himself that he was finished; that like Edward II, he, too, would lose his crown; that he, the son of the man whom God used to execute sodomitical Richard II, would be struck down; that he, the man who wanted to be, not sodomitical Edward II, but homosocial Edward III, is Edward II. In desperation, urgent to be Edward III, Henry desires to be straight, but because of his desires, he cannot be straight. Not just a problem, this doubleness poses an insoluble dilemma, since as homosocial king it is Henry's duty to destroy sodomites—to train lethal gun stones (to use the play's imagery) against tennis balls—

wherever he finds them. Henry's problem, then, is that he is, and yet he cannot be, a sodomite, and the plot as we have it, I am suggesting, traces Henry's compulsively repetitive attempts to "solve" this endlessly recurring, permanently insoluble problem without seeming to be solving any such problem at all. What applications of denial, repression, splitting, and projection will ensure the ongoing fantasy that his homosocially constructed desire not to be a sodomite will be able to make invisible, unconscious, and nonexistent his sexual desire to be a sodomite? By what means, that is, can Henry bring homosociality's lethal apparatuses of power to bear absolutely, and yet not bear at all, on his actual self? As we shall see, one effect of this doubleness is that every signifier attached to Henry has two signifieds; another is that every question a critic can ask about Henry's behavior has at least two contexts of explanation—a homosocial one and a sodomitical one.[20]

Consider Henry's remarks after declaring war against France:

> Either our history shall with full mouth
> Speak freely of our acts, or else our grave,
> Like a Turkish mute, shall have a tongueless mouth,
> Not worshipped with a waxen epitaph (1: 2, 231–34).

At first glance this claim that history will loudly and freely proclaim Henry a hero if he wins his war or forget him if he does not seems conventionally heroic, if oddly perturbed. Given a second, queer look, however, this boast also is stating a promise that Henry will control what is said about himself, and will do so by silencing anyone who could say anything other than what the official version shall speak with "full mouth." We may understand the "full mouth" / "Tongueless mouth" binary not only, that is, in the apparent sense noted above, but also as a defense against the anxieties bred by Henry's fear of exposure: Henry will literally remove the tongue from (will Turkishly "mute") any mouth which is in a position to expose him. And, by symbolic extension, Henry's act will ensure that never again will "tongues" (that is, penises) be in "mouths" (that is, orifices). In short, Henry's signifiers, oddly perturbed by the multiplication of their unsuspected signifieds, allow Henry to announce the "barbarous license" he must pursue under the guise of glorious war he will pursue. Henry wages war, that is, not only to become phallic (the homosocial and speakable context of his discourse), but to hide under the exigencies of honorable war the murder of anyone who could destroy this assumption of phallic stature (the sodomitical and unspeakable context). Henry's confidence is that no one will be able to see these homicides because, disguised as sovereign martial necessities, they will be wholly invisible. Thus, were we to ignore the perturbations by which Shakespeare's unspeakable history disturbs Henry's history of "Henry," Henry's "full mouth" would be the only mouth speaking his history (though not, thanks to the ironists, the only mouth valuing the consequences and effects of this history), and Shakespeare's unofficial history would become a tongueless mouth, *his* text a "Turkish mute."[21]

Whom does Henry murder? First Falstaff, as Nell ("the King has killed his heart") and Fluellen tell us:

> FLUELLEN: I think it is in Macedon where Alexander is porn. I tell you, captain, if you look in the maps of the orld, I warrant you sall find, in the comparisons between Macedon and Monmouth, that the situations, look you, is poth alike. There is a river in Macedon, and there is also moreover a river at Monmouth. It is called Wye at Monmouth; but it is out of my prains what is the name of the other river. But 'tis all one; 'tis alike as my fingers is to my fingers, and there is salmons in poth. If you mark Alexander's life well, Harry of Monmouth's life is come after it indifferent well; for there is figures in all things. Alexander, God knows and you know … did, in his ales and his angers, look you, kill his best friend, Cleitus.
>
> GOWER: Our King is not like him in that. He never killed any of his friends.
>
> FLUELLEN: … As Alexander killed his friend Cleitus, being in his ales and his cups, so also Harry Monmouth, being in his right wits and his good judgments, turned away the fat knight with the great pelly doublet … (4: 7, 31ff.).

What did Henry kill? A man who was to Henry what Cleitus, Alexander's sodomitical lover, was to Alexander. Homosocial critics like Richard Levin have enjoyed ridiculing Fluellen's method of comparison—the logical inconsequentiality of his comparison of "salmons" and "rivers"; but, of course, literal salmons and rivers and a literal comparison between them is not the point of Fluellen's wobbling exposition. By the logic of double signification operating in this text, salmons and rivers become simultaneously an innocent way of talking about two geographical regions, Monmouth and Macedon, *and* an extremely graphic way ("there is salmons in both") of talking about what Alexander had in Cleitus, and Henry in Falstaff, or vice versa—"Harry of Monmouth's life com[ing] after [Alexander's] indifferent well" (4: 7, 29–30). How did Henry kill Falstaff? By cutting him off cold. "I put my hand into the bed," Nell Quickly tells us, "and felt [Falstaff's feet], and they were as cold as any stone. Then I felt to his knees, and so upward and upward, and all was as cold as any stone" (2: 3, 21–24). Without desire, without love, the corpulent embodiment of sodomitical love becomes in death a symbol of what (from the perspective of homosocial space) it ought to have been in life, "as cold as any stone," just as Henry, in turning the fat knight away, himself becomes as cold as a stone. What Nell almost tells us, but does not, is that Falstaff's warm "tennis ball" testicles have also become cold stones. What she might have told us, had she lived, is that, in killing Falstaff, Henry creates the first of many "tongueless mouths."

Henry is stone cold nowhere more obviously than during the hanging of Bardolph. Here again (if we add the sodomitical to the homosocial context) a single signifier, hanging Bardolph, asserts two signifieds, Henry's official and his unofficial objectives. "We would have all such offenders so cut off," Henry asserts (3:6, 103). The official homosocial objective of this execution (as we saw above) is to cut Bardolph off as an "offending [thief] Adam"; the unofficial homicidal one is to cut Bardolph, like Falstaff, off as an "offending [sodomitical] Adam." But why "cut off" Bardolph by hanging him, and why the dark humor about his large red bulbous nose: "His face is all bubukles and whelks, and knobs, and flames o' fire, and his lips plows at his nose, and it is like a coal of fire, sometimes plue and sometimes red; but his nose is executed, and his fire's out" (3: 6, 99–103)? Officially, Bardolph is hanged because hanging is standard for thieves; but unofficially Bardolph's punishment, like Falstaff's, is symbolic in another register of signification. So if a homosocial Henry is satisfied to see Bardolph hanged as a thief, a defensively sodolethal Henry needs to see Bardolph's mortal, penile body grow stiff, his "head" become engorged with blood, his nose become even more penile than it was before.[22] It is not that Henry needs to see Bardolph executed; rather, he needs (as the text specifically asserts) to see that Bardolph's "nose is executed" as a symbolic surrogate for the erect, sodomitical penis itself. He needs to see the "sometimes [b]lue and sometimes red" head of an orgasmically twitching penile man snapped and turned cold, its fire put out, its mouth made "tongueless," its orifices "mute."

Scroop is a more difficult mouth for Henry to make tongueless, because Scroop is a more recent, a more visible "bedfellow" with standing inside homosocial space, and thus a more dangerous opponent, a mouth that could speak a more damning sodomy than Falstaff's or Bardolph's. For Henry to ask how he is going to hide the murder of Scroop is to ask how he is going to implicate Scroop in a plot along with Cambridge and Grey, so that the three can be exposed as traitors, and leave no one with grounds to suspect that, though three die as traitors, one also dies because he was Henry's lover.[23] It is also to ask how, in implicating Scroop, Henry made sure that Scroop would not prove rash enough to add slander to treason. Scroop's death is also a symbolic execution: Henry must see the stained homosocial head literally cut off, to see that same castration physically inflicted on another, on three others, which he, in a sense, is having to inflict psychically on himself: neither he nor Scroop will ever use his "head" again for pleasure. Without a head, Scroop becomes yet one more sodomite struck down by homosocial justice, one more "tongueless mouth" that cannot speak Scroop's or Henry's real name. It can be objected that all traitors of rank are beheaded, and thus that Scroop's beheading has no unusual symbolic significance. But this is exactly Henry's objective, to leave no trace: the invisible signifieds which Henry is concealing under the visible ones, $\frac{treason}{[sodomy]}$, $\frac{execution}{[murder]}$, escape detection because Henry makes the signifier of the closeted signified virtually identical to the signifier of the uncloseted one. In Shakespeare's text, however, a trace, a difference, is in fact left: Gary Taylor tells us that Henry's reaction to Scroop's betrayal is "so prolonged and excessive that it has almost never been performed in full" (1982, 45). My suggestion is that Henry's $\frac{execution}{[murder]}$ of Scroop's $\frac{treason}{[sodomy]}$ is almost never performed in full because to perform it in full would allow a scene to leave a trace which, when not performed in full, plays altogether straight.

Falstaff, Bardolph and Scroop are not, of course, the only sodomites destroyed in Henry's purge. Consider the boys who are killed guarding the baggage: "Kill the poys and the luggage?" asks Fluellen. "'Tis expressly against the law of arms. 'Tis as arrant a piece of knavery, mark you now, as can be offert" (4:7, 1–3). Did retreating French soldiers kill these baggage boys, as the official version maintains? The French are in retreat, fleeing for their lives. Perhaps it is believable that terrified French soldiers might stop long enough and be cowardly enough to slaughter baggage boys as revenge, but would they have been able, under the circumstances of chaotic retreat, to kill *every* single boy even if they had wanted to do so? "'Tis certain," Gower tells us, "there's not a boy left alive" (4:7, 5). Henry, on the other hand, has a powerful motive to have every boy killed. If he is to disguise, as a French atrocity, the murder of the boy he knew in his Eastcheap life, and thereby create yet one more "tongueless mouth," one more "Turkish mute," Henry would have had to be absolutely certain that not a single boy survived, since a survivor's tongue could wag in the direction of English, rather than the alleged French, assassins. Henry's objective in staging such an atrocity is not just, however, that there would be no boy left to speak his crime; it is also that there would be no more boys to tempt him, or make him suffer unendurable pangs of desire for what he cannot any longer enjoy, or pollute his band of celestial brothers. For further evidence of Henry's involvement, consider the subsequent scenic juxtapositioning: Fluellen's and Gower's discussion of the slaughtered boys turns directly to a discussion of whether Henry killed Falstaff as Alexander killed Cleitus.[24]

At (4:3, 129–30), the Duke of York—next in succession once Mortimer dies—petitions Henry: "My lord, most humbly on my knee I beg / The leading of the vaward [vanguard]." At (4:8, 98–100), we learn that "Edward the Duke of York, the Earl of Suffolk, Sir Richard Ketly, [and] Davy Gam" are the only English dead "of name"— York and Suffolk are being the only dead English nobility. So the play invites us to ask "why York and Suffolk are the *only* English nobility who die at Agincourt." And the play is constructed, I suggest, to provide an answer at 4: 6, 10ff., where we learn that by York's "bloody side, / . . . The noble Earl of Suffolk also lies":

> Suffolk first died; and York, all haggled over,
> Comes to him, where in gore he lay insteeped,
> And takes him by the beard, kisses the gashes
> That bloodily did yawn upon his face,
> And cries aloud, 'Tarry, my cousin Suffolk!
> My soul shall thine keep company to heaven. . . .'
> So did he turn, and over Suffolk's neck
> He threw his wounded arm and kissed his lips;
> And so, espoused to death, with blood he sealed
> A testament of noble-ending love.

This quotation, a considerably abbreviated version of Shakespeare's lengthy addition to Holinshed, is, I suggest, a test case of Alan Bray's thesis that it is not possible to tell the difference between male-male friend/lovers and male-male sex/lovers in early modern England (1990). So we can ask: Is it merely a coincidence that the only two noble

English dead "of name" are York and Suffolk? And is it a coincidence that it is York who petitioned Henry to lead the vanguard, or may we assume that York's desire became the desire of the royal Other as a result of the same sort of manipulative coercion which shaped Canterbury's desire to Henry's martial desire in Act One, and which will shape Katherine's desire to Henry's heteronormative desire in Act Five? To be sure, it is not possible to conclude with certainty that York and Suffolk were sex/lovers, or that they are being represented as such in this passage.[25] In the context of Henry's war, however, given that anyone who dies is a sodomite (since, by definition, phallic men do not die), York and Suffolk are nonetheless what Henry needs them to be: two more "tongueless mouths," two more dead lovers who will not remind Henry of his identity, and two more who, far from being "celestial spirits," will not populate/pollute Henry's English paradise or be included in Henry's "band of brothers."

In killing Falstaff, Scroop, Bardolph, the boy, York, and Suffolk, as well as the thousands of soldiers and prisoners who die (and a Dauphin who disappears) at Agincourt, Henry's motive is not just to purify England, not just to project his own sodomitical desire onto others so he can obliterate this desire in the obliteration of the sodomitical other, not just to remove temptations and witnesses, nor just to make impossible any history of his life other than his official one; Henry's motive is also to "prove" to himself that sodomites die—to "prove" that the homosocial God means exactly what he says ("no sodomite can suceed"). How can Henry persuade himself not to be what he is except by causing to happen to numerous sodomitical others that very fate which he fears will be imposed on him if he is not what he must be? It is in this respect that we understand why a victory that is not his God's would be valueless: such a victory could not "prove" what Henry needs to prove, that he is straight and that, among others, York and Suffolk are sodomites.

Critics have often pondered what Henry is doing during the night he waits for trial by combat/ordeal to prove his phallic identity. So we may also ask whether queer theory is able to illuminate Henry's disguised encounter with three common soldiers, Williams, Court, and Bates, or the briefer bracketing scenes, also frequently cut from performance, between Henry and Pistol, Pistol and Fluellen. At the outset of Act Four, the Chorus tells us:

> ... O, now, who will behold
> The royal captain of this ruined band
> Walking from watch to watch, from tent to tent. . . .
> For forth he goes and visits all his host,
> Bids them good morrow with a modest smile. . . .
> That every wretch, pining and pale before,
> Beholding him, plucks comfort from his looks. . . .
> His liberal eye doth give to every one,
> Thawing cold fear, that mean and gentle all
> Behold, as may unworthiness define,
> A little touch of Harry in the night (4: Cho., 28ff).

As numerous commentators have observed, we do not in fact behold any of this. Virtually everything that happens in the scenes that immediately follow this official account of Harry in the night contradicts the picture the Chorus paints. What we do behold is a disguised Henry who, going off (he says) to be alone, comes into contact first with Pistol, and then with three common soldiers, Williams, Court, and Bates. After a lengthy argument with the latter three turns into a heated quarrel, Williams and a disguised Henry each agree to wear the other's glove in his hat until they can meet and settle their differences. In a subsequent scene Henry asks Fluellen to wear William's glove in his hat. In a third scene, Williams challenges Fluellen, thinking him to be the disguised stranger he argued with in the night. Henry intervenes, acknowledging that he was the soldier with whom Williams quarreled, and rewards Williams by filling Williams's glove with gold.

These episodes are complicated enough to cause many directors to cut them, and many critics to wonder why Shakespeare filled his fourth act with such obscure material. If we set aside the content of Henry's and Williams's lengthy political/ethical argument as not irrelevant but secondary to the action taking place, and look instead at the relations of power and sexuality structuring the action of these scenes, we discover, I suggest, that Henry is out at night wandering among his troops for two contradictory reasons. This might be the last night he will be alive and, in his loneliness and anxiety, he is, I suggest, longing for illicit male companionship; he is also deeply worried that his men might be longing for the same thing ("a little touch of Henry in the night"). Henry has a terrible need for what he is afraid he will find: men, like himself, who are succumbing to the temptations of the penile body symbolized, in Henry's case, by the fact that he confronts these men not "like himself" but disguised by a cloak.[26] However, for his miraculous victory to transpire the next day, Henry must eradicate any possibility of penile weakness (anxiety, fear, doubt), and, more importantly, any possibility of sodomitical pleasures taking place between his men, as well as between himself and his men. So, when Henry encounters Williams, arguably a handsome enough young soldier for Henry to dally with (in contrast to the very brief, earlier exchange he has with Pistol), Henry must, if he is to live, transform his and Williams's powerful libidinal attraction to each other into homosocial anger and aggression (just as Katherine's libido is translated into aggression in the English lesson and wooing scenes). Hence the quarrel. Then, as a way of permanently fixing this translation of libido into anger and aggressivity, Henry symbolically reifies it. He moves Williams's glove—a symbolic surrogate for bodily orifices that fingers and penises may penetrate, as well as a symbolic surrogate for such penetrating appendages—from Williams's waist to his own cap, and he simultaneously moves his own glove, similarly symbolic, from his waist to Williams's cap. In this way, penile/sodomitical libidos and their bodily organs are sublimated and territorialized by being rewritten as tokens of exchange within that highly aggressive homosocial ritual, the challenge. In order to further defend against sodomitical desire, Henry then fills Williams's glove, not with semen, but with gold (here symbolic of phallic power) in order to transform penetration and filling from sodomitical to phallic acts. In short, the three scenes with Williams act out the ritualistic processes of phallicization that structure homosocial space itself. And by reenacting these constitutive formulae the night before Agincourt, Henry (in Foucault's formulation) *produces* aggressive homosocial bonding out of sodomitical libido. So if Henry is "thawing cold fear" as the Chorus proclaims, it is Henry's own fears and anxieties that are being thawed; and if anyone is getting "a touch of Henry in the night," Henry is making sure that it is an aggressive, and not a sodomitical one.[27]

But because desire is strong and repression "endlesse worke," Henry's sublimational alchemy must be compulsively repeated. In fact, the scene with Williams is already a repetition of numerous earlier instances of this process, particularly the first scene of this fourth act. Prior to meeting Williams, Henry plays out a brief version of this subli-mational process with Pistol (a character, like Hotspur, whose name and "character" create dangerously incoherent conflations of penis and phallus). Rather than recognition, friendship or nostalgia at what may be the last meeting between these two Eastcheap friends, there must now be nothing but the safe lubricants of nonrecognition and aggression, as Pistol's cudgeled head learns yet one more time in 5:1, where Pistol is forced to play out this process in far more violent fashion with Henry's surrogate, Fluellen, a scene in which Pistol's eating of Fluellen's leek (a symbolic staging of fellatio) is visually translated into Pistol's symbolic submission to Fluellen's phallic correction, and in which a penis surrogate (a leek held at Fluellen's waist) is translated into a phal-lic surrogate (a leek in Fluellen's cap).

We are now in a position to ask why Shakespeare adds four captains—an English-man, a Scot, an Irishman, and a Welshman—to the Henrician legend, given that none of these four are to be found in any of the chronicle sources. If these captains, like Henry's Eastcheap associates, disappear in criticism and in performance (as they disap-pear in Olivier's and Branagh's films) into a quotidian military mass, there is no point for Shakespeare's addition except to supply proof that support for Henry's war comes from every ethnic part of an allegedly unified nation. But if three of these captains are beautiful young men, then there is a powerful point to their diversity, their exoticism, their difference. Why would Henry not want to surround himself, at the moment he submits to homosocial law, with the most handsome *speci-men* in uniform he can find from the four quarters of his empire?[28] To love all and to be loved by all of his homoso-cial subordinates is the least he deserves in repayment for his suffocated desire. So why should not his "band of brothers" be an especially aesthetically pleasing lot, given that Gower, Jamy, and Macmorris, and the Welshman, Fluellen, are homosocial replace-ments in Henry's life for Bardolph, Nym, Pistol, and Falstaff? The question to ask, I suggest, is who is acting the part of Fluellen? And if the answer is Will Kempe, the actor who presumably played Falstaff, then the transformation of this actor's role from Henry's sodomitical to Henry's homosocial father figure is a particularly vivid theatri-cal visualization of the sublimational logic dominating Henry's behavior, a logic which transforms sodomitical libido not only into homosocial aggression but also into homosocial aestheticism. Of course, these captains can also be said to be evidence of a desperate hope surviving somewhere deep in Henry's psyche that the universal *sameness* demanded by homosocial Christianity might still have some room in it for heavily fissured differences, despite the necessity of having to be marked as same.[29]

From the perspective of those who do not want to witness, celebrate, or identify with Henry's victorious Christian/homosocial/heteronormative absolutism, Shakespeare's *The Life of King Henry the Fifth* is a tragedy, though, of course, it is also a "comedy" for those who, standing in homosocial space, need precisely to see, celebrate, and identify with such a victory. From a nonhomosocial perspective, the answer to the question, "Why is this history tragic?" is simple. Because thousands are dead. Because Henry, more and more threatened by every noncathected tongue, becomes more and more dependent on violence to perform his hyperideal identity. And because, as a result of this dependency, Henry's economy, psychic and otherwise (not to mention England's economy under Henry), inevitably degenerated into an economy of waste and decline which seemed to prosper only when it was at war, which is why Henry spent the rest of his life fighting "himself" in the fields of France.

Given such consequences, one must interrogate the cause of such a tragedy. Is it the fact that Henry is a sodomite? Would things have been different, that is, if Henry had been straight? If by "straight" one means homosocial heteronormativity, no doubt English homosociality would have gone on, nevertheless, in its own direction, and Henry would have been one more monarch hiding under his phallic identity a subjectivity riddled by autoeroticism, voyeurism, adultery, rape, pederasty, fornication, or some other sodomitical activity tolerable when hidden. But if by "straight" one means heteroromantic/reciprocal love/sex, then Henry would also have been in trouble. To be sure, had Henry simply been discovered as being straight in this sodomitical sense he would not have been executed, as Edward II was, with a red hot poker inserted into his anus, but he hardly could have commanded the respect, fear, and love of, nor could he have assumed or exerted sovereign authority over his homosocial peers. So to have kept his crown, a straight Henry (in this sense of "straight") would also have had to engage in something like the endlessly repetitive dissimulations of desire in which Henry is so thoroughly trapped.

But the larger point is that Henry's sexuality *per se* is not the cause of this tragic waste; Henry's sodomitical desire is not correctable, nor is sodomitical desire the problem Shakespeare's play is interrogating. The cause of the tragedy that is Henry's life is the cultural demand/introject, "Be straight or die," and the homosocial formation which necessitates such a demand/introject. This cause *is* correctable, and it is the problem Shakespeare's text is analyzing. The solution to Henry's problem, that is, is not the sodolethal apparatus of power Henry brings to bear upon his desire displaced onto the other, but the removal of homosociality itself, its "Be straight or die" demand/introject, its identities, aggressivities, sexual roles, protocols, relations of power, monopolies, and histories. To solve Henry's problem, a culture must be created in which a person like Henry might do something more valuable with his energies and intelligence than construct himself as a celestial spirit, England as a fascist paradise and English culture as a happy band of Christian/homosocial brothers, and something more pleasurable with his sodomitical desires than make them fodder for sadomasochistic purgation or fuel for sadistic purifications. So, though it is true that homosocial productions and homosocial readings of *Henry V*—caring more for Henry and homosociality than they do for the thousands of lives they happily sacrifice on the altars of Henrician perfection—do "draw their audiences irresistibly toward the celebration of . . . power [based on] force and fraud";[30] it is also true that Shakespeare's *Henry V* was designed to draw its audiences away from "mighty men . . . in little room . . . mangling . . . their glory" (Epi., 3–4), and draw them toward that revisionistic assault on such power, force, and fraud which we now call democracy.

In *Misrepresentations*, Graham Bradshaw argues that "history never tells us what Henry's motives were, because it can't; in this simple but important sense a history play that pretended to make Henry's motives clear would be historically irresponsible" (1993, 46–47).[31] I have been arguing, on the contrary, that Shakespeare's play makes a way to Henry's motives available, if not clear. There is in this text that which functions, in censorial circumstances, as evidence—a collocation of traces, coincidences, displacements, repetitions, overdeterminations, and juxtapositionings which register on a nonhomosocial audience. I have catalogued some of this collocation—this semiotic excess that Shakespeare added to his chronicle sources. That Olivier, Branagh, and others have had to cut so much of this excess in order to produce their versions of *Henry V* as homosocial masterpieces—and their Henries as sovereignty's best piece of poetry—suggests just how much of Shakespeare's play is irresponsible in Bradshaw's sense. Shakespeare's *Henry V* is and is not irresponsible, but, paradoxically, it is its irresponsibility that makes it so useful to some as history, just as it is its thoroughly coerced responsibility that makes it so useful to others as homosocial History.

NOTES

1. Cho. 5; all citations of this play are from *The Life of King Henry the Fifth* (*Henry V*), Shakespeare (1972). I would like to thank the editors of this volume, Louise Fradenburg and Carla Freccero, for their careful editorial attention to the argument that follows.

2. Chronicle histories: Hall (1548); Fabyan (1559); Holinshed (1587); Stow (1580). Poems: *The Battle of Agincourt* (c. 1530); Baldwin (1575); Daniel (1595). For a discussion of the earlier Henry V plays, especially *The Famous Victories of Henry the Fifth* (1598), see Taylor (1982, 3–4).

3. Holinshed (1587), in Bullough (1962; 280, 408). For discussions of Tudor chronicles as history and the complexity of Tudor representations of Henry, see: Levy (1967); Kelly (1970); Smith (1976 3–26); Patterson (1989, 71–92); Hunter (1990); Rackin (1990); and Bradshaw (1993).

4. For a recent account of Henry's life, see Hibbert 1975; for an earlier account, see Wylie, 1914–1929.

5. On quarto/folio differences see: Taylor (1982, 12–26); Patterson (1989); Graham Holderness, *et al.* (1988); Holderness and Loughrey (1993). On censorship, see: (Hill 1986, 32–71); (Clare 1990). For a discussion of Shakespeare's relation to his chronicle sources, see Tomlinson (1984); Taylor; Walter (1954); and Bullough (1962). Taylor relates the critical controversy to the quarto/folio differences: unlike the 1623 Folio, the 1600 Quarto

"removes almost every difficulty in the way of an unambiguously patriotic interpretation of Henry and his war" (12). Brennan 1992 shows that a longstanding stage tradition in which productions are generally as heavily cut as the 1600 Quarto has had much the same jingoizing effect. In other words, the play's critics have *seen* remove from the play most of what Shakespeare added to the chronicle accounts.

6. Among those attracted to Henry: Wilson (1943); Walter (1954); Humphrey (1968); Aoki (1973); Sanders (1977); Berg (1985). Among those repelled: Gould (1919), (1969), Doren (1939); Goddard (1951); Rossiter (1961); Richmond (1967); Gurr (1977); and Barber and Wheeler (1986, 198–236).

7. Rabkin (1981). Rabkin was anticipated, in the play itself, by Pistol ("I love the lovely bully"); Nym ("the King is a good King … but the King hath run bad humors on the knight [Falstaff]"); Hazlitt (1817), who termed Henry an "amiable monster" [cited in Quinn (1969, 37)]; Traversi (1957); and Hapgood (1963, 9–16). Rabkin's lead was followed by Salomon (1980, 343–56); (Pye 1990, 13–42); Brennan (1992); and Bradshaw (1993).

8. As Rabkin (1981) implicitly recognized, the longstanding debate about *Henry V* was not so much a crisis created by ironic readings of *Henry V* as a crisis within the profession occasioned by the new discourses being used to produce such readings. Thus Rabkin's effort to negotiate a solution to the *Henry V* controversy was implicitly an attempt to resolve a methodological problem which was proving increasingly divisive to the profession.

9. The theoretical work on *Henry V* to which I am particularly indebted is that of Williamson (1975); Greenblatt (1981); Mullaney (1983); Dollimore and Sinfield (1985); Erickson (1985); Wilcox (1985); Czerniecki (1988); Leggatt (1988); Berger (1989); Rackin (1990; 1991, 323–45); Newman (1991); Helgerson (1992); and Traub (1992a).

10. Goldberg (1992, 145–75). Quinn (1969) cites the relevant passage from Hazlitt (1817, 37).

11. To read Shakespeare's text as sexualizing, materializing, and thus as historicizing its central character is not to read Shakespeare's Henry as a person; rather, it is to perceive Shakespeare's Henry as a theatrical analysis of an historical subject who is recognized as having been embedded in and conditioned by social processes that produced his sexuality as a function of his cultural identity.

12. In addition to Goldberg's, the queer theory to which I am indebted includes: Foucault (1976/1980); Irigaray (1977/1985); Hocquenghem (1978); Cixous (1981); Bray (1982 and 1990); Sedgwick (1985 and 1990); Butler (1990); Bredbeck (1991); Smith (1991); and Traub (1992b).

13. In *1 Henry IV*, Falstaff mocks Hal as a "dried neat's-tongue," "a bull's pizzle," a "stock-fish"—euphemistic expressions, David Bevington's glosses at 2: 4, 240–42 tell us (1987), which are designed to point out Hal's "genital emaciation"; Falstaff's larger objective, however, as Goldberg notes, is to "point to the phallus Hal lacks" (1992, 174).

14. Holinshed quotes Christopher Ocklund's (1580) *Anglorum Praelia. Ab anno Domini 1327 usque ad annum Domini 1558* (R. Neuberie for H. Bynneman): *"Ille inter iuvenes paulo lascivior ante"* [translated by Bullough (1962) as "Previously he has been somewhat wanton among the young men" (280)].

15. For an anthropological analysis of these predatory/incorporative technologies, see Bloch (1982a), and Bloch and Perry (1982b, 1982c, 211–30).

16. It is not necessary here to outline the rise of intolerance which Boswell 1980 locates in thirteenth- and fourteenth-century Europe; Boswell's account is brilliant and well-known. It is necessary, however, to note that English homosociality became increasingly intolerant as the crown of England passed from Richard Coeur de Lion (1189–1199), to Edward II (1307–1327), Richard II (1377–1399), and to Henry V (1413–1422).

17. For recent alternative discussions of this matter, see Barber and Wheeler (1986, 227); Brennan (1992, 92–95); Bradshaw (1993, 294n26).

18.   After Foucault (1976/1980) and Bray (1982), it has become conventional to distinguish between late modern homosexual *identities* and early modern sodomitical *acts*—the former category confining sodomy to an essentialized subset of the culture, the latter regarding it as a sin everyone is capable of committing. Recently, however, this distinction has been questioned by Bruce R. Smith, who observes that in Renaissance satire "the sodomite was a distinct type rather than a universal figure" (1991, 75–76).

19.   Many critics of this scene conclude that the Dauphin is simply in error about Henry's present situation because he has not yet heard about Henry's miraculous reformation. However, the unofficial history we are watching encourages us to recognize that the Dauphin is not in error, that he knows the official myth articulating the pastness of Henry's past but simply does not believe it. The obvious reason, apart from needing something to carry them in, that the French Ambassador presents the tennis balls in a tun (*OED*, s. v. tun: a large vessel in general; a tub or vat; a chest; Holinshed writes, "a barrel of Paris balls" [545]) is to get an insulting tub-equals-Henry analogy in the King's face. Much of the force of this insult is lost, however, if Shakespeare's tun is turned (as it is in the Branagh production) into a small, elegant box.

20.   A particularly striking example of this double semiotic is Henry's relation to Salic Law. Why, we may ask, is Henry so troubled by a law that says "'*In terram Salicam mulieres ne succedant*'; | 'No woman shall succeed in Salic land'" (1: 2, 38–39)? The official answer is that if Salic law stands, Henry's claims on ancestral lands in France are invalid. But to recognize only this official, homosocial explanation would be to miss the less visible function of Salic Law in this text. In reading Salic law, Henry finds himself reading the handwriting on the wall, because for him this law bars possession of his inheritance in a sense quite different from the bar being asserted in public. For Henry, Salic Law is seen to stand as a restatement of the divine injunction against sodomy: "no sodomite shall succeed in homosocial land." Thus, for Henry to circumvent the visible law is, magically, to circumvent the less visible one. Moreover, to circumvent the invisible law is to put himself in the position, as we have seen above, of enforcing it: Henry will now ensure that "no sodomite shall succeed in homosocial space."

21.   "Tongueless mouth" has, of course, other registers of signification. This passage alludes to the myth of Tereus and Philomela in Book Six of *The Metamorphoses of Ovid* (1955). The more obvious connection is a narrative one—Tereus, having raped Philomela, his wife's sister, responds to her threat—"I shall come forward before your people, and tell my story. If I am to be kept shut up in the woods, I shall fill the forests with my voice, and win sympathy from the very rocks that witnessed my degradation"—by turning Philomela into a tongueless mouth—"But even as she poured out her scorn ... he grasped her tongue with a pair of forceps, and cut it out with his cruel sword" (162–163). The less obvious connection is the performative aspect of this barbarity: "The very acts which furthered [Tereus's] wicked scheme made people believe that he was a devoted husband [to Procne], and he was praised for his criminal behaviour" (160). A second subversive connection to *Henry V* lies in a common historiographical project: as Philomela, unable to speak Tereus' tyranny, weaves a tapestry which tells her story ("Cunningly she set up her threads on a barbarian loom, and wove a scarlet design on a white ground, which pictured the wrong she had suffered" [163]), so Shakespeare's *Henry V*, unable to proclaim Henry's barbarity, weaves a text which tells Henry's victims' stories.

22.   In the place of the conventional terms, *homophobic/homophobia*, I will be using *sodolethal*. I do so because a friend of mine asked why a term which voices the anxieties and fears of the aggressor should be used to mark the violent effects of these fears on the aggressor's victims.

23.   For a valuable discussion of this scene, see Wentersdorf (1976). For discussions of the commonplace linkage of treason and sodomy, see Bray (1982, 70–80), and Smith (1991, 41–53). For a discussion of the sodomitical puns in the scene (as throughout *Henry V* and *1 & 2 Henry IV*), see Rubenstein (1984). Among the numerous entries Rubenstein indexes

(324–25), see, in particular, "Bungle(hole), bungle Anus.... *Henry V.*" One part of this complex discussion must stand for the whole: a "'demon' (homosexual) ... 'gull'd' (buggered) Scroop.... (who, in turn, buggered Henry)" (39–40). The brunt of the entry in the *Dictionary of National Biography* —SCROPE, HENRY le, third Baron Scrope of Masham (1376?–1415 [11 years older than Henry])—is that Scrope's "complicity ... in the plot ... caused general surprise. It seemed strangely inconsistent with his character as well as his past career. He himself pleaded that he had become an accessory in order to betray the conspiracy (*Rot.Parl.iv.66)*" (1077). Is it possible, in other words, that Henry drew Scroop into this plot by "asking" his "bedfellow" to become an accessory, in much the same way that he had "asked" Canterbury to support war and Katherine to accept marriage, and then charged Scroop as an accomplice?

24.   Henry also, of course, derives military value from this atrocity. What better way to redou-ble his soldiers' efforts at a moment of potential defeat than throw a war atrocity in their faces? Henry has already used one tactic to shore up their phallic valor—making them kill their prisoners—so by killing the boys he not only provides a justification for this command but also translates fear into outraged violence.

25.   It is possible, for example, that Henry's imaginary constructs York and Suffolk as sodomites in order to justify killing York, a successor to the throne.

26.   For antecedents for Henry's disguise, see Barton (1975). One antecedent Barton does not discuss is the Christian one. In Henry's homosocial space the chief paradigm for the ritu-alistic productivity of disguise is, of course, Christ. Coming disguised as the man Jesus into the night of the fallen world, Christ puts on, like a cloak, the penile condition of man as a preface to the technologies of rephallicization by which he will rehomosocialize himself and the penile other through various forms of aggressivity against self and other. For a medieval parallel, see Fradenburg (1991, 240–41).

27.   These scenes are also working in at least two other ways: Henry is making it absolutely impossible for himself to remain "disguised," and he is proleptically rehearsing during the night the transformation from disguised penile sodomite to victorious phallic sovereign he intends to actualize the following morning.

28.   Four geographically distinct captains call to mind the imperial habit of articulating homosocial monuments with nude women, one for each corner of the empire: the Albert Memorial in London, for example, or the figures presently outside the Musee d'Orsay in Paris, or, earlier, the title-pages of Renaissance texts. The homosocial message is that empire harnesses sexuality as a means of producing civilization, even though this message is purposefully transgressed by an illicit exploitation of the colonialized subjects' sexuali-ties. Equally relevant is the recognition that these sculpted nudes offer an illicit reward to the imperial gaze—i.e., dominance over the subjected other's sexual body. Cp. also the figures of Emetreus and Lygurge in Chaucer's "Knight's Tale."

29.   Henry is so compulsive about transforming sodomitical libido into homosocial identity that he seems to have arranged events so that his miracle of Agincourt would take place on October 25, "the Feast of Crispian" (4:3, 40), a feast day celebrating two brothers, Crispianus and Crispinus, who, martyred A.D. 287, became the patron saints of shoemak-ers. But why this feast day? One answer, I suggest, is that in Henry's imaginary this day could be seen as celebrating penile brothers who become saintly brothers by containing their penile names ("-anus" and "-pinus") within their saintly phallic names (Crispianus and Crispinus) through the mediation not so much of their martyrdom as of their fetishized craft role, shoemaking. As saints, that is, one brother becomes an asexual cover (a "shoe") for the foot taken as a fetish substitution for the penis, while the other becomes an asexual surrogate for the anus taken as a fetishized receptacle (a "shoe") for the fetishized foot. As 'shoes' they no longer have a (visible) "-pinus" or "-anus."

30.   Greenblatt (1988, 20). On "territorialization" see Deleuze and Guattari (1983).

31.   Bradshaw is echoing Maynard Mack on the subject of motivation. To quote Berger "the essence of Mack's argument . . . is that since characters are not only imaginary persons but also emblems, archetypes, and exemplars, motivation is beside the point" (1985, 224).

WORKS CITED

Aoki, Keiji. 1973. *Shakespeare's "Henry IV" and "Henry V": Hal's Heroic Character and the Sun-Cloud Theme.* Kyoto: Showa Press.

Baldwin, W., ed., 1575. *A myrroure for magistrates . . .* London: Thomas Marsh.

Barber, C. L. and Richard P. Wheeler. 1986. *The Whole Journey: Shakespeare's Power of Development.* Berkeley: University of California Press.

Barton, Anne. 1975. "The King Disguised: Shakespeare's *Henry V* and the Comical History," in *The Triple Bond,* ed. Price. 92–117.

The Battle of Agincourt. c. 1530. London: John Skot.

Berg, Kent T. van den. 1985. *Playhouse and Cosmos: Shakespearean Theater as Metaphor.* Newark: University of Delaware Press.

Berger, Harry, Jr. 1985. "Text against Performance: The Gloucester Family Romance," in *Shakespeare's "Rough Magic,"* ed. Erikson and Kahn, 210–29.

———. 1989. "What Did the King Know and When Did He Know It? Shakespearean Discourses and Psychoanalysis." *The South Atlantic Quarterly* 88: 842–62.

Berman, Ronald, ed. 1968. *Twentieth Century Interpretations of Henry V.* Englewood Cliffs, NJ: Prentice-Hall.

Bevington, David, ed. 1988. *Henry V.* New York: Bantam Books.

———. 1987. *Henry V.* Oxford: Oxford University Press.

Bloch, Maurice. 1982a. "Death, Women and Power," in *Death and the Regeneration of Life,* ed. Bloch and Perry. 211–30.

Bloch, Maurice and Jonathan Perry. 1982b. "Introduction: Death and the Regeneration of Life," in *Death and the Regeneration of Life,* ed. Bloch and Perry. 1–44.

Bloch Maurice and Jonathan Perry. 1982c. *Death and the Regeneration of Life.* Cambridge: Cambridge University Press.

Boswell, John. 1980. *Christianity, Social Tolerance, and Homosexuality: Gay People in Western Europe from the Beginning of the Christian Era to the Fourteenth Century.* Chicago and London: University of Chicago Press.

Bradshaw, Graham. 1993. *Misrepresentations: Shakespeare and the Materialists.* Ithaca and London: Cornell University Press.

Bray, Alan. 1982. *Homosexuality in Renaissance England.* London: Gay Men's Press.

———. 1990. "Homosexuality and the Signs of Male Friendship in Elizabethan England." *History Workshop Journal* 29: 1–19.

Bredbeck, Gregory. 1991a. *Sodomy and Interpretation: Marlowe to Milton.* Ithaca and London: Cornell University Press.

———. 1991b. "Constructing Patroclus: The High and Low Discourses of Renaissance Sodomy," in *The Performance of Power,* ed. Case and Reinelt. 77–91.

Brennan, Anthony. 1992. *Twayne's New Critical Introductions to Shakespeare: Henry V.* New York: Twayne Publishers.

Bullough, Geoffrey, ed. 1962. *Narrative and Dramatic Sources of Shakespeare.* London: Routledge and Kegan Paul.

Butler, Judith. 1990. *Gender Trouble: Feminism and the Subversion of Identity.* New York and London: Routledge.

Candido, Joseph and Charles R. Forker. 1983. *Henry V: An Annotated Bibliography.* New York: Garland.

Case, Sue Ellen and Janelle Reinelt, eds. 1991. *The Performance of Power: Theatrical Discourse and Politics.* Iowa City: University of Iowa Press.

Charnes, Linda. 1993. *Notorious Identity: Materializing the Subject in Shakespeare.* Cambridge: Harvard University Press.

Cixous, Hélène. 1981. "The Laugh of the Medusa," in *New French Feminisms,* ed. Elaine Marks and Isabelle de Courtivron. Brighton: Harvester Press. 245–55.

Clare, Janet. 1990. *"Art Made Tongue-Tied by Authority": Elizabethan and Jacobean Dramatic Censorship.* Manchester: Manchester University Press.

Czerniecki, Krystian. 1988. "The Jest Digested: Perspectives on History in *Henry V*," in *On Puns,* ed. Jonathan Culler. Oxford: Basil Blackwell. 62–82.

Daniel, S. 1595. *The first fowre books of the civile warres betweene the two houses of Lancaster and Yorke.* London: Simon Watterson.

Deleuze, Gilles and Félix Guattari 1983. *Anti-Oedipus: Capitalism and Schizophrenia,* trans. Robert Hurley, Mark Seem and Helen R. Lane. Minneapolis: University of Minnesota Press.

———. 1987. *A Thousand Plateaus: Capitalism and Schizophrenia,* trans. Brian Massumi. Minneapolis: University of Minnesota Press.

Dollimore, Jonathan and Alan Sinfield. 1985. "History and Ideology: The Instance of *Henry V*," in *Alternative Shakespeares,* ed. Drakakis. 206–27.

Doren, Mark Van. 1939. *Shakespeare.* New York: Henry Holt.

Drakakis, John, ed. 1985. *Alternative Shakespeares.* London: Methuen.

Dutton, Richard. 1990. "The Second Tetralogy," in *Shakespeare,* ed. Wells. 337–80.

Erikson, Peter. 1985. *Patriarchal Structures in Shakespeare's Drama.* Berkeley: University of California Press.

——— and Coppélia Kahn, eds. 1985. *Shakespeare's "Rough Magic": Renaissance Essays in Honor of C. L. Barber.* Newark: University of Delaware Press.

Fabyan, Robert. 1559. *The Chronicle . . .* 4th ed. London: Jhon Kyngston.

The Famous Victories of Henry the Fifth. 1589. London: T. Creede.

Feifel, Herman, ed. 1959. *The Meaning of Death.* New York: McGraw-Hill.

Foucault, Michel. 1969/1972. *The Archaeology of Knowledge,* trans. A.M. Sheridan-Smith. New York: Harper and Row.

———. 1976/1980. *The History of Sexuality, Vol. I: An Introduction,* trans. Robert Hurley. New York: Vintage Books.

———. 1982. "The Subject and Power." *Critical Inquiry* 8: 777–95.

Fradenburg, Louise O. 1991. "The Wild Knight," in *City, Marriage, Tournament: Arts of Rule in Late Medieval Scotland.* Madison: University of Wisconsin Press.

Goddard, H. C. 1951. *The Meaning of Shakespeare.* Chicago: University of Chicago Press.

Goldberg, Jonathan. 1992. *Sodometries: Renaissance Texts, Modern Sexualities.* Stanford: Stanford University Press.

Gould, Gerald. 1919. "A New Reading of *Henry V.*" *The English Review* 29: 42–55. Reprinted in Quinn, 81–94.

Greenblatt, Stephen. 1981. "Invisible Bullets: Renaissance Authority and its Subversion, *Henry IV* and *Henry V.*" *Glyph* 8: 40–61. Revised and reprinted in *Shakespearean Negotiations,*. 21–65.

———. 1988. *Shakespearean Negotiations: The Circulation of Social Energy in Renaissance England.* Berkeley: University of California Press.

Gurr, Andrew. 1977. "*Henry V* and the Bee's Commonwealth." *Shakespeare Survey* 30: 61–72.

Hall, Edward. 1548. *The vnion of the two noble and illustre famelies . . .* London: Richard Grafton.

Hapgood, Robert. 1963. "Shakespeare's Delayed Reactions." *Essays in Criticism* 13: 9–16.

Hazlitt, William. 1817. *Characters of Shakespear's Plays.* London: C. H. Reynell for R. Hunter: reprint London: Oxford University Press, 1966.

Helgerson, Richard. 1992. *Forms of Natiohood: The Elizabethan Writing of England.* Chicago: University of Chicago Press.

Hibbert, Christopher. 1975. *Agincourt.* London: Batsford.

Hill, Christopher. 1986. *Collected Essays of Christopher Hill.* Brighton: Harvester Press.

Hocquenghem, Guy. 1978. *Homosexual Desire,* trans. Daniella Dangoor. London: Allison & Busby.

Holderness, Graham. 1988. *Shakespeare: The Play of History.* London: Macmillan Press.

———— and Brian Loughrey, eds. 1993. *The Chronicle History of Henry the Fift with his battell fought at Agin Court in France.* Lanham: Barnes & Noble.

Holinshed, Raphael. 1587. *The third volume of chronicles . . .* London: Henry Denham.

Humphrey, A.R. 1968. *Henry V.* Harmondsworth: Penguin Books.

Hunter, G. K. 1990. "Truth and Art in History Plays." *Shakespeare Survey* 42: 15–24.

Irigaray, Luce. 1977/1985. *This Sex Which Is Not One,* trans. Catherine Porter. Ithaca: Cornell University Press.

Kantorowicz, Ernst H. 1957. *The King's Two Bodies: A Study in Mediaeval Political Theory.* Princeton: Princeton University Press.

Kelly, Henry Ansgar. 1970. *Divine Providence in the England of Shakespeare's Histories.* Cambridge: Harvard University Press.

Leggatt, Alexander. 1988. *Shakespeare's Political Drama: The History Plays and the Roman Plays.* London: Routledge.

Levin, Richard. 1979. *New Readings vs. Old Plays: Recent Trends in the Reinterpretation of English Renaissance Drama.* Chicago and London: University of Chicago Press.

Levy, F. J. 1967. *Tudor Historical Thought.* San Marino: Huntington Library.

Marcuse, Herbert. 1959. "The Ideology of Death," in *The Meaning of Death,* ed. Feifel. 64–76.

Mullaney, Steven. 1983. "Strange Things, Gross Terms, Curious Customs: The Rehearsal of Cultures in the Late Renaissance." *Representations* 3: 53–62.

Newman, Karen. 1991. "Englishing the Other: '*Le tiers exclu*' and Shakespeare's *Henry V*," in *Fashioning Femininity and English Renaissance Drama.* Chicago: University of Chicago Press. 95–108.

Ovid. 1955. *The Metamorphoses of Ovid,* trans. Mary M. Innes. Baltimore: Penguin.

Patterson, Annabel. 1989. *Shakespeare and the Popular Voice.* Cambridge: Basil Blackwell.

Price, Joseph G., ed. 1975. *The Triple Bond: Plays, Mainly Shakespearean, in Performance.* University Park: Pennsylvania State University Press.

Pye, Christopher. 1990. "Mock Sovereignty: *Henry V*," in *The Regal Phantasm.* London: Routledge. 13–42.

Quinn, Michael, ed. 1969. *Shakespeare, Henry V: A Casebook.* London: Macmillan Press.

Rabkin, Norman. 1981. *Shakespeare and the Problem of Meaning.* Chicago: University of Chicago Press.

Rackin, Phyllis. 1990. *Stages of History: Shakespeare's English Chronicles.* Ithaca: Cornell University Press.

————. 1991. "Genealogical Anxiety and Female Authority: The Return of the Repressed in Shakespeare's Histories," in *Contending Kingdoms,* ed. Marie Rose Logan. 323–45. Detroit: Wayne State.

Richmond, H.M. 1967. *Shakespeare's Political Plays.* New York: Random House.

Rossiter, A. P. 1961. "Ambivalence: The Dialectic of the Histories," in *Angels with Horns.* New York: Theatre Arts Books. 40–64.

Rubenstein, Frankie. 1984. *A Dictionary of Shakespeare's Sexual Puns and Their Significance.* London and Basingstoke: Macmillan Press.

Salomon, Brownell. 1980. "Thematic Contraries and the Dramaturgy of *Henry V.*" *Shakespeare Quarterly* 31: 343–56.

Sanders, Norman. 1977. "The True Prince and the False Thief: Prince Hal and the Shift of Identity." *Shakespeare Survey* 30: 29–34.

Sedgwick, Eve Kosofsky. 1985. *Between Men: English Literature and Male Homosocial Desire*. New York: Columbia University Press.

————. 1990. *Epistemology of the Closet*. Berkeley: University of California Press.

Shakespeare, William. 1972. *The Life of King Henry the Fifth*, ed. Alfred Harbage. Middlesex: Penguin.

Smith, Bruce R. 1991. *Homosexual Desire in Shakespeare's England: A Cultural Poetics*. Chicago and London: University of Chicago Press.

Smith, Gordon Ross. 1976. "Shakespeare's *Henry V*: Another Part of the Critical Forest." *Journal of the History of Ideas* 37: 3–26.

Stow, John. 1580. *The Chronicles of England* . . . London: Ralphe Newberie.

Taylor, Gary, ed. 1982. *Henry V*. Oxford: Clarendon.

Tillyard, E. M. W. 1944. *Shakespeare's History Plays*. London: Chatto & Windus.

Tomlinson, Michael. 1984. "Shakespeare and the Chronicles Reassessed." *Literature and History* 10: 46–88.

Traub, Valerie. 1992a. "Prince Hal's Falstaff: Positioning Psychoanalysis and the Female Reproductive Body," in *Desire and Anxiety: Circulations of Sexuality in Shakespearean Drama*. London: Routledge. 50–70.

————. 1992b. "The (In)significance of Lesbian Desire in Early Modern England," in *Erotic Politics*, ed. Zimmerman. 150–69.

Traversi, Derek. 1957. *Shakespeare: From "Richard II" to "Henry V."* Stanford: Stanford University Press.

Walter, J. H., ed. 1954. *Henry V.* London: Arden.

Wells, Stanley, ed. 1990. *Shakespeare: A Bibliographical Guide, New Edition*. Oxford: Clarendon Press.

Wentersdorf, Karl P. 1976. "The Conspiracy of Silence in *Henry V*." *Shakespeare Quarterly* 27: 264–87.

Wilcox, Lance. 1985. "Katherine of France as Victim and Bride." *Shakespeare Survey* 17: 61–76.

Williamson, Marilyn L. 1975. "The Courtship of Katherine and the Second Tetralogy." *Criticism* 17: 326–34.

Wilson, John Dover. 1943. *The Fortunes of Falstaff*. Cambridge: Cambridge University Press.

Wylie, J. H. 1914–1929. *The Reign of Henry the Fifth*. 3 vols. Reprint 1968. New York: Greenwood Press.

Zimmerman, Susan ed. 1992. *Erotic Politics: Desire on the Renaissance Stage*. New York: Routledge.

Part Two

MEDICINE
AND LAW

"*Ut cum muliere*"   **5**

A Male Transvestite Prostitute
in Fourteenth-Century London

Ruth Mazo Karras and David Lorenzo Boyd

Although legal records provide much valuable information on the practice of "sodomy" in late medieval Italy, such evidence is remarkably scant for other parts of Europe (Rocke 1989; Ruggiero 1985, 109–45). The document presented here stands practically alone for medieval England as a description of same-sex intercourse as well as male transvestism.[1] It thus helps assess how medieval English society viewed such behavior. Medieval ideas about what modern people call "sexuality" cannot be elucidated only from the writings of canonists and theologians (Brundage 1987; Payer 1993), but must also be sought from documents recording social practice. First-person accounts on which scholars might base a reconstruction of an individual's sexual subjectivity are rare in the Middle Ages. When such accounts do appear, they are likely to have arisen in a legal context and to be subject to all sorts of problems of interpretation.[2] Nevertheless, as they reflect both the way individuals saw themselves and the way the legal system interpreted their behavior, such accounts are important avenues into medieval constructions of sexuality.

Read within the context of current understandings of the legal regulation and cultural construction of sexualities in the Middle Ages, this document indicates that gender distinctions, rather than those of sexual behavior or "identity," were most crucial. Recognizing that there is no way of verifying the facticity of Rykener's account, we base our analysis here on the premise that if the account is a fiction, it is a verisimilar one, and that what is important is not the actual behavior of this individual, but the construction of sexuality that his account implies (Strohm 1992, 4).

The document translated as the Appendix to this article (the first case on membrane 2 of Plea and Memoranda Roll A34, Corporation of London Records Office), describes the testimony of John Rykener, "calling himself Eleanor," who was apprehended in women's clothing having sex with another man in a London street one night in December 1394.[3] Rykener claimed that he had worked as a prostitute in

London, having been initiated by women who taught him to cross-dress. He then worked in Oxford as an embroideress, having sex with several students, and in Burford as a tapster, again also practicing prostitution. His partners included priests, Franciscans, and Carmelites. He also reported having sex with many women, including nuns, but not apparently for money.

Unfortunately, the result of the case does not survive, if indeed any formal action was ever taken. It is not entirely clear why the examination of Rykener was entered on the roll, but the maintenance of "public order" may have been a reason, although Rykener's offense was never labeled prostitution (the main sexual offense that the courts treated as a threat to public order). Nothing in the document indicates that any sort of formal legal process was under way. What is clear—from the case's physical placement on the roll and the hand in which it is written—is that it is not a later interpolation.

It was rare indeed for a temporal court in England to deal with cases of sodomy, which is one way Rykener's case could have been legally classified. Sexual matters, in England as elsewhere in Europe, were within the jurisdiction of the church courts, and had been so since at least the twelfth century (although temporal authorities also regulated sexual matters when they deemed them relevant to public order). Though canon lawyers, the theorists of the law applied in the church courts, had a good deal to say about sodomy, in actual cases the charge of sodomy appears most often as a further accusation to hurl at heretics. Even so, it does not appear frequently in English church court records of the later Middle Ages; only one case, for example, turns up among the thousands of cases in the records from the London diocese for the late fifteenth century (Wunderli 1981, 83–84).[4] As no late fourteenth-century church court records survive for that jurisdiction, it is not possible to determine whether Rykener and his partner were prosecuted under ecclesiastical jurisdiction.

Despite the general rule that sexual offenses were matters for the church courts, in some cases the city of London took charge of these offenses. Prostitution and procuring, for example, involved public order, and the temporal courts dealt with them for that reason, so that the same people might be prosecuted in both jurisdictions for the same offense. Even a few adultery and fornication cases ended up in the city courts, most involving priests.[5] The city authorities seem to have been particularly eager to bring clerics' sexual transgressions to light, and this may be why they recorded the examination of Rykener. Indeed, awareness of their interest in rooting out clerical offenses may have prompted Rykener's concluding remark that he preferred priests to his other customers. The emphasis on priests does not explain why the authorities were interested in Rykener's cross-dressing in the first place—as we argue below, his gender transgression was the most important factor here—but it does explain why the details of his testimony were so carefully recorded.

Rykener's interrogation raises issues central to our understanding of the role of sexuality in medieval culture. These include the construction, or lack thereof, of specific sexualities; the deployment of the concept of sodomy to impugn the masculinity of a celibate clergy; the relation between the grammatical subject/object relation and the social subject/object relation; and the medieval understanding of gender as performative and the issues of "passing" that arise from it. These questions are a heavy burden for John/Eleanor Rykener to bear alone, but the document is at least a starting point for considering them.

Before discussing the information the document brings to bear on these questions, we need first to consider the discursive context in which the case was situated. In modern terms, Rykener would be described as a transvestite (because he cross-dressed) and a prostitute (because he took money for sex), and probably a bisexual. The relevance of the last term is the most problematic. According to his account, Rykener had sex with both men and women, but all his sexual encounters with men were for money, while those with women were not. This raises the question of whether his motivation for sex with men was more financial than libidinal; he may have been bisexual in his choice of partners but not in his desires. In medieval terms the question of bisexuality would not even have arisen. While people would certainly have been aware that there were some men who had sexual desire for both males and females, this was not seen as a fixed orientation, and did not define a particular type of individual.[6]

For that matter, transvestism would not have been seen as a sexual orientation. Medieval culture is full of stories of women who cross-dressed, but few such stories concern men, and when they did medieval authors did not see cross-dressing as a sexual preference, but rather as a means of gaining access to women (Bullough and Bullough 1993, 45–73). Rykener's case gives no indication that cross-dressing brought him any sexual gratification. We have no idea how he felt about it himself, although the fact that he named the woman who "first dressed him as a woman" indicates that someone else may have suggested the cross-dressing because of the earning opportunities it presented.

In medieval terms, then, what was Rykener? How would medieval culture have viewed his sexuality? Medieval texts, legal and literary, suggest two common cultural categories into which he might have fallen. First, he might have been a prostitute. That is certainly what the man with whom he was arrested took him for. Second, he might have been a sodomite, the common medieval term for a man who had sex with another man (although Rykener was apparently the "passive" partner and this term was sometimes used only for the active one) (Boyd 1994, 69–70).

Perhaps surprisingly, Rykener does not seem to have been treated under either of these two categories. The language used in the confession itself suggests that Rykener might have been seen as a woman, and that it was the gender-crossing, rather than the sexual behavior, that constituted his identity. The following discussion of the cultural categories of prostitution and sodomy will indicate why Rykener did not really fit into them, and we will then turn to an analysis of the document's focus on gender transgression.

It may seem somewhat strange to speak of prostitution in terms of a sexual identity or sexual orientation, because, to a modern sensibility, prostitution is an act, the exchange of sex for money. Prostitution was until relatively recently a status offense (that is, one could be arrested for *being* a prostitute), but now—legally and in most people's minds—it is defined in terms of specific behavior.[7] In the Middle Ages, however, although prostitution was never clearly defined in the law, the offense for which women were presented and prosecuted in both church and temporal courts was that of being a prostitute (*meretrix, feme publique, gemeine fraw,* common woman, and so on), rather than soliciting sex.[8] Prostitutes in many towns had to wear distinguishing clothing (Brundage 1987, 346, 351–52; Schuster 1992, 145–53; Karras 1996). Some municipalities had officially recognized brothels in order strictly to demarcate prostitutes from other women. Under these circumstances, it may not be pushing the evidence too far to argue that a prostitute was seen as a certain type of person rather than as a person who did certain things. In this sense, prostitution was a sexual orientation, an important component of personal identity.

The way prostitution was defined, when medieval writers did go to the trouble to define it, also indicates that it involved being a certain type of person, rather than engaging in sex for money. Medieval people were certainly aware that those they called *"meretrix"* commonly did engage in sex for money, but it was not that which distinguished them as a category. Indeed, "whore" is probably a better translation of *"meretrix"* than "prostitute," because the term had a wider meaning. Although canonists certainly recognized that those they called *"meretrices"* operated commercially, they did not consider that this was what made them *meretrices;* rather it was the public nature of their sexual activity, or the fact that they did not refuse any partner, or the number of partners they had, that placed them in that category (Brundage 1987, 248, 389–90). The practice of the church courts followed the canonists' analysis: while the fact of taking money was occasionally alleged as evidence that a given woman is a whore, the fact of her having sex with several men, or with one man who was a priest, could also be cited as evidence (Karras 1992, 6–8).

It is true that other medieval writers recognized financial exchange as one of the factors defining the category "whore," but only one among many, and not the defining one. The early thirteenth-century moral theologian Thomas of Chobham, for example, cites several different meanings of *"meretrix"*: a woman who has sex outside marriage; a woman who has sex with many men; a woman who denies herself to none; a woman whose sin is public; and a woman who sells herself (Thomas of Chobham 1968, 346–47). The fourteenth-century English handbook for preachers, *Fasciculus Morum,* in discussing the types of lust, defined fornication as follows:

> While fornication is any forbidden sexual intercourse, it particularly refers to intercourse with widows, prostitutes (*meretrices*), or concubines. But the term "prostitute" (*meretrix*) must be applied only to those women who give themselves to anyone and will refuse none, and that for monetary gain (Wenzel 1989, 669).

Here the author seems to have an understanding similar to the modern understanding of the prostitute. Yet it is noteworthy that this text does not have a category for single women who fornicate, other than widows, whores or concubines. Any sexually active woman who is not attached to a particular man is defined as a *meretrix*. The category of prostitute included more than just women who took money for sex.

This terminological conflation of all women who had sex with multiple partners and commercial prostitutes is the key to understanding the deployment of the concept of *meretrix* in medieval society. Those who had sex for money were a recognized group; but because of the way whoredom or prostitution was defined, any woman who was sexually deviant, or any woman who was not under the control of a man, could be placed in that group as well. The classification of sexually independent women as *meretrices* could thus be used as a warning, a tool to control all women (Karras 1989, 425–26; Karras 1996).

In this way, prostitution was intimately tied up with femininity. The whore was the extreme case of what all women could be, and any woman risked classification as a whore if she stepped out of line. For a man to be considered a prostitute, then, would have been an oxymoron. A whore was first and foremost a sinful woman, although probably one who happened to take money for her sin. A man who took money for sex did not fall into the same category. This may explain why Rykener was not accused of prostitution in the London court.

Men could, of course, be prosecuted for sexual offenses in the same way women could; they were also accused and convicted of fornication and adultery. There is, however, no case extant from the medieval English ecclesiastical courts (or in fact from any other medieval courts, as far as we know) in which a man was accused, let alone convicted, of prostitution. Men's other sexual offenses typically involved their control over women: they were pimps or procurers. Even if we look at common sexual defamations or insults directed at men and women, men are rarely called sodomites and never prostitutes; the sexual insults involved women under their control, as they were called cuckolds or whoremongers (Poos 1995; Karras 1996). Little wonder that once Rykener's biological sex had been determined, he was not accused of prostitution. He may have operated in the same way and in the same milieu as women who were accused of prostitution, but in medieval terms his offense was not the same as theirs.[9]

If Rykener cannot be considered a prostitute in terms of medieval understandings of the concept, then, to what extent can he be considered a sodomite? It is telling that he never referred to himself as a sodomite, or to his activities as sodomy, in his confession. The phrases "detestable, unmentionable, and ignominious vice," "libidinous and unspeakable act" and "abominable vice" were used, however, and "unmentionable" and "unspeakable" are often connected with sodomy in medieval discourses about sex. These words may have been spoken by Rykener, who would have been familiar with them from the confessional (Rykener, who was not a cleric, almost certainly did not give his deposition in Latin, so the phrases must be the scribe's interpretation of what he said). Other European jurisdictions in this period were not afraid to use the term "sodomy," and the hesitancy to do so here may signify indecision or confusion about the nature of Rykener's activity and, indeed, of sodomy itself.[10]

It is important to note that the legal crime of sodomy did not mean "having the status of being a homosexual" or "being attracted to men." Legally, it was an act, usually though apparently not always, the act of anal intercourse.[11] In discussing here whether or not Rykener was a sodomite, we are not discussing whether or not he was exclusively attracted to men; a sodomite convicted because of a sex act with a man could also have had sex with women, and in fact Rykener testified that this was so in his case.

But not every act of anal intercourse was necessarily considered sodomy. Alan Bray (1982, 67–69) has argued that, in Renaissance England, routine sex between men was taken more or less for granted and was not equated with sodomy, a vice connected mainly with the debauched court. If Bray is correct, it is also possible that this was true at an earlier period as well, and it may account for the lack of visible enforcement of the antisodomy law in England. This renders problematic any attempt to determine whether Rykener would have been considered a "sodomite."

The logic behind the condemnation of sodomy also problematizes Rykener's case. Is the problem of the unmentionable vice the vice itself or, rather, the disruption of social norms it represents? The more one reads medieval texts concerning sodomy, the more apparent it becomes that it was not the act of sodomy *per se* that constituted wrongdoing. Sodomy was only one of the manifestations of a more important issue subtending the denunciation of male homosexual contact in medieval culture: gender transgression and conflation (Boyd 1994). As we shall see, this gender transgression is precisely what is at issue in Rykener's case. The concern with homosexual behavior as gender disruption surfaces constantly throughout both Latin and vernacular writing, beginning as early as Ennodius' epigrams, which mark the way that sodomy disrupts a stable sex/gender system:

> Vir facie, mulier gestu, sed crure quod ambo,
> jurgia naturae nullo discrimine solvens,
> es lepus, et tanti conculcas colla leonis.
>
> Respice portentum permixtu jure creatum,
> communis generis, satius sed dicitur omnis.
>
> Ludit in ancipiti constans fallacia sexu:
> femina cum patitue, peragit cum turpia, mas est.

> Your face is masculine, your gestures feminine, but your thighs are both
> You resolve an opposition in nature by negating the difference.
> You are a rabbit and trample the neck of a great lion.
>
> Look at this monster created by promiscuous rule
> Of common gender or, rather, of all genders.
>
> There is a constant deception at play in his double sex:
> He's a woman when passive, but when active in shameful deeds, he's a man
> (Stehling 1984, 6–7).

That man can couple with man as with a woman threatens to obscure sharp distinctions between gendered bodies—and gendered orifices. From this perspective, it is little wonder that theologians such as Peter Damian found the flexibility of gender identity dangerous and in need of immediate disciplinary action: the male body under no circumstances should be feminized (Boyd 1994). Vernacular literary texts such as the *Romance of the Rose* and *Eneas* treat the issue of sodomy in similar fashion.

Similar concerns over sodomy as part of a larger issue of gender transgression also surface in fourteenth-century English poems, literary productions close to Rykener's cultural situation and to the textualization of his confession as a written document. Here the literary constructions of sodomy emphasize not the act itself but the feminizing subversiveness of the activity. In both *Sir Gawain and the Green Knight* and *The Miller's Tale*, the substitution of the male for the female (or a male orifice for a female one) becomes the focal point of transgression.[12] The concern with gender arises perhaps most clearly in *Cleanness*, also written by the author of *Sir Gawain*. Speaking to Abraham in *Cleanness*, God describes the activities of the Sodomites and condemns homosexual sodomy as both unclean and antithetical to heterosexual intercourse:

> þay han lerned a lyst þat lykez me ille,
> þat þay han founden in her flesch of fautez þe werst:
> vch male matz his mach a man as hymseluen,
> And fylter folyly in fere on femmalez wyse.
> I compast hem a kynde crafte and kende hit hem derne,
> And amed hit in Myn ordenaunce oddely dere,
> And dyȝt drwry þerinne, doole alþer-swettest,
> And ȝe play of paramorez I portrayed Myseluen,
> And made þerto a maner myriest of oþer:
> When two true togeder had typed hemseluen,
> Welnyȝe pure paradys moȝt preue no better;
> Elles þay mot honestly ayþer oþer welde,
> At a stylle stollen steuen, vnstered wth syȝt,
> Luf-lowe hem bytwene lasched so hote
> þat alle þe meschefez on mold moȝt hit not sleke.
> Now haf þay skyfted My skyl and scorned natwre
> And henttez hem in heþyng an vsage unclene
> (ll. 693–710).

> They have learned a lust [pleasure] that ill-pleases me,
> That they have founded in their flesh the worst of faults:
> Each male takes for a mate a man as himself,
> And they join together lewdly as [a man] with a woman.
> I devised for them a natural [lawful] craft and taught it to them in secret,
> And esteemed it as singularly precious in my ordinaunce,

And ordained lovemaking therein, intercourse as the sweetest of all

And the play of paramours I fashioned myself,

And made the manner of it the merriest of all:

When two people joined themselves together,

Pure paradise might prove itself no better;

If they would honestly possess one another

At a private, secret rendezvous, undisturbed by sight,

The love-flame between them would burn so hotly

That all the mischief in the world might not quench it.

Now they have altered my devising and scorned nature

And contemptuously founded [in themselves] an unclean custom

(Andrew and Waldron 1978).

As an unclean usage of male bodies that feminizes one of them, homosexual activity scorns the sweet heteronormativity sanctioned by Nature and God, and disregards the proper, gendered use of male bodies. They, much like Rykener, act *"ut muliere"* ("as a woman").

Finally, the portrait of Chaucer's much discussed Pardoner in the *General Prologue* to *The Canterbury Tales* also privileges gender transgression over sodomy. When Chaucer describes this ambiguous and effeminate character, he expresses confusion over whether the Pardoner is a gelding or a mare ("mare" probably being slang for one who engages in homosexual activity while taking the passive role) (McAlpine 1980). But the Pardoner's uninterpretability does not dominate the description; rather, it appears as a way of proving, of explaining, the effeminacy already described in the Pardoner's features and the gender instability already expressed amply throughout the text. Perhaps even more telling is that the greatest hint of the Pardoner's sodomitical behavior comes in the Summoner's portrait, where we learn that the Summoner supplies the Pardoner with a stiff "burdoun"—a *double entendre* possibly meaning both musical accompaniment and penis. By focusing on the ambiguous gender of the Pardoner—and on the ambiguity of his (male?) body—the *General Prologue* succeeds in highlighting the disruptive influence that gender transgression might have had on medieval culture's systems of order and interpretation (Burger 1992).

In light of this medieval focus on gender, it is less surprising that the account of Rykener's confession makes no explicit mention of sodomy, but rather employs words such as "unmentionable," "nefarious," and "vice"; focusing on sodomy itself might have taken away from the larger issue about gender that Rykener's case shares with the literature discussed above. We are thus left with a fascinating scenario: while Rykener might have engaged in prostitution, he was not identified as a prostitute; while he might have practiced sodomy, he was not clearly identified as a sodomite. He was identified as a man who had forsaken his gendered identity and had become a woman, engaging in sexual intercourse with men "as a woman." This is why his "confession" of what could have been called, but were not called, sodomy and prostitution, does not seem to be of primary interest to the authorities in this case. That he prostituted himself and engaged in sodomy only confirm his gender loss and conflation. While "sodomite" is largely (though not entirely) a question of choice of orifice, "effeminate" is a question of transgression of gender roles. Hence, not only did his clients think that Rykener was a woman (at least he dressed as one, and never said that his clients knew otherwise), but he had in effect become a woman, allowing them to have sex with him "as with a woman." His "error," to use a medieval phrase, was not primarily, then, that he committed these "sins," but, rather, that he renounced his male body and the privilege that masculine morphology entailed, a renunciation that allowed these sins subsequently to take place.

Not surprisingly, then, the document repeatedly treats Rykener as a woman. He commits the sex act *"modo muliebri"* ("in a womanish manner") and men have sex with him *"ut cum muliere"* ("as with a woman") or *"ut cum femina,"* ("as with a female"), while when he has sex with women, he does it *"ut vir"* ("as a man") or *"modo virili"* ("in a manly fashion"). It is not object choice that affects his sexual identity, but the role he plays. When he acts as a man, he is the subject of the verb *"concubo"* ("to lie with, to have sex with"), but when he acts as a woman, he is its object; his sexual passivity is inscribed in the Latin verbal construction. The text does not persistently stress the sinful or criminal nature of his behavior: on several occasions when he acts "as a woman," his partners alone are said to "commit that vice," as though the feminine partner has disappeared. A male who dressed as a woman provided the extreme case for the medieval habit of gendering any "passive" partner (the one who is penetrated) as feminine (Boswell 1989, 33–34).[13]

Rykener's case suggests that gender was seen as performative, that it was behavior and not intrinsic nature that made one a man or a woman. As Judith Butler (1990, 25) has argued, gender "is always a doing ... [gender] identity is performatively constituted by the very 'expressions' that are said to be its results."[14] That gender is constituted by behavior can clearly be seen in this medieval case. The male-dominated medieval social order, built upon clearly delineated and constantly reenforced gender roles, naturalized and maintained these roles through a variety of practices: differences in dress, mannerisms, sexual positions and activities, social pastimes, occupations, familial roles, legal rights, and duties all functioned to distinguish the masculine from the feminine.[15] Male cross-dressing undermined the male dominance and status that these practices created, exposing gender roles as performative and constructed. It is also for this reason, among others, that sodomy, disrupting the "natural" order and use of male and female bodies and orifices, was condemned, for it turned men into women through the *performance* of sexual acts.[16] Thus, this disruption of masculine and feminine gender differences becomes an offence not only against nature but against the "natural" social order as well.

John Rykener, by describing himself in the terminology of gender transgression rather than sodomy or prostitution, represents such disruption in two interrelated ways. First, by dressing as female and naming himself Eleanor, Rykener's performance as a woman marks him *as a woman*, so much so that periodically he is linguistically gendered feminine in the Latin document.[17] Second, as a male adopting a passive or feminine function with men during sex, he undermines the use of sexual performance and activity to construct masculine and feminine gender roles, and blurs the distinction between the male and the female. These roles are emphasized in the text as constructed behaviors: he learns his sexual behavior from a prostitute named Anna, and his transvestism from Elizabeth Brouderer. Hence, performatively gendered both through sexual activity and dress, Rykener is doubly feminized and disempowered through being perceived as a woman and used sexually by other males. What makes Rykener's case so interesting theoretically is not that he practiced transvestism or the unspeakable vice, but rather that he did both simultaneously. It is in the relationship between the two performances that the politics of medieval gender emerge.

Rykener's position as a male who is gendered feminine cannot be taken as typical of all men at the time who engaged in same-sex relations; the fact that he dressed in women's clothing and that at least some of his partners thought he was a woman certainly contributed to his gendering as feminine. The medieval understanding of Rykener's behavior is much closer to a nineteenth-century concept of "sexual inversion" (a person born into the wrong sexed body) than a modern concept of "homosexuality" focused mainly on object choice (Chauncey 1982–1983). Yet it cannot be concluded that this would have been the way medieval culture understood all or most men who were involved in sexual relations with other men.

What, then, was Rykener in medieval terms? He was feminine, if not literally a woman; but this was not a crime. He was not a prostitute as medieval people understood that concept, and it was unclear whether he was a sodomite. Our perplexity as to where medieval culture would have classified him may well parallel that of the London civic officials. If, in fact, they did not prosecute him, but took his statement and released him, this may have been because they did not know quite what to make of him. He disrupted the traditional boundaries. There may not have been a category in medieval England for Rykener; as a gender-crosser, he was strange, unusual, queer.

Although arguing from negative evidence is always dangerous, it is interesting to speculate on why no further information about Rykener's case appears in the record. Was further action taken and recorded elsewhere, in a document that does not survive? Did the authorities release Rykener without any further action because they did not find his behavior criminal, at least not according to any of the established categories of criminal behavior? Did they not record any further information about him because his crime was so abominable and unmentionable it could not be publicly discussed? Or did they abandon the case out of confusion about what to do? What we can say for certain is that Rykener did not fit the expectations of normal masculine behavior (or even criminal behavior) in fourteenth-century English society and culture.

APPENDIX

Corporation of London Records Office, Plea and Memoranda Roll A34, m. 2 (1395)

This case is found at the top of the membrane, and is followed by several unrelated cases in the same hand.[18] A transcription of the original Latin of this document can be found in *GLQ* 1 (1994), 461–62.

On 11 December, 18 Richard II, were brought in the presence of John Fressh, Mayor, and the Aldermen of the City of London John Britby of the county of York and John Rykener, calling [himself][19] Eleanor, having been detected in women's clothing, who were found last Sunday night between the hours of 8 and 9 by certain officials of the city lying by a certain stall in Soper's Lane[20] committing that detestable, unmentionable, and ignominious vice.[21] In a separate examination held before the Mayor and Aldermen about the occurrence, John Britby confessed that he was passing through the high road of Cheap on Sunday between the above-mentioned hours and accosted John Rykener, dressed up as a woman, thinking he was a woman, asking him as he would a woman if he could commit a libidinous act with her. Requesting money for [his] labor, Rykener consented, and they went together to the aforesaid stall to complete the act, and were captured there during these detestable wrongdoings by the officials and taken to prison. And John Rykener, brought here in woman's clothing and questioned about this matter, acknowledged [himself] to have done everything just as John Britby had confessed. Rykener was also asked who had taught him to exercise this vice, and for how long and in what places and with what persons, masculine or feminine, [he] had committed that libidinous and unspeakable act. [He] swore willingly on [his] soul that a certain Anna, the whore of a former servant of Sir Thomas Blount, first taught him to practice this detestable vice in the manner of a woman. [He] further said that a certain Elizabeth Brouderer[22] first dressed him in women's clothing; she also brought her daughter Alice to diverse men for the sake of lust, placing her with those men in their beds at night without light, making her leave early in the morning and showing them the said John Rykener dressed up in women's clothing, calling him Eleanor and saying that they had misbehaved with her. [He] further said that a certain Phillip, rector of Theydon Garnon,[23] had sex with him as with a woman in Elizabeth Brouderer's house outside Bishopsgate, at which time Rykener took away two gowns of Phillip's, and when Phillip requested them from Rykener he said that [he] was the wife of a certain man and that if Phillip wished to ask for them back [he] would make [his] husband bring suit against him. Rykener further confessed that for five weeks before the feast of St. Michael's last [he] was staying at Oxford and there, in women's clothing and calling himself Eleanor, worked as an embroideress; and there in the marsh three unsuspecting scholars—of whom one was named Sir William Foxlee,[24] another Sir John, and the third Sir Walter—practiced the abominable vice with him often. John Rykener further confessed that on Friday before the feast of St. Michael [he] came to Burford in Oxfordshire and there dwelt with a certain John Clerk at the Swan in the capacity of tapster for the next six weeks,[25] during which time two Franciscans, one named Brother Michael and the other Brother John, who gave [him] a gold ring, and one Carmelite friar and six foreign men committed the above-said vice with him, of whom one gave Rykener twelve pence, one twenty pence, and one two shillings. Rykener further confessed that [he] went to Beaconsfield[26] and there, as a man, had sex with a certain Joan, daughter of John Matthew, and also there two foreign Franciscans had sex with him as with a woman. John Rykener also confessed that after [his] last return to London a certain Sir John, once chaplain at the Church of St. Margaret Pattens,[27] and two other chaplains committed with him the aforementioned vice in the lanes behind St. Katherine's Church by the Tower of London. Rykener further said that he often had sex as a man with many nuns and also had sex as a man with many women both married and otherwise, how many [he] did not know. Rykener further confessed that many priests had committed that vice with him as with a woman, how many [he] did not know, and said that [he] accommodated priests more readily than other people because they wished to give [him] more than others.

NOTES

The authors wish to thank Sheila Lindenbaum for initially drawing our attention to the document, and the Corporation of London Records Office for permission to publish it in *GLQ*; in addition, Laurence Helfer, Cynthia Herrup, Christopher Karras, E. Ann Matter and Paul Strohm, for comments and advice, and the late John Boswell for his inspiration as well as his criticism. Ruth Karras presented a previous version of this article at the Medieval Academy of America meeting in April 1993 and David Boyd another version at the International Medieval Congress, Kalamazoo, in May 1994.

1. Boswell (1980) provides the most thorough treatment of the general subject; see also Goodich (1979). Bullough and Bullough (1993), in their chapter on the medieval period (45–73), generally do not associate male transvestism with homosexuality. They adduce instances of ritual transvestism but none of prostitution.

2. Such legal accounts may reflect the kinds of questions that were put and therefore the way the legal system constructed sexuality, rather than the way the individual experienced it subjectively. See the interrogation of Arnold of Vernioulles, translated in Goodich (1979, 89–123).

3. The modern editor of the Plea and Memoranda Rolls suppressed this case by omitting the details from the published calendar, which is in most cases very detailed and reliable. To describe this case he wrote just a single sentence: "Examination of two men charged with immorality, of whom one implicated several persons, male and female, in religious orders" (Thomas 1924–1932, 228). He thus made invisible the nature of the "immorality" with which they were charged, although he claimed that "care has been taken ... to include all passages which seem to add in any way to our knowledge of the times" (vii). For fuller discussion, see the earlier version of this article in *GLQ* 1 (1994), 459–60.

4. For another example, see York Minster Library, Ms M2(1)f (Dean and Chapter, Court of Audience Register of Comperta 1357–1420 with Chapter act material 1359–1485), fol. 32r.

5. See e.g. Corporation of London Records Office, Letter-Book I, fols. 286r–290r. These date from the early fifteenth century.

6. A great many medieval writers assumed that males and females were in some ways fungible as sex partners. See Boyd (1994); Karras forthcoming.

7. For example, Pennsylvania Consolidated Statutes §5902 provides that "A person is guilty

of prostitution; a misdemeanor of the third degree, if he or she: (1) is an inmate of a house of prostitution or otherwise engages in sexual activity as a business; or (2) loiters in or within view of any public place for the purpose of being hired to engage in sexual activity." The statute goes on to define several other terms ("inmate," "house of prostitution," "sexual activity"). See George (1962, 720), on the use of "common prostitute" in US law; for popular understandings of the term see Swatos and Klein (1978).

8. In some jurisdictions—York, for example—the ecclesiastical courts did not prosecute women as *meretrices*; rather, they charged them with multiple acts of fornication or adultery, focusing on acts rather than on status but ignoring the issue of money. See Borthwick Institute for Historical Research, D/C AB (Dean and Chapter Act Book) 1 (1387–1494).

9. The case of Rolandino Ronchaia, from fourteenth-century Venice, suggests the same thing: he was a male transvestite working as a prostitute, but he was accused of sodomy, not prostitution (Ruggiero 1985, 136).

10. The confusion about whether Rykener's activity amounted to sodomy cannot be entirely resolved by modern scholars, for we do not know what the law of sodomy actually was. Thirteenth-century lawbooks prescribed the death penalty for it, but these are textbooks, not law codes, and actual legislation does not survive, nor do any examples of enforcement of such legislation (Richardson and Sayles 1955, 2:90; Nichols 1865, 1:42; Boswell 1980, 292–93). Examples do, however, survive from other parts of Europe of the harsh punishment of sodomy in the fourteenth and fifteenth centuries, including castration and death (Goodich 1979, 71–88; Rocke 1989; Ruggiero 1985, 109–45; Pavan 1980; Chiffoleau 1984, 191–95; Krekić 1987; Labalme 1984). For a slightly later period, cf. Perry (1989) (where the *pecado nefando* was clearly anal intercourse); Monter (1981).

11. This is not to say that there was in late medieval Europe no category of "sodomite" based on sexual preference rather than on discrete acts; this is not an issue that legal discourse alone can resolve. See Gaunt, this volume, 155–73.

12. Sir Gawain in particular has recently been subject of such analyses. See Dinshaw (1994) and Boyd forthcoming.

13. See Halperin (1989, 46–47, 50–51), on the ancient period. For a similar phenomenon in a rather different medieval society, see Meulengracht Sørensen 1983.

14. On the applicability of this notion to the Middle Ages, see the essays in *Medieval Feminist Newsletter* 13 (1992).

15. Medieval misogyny also enforced this distinction. See Kendrick (1990); Hanawalt (1987).

16. On sodomy as "unnatural," see Boswell (1980, 303–32). The passive role was typically understood as a type of "gender switch," or inversion from masculine to feminine, throughout the Middle Ages, as well as before and after the period.

17. For example, when Rykener describes being shown to his alleged customers by Elizabeth Brouderer, the record describes him as *"ipsa"* ("she").

18. For the cases that precede and follow, see Thomas (1924–1932, 3: 228–30).

19. We have put in brackets the places where the Latin pronoun used for Rykener is of indeterminate gender, or where we supply a pronoun that the Latin omits. Where we use an unbracketed masculine or feminine pronoun to refer to Rykener, this is because the Latin so specifies. The feminine is only used twice to refer to Rykener, both in indirect speech, so it seems reasonable and consistent to translate the indeterminate pronouns as masculine. We have indicated, however, where we have thus disambiguated the text.

20. Soper's Lane, in Cheap and Cordwainer wards, ran south from Cheapside. The name probably comes from *soparii*, shopkeepers, not soapmakers (Lobel 1989, 94).

21. Since this language is stronger than that used to refer to prostitution in the legal records,

it probably refers to sodomy here. See Karras (1996, Chapter 3), for the legal language employed in reference to prostitutes. On the unmentionability of sodomy, see Boyd nd.

22. This may not be a surname but a byname for an embroideress. She may be the same woman as Elizabeth, wife of Henry Moryng, who was convicted in 1385 of bawdry for taking on young women as apprentice embroideresses and then prostituting them. Elizabeth Moryng lived in Broad Street Ward, in the parish of All Hallows Next the Wall, and Elizabeth Brouderer ten years later lived nearby, outside Bishopsgate. Corporation of London Records Office, Letter-Book H, fol. 194; English translation in Riley (1868, 484).

23. In Essex, near Epping.

24. The title "Dominus" or "Sir" was commonly used for priests. No William Foxlee (or any other Foxlee at that date) is found in Emden 1957–1959.

25. Tapsters were often connected with prostitution, and indeed taverns were suspect places for this reason. See Goldberg (1988, 118).

26. Beaconsfield in Berkshire.

27. St. Margaret Pattens in Tower Ward, between Fanchurch Street and East Cheap.

WORKS CITED

Andrew, Malcolm and Ronald Waldron, eds. 1978. *The Poems of the Pearl Manuscript*. Berkeley: University of California Press.

Borthwick Institute for Historical Research, York. MS D/C AB 1.

Boswell, John. 1980. *Christianity, Homosexuality, and Social Tolerance: Gay People in Western Europe from the Beginning of the Christian Era to the Fourteenth Century*. Chicago: University of Chicago Press.

———. 1989. "Revolutions, Universals, and Sexual Categories," in *Hidden From History: Reclaiming the Gay and Lesbian Past*, ed. Martin Duberman, Martha Vicinus, and George Chauncey, Jr. New York: Penguin. 17–36.

Boyd, David Lorenzo. 1994. "Disrupting the Norm: Sodomy, Culture and the Male Body in Peter Damian's *Liber Gomorrhianus*," in *Essays in Medieval Studies*. Vol. 11, ed. Allen J. Frantzen and David J. Robertson. Chicago: Illinois Medieval Association. 63–74.

———. n.d. *Sodomy, Silence and Social Control: Queer Theory and Medieval Texts*.

———. Forthcoming. "Sodomy, Misogyny, and the Displacement of Queer Desire in *Sir Gawain and the Green Knight*." *Arthurian Interpretations*.

Bray, Alan. 1982. *Homosexuality in Renaissance England*. London: Gay Men's Press.

Brundage, James A. 1987. *Law, Sex, and Christian Society in Medieval Europe*. Chicago: University of Chicago Press.

Bullough, Vern L. and Bonnie Bullough. 1993. *Cross Dressing, Sex, and Gender*. Philadelphia: University of Pennsylvania Press.

Burger, Glen. 1992. "Kissing the Pardoner." *PMLA (Proceedings of the Modern Language Association)* 107: 1143–56.

Butler, Judith. 1990. *Gender Trouble: Feminism and the Subversion of Identity*. New York: Routledge.

Chauncey, George. 1982–1983. "From Sexual Inversion to Homosexuality: Medicine and the Changing Conceptualization of Female Deviance." *Salmagundi* 58–59: 114–46.

Chiffoleau, Jacques. 1984. *Les Justices du Pape: délinquance et criminalité dans la région d'Avignon au quatorzième siècle*. Histoire ancienne et médiévale 14. Paris: Publications de la Sorbonne.

Corporation of London Records Office. Letter Book H.

———. Letter Book I.

Dinshaw, Carolyn. 1994. "A Kiss is Just a Kiss: Heterosexuality and its Consolations in *Sir Gawain and the Green Knight*." *diacritics* 24: 205–26.

Emden, A. B. 1957–1959. *A Biographical Register of the University of Oxford to A.D. 1500*. Oxford: Oxford University Press.

George, B. J., Jr. 1962. "Legal, Medical and Psychiatric Considerations in the Control of Prostitution." *Michigan Law Review* 60: 717–60.

Goldberg, P. J. P. 1988. "Women in Fifteenth-Century Town Life," in *Towns and Townspeople in the Fifteenth Century*, ed. J. A. F. Thompson. Gloucester: Alan Sutton. 107–28.

Goodich, Michael. 1979. *The Unmentionable Vice: Homosexuality in the Later Medieval Period*. Santa Barbara: Ross-Erickson.

Halperin, David. 1989. "Sex Before Sexuality: Pederasty, Politics, and Power in Classical Athens," in *Hidden from History: Reclaiming the Gay and Lesbian Past*, ed. Martin Duberman, Martha Vicinus and George Chauncey, Jr. New York: Penguin. 37–53.

Hanawalt, Barbara. 1987. "Golden Ages for the History of Medieval English Women," in *Women in Medieval History and Historiography*, ed. Susan Mosher Stuard. Philadelphia: University of Pennsylvania Press. 1–24.

Karras, Ruth Mazo. 1989. "The Regulation of Brothels in Later Medieval England." *Signs: Journal of Women in Culture and Society* 14: 399–433.

———. 1992. "The Latin Vocabulary of Illicit Sex in English Ecclesiastical Court Records." *Journal of Medieval Latin* 2: 1–17.

———. 1996. *Common Women: Prostitution and Sexuality in Medieval England*. New York: Oxford University Press.

———. Forthcoming. "Sexuality and Marginality," in *Peripheral Visions: Reading the Margins in the Middle Ages*, ed. James W. Earl.

Kendrick, Laura. 1990. "Transgression, Contamination, and Women in Eustache Deschamps's *Miroir de Mariage*." *Stanford French Review* 14: 211–30.

Krekić Bariša. 1987. "Abominandum Crimen: Punishment of Homosexuals in Renaissance Dubrovnik." *Viator* 19: 337–45.

Labalme, Patricia H. 1984. "Sodomy and Venetian Justice in the Renaissance." *Tijdschrift voor rechtsgeschiedenis/Revue d'histoire du droit* 52: 217–54.

Lobel, Mary D., ed. 1989. *The City of London from Prehistoric Times to c. 1520*. Vol. 3 of *The British Atlas of Historic Towns*. Oxford: Oxford University Press.

McAlpine, Monica. 1980. "The Pardoner's Homosexuality and How It Matters." *PMLA (Publications of the Modern Language Association)* 95: 8–22.

Meulengracht Sørensen, Preben. 1983. *The Unmanly Man: Concepts of Sexual Defamation in Early Northern Society*, trans. Joan Turville-Petre. Odense, Denmark: Odense University Press.

Monter, E. William. 1981. "Sodomy and Heresy in Early Modern Switzerland," in *Historical Perspectives on Homosexuality*, ed. Salvatore J. Licata and Robert P. Petersen. New York: Haworth. 42–55.

Nichols, Francis Morgan, ed. 1865. *Britton*. Oxford: Oxford University Press.

Pavan, Elisabeth. 1980. "Police des mœurs, société et politique à Venise à la fin du Moyen Age." *Revue Historique* 264: 241–88.

Payer, Pierre J. 1993. *The Bridling of Desire*. Toronto: Toronto University Press.

Perry, Mary Elizabeth. 1989. "The 'Nefarious Sin' in Early Modern Seville," in *The Pursuit of Sodomy: Male Homosexuality in Renaissance and Enlightenment Europe*, ed. Kent Gerard and Gert Hekma. New York: Haworth. 67–89.

Poos, L. R. 1995. "Sex, Lies, and the Church Courts of Pre-Reformation England." *Journal of Interdisciplinary History* 25: 585–607.

Richardson, H. G. and G. O. Sayles, eds. 1955. *Fleta*. Selden Society, vol. 72. London: Selden Society.

Riley, H. T. 1868. *Memorials of London and London Life*. London: Longmans, Green & Co.

Rocke, Michael J. 1989. *Male Homosexuality and its Regulation in Late Medieval Florence.* Ph.D. thesis, State University of New York, Binghamton.

Ruggiero, Guido. 1985. *The Boundaries of Eros: Sex, Crime and Sexuality in Renaissance Venice.* New York: Oxford University Press.

Schuster, Peter. 1992. *Das Frauenhaus: Städtische Bordelle in Deutschland (1350-1600).* Paderborn, Germany: Ferdinand Schöningh.

Stehling, Thomas, ed. and trans. 1984. *Medieval Latin Poems of Male Love and Friendship.* New York: Garland.

Strohm, Paul. 1992. *Hochon's Arrow: The Social Imagination of Fourteenth-Century Texts.* Princeton: Princeton University Press.

Swatos, William H., Jr. and Judith A. Klein. 1978. "The Lady is Not a Whore: Labeling the Promiscuous Woman." *International Journal of Women's Studies* 1: 159–66.

Thomas of Chobham. 1968. *Thomae de Chobham Summa Confessorum,* ed. F. Broomfield. Analecta Mediaevalia Namurcensia, 25. Louvain, Belgium: Éditions Nauwelaerts.

Thomas, A. H. 1924–1932. *Calendar of Select Pleas and Memoranda of the City of London, a.d. 1381–1412.* 3 vols. Cambridge, UK: Cambridge University Press.

Wenzel, Siegfried, ed. 1989. *Fasciculus Morum: A Fourteenth-Century Preacher's Handbook.* University Park: Pennsylvania State University Press.

Wunderli, Richard. 1981. *London Church Courts and Society on the Eve of the Reformation. Speculum* Anniversary Monographs, 7. Cambridge, MA: Medieval Academy of America.

York Minster Library. MS M2(1)f.

The Hermaphrodite and the Orders of Nature

6

Sexual Ambiguity in Early Modern France[1]

Lorraine Daston and Katharine Park

In his 1614 treatise, *Discourse on Hermaphrodites*, the distinguished Parisian physician, Jean Riolan, professed himself quite unsurprised that a hermaphrodite should turn up in Paris "to inform the learned and the curious of the secrets of nature, the composition of Hermaphrodites"; after all, Riolan noted, Paris was "the précis of the universe, which contains in itself all the marvels, beauties, and imperfections of the world" (Riolan 1614, 3, 2). But Paris had no monopoly on hermaphrodites, as Riolan well knew, since his treatise was in large part inspired by the case of a hermaphrodite in Rouen. Judging from the frequency with which they appeared in the pages of both learned and popular works of this period, one might indeed conclude that hermaphrodites were ubiquitous. At least they were objects of intense interest and speculation: their causes, classification and status were much discussed, and accounts of particular cases greedily read.

In this essay we wish to argue for the singularity of this early modern fascination with hermaphrodites. The attention lavished on them by late sixteenth- and seventeenth-century authors differs quantitatively and qualitatively from both medieval and modern writing on the topic. Even within the restricted domain of medical and legal works that will be our focus here, hermaphrodites come to be lodged within new explanatory frameworks, and linked with new fields of gender associations during this period. Moreover, sixteenth- and seventeenth-century views and attitudes concerning hermaphrodites did not create the mold for later, more familiarly "modern" accounts, any more than they simply echoed medieval writings.

This early modern singularity complicates the conventional binary periodization of sexuality into "modern" and "premodern." We would like to complicate the situation still further by insisting on the heterogeneity within early modern accounts of hermaphrodites. Not only did medical texts not exercise hegemony over other literary, legal and political discussions; the medical literature itself was hardly unified on this theme. Hippocratics debated Aristotelians over the nature of hermaphrodites; university-trained anatomists gainsaid midwives and surgeons; French provincial physicians contradicted their Parisian colleagues; and there are clear differences between national medical traditions. The early modern literature on hermaphrodites is veined with fault lines that run along many different axes. As Patricia Parker has recently pointed out in the case of early modern accounts of sex changes, here one simplifies and generalizes at one's peril (Parker 1993).[2]

We thus concentrate on the learned culture of physicians and jurists, not because we believe that their views necessarily dictated how early moderns understood hermaphrodites, although professional opinions were not without influence in more political and popular spheres. Rather, we choose this narrowed focus because there is a good deal of untangling of positions and implications to be done, even in such a restricted domain. We undertake this untangling in two stages. First, we describe the spectrum of medical and natural philosophical views on sex determination, focusing on sixteenth-century France as the time and place when hermaphrodites first became strongly associated with sexual ambiguity and thence with the otherwise unrelated phenomena of sexual metamorphosis, transvestism, and sodomy. After tracing the emergence of this particular view of hermaphroditism, we examine the several conceptions of the natural and the nonnatural on which it depended. We argue in conclusion that not only must notions of sexual identity be denaturalized through history, but also that the analytic categories of nature and culture must themselves be historicized.

DOUBLE OR BETWEEN?
MEDIEVAL AND EARLY MODERN MODELS OF HERMAPHRODITISM

Riolan was not by any means the only medical writer of the later sixteenth and early seventeenth centuries to demonstrate a special interest in hermaphrodites; in addition to chapters on the subject in numerous more broadly conceived treatises on medicine, such as Ambroise Paré's *On Monsters and Prodigies*, first published in 1573 (Paré 1971, 24–28), we find at least three extended monographs on the subject by medical authors: Riolan's *Discourse*, Jacques Duval's *Treatise on Hermaphrodites* (1612), and *On the Nature of Births of Hermaphrodites and Monsters* (1614) by Gaspard Bauhin. The range and intensity of this medical interest in the topic was distinctly new—in contrast to the relatively brief and general references in earlier treatises—as was the urgency of the moral and social concerns that they expressed. Nonetheless, these works fell clearly within a long-established tradition of ancient and medieval reflection on generation and sexual difference, and they must in the first instance be understood in that context.

The core of this earlier tradition lay in the theories of generation developed and transmitted by writers on medicine and natural philosophy.[3] This tradition was more complicated and internally diverse than appears in the recent account by Thomas Laqueur (1990).[4] As many historians have emphasized, most recently and authoritatively Joan Cadden, postclassical European accounts of generation were dominated by two distinct and, in many ways, contradictory theoretical traditions, Hippocratic and

Aristotelian (Cadden 1993, esp. 13–53; Baldwin 1994, 94–96; Park 1996). These traditions differed in a number of important ways, and from them the early modern period inherited two contrasting models of hermaphroditism with radically different sexual— and ultimately social—implications. The oldest, associated with the Hippocratic writers and (in this respect) with Galen, viewed hermaphrodites as beings truly intermediate in sex, neither male nor female, but exactly in between.[5] According to this theory, the sex of the fetus was determined by two important oppositions: between the male and female principles in the maternal and paternal seed, and between the left and right sides of the uterus.[6] Depending on which seed from which parent was dominant and the position of the fetus in the womb, the offspring would occupy one of a number of possible points on a sexual spectrum, ranging from unambiguously male (male seed contributed by both mother and father lodged in the right side of the uterus) to wholly female (female seed contributed by both mother and father lodged in the left side of the uterus). Other combinations were thought to produce offspring of intermediate sexual nature: fragile and effeminate males, strong and virile females, and—in the rare event of perfectly balanced male and female factors—the occasional hermaphrodite.[7]

The second model inherited by early modern writers viewed hermaphrodites not as beings of intermediate sex, but as beings with doubled or redundant genitalia—a particular and unusual case of twins *manqués*. This model had its roots in the works of Aristotle, most notably the *Generation of Animals*, where he discussed hermaphrodites in the context of multiple births.[8] According to Aristotle, hermaphrodites were produced when the matter contributed by the mother—unlike the Hippocratic writers, he denied the existence of female seed—was more than enough for one fetus, but not enough for two. A large amount of extra matter would yield conjoined twins, each almost perfect in form. A small amount would go to make only an extra member, either internal or external, depending on where in the body it happened to be located. On the foot, for example, it would produce a sixth toe; in the groin, a second set of genitals. In this latter case, if the paternal seed had fully mastered or been mastered by the maternal matter—the basis of Aristotle's general account of sex determination— both sets of genitals would be either male or female; but if the seed mastered the matter in one part but not in the other, the fetus would have one of each. Even in this case, however, the sex of the hermaphrodite was never more than apparently ambiguous, since the sex of the whole fetus was determined by the heat of the heart, which in turn determined the complexion of the body as a whole (Aristotle 1953, 391–93; bk. 4, ch. 1; 766a30–b8).

This model expressed the characteristic Aristotelian interpretation of sexual difference, which presented male and female less as points on a spectrum, in the Hippocratic manner, than as polar opposites admitting no meaningful mediation.[9] Thus from the Aristotelian point of view, hermaphroditism was a condition only of the genitals—the product of a local excess of matter and imbalance of male and female principles— rather than of the entire organism. There could be no true hermaphrodites in the sense of the Hippocratic model; the animal was either male or female, and the other set of genitals was always inoperative, resembling in that respect a tumor or growth (Aristotle 1953, bk. 4, ch. 4; 772b26–35).

Although both the Hippocratic and the Aristotelian accounts were purely natural-istic, they differed greatly from each other in their sexual implications. The Hippocratic model was sexually charged; allowing for a spectrum of intermediate sexual possibili-ties, it posed a potential challenge to the male-female dichotomy, and to the whole social and sexual order based on that dichotomy. The Aristotelian model, on the other hand, had none of those resonances; the sexual ambiguity of the hermaphrodite was never more than superficial, leaving the bipolar sexual order intact.

Over the course of more than a thousand years, these two contrasting, ancient accounts of hermaphroditism were transmitted to medieval and early modern medical theorists in a number of stages, both directly—as various of the key texts were succes-sively translated from Greek into Latin—and indirectly, through the intermediary of Arabic writers such as Avicenna (Cadden 1993, 39–110). The result of this piecemeal transmission was a complicated intellectual situation, in which Hippocratic and Aristotelian interpretations wove their way through medieval and early modern medi-cine and natural philosophy, sometimes in counterpoint, more often in uneasy synthe-sis. In general, the "Hippocratic" model dominated writing on the subject in the early Middle Ages (Cadden 1993, 53–104; Baldwin 1994, 94–96). With the Aristotelian revival of the thirteenth century, however, the situation became more complex. Although Aristotle's theory of generation generally gained the upper hand, it was strongly tempered with a distinct admixture of Hippocratic and Galenic elements. The result was a subtle and eclectic body of theory that admitted both debate and difference of opinion on virtually all of the central issues raised by the problem of generation (Cadden 1993, 197–201).

One of the striking things about later medieval and early Renaissance medical writ-ing on hermaphrodites, to someone versed in the sixteenth- and seventeenth-century material, is its remarkable blandness and lack of development. In part, this may reflect the influence of the Aristotelian tradition, which tended to reject the possibility of the true hermaphrodite, the being of truly intermediate sex, with all of the problems it posed concerning sex and gender. From this point of view, hermaphroditism presented itself less as an ideological than as a surgical challenge—a condition tantamount to possessing a redundant limb. Thus most later medieval medical discussions of hermaphrodites appear in works written by and for surgeons, since they were the group who treated localized external conditions such as tumors. In the mid-fourteenth century, for example, the surgical writer, Guy de Chauliac, drew on Arabic sources for his rudimentary typology of hermaphroditism based on the shape of the genitals. "As Avicenna notes," he wrote, "it is often treated by excision, although not of that part used to urinate, according to Albucasis" (Guy de Chauliac 1890, 547).[10]

But even within the Aristotelian framework, this picture was blurred and compli-cated by Hippocratic and Galenic influences (generally mediated through the Arabic writer Avicenna), which caused medieval writers to stress, much more than Aristotle had, the potential *practical* difficulties in determining the true sex of the hermaphrodite. We can see this effect even in an author like Albertus Magnus, who was writing within the natural philosophical tradition, and was thus inclined to follow a generally Aristotelian line. In *On Animals*, Albertus described hermaphroditism as a local condition of the groin, related to the phenomenon of multiple births. Nonetheless, he noted:

> sometimes the shape of both members is so complete that it is not evident to sight or touch which sex prevails. It is not impossible for such a being to have two bladders and to urinate through each [set of genitals] and to have sex in both ways, although I don't think that it may both impregnate and be impregnated. But its principal set of genitals will be the one that concords with the complexion of the heart, although sometimes the complexion of the heart is so intermediate that it is hardly possible to determine which sex should prevail (Albertus Magnus 1916–1921, 2:1225; bk. 18, tract. 2, ch. 3).

As the uncertainties and hesitations of this passage indicate, by the later thirteenth century the simple dichotomies between Aristotelian and Hippocratic models had become blurred and complicated by a welter of distinctions and mutual accommodations. The result was to compromise the sexually neutral Aristotelian model of hermaphroditism, and to give it a vague aura of moral and sexual disreputability; Albertus described hermaphrodites, viragos and effeminate males as liars, whose bodies and behaviors mislead (Cadden 1993, 212–13). But there is almost no trace of these concerns in the medical literature proper, which characteristically avoided moral judgments and, when faced by behaviors such as sodomy, which were virulently condemned by contemporary canonists and theologians, chose not to fulminate but to evade (Jacquart and Thomasset 1985, 156–59).

In contrast, the medical literature produced after about 1550 not only devoted far more attention to hermaphroditism but also associated it to a far greater extent with the sexually, theologically, and morally charged issues of sodomy, transvestism, and sexual transformation. The chapter on hermaphroditism in *On Monsters and Prodigies*, by the French surgeon, Ambroise Paré, offers an instance of this later cluster of associations. After a general discussion of hermaphrodites, together with several illustrated examples (a set of conjoined twins from Heidelberg, a four-armed child from Italy, a "monster" from Ravenna equipped also with wings, a horn, and the foot of a griffon), he immediately moves to a long discussion of sex between women and then, in the following chapter, to a series of what he terms "memorable stories of certain women who degenerated into men" (Paré 1971, 24–30; ch. 6–7).[11]

To what can we attribute this striking shift? A preliminary answer is suggested by Paré's remarks on the causes of hermaphroditism. Rather than invoking Aristotelian considerations of excess maternal matter, only partially mastered by the paternal seed, he offers a frankly Hippocratic explanation: "it is because the woman provides proportionally as much seed as the man," with the end result that "in a single body are sometimes found two sexes, which we call Hermaphrodites" (Paré 1971, 24).

During the sixteenth century, in fact, we find a clear resurgence of interest in more purely Hippocratic theories concerning generation and sexual difference, one aspect of a general and self-conscious Hippocratic revival that drew on the new humanist translations and editions of that author and that was particularly pronounced in Parisian medical circles (Maclean 1980, 155–74; Lonie 1985).[12] These new ideas did not wholly supplant the older, eclectic tradition, with its clear Aristotelian cast; this remained vital well into the seventeenth century. But they did provide a clear alternative to them.[13]

The Hippocratic view of the hermaphrodite as a being of intermediate sex, flanked in the sexual spectrum by the virago and the effeminate male, tended to associate it more strongly with the sodomite—the woman who has sex with women or the man who has sex with men. This association appears in later medieval writing, but only occasionally and in a brief and casual way; the (male) sodomites in Dante's *Purgatory*, for example, describe their sin as "hermaphroditic" (Dante 1973, 285; canto 26, l. 82), while the rubric "hermaphroditus" was used to refer to a French case of sodomy between women from 1405 (Du Cange 1937–1938, 4:202).[14] The term is not glossed, however, but seems to refer generally and figuratively to what the authors consider an unseemly cross-mixture of gender and behavior (men acting like women and vice versa); there is no indication that the authors are thinking about anatomical hermaphrodites, and medical writers, who do deal with anatomical hermaphrodites, do not employ this metaphorical usage at all.

Less obvious than the newly urgent association between physical hermaphroditism and sodomy is the link with transvestism. At least within the spiritual context of hagiography, transvestism had been treated as largely positive during the Middle Ages: there was a long tradition of female and (to a lesser degree) male saints, who aspired to the spiritual qualities and in some cases the dress of the opposite sex.[15] Here the connection seems to have been a looser and more symbolic one: once the hermaphrodite came to be seen primarily as a being of intermediate (rather than doubled) sex, it also became emblematic of all kinds of sexual ambiguity, and associated with all practices that appeared to blur or erase the lines between the sexes. It is no coincidence that this was occurring precisely at the moment that many of these practices were becoming objects of increasing public concern, as we will see below.

Perhaps the most obvious sign of the development of a discourse that sexualized the hermaphrodite was its increasing association with pornography. The authors of vernacular medical works relating to generation, such as Paré and the physician Jacques Duval, hoped to boost sales by a veiled or not so veiled appeal to the prurient interests of the growing popular audience for printed books—an appeal often enhanced by the copious use of illustrations. In this context, hermaphrodites loomed large. When the Paris faculty of medicine took Paré to task for the various obscenities contained in his book on monsters, they particularly stressed the chapter on hermaphrodites, with its coda on what we would call lesbian anatomy and practices, which they branded "unfit to be read, recited, and heard by Christians," according to Paré. (They expressed particular concern for its potential female readers, to whom, they feared, it would give the wrong idea.)[16] Frankest of all was Duval, who in the introduction to his book on hermaphrodites assured his reader of delights to follow. "Powerful Nature," he wrote,

> that excellent artisan, desiring to encourage men to the propagation of their species, was not content to produce great enjoyment when we actually use our genitals, but also—moved by what instinct I do not know—arranged that we would experience such pleasurable titillation and lustful attraction when they are but named or indicated, that even if I were to use hieroglyphics borrowed from the Egyptians … to designate them … I could not eliminate the simple wantonness with which Nature has ornamented and decorated their commemoration (Duval 1880, 11).

HERMAPHRODITES AND THE ORDER OF NATURE

Duval connected hermaphrodites with sex pure, simple, and pleasurable, but for many of his contemporaries the associations were both more complicated and more disquieting. As emblems of sexual ambiguity, hermaphrodites—once consigned to the margins of legal, theological, medical and philosophical treatises—became an urgent topic. The burning question they raised for early modern writers was one of both authority to judge and criteria for judgment: Who decided the hermaphrodite's sex, and on what grounds? When moderns confront these questions, they test the resilience of powerful and contested polarities: male versus female, individual versus society, and nature versus culture. This is certainly one reason why early modern deliberations on sexing hermaphrodites have attracted so much recent historical attention. It is important to remember, however, that early modern categories were not our own, and that the opposition between nature and culture—sex versus gender and medicine versus law being but special cases of this opposition—would have made little sense to early modern writers on hermaphrodites. Early modern thinkers parsed phenomena like hermaphrodites in terms of the dichotomies that were meaningful to them: natural versus artificial, natural versus preternatural, and natural versus unnatural. In these dichotomies and more generally, the natural was usually the normative. In this section, we shall argue that, although early modern writers planted hermaphrodites firmly on the natural side of the natural/supernatural divide, their location within the oppositions of natural versus artificial, natural versus preternatural and natural versus unnatural shifted precariously toward the nonnatural pole during this period.

Before analyzing the metaphysical and moral framework erected around the meanings of the natural, let us first consider the specific medical and legal doctrines and practices involved in sexing hermaphrodites. Early modern legal and medical authorities worked hand in hand to determine the sex to which the hermaphrodite belonged. In a sexually bifurcated society such as early modern France, jurists could tolerate no middle ground between male and female: sex, like rank and age, was a legal "condition" that fitted or unfitted a person from marrying, inheriting property, bearing witness, and so forth, and was thus an essential determinant of legal identity.[17] Nor were medical writers more comfortable with creatures who straddled the divide: whether they spoke the Aristotelian language of "true" sex or the more Hippocratic language of "dominant" sex, most were eager to resolve the theoretical dilemma posed by hermaphrodites, even when practical exigencies did not press them to do so. (Like Albertus Magnus, most early modern doctors continued to express deep scepticism over the existence of the "perfect" hermaphrodite—one with well formed and fully functional genitals of both kinds—since such cases were never encountered and rarely even alleged.)[18] Thus the relevant judicial rule in both civil and canon law assigned identity by predominant sex; once typed as male or female, according to most legal opinion, the hermaphrodite was entitled, with a few exceptions, to all the prerogatives of that sex (Domat 1713, 1:12; Bauhin 1614, 393–400; Tiraqueau 1546, fol. 144r).[19]

Thus far, the Renaissance medical and legal treatment of hermaphrodites accorded in practice with medieval norms, despite the pressure of a new, theoretical understanding of hermaphroditism. The novelty of sixteenth-century legal practice lay in its increasing reliance on outside testimony to determine the hermaphrodite's predominant sex. Prior to this period, it had been widely assumed that the mature hermaphrodite could be depended on to know and choose which sex predominated, for it was one's "nature" that spoke in the urgent tones of attraction to the "opposite" sex, and what possible motive could there be to dissimulate? Choice of sex was not free in Foucault's sense; this would have been the case only for the mythical "perfect" hermaphrodite, and even then only regarding marriage, since perfect hermaphrodites were otherwise treated as juridically female (Martin 1880, 108). But the individual in question could usually be charged with the decision, without further consultation of authorities, medical or otherwise. Even if midwives or parents had initially mistaken the child's predominant sex, puberty would eventually clarify the situation, when the young hermaphrodite's sexual inclinations made themselves known.

However, once hermaphrodites came to stand for sexual ambiguity of all kinds, including the associated transgressions of sodomy and cross-dressing, the testimony of the hermaphrodite as to predominant sex became problematic. These problems were dramatized in the case of Marie le Marcis, a twenty-year-old hermaphrodite accused of sodomy in 1601, when she abandoned female dress, changed her name to Marin, and announced her intention to marry a fellow maidservant, the widow Jeane le Febvre. Jacques Duval, author of the treatise on hermaphrodites cited earlier, served on a medical commission that advised the court of the Parlement of Rouen in this sensational case. Thanks to Duval's expert testimony, which contradicted that of several other doctors and midwives, that le Marcis possessed a male member that emerged from her/his vagina only when aroused, Marie/Marin was saved. The original death sentence, to be hanged and then burned, was commuted to a probationary period of several years, during which she was to live and dress as a woman and to use neither set of genitals for sex, until it became clear to which of the two "the force of nature inclined her more," as Duval put it (Duval 1880, 10).[20] Another, similar case involved the daughter of a Parisian lawyer accused of having sex with another woman, who was examined by a court-appointed delegation of physicians, surgeons, and midwives. Once revealed to be a hermaphrodite with a hidden penis, she was allowed to assume male dress and to study humane letters and philosophy (Duval 1880, 350–51).

Marie/Marin and the Parisian student were the kind of hermaphrodites that preoccupied Renaissance doctors and lawyers: these were vexed cases, where the evidence was equivocal and accusations of sodomy hung heavily in the air. In such cases, the courts turned to commissions of medical authorities to rule on predominant sex. It was not that legal proceedings on sexual matters had become newly medicalized; doctors had been consulted in cases of sexual incapacity or suspected adultery from at least the thirteenth century (Esmein 1968, 1:254; Hewson 1975, 213–216; Darmon 1979). Nor was it true that medical claims to pronounce upon the "natural" carried more authority than mere legal conventions; both medicine and the law were custodians of the natural during this period, as we shall see shortly. Rather, it was the new fear of sexual fraud and malfeasance surrounding all forms of sexual ambiguity that disqualified the hermaphrodite's own testimony, and demanded that of doctors, surgeons, and midwives instead.

Suspicion concerning sexual imposture reached such a pitch that even hermaphrodites not accused of sodomy or deliberate deception came under severe medical and legal scrutiny. Such was the case of Marguerite Malaure, a pretty maidservant in Toulouse, declared by doctors to be a predominantly male hermaphrodite in 1686. Sexually inexperienced, bewildered, and ashamed, Marguerite lost her livelihood when the municipal magistrates, upon medical consultation, forced her to assume the dress and identity of Arnaud Malaure, which she found "unbelievably painful." Jailed for backsliding into female identity, desperate, and penniless, she travelled to Paris to plead her case to the king, who—on the advice of a commission of physicians and surgeons— eventually reinstated her as a woman (Pitaval 1772–1788, 6: 401–15; Veay 1687).

Throughout Marguerite's ordeal as Arnaud, she insisted vehemently that "she believed she heard nature always calling her to the sex she had been forced to abdicate" (Pitaval 1772–1788, 405); similarly, Marin le Marcis defended himself before the magistrates by claiming that "he had only made use of what nature had formed in him" (Duval 1880, 364). It continued to be assumed that nature dictated predominant sex, but by the early seventeenth century, the issue had become which nature—sexual attraction? genital conformation? temperament?—and who was to interpret nature's often enigmatic decrees. Anxiety over sexual ambiguity had taken the decision out of the hands of the hermaphrodite and its family, as these cases show, placing it in the hands of the court, which was largely guided, in turn, by expert medical opinion. As Riolan put it in 1614: "it belongs to the physician to know the sex of hermaphrodites, and to judge that [sex] which suits them, without giving them the option to elect and choose the sex they would like" (Riolan 1614, 30).

The reasoning about hermaphrodites had always centered on nature, and continued to do so. However, Renaissance conceptions of nature could embrace considerations as familiar to modern ears as anatomy and as unfamiliar as complexion. Key to almost all these meanings was a blending of the descriptive and the normative, which explains why they cut across the distinctions that inform modern thought. On the one hand, the natural described what happened always or mostly—nature's custom. On the other hand, nature prescribed what *should* happen, because a teleological principle required that outcome, either because such ends were built into nature or because nature executed God's will.

At the very heart of high medieval and Renaissance notions of nature was the traditional image of the goddess Natura, protectress of heterosexual, procreative sex. Whether personified in all her splendor in poems or satires,[21] or invoked pale and abstract, in treatises on natural law (Boswell 1980, 313–22), her mission was to insure the continuance of the human species through sexual congress between man and woman. Thus the very word "nature" became a synonym for the genitals. Natura's laws simultaneously partook of the descriptive (heterosexual relations were in fact more common than homosexual ones) and of the normative (heterosexual relations ought to prevail).

Early modern writers, like their medieval predecessors, were well aware that nonprocreative sexual conduct such as masturbation and sodomy was possible: this is why Natura had to lodge the occasional "complaint."[22] Thus, to them, the order of nature connoted not inviolable natural laws,[23] but rather, what nature intends and therefore usually brings to pass. Her intentions were multifarious, summarized by such commonplaces as "nature always perfects" (often invoked as the reason girls sometimes turn into boys, but never the reverse) (Bouchet 1873–1882, 3:96–97; Renaudot 1660, 2:866) or "nature delights in variety" (cited to explain any number of anomalies, including hermaphrodites) (Duval 1880, 382).[24] Because the natural pertained at once to moralized ends and to what ordinarily happens, nature and custom often made common cause.

This was nowhere more evident than in the natural law (here used in the older, juristic sense) framework that regulated the civil status of hermaphrodites. Amongst the indications of rank and condition, distinctions between the sexes counted as one of the "natural" marks of status, as opposed to merely human conventions such as slavery—but then, so did the distinction between legitimate and illegitimate birth, and the "obligations of children toward parents" (Domat 1713, 1:10–12; bk. 1, tit. 2). In the case of hermaphrodites, natural law dictated that sex should follow not only procreative capability, but also the other, related signs, such as activity and passivity, that distinguished men from women. The "natural" might easily embrace character and conduct, as well as anatomy and physiology, since according to medieval and early modern medical theory, "complexion"—the proportions of hot, cold, wet, and dry elements in one's constitution—played a determining role in all of these (Cadden 1993, 170–77). The fundamental opposition of male and female signs of temperament and desire was enough to make some doubt the possibility of perfect hermaphrodites on grounds of natural law alone. According to one of the speakers at a 1636 meeting of the Parisian Bureau d'Adresse, for example:

> natural reason rejects hermaphrodites—not those who only have the appearance of
> [both] genitals ... but those who have the use and perfection of them, which consists in

generation. For nature never places in the same subject an interior and fundamental principle involving two simultaneous, contradictory desires.... And because the [desire] of a man is opposed to that of a woman—the one consisting in activity and the other in passivity, the one in giving and the other in receiving—they cannot be present in the same individual (Renaudot 1660, 2:862).

Here the signs of genital conformation, procreative function, sexual desire, sexual positions, and dispositions all converge in the natural.

The medical commissions of physicians, surgeons, and midwives charged with ascertaining the predominant sex of the hermaphrodite worked with a similarly capacious definition of the natural—one that included elements that we would ascribe to upbringing and socialization. Thus Paré advised medical consultants to inspect not only the genitals, to see "if the feminine sex [i.e. vagina] has the proper dimensions to receive the male member and if the menses flow from there," but also the face, and whether the hair is coarse or fine, the speech "virile or delicate," the carriage "robust or effeminate," the personality "bold or timid" (Paré 1971, 25–26). What might appear to modern eyes as the social constructs of gender struck early modern medical writers as fully as "natural" as the anatomical signs of sex, just as legitimate or bastard birth struck contemporary jurists as fully as "natural" as sex or age.

However, the attention of physicians concentrated on the genitals, for these held the key to the all-important question of procreative capability, which was, as we have seen, invested with considerable normative significance. This is amply demonstrated by the writings of Duval and the Parisian anatomist Jean Riolan regarding the le Marcis case. Despite their ensuing controversy, moreover, both held the *internal* anatomical conformation of the genitals to be decisive in the case. Duval believed he had found a hidden penis, where Riolan diagnosed a prolapsed uterus,[25] but both had absorbed enough of the teachings and prestige of the new, post-Vesalian anatomy to condemn the other members of the Rouen commission who had been content with a Paré-style external examination. Duval elaborated the preeminence of internal anatomy into a principle, which stiffened his resolve to push on, or rather in, when his colleagues had hesitated: "natural things," he wrote,

which have the beginning of motion and rest in themselves, are much more polished, ornamented and decorated in their interior ... quite the opposite from that which is made by human artifice, whose external parts are the only ones well polished, ornamented, and elaborated, the internal ones [being] left as useless with little or no display and ornament (Duval 1880, 371).

As this passage suggests, oppositions between the natural and the various forms of the nonnatural—artificial, preternatural, supernatural, and unnatural (*contra naturam*)—could also carry a normative charge.

For early modern authors, hermaphrodites partook in varying degrees of the artificial, the preternatural, and the unnatural,[26] and the first and last of these rubrics could be highly negative. The artificial encompassed all that was made by human industry; according to Aristotle, the artifact lacks a true "nature," that is, "the distinctive form or quality of such things as have within themselves a principle of motion" (Aristotle 1968–1970, 1:115; bk. 2, ch. 1; 193b3–5).[27] Preternatural phenomena were rare and unusual, outside the ordinary course of nature, but in principle fully explicable by natural causes. These were marvels, not miracles, and included petrifying springs, rains of iron or frogs, sleepers who dozed for months at a stretch, and hermaphrodites.[28] Finally, unnatural acts transgressed the moral dictates laid down by the "author of Nature"; stock examples included a mother murdering her children (Cadden 1993, 223), or bestiality (Aquinas 1946–1948, 2:1825–1827; bk. 2, pt. 2, question 154, art. 11–12). Classed as preternatural, hermaphrodites basked in the positive glow of the marvelous, as in the works of Paré and Duval. But to call a hermaphrodite "artificial" was to insinuate sexual imposture, and to call one "unnatural" was to charge it with a heinous crime.

In most Renaissance oppositions of the natural and the artificial, the natural was strongly preferred, and sexual matters were no exception. When Jeane le Febvre testified that Marin le Marcis had performed manfully, "three or four times," in bed, she emphasized that he had satisfied her "naturally, and adequately accomplished the works of marriage, with equal or greater pleasure than she had had with her deceased husband, with whom she had engendered children" (Duval 1880, 365). In addition to the all-important reference to procreation, the key word here is "naturally," for women accused of playing the male part artificially, that is, with a dildo, faced draconian punishments in this period. Thus Montaigne records how he arrived in the town of Vitry just a few days after a young woman had been hanged for having disguised herself as a man, married a local girl, and used in bed "illicit inventions to supply the deficiencies of her sex" (Montaigne 1967, 456).[29] Similarly, Claude de Tesserant, in his *Prodigious Stories*, contrasted the admirable "natural" transformation of women into men, when an infusion of heat extruded their genitals, with the "artificial" sex changes that turned men into women by their own abominable choice—a degeneration that nature herself, always seeking perfection, would never have countenanced. Dwelling with fascination and feigned horror on the transvestite and homosexual antics of Nero and his court—doubtless a veiled reference to the goings-on associated with Henri III— Tesserant deplored these artificial transformations: an indication of the dangerous company that hermaphrodites had begun to keep in the minds of sixteenth-century authors (Boaistuau 1598, 2:25–28).[30]

Early modern hermaphrodites also risked falling on the wrong side of the natural/unnatural divide. Although celebrated as marvels by some writers, such as Duval, their new proximity to sodomy, the most flagrant form of unnatural behavior,[31] in general brought them other unwelcome neighbors. Tesserant, as we have seen, called transvestites and sodomites "artificial" hermaphrodites and linked these in turn with heinous crimes, murders, and sexual deviations, all lumped together as "strangely against nature" (Boaistuau 1598, 2:36). By the early eighteenth century, the Parisian chronicler, Henri Sauval, classed hermaphrodites with "unnatural sons" who killed their parents, and spouses who murdered in order to remarry (Sauval 1969, 566). These were, of course, associative rather than reasoned connections, but they were nonetheless telling. Once hermaphrodites had entered the precincts of sexual ambiguity, their very existence a challenge to a secure boundary between male and female in a period tense over such uncertainties, their lot could only deteriorate.

CONCLUSION

Why did hermaphrodites so preoccupy early modern writers, and whence the penumbra of conflicting associations that surrounded them in this period? We do not mean to imply that the Hippocratic revival of the mid-sixteenth century created the popular fascination with hermaphrodites. We see, rather, a conjunction of changing medical ideas with a general climate of acute male anxiety about the very issues showcased by the new interpretation of the hermaphrodite as a being of intermediate sex: sodomy and other sexual crimes, and the proper relationship and boundaries between men and women.

This sexual anxiety manifested itself in a number of other ways, some of which are directly relevant to contemporary French views on hermaphroditism. It appears, for example, in the intensification of concern about nonprocreative sexuality associated with the Counter-Reformation. The post-Tridentine church took an increasingly strict line on impediments to marriage, as is clear from the literature on impotence and the marriageability of eunuchs (Esmein 1968, 2:274; Ancillon 1707), as well as on masturbation (now classed as worse than fornication or adultery) and sodomy, especially on the part of women. Thus, although sodomy had been heavily criminalized since the late thirteenth century—the most commonly prescribed penalty was burning alive—most of the legislation and the litigation emphasized male offenders; in the later sixteenth and seventeenth century, this concern was extended increasingly to women, especially in Catholic countries (Park 1996; Brundage 1987, 57, 472–74, 533–35, 570–71).[32] It is revealing both of the new worries about female sodomites and of their association with hermaphrodites that Riolan reclassified a number of alleged hermaphrodites as women with enlarged clitorises, and then branded them as "lesbians" (*tribades*) (Riolan 1614, 72–73, 79; Park 1996).[33]

The new emphasis on female sodomy signals another, even greater source of sexual anxiety: the male concern with female pretensions to masculine status and prerogatives that is so visible in the popular literature and to some extent in the ritual practice of the period. This concern also crystallized in disapproval of female cross-dressing.[34] At least in the context of hagiography, medieval writers had often spiritualized female transvestism as a metaphor of saintly aspiration, as we have already mentioned. In the sixteenth and early seventeenth centuries, it became an obsessive theme in the works of male authors and a figure for the monstrous pretensions and actions of ordinary women—the "new hermaphrodites" of *Hic Mulier, or the Man-Woman*, the famous English pamphlet on female cross-dressing (Jardine 1983, 93, 154–55; Woodbridge 1984, 139–51). In France, even when not associated with sexual fraud and license, as in the case cited by Montaigne, it was treated as clearly unacceptable. The pathetic example of the would-be saint, Antoinette Bourguignon, shows how dramatically the meaning of female transvestism had changed by the seventeenth century, even in a religious context. Emulating the medieval transvestite saints, Antoinette interpreted a vision in which Christ directed her to become "more virile" as a command to don male dress, but all she got for her trouble was a tongue-lashing from the archbishop for her impudence and imprudence (Delcourt 1958, 17).[35] This association between hermaphroditism, cross-dressing, and female presumption does much to explain the identification of hermaphrodite and *tribade* that is one of the most peculiar and striking elements of the literature of the period (Park 1996).[36]

We draw two historiographic morals from our story. The first is in line with much recent work on the history of sexuality:[37] the medical understanding and cultural significance of hermaphrodites depend heavily on time and place, just as do the meanings of femininity and masculinity. There is no straight line connecting early modern with either medieval or modern views on these topics. The second moral is that the terms of analysis on which the first, historicist moral depends are themselves in need of historical scrutiny. Epitomized by the sex/gender distinction, the aim of many studies has been to shift sexual identities from the category of the natural to that of the cultural, and to challenge thereby the inevitability of our own commonplaces on such matters. This project has been pursued with great *éclat,* and has contributed to a far-reaching rethinking of the assumptions and values that structure our own sexual arrangements. We wish to suggest, however, that the categories of the "cultural" and, especially, the "natural" also have a history. The opposition nature versus culture, so illuminating for us in our attempts to sort out the humanly universal from the culturally local, can be deeply misleading when imposed upon earlier periods. In the early modern period, nature was regulated by "customs" rather than ironclad laws, encompassed much of the psyche as well as the body, and bristled with moral directives. Within this conceptual world, to medicalize was not *ipso facto* to naturalize in our sense. At stake, in part, is the authority of nature, now conceived as the authority of the necessary rather than the normative, but no less powerful for that. Unless we historicize nature, we cannot understand, much less challenge, the sources and scope of that authority.

NOTES

1. This article is a revised version of a paper entitled "The Hermaphrodite and the Order of Nature: Sexual Ambiguity in Renaissance Europe," originally presented in 1990 at the Centennial Symposium in the History of Science at the University of Oklahoma.
2. The early modern hermaphrodite has attracted a good deal of recent scholarly attention, beginning with Foucault's discussion (1980, esp. vii–viii). See also Greenblatt (1988); Jones and Stallybrass (1991); Daston and Park (1985); Park (1993); Freccero (1986); Schwartz (1978).

3. We are not concerned here with the rather specialized fields of alchemy, neo-Platonic philosophy and literary allegory, in which the hermaphrodite figured as a metaphoric or mythical figure, along the lines of Plato's androgyne (*Symposium* 189C–193D), Ovid's Hermaphroditus (*Metamorphoses* IV, 285–388), or Pliny's race of Androgyni (*Natural History* VII, 2). The literature with which we are concerned focused on what their authors took to be actual, individual cases of hermaphroditism, both animal and (especially) human. For the classical roots and contours of ideas concerning the mythical hermaphrodite, see Delcourt (1961).

4. In particular, Laqueur elides the significant distinctions between Hippocratic and Aristotelian ideas, producing a totalizing synthesis (the supposed "one-sex model") that does not do justice to the complexities of the tradition; see Park and Nye (1991).

5. The core texts in this tradition were the Hippocratic treatises *On the Seed* and *On the Nature of the Child*, and two works attributed to Galen called *On the Seed*, one authentic and one pseudonymous. See in general Cadden (1993, 15–21) (on the Hippocratic tradition) and 30–37 (on Galen); Lloyd (1983, 58–111); Boylan (1984); Preus (1977).

6. Although some Greek writers also emphasized the role of the right and left testicles of the father, this idea seems to have had relatively little influence in the postclassical medical tradition; cf. Lloyd (1962, 60).

7. See, e.g., pseudo-Galen, *De spermate,* as cited in Jacquart and Thomasset (1985, 195). The simplest form of this doctrine appears in the theory of the seven-celled uterus: the three right-hand cells produce males, the three left-hand cells, females, while the seventh, in the center, produces a hermaphrodite; see Kudlien (1965).

8. Aristotle (1953, 425–43; bk. 4, ch. 1 and bk. 4, ch. 4, esp. 770b27–773a2). See also Cadden (1993, 21–26), and other references in note 5 above. Aristotle nowhere uses the term "hermaphrodite," referring only to animals "having two sets of genitals."

9. As Cadden (1993) notes (24–25), although the opposition between hot and cold can be mediated, other polarities fundamental to the Aristotelian interpretation of sex difference—active and passive, perfect and imperfect, ability to produce semen and the corresponding inability—cannot.

10. See also Albucasis (1973, 424), and Avicenna (1964, fol. 356r; bk. 3, fen 20, tract. 2, ch. 43). According to Guy, there are two kinds of predominantly male hermaphrodite, one with a vulva between the testicles and the other with a vulva in the perineum, and one female kind, in which the male genitals appear in front of and above the vulva; he recommended excision particularly in this last case. Guy's three divisions seem to represent a simplification of the fourfold typology of Paul of Aegina (1855, bk. 6, ch. 69), citing Leonidas of Alexandria.

11. The material on lesbians was expanded in the second edition, from 1575, but removed from later editions after a strenuous protest from the Paris medical faculty; see Céard's introduction in Paré (1971, xiv–xvi). Note that in order to incorporate this material, Paré had to deviate from his previously elaborated typology of monsters, inserting the linked topics of hermaphrodites, lesbians, and sexual transformation between the chapters on monsters arising from too much and too little seed, discussed in chapters 5 and 6 respectively—a testimony to the continuing strength of the Aristotelian association between hermaphrodites and multiple births or supernumerary members.

12. See also Roger (1963, 49–94); Deer (1980).

13. For an example of a strongly argued Aristotelian position, see Riolan (1614). Often the strongest Hippocratic stance was taken by the more marginal members of the medical profession, who used it to contest the traditional authority and power structure of the profession; examples include the surgeon Paré or the provincial physician Jacques Duval. Probably for this reason, it is more prominent in vernacular than in Latin medical writing of the late sixteenth century.

14. Cf. Cadden (1993, 222–25), and Boswell (1980, 185, 375–76, n. 50). *Pace* Boswell, our own research does not reveal a "lively scientific interest in hermaphrodites" at any time during the Middle Ages, nor does it confirm that the use of the term "hermaphrodite" or "androgyne" to refer to sodomites became more common in the thirteenth and fourteenth centuries; cf. Boswell (1980, 375–76, n. 50).

15. See Anson (1974); Delcourt (1958); Bynum (1984); Bullough (1974); Patlagean (1976); and Simon Gaunt's contribution to this volume. There is some evidence of a more critical attitude toward female transvestism in a secular context, at least in fourteenth-century England; see Knighton (1965, 2:57–58), and Fradenburg (1991, 215–16).

16. See Céard's introduction to Paré (1971), xiv–xvi, and Paré's defense in Le Paulmier (1884, 223–48, esp. 230–33). Pare's riot of show-all woodcuts contrasted signally with the more sober and self-consciously responsible Latin discussion of the physician Jacob Rueff, who omitted all pictures from the section on hermaphrodites in his otherwise heavily illustrated work on generation: Rueff (1554, fol. 48r).

17. See e.g. Domat (1713, 1:10–11; bk. 1, tit. 2).

18. Paré (1971, 25), and Duval (1880, 274), both imply that such may exist, but cf. Rueff (1554, fols. 47v–48r); Bodin (1597, 549–50); Riolan (1614); Renaudot (1660, 2: 861–62).

19. See also Martin (1880, 108). The principal exceptions were (for the male hermaphrodite) serving as a lawyer, judge or rector of a university.

20. Ten years after the court's decision, Duval tells us, Marin was living as a man, working as a tailor, and wearing a beard.

21. E.g. Alain de Lille (1980); see also Economou (1972, 83–85).

22. On the idea of "contra-natural" sex, see Brundage (1987, 212–13, 286–87, 533, 571); Boswell (1980, 312–13).

23. On the emergence of the natural law concept in natural philosophy, see Milton (1981); Oakley (1984, 82–113); and Ruby (1986).

24. See Céard (1977, 229–314).

25. Although he had not examined Le Marcis firsthand, Riolan (1614, 45–46) argued *a priori* that there was insufficient space in the vulva to accommodate the anatomical structures necessary for male erection and ejaculation.

26. Hermaphrodites had had strong supernatural associations in classical antiquity, but lost this supernatural sheen very early on—by the first century, if Pliny is to be credited—and appeared in the Middle Ages and the Renaissance almost completely shorn of portentous significance: Delcourt (1961, 44–46); Pliny, *Natural History*, VII, 3; Daston and Park (1985, 5–6).

27. *Physics*, II, 1–2 remained the *locus classicus* for the nature/art distinction until the mid-seventeenth century.

28. On the category of the preternatural and its relationship to the natural and supernatural, see Clark (1984, esp. 361–63); Daston (1991, esp. 95–100).

29. All the cases of women executed for sodomy in the sixteenth century cited by Louis Crompton (1980–1981, 17) involved a dildo. This position was explicitly argued by the Spanish legal writer, Antonio Gomez (Crompton 1980–1981, 19). See in general Park (1996).

30. This topic gained special urgency from the rumors of transvestism and homosexuality at the court of Henri III, to whom the image of the hermaphrodite was satirically applied; see Schwartz (1978, 125–26), citing Agrippa d'Aubigné's *Les tragiques*, Pierre de l'Estoile (1982), and Artus (1605).

31. See Boswell (1980, 318–29) for the traditional theological analysis.

32. See also Crompton (1980–1981, 11–25); Brown (1986, 117–28). English law was almost unique in not criminalizing lesbian acts as sodomitical.

33. See Park (1993) and, on the issue of terminology, Traub (1992).

34. See, in general, Davis (1975). The causes of this anxiety are less clear. Lawrence Stone (1977, 109–46) argues, like Davis, that this period saw a general, largely successful attempt to reinforce patriarchal power within the family. The coincidental appearance of a cohort of female rulers in the mid-sixteenth century, including Mary Tudor, Catherine de' Medici and Elizabeth I, may also have contributed to the male sense of threat.

35. The late sixteenth century went so far as to rewrite even the story of the most famous French transvestite saint, Joan of Arc, attributing to her anguished scruples about cross-dressing wholly lacking from her trial testimony; see Warner (1982, 139–40). For a sermon from 1561 chastising male and female transvestism, see Jean Montluc, *Sermons de l'évêque de Valence*, (1561, 349) (cited in Schwartz 1978, 130, n. 18).

36. In the nineteenth century, in contrast, the hermaphrodite was identified above all with the male homosexual; see Nye (1989, esp. 39).

37. See for example Foucault (1978); Davidson (1987); Halperin (1990).

WORKS CITED

Alain de Lille. 1980. *The Plaint of Nature*, trans. James J. Sheridan. Toronto: Pontifical Institute of Mediaeval Studies.

Albertus Magnus. 1916–1921. *De animalibus libri XXVI*. Beiträge zur Geschichte der Philosophie des Mittelalters, Texte und Untersuchungen, 15–16. 2 vols. Münster i. W.: Aschendorff.

Albucasis. 1973. *On Surgery and Instruments: A Definitive Edition of the Arabic Text with English Translation and Commentary*, ed. M. S. Spink and G. L. Lewis. Berkeley: University of California Press.

Ancillon, Charles. 1707. *Traité des eunuques, dans le quel on explique toutes les différentes sortes d'eunuques*. N.p.: n.p.

Anson, John. 1974. "The Female Transvestite in Early Monasticism: The Origins and Development of a Motif." *Viator* 5:1–32.

Aquinas, Thomas. 1946–1948. *Summa theologiae*, trans. the Fathers of the English Dominican Province. 3 vols. New York: Benziger.

Aristotle. 1953. *Generation of Animals*, trans. A. L. Peck. Cambridge, MA: Harvard University Press.

———. 1968–1970. *Physics*, trans. Philip H. Wicksteed and Francis Cornford. 2 vols. Cambridge, MA: Harvard University Press.

Artus, Thomas. 1605. *L'Isle des hermaphrodites nouvellement descouverte*. N.p.: n.p.

Avicenna. 1964. *Liber canonis*. 1507. Reprint. Hildesheim, Germany: Georg Olms.

Baldwin, John W. 1994. *The Language of Sex: Five Voices from Northern France around 1200*. Chicago: University of Chicago Press.

Bauhin, Gaspard. 1614. *De hermaphroditorum monstrorumque partuum natura ex theologorum, jureconsultorum medicorum, philosophorum et rabbinorum sententia libri duo*. Oppenheim: de Bry.

Boaistuau, Pierre, et al. 1598. *Histoires prodigieuses extraictes de plusieurs fameux autheurs, Grecs et Latins, sacrez & prophanes. . . .* 6 vols. Paris: Cavellat.

Bodin, Jean. 1597. *Théatre de la nature universelle*, trans. François de Fougerolles. Lyon, France: Pillehotte.

Boswell, John. 1980. *Christianity, Social Tolerance, and Homosexuality: Gay People in Western Europe from the Beginning of the Christian Era to the Fourteenth Century*. Chicago: University of Chicago Press.

Bouchet, Guillaume. 1873–1882. *Les serées de Guillaume Bouchet, Sieur de Brocourt*, ed. C. E. Roybet. 6 vols. Paris: A. Lemerre.

Boylan, Michael. 1984. "The Galenic and Hippocratic Challenges to Aristotle's Conception Theory." *Journal of the History of Biology* 17: 83–112.

Brown, Judith. 1986. *Immodest Acts: The Life of a Lesbian Nun in Renaissance Italy*. New York: Oxford University Press.

Brundage, James A. 1987. *Law, Sex, and Christian Society in Medieval Europe*. Chicago: University of Chicago Press.

Bullough, Vern. 1974. "Transvestites in the Middle Ages." *American Journal of Sociology* 79: 1381–94.

Bynum, Caroline Walker. 1984. "Women's Stories, Women's Symbols: A Critique of Victor Turner's Theory of Liminality," in *Anthropology and the Study of Religion*, ed. Robert L. Moore and Frank E. Reynolds. Chicago: Center for the Scientific Study of Religion. 105–25.

Cadden, Joan. 1993. *Meanings of Sex Difference in the Middle Ages: Medicine, Science, and Culture*. Cambridge: Cambridge University Press.

Céard, Jean. 1977. *La nature et les prodiges: l'insolite au XVIe siècle, en France*. Geneva: Droz.

Clark, Stuart. 1984. "The Scientific Status of Demonology," in *Occult and Scientific Mentalities in the Renaissance*, ed. Brian Vickers. Cambridge: Cambridge University Press. 351–74.

Crompton, Louis. 1980–1981. "The Myth of Lesbian Impunity: Capital Laws from 1270 to 1791." *Journal of Homosexuality* 6: 11–25.

Dante Alighieri. 1973. *Purgatory*, trans. Charles S. Singleton. Princeton: Princeton University Press.

Darmon, Pierre. 1979. *Le tribunal de l'impuissance*. Paris: Editions du Seuil.

Daston, Lorraine. 1991. "Marvelous Facts and Miraculous Evidence in Early Modern Europe." *Critical Inquiry* 18: 93–124.

Daston, Lorraine and Katharine Park. 1985. "Hermaphrodites in Renaissance France." *Critical Matrix* 1/5:1–19.

Davidson, Arnold I. 1987. "How to Do the History of Psychoanalysis: A Reading of Freud's *Three Essays on the Theory of Sexuality*." *Critical Inquiry* 13: 252–77.

Davis, Natalie. 1975. "Women on Top," in *Society and Culture in Early Modern France*. Stanford: Stanford University Press. 124–51.

Deer, Linda Allen. 1980. "Academic Theories of Generation in the Renaissance: The Contemporaries and Successors of Jean Fernel." Ph.D. diss., Warburg Institute, University of London.

Delcourt, Marie. 1958. "Le complexe de Diane dans l'hagiographie chrétienne." *Revue de l'histoire des religions* 77: 1–33.

———. 1961. *Hermaphrodite: Myths and Rites of the Bisexual Figure in Classical Antiquity*, trans. Jennifer Nicholson. London: Studio Books.

Domat, Jean. 1713. *Les loix civiles dans leur ordre naturel*. Rev. ed. 2 vols. in 1. Paris: Nicholas Gosselin.

Du Cange, Charles du Fresne. 1937–1938. *Glossarium mediae et infimae latinitatis*. 10 vols. Paris: Librairie des sciences et des arts.

Duval, Jacques. 1880. *Traité des hermaphrodits, parties génitales, accouchements des femmes, etc.* 1612. Reprint, Paris: Liseux.

Economou, George. 1972. *The Goddess Natura in Medieval Literature*. Cambridge, MA: Harvard University Press.

Epstein, Julia. 1990. "Either/Or-Neither/Both: Sexual Ambiguity and the Ideology of Gender." *Genders* 7:99–142.

Esmein, E. 1968. *Le mariage en droit canonique*. 1891. 2 vols. Reprint. New York: B. Franklin.

Foucault, Michel. 1978. *The History of Sexuality: Volume I: An Introduction*, trans. Robert Hurley. New York: Random House.

———. 1980. *Herculine Barbin: Being the Recently Discovered Memoirs of a Nineteenth-Century French Hermaphrodite*, trans. Richard McDougall. New York: Pantheon.

Fradenburg, Louise Olga. 1991. *City, Marriage, Tournament: Arts of Rule in Late Medieval Scotland*. Madison: University of Wisconsin Press.

Freccero, Carla. 1986. "The Other and the Same: The Image of the Hermaphrodite in Rabelais," in *Rewriting the Renaissance: The Discourses of Sexual Difference in Early Modern Europe*, ed. Margaret W. Ferguson, *et al.* Chicago: University of Chicago Press. 145–58.

Greenblatt, Stephen. 1988. "Fiction and Friction," in *Shakespearean Negotiations: The Circulation of Social Energy in Renaissance England*. Berkeley: University of California Press. 66–93.

Guy de Chauliac. 1890. *La grande chirurgie de Guy de Chauliac . . . composée l'an 1363*, ed. E. Nicaise. Paris: F. Alcan.

Halperin, David. 1990. *One Hundred Years of Homosexuality and Other Essays on Greek Love*. New York: Routledge.

Hewson, M. Anthony. 1975. *Giles of Rome and the Medieval Theory of Conception*. London: Athlone.

Hic Mulier: Or, the Man-Woman: being a Medicine to cure the Coltish Disease of the Staggers in the Masculine-Feminines of our Times. 1620. London: J. T.

Jacquart, Danielle and Claude Thomasset. 1985. *Sexualité et savoir médical au Moyen Age*. Paris: Presses universitaires de France.

Jardine, Lisa. 1983. *Still Harping on Daughters: Women and Drama in the Age of Shakespeare*. Totowa, NJ: Barnes and Noble.

Jones, Ann Rosalind and Peter Stallybrass. 1991. "Fetishizing Gender: Constructing the Hermaphrodite in Renaissance Europe," in *Body Guards: The Cultural Politics of Gender Ambiguity*, ed. Julia Epstein and Kristina Straub. New York: Routledge. 80–111.

Knighton, Henry. 1965. *Chronicon Henrici Knighton, vel Cnitthon, monachi leycestrensis*, ed. Joseph Rawson Lumby. 1889. 2 vols. Reprint. Wiesbaden: Kraus Reprint.

Kudlien, Fridolf. 1965. "The Seven Cells of the Uterus: The Doctrine and its Roots." *Bulletin of the History of Medicine* 39: 415–23.

Laqueur, Thomas. 1990. *Making Sex: Body and Gender from the Greeks to Freud*. Cambridge, MA: Harvard University Press.

Le Paulmier, Claude Stephen. 1884. *Ambroise Paré d'après de nouveaux documents*. Paris: Charavay Frères.

L'Estoile, Pierre de. *Mémoires-journaux, 1574–1611*. 12 vols. Paris: Tallandier, 1982.

Lloyd, G. E. R. 1962. "Right and Left in Greek Philosophy." *Journal of Hellenic Studies* 82: 56–66.

———. 1983. *Science, Folklore and Ideology: Studies in the Life Sciences in Ancient Greece*. Cambridge: Cambridge University Press.

Lonie, Iain M. 1985. "The 'Paris Hippocratics': Teaching and Research in Paris in the Second Half of the Sixteenth Century," in *The Medical Renaissance of the Sixteenth Century*, ed. Andrew Wear *et al.* Cambridge: Cambridge University Press. 155–74.

Maclean, Ian. 1980. *The Renaissance Notion of Woman: A Study in the Fortunes of Scholasticism and Medical Science in European Intellectual Life*. Cambridge: Cambridge University Press.

Martin, Ernest. 1880. *Histoire des monstres depuis l'antiquité jusqu'à nos jours*. Paris: C. Reinwald.

Milton, John R. 1981. "The Origin and Development of the Concept of 'Laws of Nature'." *Archives of European Sociology* 22: 173–95.

Montaigne, Michel de. 1967. *Journal de voyage en Italie*, in *Oeuvres complètes*, ed. Robert Barral and Pierre Michel. Paris: Editions du Seuil.

Nye, Robert. 1989. "Sexual Difference and Male Homosexuality in French Medical Discourse, 1830–1930." *Bulletin of the History of Medicine* 63: 32–51.

Oakley, Francis. 1984. *Omnipotence, Covenant, and Order: An Excursion in the History of Ideas from Abelard to Leibniz*. Ithaca: Cornell University Press.

Paré, Ambroise. 1971. *Des monstres et prodiges*, ed. Jean Céard. Geneva: Droz.

Park, Katherine. 1993. "Hermaphrodites or Lesbians? Sexual Anxiety and Renaissance Medicine." Ninth Berkshire Conference on the History of Women. Vassar College. June.

———. 1996. "The Rediscovery of the Clitoris: French Medicine and the *Tribade*, 1570–1620," in *The Body in Parts: Discourses and Anatomies in Early Modern Europe*, ed. Carla Mazzio and David Hillman. New York: Routledge.

Park, Katharine and Robert Nye. 1991. "Destiny is Anatomy." Review of *Making Sex: Body and Gender from the Greeks to Freud*, by Thomas Laqueur. *The New Republic*. February 18. 53–57.

Parker, Patricia. 1993. "Gender Ideology, Gender Change: The Case of Marie Germain." *Critical Inquiry* 19: 337–64.

Patlagean, Evelyne. 1976. "L'histoire de la femme déguisée en moine et l'évolution de la sainteté féminine à Byzance." *Studi Medievali*, 3rd ser., 17: 597–623.

Paul of Aegina. 1855. *Chirurgie de Paul d'Egine*, ed. and trans. René Briau. Paris: Victor Masson.

Pitaval, François Gayot de. 1772–1788. *Causes célèbres et intéressantes*, ed. Richer. 22 vols. Amsterdam: Michel Rhey.

Pliny. 1938–1962. *Natural History*, trans. H. Rackham. 10 vols. Cambridge, MA: Harvard University Press.

Preus, Anthony. 1977. "Galen's Criticism of Aristotle's Conception Theory." *Journal of the History of Biology* 10: 65–85.

Renaudot, Théophraste. 1660. *Recueil general des questions traitées ès conférences du Bureau d'addresse*. 2 vols. Paris: Loyson.

Riolan, Jean. 1614. *Discours sur les hermaphrodits. Où il est demonstré contre l'opinion commune, qu'il n'y a point de vrays Hermaphrodits*. Paris: Pierre Ramier.

Roger, Jacques. 1963. *Les sciences de la vie dans la pensée française du XVIIIe siècle: la génération des animaux de Descartes à l'Encyclopédie*. Paris: Armand Colin.

Ruby, Jane E. 1986. "The Origins of Scientific 'Law'." *Journal of the History of Ideas* 47: 341–59.

Rueff, Jacob. 1554. *De conceptu et generatione hominis, et iis quae circa hec potissimum consyderantur libri sex*. Zurich: C. Froschoverus.

Sauval, Henri. 1969. *Histoire et recherches des antiquités de la ville de Paris*. 1724. Reprint. Westmead: Gregg International.

Schwartz, Jerome. 1978. "Aspects of Androgyny in the Renaissance," in *Human Sexuality in the Middle Ages and Renaissance*, ed. D. Radcliff-Umstead. Pittsburgh: University of Pittsburgh Press. 121–31.

Stone, Lawrence. 1977. *The Family, Sex, and Marriage in England, 1500–1800*. London: Weidenfeld and Nicholson.

Tiraqueau, André. 1546. *De legibus connubialibus et iure maritali*. Paris: Jacob Keruer.

Traub, Valerie. 1992. "The (In)significance of 'Lesbian' Desire in Early Modern England," in *Erotic Politics: Desire on the Renaissance Stage*, ed. Susan Zimmerman. New York: Routledge. 150–69.

Veay. 1687. "An Extract of a Letter written by Mr. Veay Physician at Toulouse to Mr. de St. Ussans concerning a very extraordinary Hermaphrodite in that City." *Philosophical Transactions of the Royal Society of London* 16: 282–83.

Warner, Marina. 1982. *Joan of Arc: The Image of Female Heroism*. New York: Vintage.

Woodbridge, Linda. 1984. *Women and the English Renaissance: Literature and the Nature of Womankind, 1540–1620*. Urbana: University of Illinois Press.

Don't Ask, Don't Tell 7

Murderous Plots and Medieval Secrets

Karma Lochrie

> Instead of the question "What does secrecy cover?" we had better ask "What covers secrecy?" What, that is, takes secrecy for its field of operations?
>
> —D. A. Miller, *The Novel and the Police*[1]

In July, 1993, the Pentagon and the Joint Chiefs of Staff delivered their policy governing gays and lesbians in the military to President Clinton. This policy, which is popularly called "don't ask, don't tell," claimed to release gays and lesbians from the pressures of interrogation about their sexuality under the condition that they maintain silence about it and that they not engage in any homosexual conduct which would "tell" on them. If a gay man or woman is accused of engaging in such acts, according to Pentagon logic, suddenly the prescription against telling becomes transformed into that mysterious thing called the "rebuttable presumption," which in effect makes telling compulsory. "Don't tell," so the policy goes, unless you are rebutting the presumption that you are homosexual, and then *you must tell* by rebutting the accusation with the "heterosexual truth about yourself" or by confirming it.[2] The prohibition against telling rests in troubling conjunction with the requirement of disclosure, and the presumption of ignorance in disturbing relation to that of knowledge. The emphasis of this policy on not telling/rebutting the presumption produces an incoherence which is necessary to contain male heterosexual anxiety by rendering gay and lesbian service people secrets—open secrets whose telling is forbidden, even as the knowledge of their sexuality is not.

Like many of the juridical rulings on homosexuality, this policy institutes what Eve Kosofsky Sedgwick calls "an excruciating system of double binds, systematically oppressing gay people, identities, and acts by undermining through contradictory constraints on discourse the grounds of their very being" (Sedgwick 1990). The double binds here work to prohibit public telling while permitting private talk, to allow queer identity but curtailing any meaningful exercise of that identity through acts (a term which includes behaving in a "homosexual manner" but not reading queer journals)—in short, the policy endeavors to render gay military personnel open secrets, known to be gay but prevented from telling or acting gay.

The "social function of secrecy," as D. A. Miller describes it, "is not to conceal knowledge, so much as to conceal the knowledge of the knowledge" (1988, 206)—in this case, *from heterosexuals.* The heterosexual military insists at the same time on knowing the secret, and on keeping it. The function of the Pentagon's policy is to define the heterosexual position as one marked by the imperative of "privileged unknowing," while the gay position is implicated in that unknowing by its own knowing silence, its "epistemological transparency." Ironically, then, it is heterosexual ignorance (or the desire for it) which "structures and enforces" this particular knowledge of gay iden-tity/activity.[3] The real secret of this policy, it turns out, is not gay and lesbian sexuality or conduct, but heterosexual fear of contamination by the *knowledge* of it.

Yet as Miller also notes, in the passage I quoted at the outset of this essay, what the secret covers here is not so important as what cultural operations, or representations, take secrecy for their technology. Sedgwick describes the dynamics of secrecy as a cultural operation in her book, *The Epistemology of the Closet.* Claiming that the closet is "the defining structure of gay oppression in this century," Sedgwick is interested in how the principle of secrecy informs the representational practice of the closet, and how it impli-cates other ideologies in its cultural work (1990, 71). Further, she challenges historians of sexuality not to limit themselves to studying specific acts, behaviors and objects of desire, but to interrogate as well larger representational practices (and their affiliations), such as that of secrecy:

> I want to argue that a lot of the energy of attention and demarcation that has swirled around issues of homosexuality ... has been impelled by the distinctively indicative rela-tion of homosexuality to wider mappings of secrecy and disclosure, and of the private and the public, that were and are critically problematical for gender, sexual, and economic structures of the heterosexist culture at large, mappings whose enabling but dangerous incoherence has become oppressively, durably condensed in certain figures of homosexuality. "The closet" and "coming out," now verging on all-purpose phrases for the potent crossing and recrossing of almost any politically charged lines of representa-tion, have been the gravest and most magnetic of those figures (1990, 71).

Sedgwick thus calls for the interrogation of the "enabling but dangerous incoherence" at stake in heterosexist mappings of secrecy; she also implicates these mappings in the histories of gender, sexuality, and economic structures, and allies them with a "whole cluster of the most crucial sites for the contestation of meaning in twentieth-century Western culture," including some I have already mentioned: knowledge/ignorance, masculine/feminine, majority/minority and natural/artificial, among others. Under the historical span of the "enabling but dangerous incoherence" of these mappings of secrecy and disclosure "have unfolded both the most generative and the most murderous plots of our culture," she asserts (1990, 72, 90).

If the contemporary figure of the closet and the military policy "don't ask, don't tell" together constitute one particular plot within this historical span, I would like to consider how earlier discourses of sexuality took secrecy for their field of operation, as Miller has it. In plotting our own narratives of sexualities, Sedgwick offers a caution against limiting ourselves to historical distinctions between particular sexual acts and contemporary sexual identities. Instead she points to the larger cultural mappings and representational practices, such as those of secrecy and disclosure, that are problematical not only for contemporary queer identity and theory but for "gender, sexual, and economic structures of the heterosexist culture at large." I want to consider three plots: a medieval plot, the military's gay policy, and the metaplot of histories of sexuality within which the other two plots are contained. In Murderous Plot I, gynecology takes secrecy for its field of operations, implicating gender and sexuality in that field. This plot is not the precursor of the Pentagon's closet plot (II), so much as it is part of my own plot to map representational alliances between contemporary structures of oppression attaching to homosexuality, on the one hand, and medieval gender and sexuality, on the other, and to offer an alternative to current history-of-sexuality plots (Murderous Plot III).

Such a cluster of plots, I believe, is one way of addressing the problems in current queer theory raised by Louise Fradenburg and Carla Freccero in their introduction to this volume. According to Fradenburg and Freccero, queer theory needs to "intensify its scrutiny" of the current construction of the historical divide between premodern and modern sexuality that began with Foucault.[4] By way of critique, they suggest that the contrast between premodern sexual acts and modern sexual identity might serve as much to "stabilize the identity of 'the modern'" as it does to contest transhistoricist and universalizing histories of sexuality. Finally, they question whether an alternative to the universalist (and essentialist) versus social constructionist visions of history is possible, one in which "continuities" or "identities" are found across historical periods without "inevitably produc[ing] a 'transhistoricist' or 'universalizing' effect."[5]

The first two plots of this essay attempt just such an alternative, while plot III reflects upon the urgency for such alternatives. All three plots make a crucial case for the need to complicate current constructions of sexuality, historical and contemporary, by interrogating their complicity with gender construction. Sedgwick's theory about the "wider mappings of secrecy" that extend from the construction of queer identity since the nineteenth century insists upon the affiliations between gender and sexuality. It also makes an historical claim for the analogous workings of structures of oppression. This seems to me to be a particularly promising hypothesis from which to study sexuality, for it preserves historical difference and continuity without foreclosing either.

The juxtaposition of these three plots, however, is not meant to produce a single, all-encompassing plot like the acts-to-identity one. Instead, I want it both to unsettle the imperiousness of current social constructionist plots and to provide a direction for alternative plots. In addition, my plots allude to the real and painful effects of these congruent acts of representation. "Murderous" is, perhaps, strong language to attach to the military gay policy, medieval gynecological discourse, and histories of sexuality. Following Sedgwick, from whom this language is derived, I use it to emphasize the violence subtending plots of secrecy, their "exactions, ... deformations, ... disempowerment, and sheer pain."[6] In using the word "murderous" to track lines of affiliation among these three plots, I am insisting upon the exacting, deforming, disempowering and painful consequences of those acts of representation that secrecy licenses for human subjects, medieval women, and contemporary gays and lesbians.

MURDEROUS PLOT I

In 1322, a woman named Jacquéline Félicie was accused of illegally practicing medicine in Paris in violation of the 1271 statute prohibiting unlicensed persons from medical practice. In her defense, Félicie argued that, where "women's secrets" are concerned, women—and not men—are the best physicians:

> It is more fitting and honest that a wise woman, experienced in the art of medicine, should visit a sick woman, to examine her and to inquire into the hidden secrets of her nature, than that a man, who is not permitted to examine her, nor to investigate or feel women's hands, breasts, stomach and feet, etc. should do so; on the contrary the man should avoid the secrets of women and flee their intimate society as much as he is able. Also a woman would allow herself to die rather than reveal the secrets of her illness to a man because of the virtue of the female sex and because of the shame she would be exposed to by revealing them.[7]

What is interesting in Félicie's formulation is the convergence of fantasies—legal, social, moral, and medical—she employs to mystify women's secrets. First, she asserts that it is more fitting that a wise woman "inquire into the hidden secrets of her [woman's] nature" ("*inquirat secreta nature et abscondita ejus*"), suggesting that women's natures conceal these secrets *naturally*. Yet she implies in the same sentence that women's hands, breasts, stomach, and feet are secrets that are protected by social taboos and protocols of medical procedure ("*cui non licet predicta videre, inquireren, nec palpare*"). Then she advises men to avoid the "secrets of woman" ("*mulierum secreta*") and their "intimate society" ("*societates secretas*"), implicating the feminine nature itself in a larger social danger to men. Here she implicitly invokes the misogynist convention of the moral and physical danger represented by the feminine, quite apart from the *licet*— the social taboo—governing inquiry into the female body. Finally, she appeals to that feminine nature, not in its masculine representative capacity as physical and moral danger, but as shame and discretion. The defense as a whole thus proliferates the referents of women's secrets, from nature, to bodies, to illnesses, to female society; it also makes everything dependent on women telling (or withholding), rather than on masculine inquiry. By restricting the telling of women's secrets to female physicians, and by mystifying those secrets, Félicie exploits (to her own and women's advantage) the incoherence within masculine representations of women's natures as secret(ive), necessitating flight and inquiry at the same time.

"Silence and secrecy are a shelter for power, anchoring its prohibitions ... ," Foucault notes (1990, 101). The discourse of women's secrets is a shelter for masculine power, anchoring its prohibitions against feminine secrets, including their natures, bodies, and sexuality. Félicie's defense assumes meaning within the practice of secrecy found elsewhere in medieval medicine—a practice which likewise obscures (for different reasons) the relationship between women and secrets/secrecy and among the activities of inquiring into, knowing and telling those secrets. Secrecy represents a discourse and ideology that includes those virtues associated with femininity—particularly shame—and the physiological code of femininity in medieval gynecological texts.

One of the most popular of these texts was *De secretis mulierum* ("Concerning the Secrets of Women," hereafter called the *Secrets of Women*), which was ascribed to Albertus Magnus, though it was probably written by a student of his in the late thirteenth or early fourteenth centuries. Its popularity is attested by the 83 manuscripts and 120 printed editions of it from the fifteenth and sixteenth centuries.[8] The treatise's field of inquiry includes the topics found in its chapter headings: the generation of the embryo, the formation of the fetus, the influence of the planets on the fetus, the exit of the fetus from the uterus, the signs of conception, the features distinguishing male and female fetuses, chastity and its corruption, the defects of the womb, the impediments to conception, and the generation of sperm. While the nature of the material included in the treatise seems commonplace by medieval standards, the author claims that it "bring[s] to light certain hidden, secret things about the nature of women" (Lemay 1992, 59). Like Félicie, pseudo-Albert implies that these "secret things"—specifically, embryology, fetal development, female reproductive functions and dysfunctions and female sexual behavior—are "hidden" by women, and that therefore, these subjects require masculine inquiry.

The author's pretext for disclosing these secrets is the request of his male reader, his "dear companion and friend in Christ." Written within and for a male monastic community, the *Secrets of Women* eventually included among its readership aristocratic and bourgeois men outside the cloister. Interestingly enough, medieval gynecological literature was transmitted chiefly through male monastic culture, presumably for medical purposes. However, Monica Green observes that we do not really know how these treatises were used, whether "to satiate monkish curiosity about the female nature or to serve as the basis of real medical practice."[9] The author explicitly excludes children and "anyone of a childlike disposition," a warning that was, in one French version, extended under threat of excommunication to include women. Indeed, the fifteenth-century writer Christine de Pizan complains, in *The Book of the City of Ladies,* about the prohibition against women reading the *Secrets of Women,* viewing it as a masculine plot:

> It was done so that women would not know about the book and its contents, because the man who wrote it knew that if women read it or heard it read aloud, they would know it

was lies, would contradict it, and make fun of it. With this pretense the author wanted to trick and deceive the men who read it.[10]

Interestingly enough, Christine characterizes the book as the product of masculine secrecy and fear, not the scientific "bringing to light" of feminine secrets. This masculine plot guards the contents of the treatise—as Christine understands it, a discussion of "the constitution of [women's] natural bodies and especially their great defects"—and it prompts her to defend Nature and the perfection of women's bodies (Pizan 1982, 22, 23–26). Her reading of the *Secrets of Women* construes Nature and women's natural bodies as the secret of the hostile treatise, while modern scholars of the text see female sexuality as "the secret."[11] This slippage of secrecy's "field of operation" is likewise characteristic of the treatise and its commentaries; such slippages are produced by the unstable relations governing the gendered body: relations of having/not having, being/not being, knowing/not knowing the secret.

Masculine motivation for disclosing women's secrets is more fully explicated in the commentaries on the text. One commentary, dating from 1353, claims that the purpose is so that "we might be able to provide a remedy for their [women's] infirmities, and so that in confessing them we might know how to give suitable penances for their sins" (Lemay 1992, 59). Yet there is little in the substance of the treatise that would provide penitential guidance for a male confessor; nor does the treatise offer a system of remedies for treating gynecological disorders, leading Green to claim that, strictly speaking, the *Secrets of Women* is not a gynecological treatise (Green 1990, 145). The commentator further mystifies the reason for "bringing to light" the hidden nature of women by adding a caution:

> The reason for this [disclosure of women's secrets] is that women are so full of venom in the time of their menstruation that they poison animals by their glance; they infect children in the cradle; they spot the cleanest mirror; and whenever men have sexual intercourse with them they are made leprous and sometimes cancerous. And because an evil cannot be avoided unless it is known, those who wish to avoid it must abstain from this unclean coitus, and from many other things which are taught in this book" (Lemay 1992, 60).

Félicie's warning to men to flee women's secrets could find no stronger support than this rationale for the *Secrets of Women.* Nor could the slippage of "the" secret in her defense find a more apt elaboration. The discrepancies registered by these accounts— pseudo-Albert and his commentators, Christine de Pizan and modern scholars—alert us to the radical indeterminacy surrounding the contents of the treatise and, not coincidentally, the representation and location of female sexuality. Such indeterminacy, finally, points us to an "elsewhere" of masculine secrecy.

Nature, female bodies, embryos, astrological inflection of embryos, menses, conception, and sexual intercourse are all collapsed in this treatise under the rubric of "women's secrets," while masculine fears of their danger also erupt into the text. Although the contents themselves are cultural clichés, the representation of the topics as secrets that Nature forbids women to tell charges them with danger and excitement. Further, the opposition between the masculine "desire to know" and the feminine refusal to tell constructs a "regime ... of epistemological enforcement" throughout the treatise.[12] Men, by definition, are not secrets, but they must protect themselves against dangerous feminine secrets by *knowing* them. The priest's desire to know the nature of women derives from his own "natural appetite," notes the commentator, "for men naturally desire to know" (Lemay 1981, 60). Knowledge/ignorance, in conjunction with masculine/feminine, thus precipitates the regime of epistemological enforcement in the treatise. Women's bodies and their bodily functions, such as menses, must be forced to render up their secret dangers through masculine interrogation and exposure, by which women are dispossessed of their secrets. It is crucial to note that this formulation does not grant women (or their bodies), thus constituted as secrets, the *possession* of any knowledge about those secrets. In fact, women are ignorant of the very secrets that they are.

Although women do not *know*, they manage to work harm from the secrets of their nature. The *Secrets of Women* explicitly warns men against women who conceal iron in their vaginas to damage the penis during intercourse:

> O my companions you should be aware that although certain women do not know the secret cause of what I shall describe, many women are familiar with the effect, and many evils result from this (Lemay 1981, 88).

What the cunning women do not know—the cause of the evil they inflict—the author refuses to divulge: "[B]ecause I fear my creator I shall say nothing more about these secrets at present (Lemay 1981, 88). At this point an "enabling but dangerous incoherence" is visible in this regime of secrecy. The boundary between masculine and feminine so clearly drawn in the preface and commentary to the treatise is thus obscured. Men's desire to know justifies their disclosure: knowledge is disclosure. Women's desire to conceal is not compromised by their ignorance: they know how to harm men but they do not know the "secret itself" nor its cause. Yet in the act of disclosing, the male author becomes the one who conceals and at the same time *keeps* women's secrets. The dangerous incoherence of the author's activity is twofold. It contradicts the premise that women do not know the secret in the first place, since they so successfully hide it. Moreover, the author's ultimate refusal to divulge these secrets leads to the uncomfortable paradox that, though men deserve to know women's secrets, the process of coming to know cannot occur without some withholding of their own. So the author interrupts the discourse to withhold indefinitely the secrets of women from his reader. If we remember Miller's claim that secrecy is not meant so much to conceal knowledge as it is to "conceal the knowledge of the knowledge," we can begin to understand how the author of the *Secrets of Women* refigures masculine fear as *auctoritas* by means of the

paradoxical appropriation of the feminine, that is, secrecy. He also exercises the principle of "privileged unknowing" by which he discursively enacts ignorance as much as he
reveals actual knowledge.

Secrecy finds its fulfillment not so much in the "special nature of the contents
revealed," according to Miller (1988, 195), but elsewhere: in the masculine intimacy and
eroticization of the discourse enacted through epistemological enforcement. A good
illustration of this comes from a French treatise in the same genre as the *Secrets of Women*.
Written in the last quarter of the thirteenth century, *Placides et Timéo* is a fictional
dialogue between the philosopher, Timéo, and the son of a prince, Placides, on the
subjects of reproduction and female sexual functions and dysfunctions. In one particular section of the text, Timéo instructs Placides on the physiological symptoms accompanying coitus. One of these symptoms is that during coitus, the woman, whose
nature is cold and moist, according to medieval theory of the humors, begins to steal
the man's heat, for men are naturally hot and dry.[13] At this critical juncture in the
narrative, Timéo's instruction breaks off abruptly, and he turns from women's desire to
that of Placides and his reader:

> And the more she [the woman during intercourse] feels [the man's heat], the more she
> desires, and in this matter, when you have been more obedient, when I have received
> from you more marks of affection, then I will tell you the deep secrets that must not be
> revealed to anyone, except to one's dearest friend: it is the essence of the secrets of nature
> which should not be written, the philosophers say, except in slender, small, and feeble
> letters, that are hard to make out, and on poor quality parchment that is hard to read and
> does not last long, and in hidden meanings, because that which is surrendered easily is
> vile and that which is discovered with difficulty is dear and precious.[14]

The master's desire to render his knowledge illegible through a crabbed script on feeble
parchment is belied by the manuscript in which it is preserved. Not only are his words
legible and the parchment intact, but the two surviving manuscripts are resplendent
examples of late medieval book culture (Jacquart and Thomasset 1988, 128). The
master's fiction is partly a version of the principle of Augustinian poetics alluded to in
the last few lines of the passage, that understanding is only precious when it is achieved
with difficulty (St. Augustine 1958, 3.5.7–9). However, the withholding of woman's
desire and the masculine technologies of authority, knowledge, and representation are
not within this hermeneutic. Timéo performs *coitus interruptus* discursively by interrupt-
ing his disclosure of female desire, and truncating the student's discovery of it.
Women's desire—that essence of the secrets of nature—is thus withheld, remaining
contingent upon masculine affection, obedience, and power.[15] The rhetoric of mastery
in the *Secrets of Women* is thus eroticized through the deferral of female desire by masculine intimacy—perhaps even by masculine desire. Just as the woman desires more of
the man's heat during intercourse, so Placides desires the master's knowledge, which
the master in turn withholds during the discourse about coitus. Such an interaction

performs the "elsewhere" of secrecy as a rhetorical practice. Michel de Certeau defines secrecy, in connection with seventeenth-century mysticism, as a system of relationships, and not simply as "that which is concealed":

> Secrecy is not only the state of a thing that escapes from or reveals itself to knowledge. It designates a play between actors. It circumscribes the terrain of strategic relations between the one trying to discover the secret and the one keeping it, or between the one who is supposed to know it and the one who is assumed not to know it (the "vulgar") (de Certeau 1992, 97).

The example of *discursus interruptus* from *Placides et Timéo* suggests that the secrecy of these medical treatises is as much about the master-student relationship as it is about feminine natures, bodies and dangers. The "play between actors" we find so explicit in *Placides et Timéo* and so subtextual in *Secrets of Women* circumscribes the terrain of strategic relations governing masculine knowledge, and the terms of this play are women's secrets. Further, this terrain is eroticized through the creation and deferral of women as secrets within the masculine master-student community.

In the Latin *Secrets of Women,* female desire is likewise averted. While medical literature of the Middle Ages commonly described female desire and pleasure during intercourse, the *Secrets of Women* does not. One of the most urgent questions of medieval medical treatises was: Who receives greater pleasure, men or women?[16] One answer, provided by Albertus Magnus, used Aristotle to argue that "pleasure is greatest and desire is greatest in woman" because of her greater lack in humoral vigor.[17] Yet Albertus, like other scholastic authors, also made qualitative distinctions between male and female pleasure, which tended to imply the superiority of male pleasure because it was *intensively greater,* while female pleasure was *extensively* greater. Pseudo-Albert never addresses the question of female desire, but instead subsumes it under performances of male authority.

These performances also serve the function, mentioned earlier, of concealing the knowledge of knowledge and attenuating masculine anxiety. In his discussion of hysteria in the *Secrets of Women,* pseudo-Albert borrows from Galen his definition of hysteria as a condition in women where "the womb is taken from its proper place," usually to the throat, causing the woman to suffocate. Pseudo-Albert cites a famous report by Galen of this malady and its cure:

> The great doctor Galen tells about a certain woman who was suffering a suffocation of the womb so serious that it prevented her from talking, and she fell down as if she were dead, with no sign of life. Many doctors were called who looked at her and, not knowing the cause of these symptoms, pronounced her dead. Galen then came on the scene, considered the cause, and freed the woman from this illness (Lemay 1992, 132).

The author never elaborates on Galen's cure; instead, he blames this condition on retained menses, and recommends as a cure that women afflicted with it not be prevented "from having sex with the man they choose" even though this "goes against custom" (Lemay 1992, 132). What pseudo-Albert conceals from Galen's account is the solution offered by the female midwife, not Galen the master: stimulation of the woman's vulva with heat and manual manipulation. Galen thus recommends either masturbation or stimulation by a female midwife as the cure if sexual intercourse is not possible (Galen 1976, 185). Neither of these alternatives is offered in the *Secrets of Women*. The regime of epistemological enforcement here exhibits its other aspect, that is, its function of concealing the knowledge of a particular knowledge, namely, that female desire and pleasure may find remedy in stimulation by a woman, and further, that masculine mastery is no more than hearsay.

The independence of female desire from heterosexual sex and the polymorphous-ness of female pleasure implied in the Galenic source are placed under masculine inter-diction in the *Secrets of Women*. The specific act of a female midwife bringing the afflicted female patient to orgasm is pure therapy, implying nothing about the identities or sexualities of either woman. And yet it bears larger implications, for medical authority, for female sexuality and for masculine rhetorics of secrecy. Joan Cadden's study of sex difference in medieval medicine argues against the notion of deliberate suppression:

> Unlike hermaphrodites, eunuchs, and members of one sex possessing traits of the other, homosexuals and homosexuality had neither a name nor a natural explanation. Scientific and medical learning confirmed this exclusion by its relative silence (Cadden 1993, 226).

Yet pseudo-Albert suppresses the example (and the authority) of the female midwife and her story in his account of Galen's cure. Furthermore, other writers using Galen also felt compelled to revise Galen.[18] Clearly, there is more to this "act" than medical therapy, and more is at stake in it. Female pleasure strays outside masculine authority in Galen's example, just as it defies heteronormative scripting. Pseudo-Albert repairs this, by returning the solution to Galen and prescribing heterosexual sex for the afflicted woman. Female pleasure is thus safely reinstated within the realm of mascu-line secrecy and authority.

By attributing the hidden solution to the "great doctor" Galen, the author of the *Secrets of Women* places women's secrets securely back into the domain of masculine medicine. The treatise's discourse of secrecy shares the monastic context of its produc-tion with the historical context of the professionalization of medieval medicine as it is evident in the University of Paris's prosecution of Jacquéline Félicie. The masculine rhetoric of secrecy in the *Secrets of Women* was popularized during a time when male physicians were engaged in circumscribing and insulating their practice. Félicie is not the only woman to be cited under new licensing laws that sought to exclude women practitioners, as well as Jews and Saracens, from the practice of medicine. In addition to enforcing the licensing of physicians, medical practitioners formed guilds and protec-tive societies, as the rivalry emerged between university-trained physicians and nonuni-versity practitioners (barbers, surgeons, and apothecaries).[19]

The construction of female sexuality as a secret and the discourse of secrecy are symptomatic of a larger professional struggle. Though the pseudo-Albert treatise was not produced in the universities, it imitates university discourse about sex, including "the ambiguity of university-style formality, which lent cool legitimacy to topics fraught with danger" (Cadden 1993, 116). In so doing, the treatise charges the masculine discourse of knowledge with danger, intimacy, and eroticism. At the same time, it preserves the privilege of unknowing in a masculine readership.

What "murderous plot" does this treatise perform in the service of medieval ideologies of gender and sexuality? What "dangerous incoherences" are produced by this discourse of secrecy in medieval culture as a whole?

MURDEROUS PLOT II

As I suggested in the beginning of this essay, the "enabling but dangerous incoherence" of the military policy, "don't ask, don't tell," resides in the contradictory requirements of disclosure for gay service people, making it both compulsory and forbidden. This incoherence renders gay and lesbian military personnel "open secrets" who are caught in the interstices between public and private, disclosure and silence, knowledge and ignorance. The military policy "don't ask, don't tell" reinforces and enforces this incoherence by demanding knowledge and ignorance, publicity and privacy, disclosure and concealment at the same time. Gay military personnel cannot publicly tell, but they must if they are investigated for homosexual behavior; their sexuality is defined as private, yet it is also regarded solely as a public problem for military (heterosexual) morale. The incoherence of the policy is dangerous for gays and lesbians because it renders them at once transparent and opaque—open secrets whose telling is prohibited—while it privileges heterosexual unknowing and presumption to know at the same time.

Medieval medical discourse implicates this policy in larger mappings of secrecy and disclosure that include gender and sexuality. The representation of women's bodies as the "domain of trickery, of seeming, of lies," and of their nature as secret is tailored to the requirements of patriarchal power (Pouchelle 1990, 191). They, too, are rendered opaque to the masculine "desire to know," and dispossessed of the very secret that they are. Out of the representation of female genitals and feminine sexuality as secrets came the academic debates in the university on the question: Can a woman keep secrets? (Pouchelle 1990, 136).

The historical span of secrecy I have sketched out here is not meant to collapse historical, cultural, and experiential distinctions between medieval representations of women's secrets and contemporary representations of the closet. In plotting analogous structures of secrecy in medieval and contemporary cultures, I am keenly aware of the historical specificity of each. The medieval representation of women's secrets is historically and culturally specific to the Western Middle Ages, but it bears ideological affiliations with contemporary gender and sexual structures of oppression as well. The closet as the primary figural representation of homosexuality is very recent, but the attachment of secrecy to sexuality and to groups of people is not.

The category of secrecy during the Middle Ages incorporated a range of social institutions into its fabric of representation. Félicie's testimony implicates moral and religious representations in its physiological construction. Women's shame as a virtue depends upon women's bodies, sex, and reproductive lives being represented as secrets in medical literature. While secrecy may not have constituted an identity for medieval women in the way that closetedness conditions homosexual identity today, nevertheless it operated as a structure of oppression in a similar way, by rendering woman's nature opaque to masculine, heterosexual knowledge.

By placing the *Secrets of Women* next to contemporary ideologies of closetedness, we can produce our own plot of the murderousness of structures of oppression that embrace gender and sexuality, and that historically refabricate themselves for complicitous ideological ends. In medieval medical discourse secrecy constructs women's bodies, particularly their sexual and reproductive functions, to dispossess women of knowledge and power and, at the same time, to define masculinity in terms of men's knowledge of women's secrets. Yet this very knowledge is always lined with a kind of privileged unknowing by which heterosexual masculinity protects itself from the knowledge of women. In a similar way, the closet works to alienate gays and lesbians from their sexuality through a complex system of disclosure and secrecy that both protects heterosexuals from knowledge of homosexuality and controls their knowledge of it. "No doubt an analysis of the kinds of knowledge it is needful to cover in secrecy would tell us much about a given culture or historical period," claims Miller (1988, 206). Indeed, secrecy tells on cultures and historical periods, even as it speaks across them.

MURDEROUS PLOT III

One of the chief plots of contemporary historians of sexuality, as I pointed out in the beginning of this essay, derives from Foucault, dividing premodern sexual acts from modern sexual identities and sexualities. The "acts-to-identity" model for homosexuality, in particular, has succeeded in changing the way medievalists think about "sexuality" in the Middle Ages. Cadden, in her study, *Meanings of Sex Difference in the Middle Ages,* is careful not to use terms such as "homosexuality" or "sexuality." She nevertheless argues that the Middle Ages might have something to teach us about sexuality as we know it: "we can learn something about the complexity, fragmentation, and difference of what we call 'sexuality' in the Middle Ages when we refrain from lending coherence to this multiplicity by our use of unifying terminology" (1993, 7–8). Simon Gaunt likewise argues for a more pluralistic construction of sexuality in the Middle Ages than the social constructionist notion of "acts" permits.[20]

The danger of juxtaposing premodern with modern plots of sexuality is, as Daston and Park have argued elsewhere in this collection, that it often does little to further our understanding of the past, and that instead, the past once again is rendered other in the interests of critiquing the present.[21] Cadden offers the suggestion that we seek out the difference as well as complexity of what we call sexuality in the Middle Ages, without surrendering to the temptation to "lend coherence" to it.

Yet the issues involved in studying sexualities of the past are as much about plots, and our own stakes in them, as they are about historical method. The stakes in the social-constructionist plot of historical sexualities are aptly framed by David Halperin:

> we must struggle to discern in what we currently regard as our most precious, unique, original, and spontaneous impulses [of our sexuality] the traces of a previously rehearsed and socially encoded ideological script (1990, 40).

If secrecy is the governing construction of medieval gender and contemporary homosexuality, it is appropriate, and ironic at the same time, that discernment should be the sexuality historian's project. What are we attempting to discern? The search for traces of a previously rehearsed and socially encoded ideological script is, I want to argue, a task which cannot be limited to the study of sexuality. As Margaret Hunt writes, queer histories need to "cast their nets widely if they hope to decipher the connections between sexuality and power, . . ."[22] This means not limiting our discernment even to medieval categories, such as sodomy, nor to "acts" that constitute sexual behaviors. The connections between sexuality and power are not limited to that ideological script governing past and present "spontaneous impulses."

The reach of ideological scripts extends beyond the field of sexuality and, as Sedgwick suggests, beyond and between historical periods. In her essay, "Critically Queer," Judith Butler insists that "it seems crucial to retain a theoretical apparatus that will account for how sexuality is regulated through the policing and the shaming of gender." Without reducing the relationship between gender and sexuality to one of cause and effect, Butler says, "it ought to be possible . . . not only to link feminism and queer theory, as one might link two separate enterprises, but to establish their constitutive interrelationship (1993, 239, 240). Her proposal for such a linkage is "to muddle the lines between queer theory and feminism." This essay attempts such a muddling, in an effort to explore the ideological script of the closet by crossing historical and categorical boundaries. In casting our nets more widely, and muddling the lines between queer theory and feminism, we need to risk more engagement and critique between the two enterprises.

The stakes in this muddling are high. Failure to interrogate the larger structures of power of which sexuality is a part stands to replicate the oppressive discourse we seek to discern. Studies of premodern sexuality that are narrowly limited to sodomitic discourse or acts create their own plot, or in Butler's words, "a reverse-discourse in which the defiant affirmation of queer dialectically reinstalls the version it seeks to overcome" (1993, 21). Perhaps it is no coincidence that the social-constructionist plot distinguishing premodern acts from modern identities coincides with the military policy of bracketing off homosexual acts from identities. At the very least, this queer juxtaposition of social-constructionist history and military policy suggests the potential for a reverse-discourse in the acts-to-identity theory of queer history, that is, its potential for new and more repressive ideological scripts.

Gender and sexuality are both part of secrecy's plot and its historical span, and if we don't ask or pursue these aspects of the plot together, we shall merely be protecting ourselves from the reaches of that ideological script and the murderous plots it generates. Secrecy allows for a larger cultural and historical cartography of that encoded ideological script, and for a greater discernment than does the study of medieval sexual acts. At stake are the plots of our culture—sometimes murderous, more often simply insidious.

NOTES

1. Miller (1988, 207). In the writing of this essay, I have benefited greatly from the extensive and thoughtful comments of Carla Freccero and Louise Fradenburg. I also wish to thank Peggy McCracken for reading an early draft of this piece. Finally, I would like to thank E. Ann Matter and the University of Pennsylvania Committee on Medieval Studies for giving me an opportunity to work through the ideas in this essay, and I am grateful for their comments.

2. For summaries of this policy and its subsequent elaboration, see "Text of Pentagon's New Policy Guidelines," *New York Times* 1993. and "Military Policy on Gays Issued," *Los Angeles Times* 1993.

3. I am borrowing this term, "epistemological transparency," from Rita Goldberg (quoted in Sedgwick 1993, 31). Sedgwick equates the condition of "epistemological transparency" with that of "pure knowing" as distinct from the condition of "pure unknowing." My own discussion of privileged unknowing is indebted to Sedgwick's in this essay and in *Epistemology of the Closet,* (5–8, 73–74, and 94–104). Sedgwick shows how "*particular* ignorances structure and enforce *particular* knowledges" (25). In the case of the Pentagon policy on gays, heterosexual ignorance is at stake against that "knowledge of the knowledge" of gay sexuality.

4. See Michel Foucault (1990). Foucault defines sexuality as "the set of effects produced in bodies, behaviors, and social relations by a certain deployment" of "a complex political technology" (127). Two examples of the social constructionist argument are David M. Halperin (1990); Padgug (1989, 54–64); Weeks (1981, 76–111); and D'Emilio (1993, 467–476).

5. See the Introduction to this volume, (vii–xii).

6. These are the words Sedgwick uses to describe the consequences of the closet as cultural construct, and she warns against writing histories that present these consequences "as inevitable or somehow valuable." See Sedgwick (1990, 68).

7. Denifle (1891, II, 264). My translation.

8. Lemay (1992, 1). Margaret Schleissner recently estimated the number of manuscripts at "nearly 100" and of Latin incunables at 55. See Schleissner (1991, 110).

9. For the audience of the *Secrets of Women,* see Lemay (1992, 7–16). For Green's comments, see Green (1985, 202). Also quoted in Lemay (1992, 8). Lemay says that the audience of the treatise is a puzzle, but that "origin in a religious community is likely for the text, given the internal evidence" (7). For evidence of non-monastic audiences for the text, Schleissner cites the example of Johann Hartlieb's German translation of *De Secretis mulierum,* in which the author claims to speak to married people but in fact addresses the aristocratic bachelor, Siegmund. See Schleissner (1991, 114). For another German translation and its bourgeois audience, see Green (1989, 67).

10. Pizan (1982, 22–23). See Schleissner (1991, 113), where she cites this very prohibition: "… deffandus de reveler a fame par nostre sainct pere le pape sus paine descommuniement en le Decretal ad meam decretam."

11. Lemay says, "For Pseudo-Albert, this term clearly refers to matters pertaining to sexual

and reproductive life" (1992, 32), while Cadden views the title more generally to refer to "material relating to sexuality, reproduction, gynecology, and obstetrics" (1993, 115). Jacquart and Thomasset characterize the treatise as being about embryology with an air of "deceit about the character of the merchandise being purveyed" (1988, 128). There is enough slippage in these three accounts to warrant suspicion, in my view, about the use of secrecy in the treatise and its mystification of the subject(s).

12.   I am borrowing language used by Sedgwick in the radically different context of Diderot's *The Nun,* where the regime of "sexual ignorance" in the character of Suzanne sets up a similar incitement to "epistemological enforcement," which Sedgwick rightly regards as an incitement to violence. See her essay on the novel in Sedgwick (1993, 48).

13.   For a summary of medieval theory on the humors, see Cadden (1993, 16–17, 80–81, and 183–88). Cadden maintains that the primary index of sexual difference and gender in medieval medicine was the humoral physiology of men and women.

14.   Thomasset (1980, 122–23). My translation.

15.   Thomasset comments on this gesture of initiation and performance of Placides's mastery in his commentary on the text, *Une vision du monde à la fin du XIIIe siècle* 1982, 73. Foucault also discusses the pleasure connected with secrecy and mastery, (1990, 35, 49, 57–61).

16.   For a good summary of this debate see Cadden (1993, 150–62); Laqueur (1990, 43–52).

17.   Quoted in Cadden (1993, 153).

18.   Lemay notes that physicians after Galen, such as William of Saliceto, were reluctant to prescribe this cure, though they agreed with the diagnosis. She attributes this reluctance to "modesty or sexual taboos." See Lemay (1981, 178).

19.   On the professionalization of medicine, see Green (1989, 52); and Rowland (1981, 9–10). However, as Green points out, no study has been made of how this professionalization affected women in particular (52 n.).

20.   See Gaunt in this volume, (155–73).

21.   See Daston and Park in this volume, (117–36).

22.   Afterword, in Goldberg 1994, (373).

WORKS CITED

Abelove, Henry, Michèle Aina Barale, and David M. Halperin, eds. 1993. *The Lesbian and Gay Studies Reader.* New York and London: Routledge.

Augustine. 1958. *On Christian Doctrine,* trans. D. W. Robertson, Jr. Indianapolis: Bobbs-Merrill.

Bennett, Judith M., Elizabeth A. Clark, Jean F. O'Barr, B. Anne Vilen, and Sarah Westphal-Wihl, eds. 1989. *Sisters and Workers in the Middle Ages.* Chicago: University of Chicago Press.

Butler, Judith. 1993. *Bodies that Matter: On the Discursive Limits of "Sex."* New York and London: Routledge.

de Certeau, Michel. 1992. *The Mystic Fable, Volume I: The Sixteenth and Seventeenth Centuries,* trans. Michael B. Smith. Chicago: University of Chicago Press.

D'Emilio, John. 1993. "Capitalism and Gay Identity," in Abelove, *et al., The Lesbian and Gay Studies Reader.* 467–76.

Denifle, Henri, ed. 1891–1899. *Chartularium Universitatis Parisiensis.* Vol. 2. Paris. 1891. 4 vols.

Duberman, Martin, Martha Vicinus, and George Chauncey, Jr., eds. 1989. *Hidden from History: Reclaiming the Gay and Lesbian Past.* New York: Penguin.

Foucault, Michel. 1990. *The History of Sexuality. Volume 1: An Introduction,* trans. Robert Hurley. New York: Vintage.

Galen. 1976. *Galen on the Affected Parts,* trans. Rudolph E. Siegel. Basel: S. Karger.

Goldberg, Jonathan. 1994. *Queering the Renaissance.* Durham, NC: Duke University Press.

Green, Monica. 1989. "Women's Medical Practice and Health Care in Medieval Europe," in Bennett *et al., Sisters and Workers.* 39–78.

———. 1990. "Female Sexuality in the Medieval West." *Trends in History* 4: 127–58.

Halperin, David M. 1990. *One Hundred Years of Homosexuality and Other Essays on Greek Love.* New York: Routledge.

Jacquart, Danielle and Claude Thomasset. 1988. *Sexuality and Medicine in the Middle Ages,* trans. Matthew Adamson. Princeton: Princeton University Press.

Laqueur, Thomas. 1990. *Making Sex: Body and Gender from Greeks to Freud.* Cambridge, MA: Harvard University Press.

Lemay, Helen Rodnite. 1981. "William of Saliceto on Human Sexuality." *Viator* 12: 165–81.

———, trans. 1992. *Women's Secrets: A Translation of Pseudo-Albertus Magnus'* De Secretis Mulierum *with Commentaries.* Albany: State University of New York Press.

"Military Policy on Gays Issued; Lawsuit Vowed." 1993. *Los Angeles Times* December 23, A1, 18.

Miller, D. A. 1988. *The Novel and the Police.* Berkeley: University of California Press.

Padgug, Robert. 1989. "Sexual Matters: Rethinking Sexuality in History," in Duberman, *et al., Hidden from History.* 54–64.

Pizan, Christine de. 1982. *The Book of the City of Ladies,* trans. Earl Jeffrey Richards. New York: Persea Books.

Plummer, Kenneth, ed. 1981. *The Making of the Modern Homosexual.* London: Hutchinson.

Pouchelle, Marie-Christine. 1990. *The Body and Surgery in the Middle Ages,* trans. Rosemary Morris. Cambridge: Polity.

Schleissner, Margaret. 1991. "A Fifteenth-Century Physician's Attitude toward Sexuality: Dr. Johann Hartlieb's *Secreta mulierum* Translation," in *Sex in the Middle Ages: A Book of Essays,* ed. Joyce E. Salisbury. New York: Garland. 110–25.

Sedgwick, Eve Kosofsky. 1990. *Epistemology of the Closet.* Berkeley: University of California Press.

———. 1993. *Tendencies.* Durham, NC: Duke University Press.

"Text of Pentagon's New Policy Guidelines on Homosexuals in the Military." 1993. *New York Times* July 20, A12.

Thomasset, Claude Alexandre, ed. 1980. *Placides et Timéo ou Li secrés as philosophes.* Geneva: Librairie Droz.

———. 1982. *Une vision de monde à la fin du XIIIe siècle: Commentaire du Dialogue de Placides et Timéo.* Geneva: Librairie Droz.

Weeks, Jeffrey. 1981. "Discourse, Desire and Sexual Deviance: Some Problems in a History of Homosexuality," in Plummer, *The Making of the Modern Homosexual.* 76–111.

Part Three

SEXUALITY

AND

SANCTITY

Straight Minds/ "Queer" Wishes in Old French Hagiography

La Vie de Sainte Euphrosine

Simon Gaunt

Sexuality—the configuration of discourses and drives that generate and regulate desire—is central to the construction of sanctity in the Middle Ages. Medieval saints' lives repeatedly celebrate virginity, celibacy, or repentance for past sexual activity. Rather than being effaced through the renunciation of genital sex, sexual agency—the right to dispose sexually of one's body as one sees fit—becomes a crucial element in the construction of a saint's identity as a saint. Medieval saints' lives reinscribe sexuality even as they ostensibly seek to deny it; thus a saint's desire not to have sex is often expressed in erotic terms, as when female virgin martyrs resist seduction, marriage, or rape, but are described as nubile "brides of Christ," eagerly awaiting union with their "lover." Moreover, other ingredients in the construction of medieval sanctity—such as pain, suffering, humility, and patience—are often associated with the erotic discourse that describes a saint's ascension to sanctity: for example, virgin martyrs happily submit to torture, often of a sexually charged nature, at the hands of male pagan tyrants in order to achieve the desired union with Jesus, their "spouse."

When the particular body of texts with which this article will be concerned— vernacular hagiography—is set in its broader literary context of contemporary vernacular genres, it is striking that saints' lives emerge as more overtly concerned with sexual activity and sexuality than most profane texts. Even in the *fabliau,* or in the beast epic, only a minority of extant texts feature sexual activity. Similarly, although sexuality is a ubiquitous subtext to courtly genres like romance or lyric, devoted as they are to "love," sexual activity is rarely discussed openly. The sexual activity of saints, or its *ascesis,* is always, however, closely scrutinized. For instance, and perhaps most famously, Alexis in the *Vie de Saint Alexis,*[1] one of the earliest surviving Old French literary texts, flees his bride's bed on his wedding night for a life of celibacy and asceticism. He fears that if he has sex, he will "lose God" (lines 59–60); his decision to remain a virgin is thus a prerequisite to his sanctity. The scenario of a putative saint rejecting marriage and opting for virginity is enacted repeatedly in hagiography, making the sexuality of the hero or heroine an explicit issue, in a manner wholly different from other vernacular genres, where the rituals of (heterosexual) desire are almost always taken for granted.[2] Moreover, in comparison to the more humdrum boy-meets-girl narratives encountered in other Old French literary genres, hagiography offers accounts of diverse and unorthodox sexual activities: lascivious tales of the prerepentance activities of repentant whores (*Marie l'Egyptienne, Thais*); sadistic, sexually charged and voyeuristic accounts of the torture by men of teenage girls (*Catherine, Marguerite, Foi*); a complex story of sexual abuse and double incest (*Grégoire*).[3]

The first aim of this article is to offer a reading of a little-known text—*La Vie de Sainte Euphrosine* (c. 1200)—which may be of interest not only to scholars working on the construction of sexuality in Old French texts, but also to a wider audience concerned with the history of sexuality. My second aim is to draw attention to a body of material —vernacular hagiography—which is seldom read, but nonetheless central to European culture, and to the construction of sexuality therein. In order to set my reading of *Sainte Euphrosine* within the context of the genre to which it belongs, and in order to set my own reading of it in perspective, I shall first outline briefly some of the issues, historical, then more theoretical, which lead me to read this text as I do.

The use in vernacular hagiography of the "bride of Christ" metaphor, common in Latin texts from early Christian times, illustrates how the meaning of discourses of sexuality that appear to transcend history may change with historical circumstances. In Latin this lexis bears witness to the enormous influence of the tradition of erotically ambiguous allegorical interpretations of the *Song of Songs*; translated into the vernacular in the twelfth and thirteenth centuries, it resonates strongly with "courtly" overtones. Christ is the woman saint's *"ami"* ("lover") or *"drut"* ("lover") as well as her *"espos"* ("spouse"); the poet addresses the woman saint as *"dame"* ("lady") or *"domna"* ("lady"), terms used in profane texts to designate a lover's beloved. This shared lexis enables vernacular hagiography to inscribe competing discourses of gender and sexuality, and the genre thus contests new, profane models at the same time as it becomes partially contained by them.[4] Where profane texts treat women as objects of exchange within feudal marriage practices, hagiography appears to empower women to opt for virginity as a way of life (and death), and thereby to reject the rights that their male kin have in their sexuality, only then to reinscribe them within an erotic discourse, this time with God as desired object and desiring subject. Erotic discourse is thus (re)appropriated by the church, and this during a period in which it is seeking to control and regulate lay marriage practices. Whereas, in aristocratic society, an individual's family chose her or his partner, a key feature of the church's model of marriage was the consent of both partners. If the church turned a blind eye to a good deal of coercion, the growing importance of consent had a clear impact on vernacular texts of all genres, producing a slow but profound sexual revolution that enshrined sexuality (and above all sexual agency) as central to European constructions of the subject.[5]

Is there any room in hagiography, amidst the celibacy or alongside the implicitly heterosexual "bride of Christ" metaphor, for nonheterosexual sexualities, indeed for the "queer" wishes alluded to in my title? The phrasing of my question raises important and much-debated theoretical problems, in that I am assuming that it is possible to make a hetero/homo distinction in a premodern culture. What do I mean by the term "heterosexual" when referring to medieval culture? Can one talk about the "heterosexual," or its implicit, modern, binary opposite, the "homosexual," seven hundred years before the words were coined? And, if one can, are representations of homosexuality simply a mechanism whereby heterosexual hegemony reimposes itself? Or can they articulate "queer wishes"—a term I use to avoid the question of agency—and thereby exceed the boundaries which they help construct and which ostensibly contain them?

If one uses words like "heterosexual," "homosexual," or "gay" to mean what they mean today, they are, of course, inappropriate to medieval culture. However, we cannot take the meaning of these words for granted in modern culture: there is no single "heterosexual," "homosexual," or "gay" identity today; rather, such constructions are geographically and historically specific, interacting with other hierarchical structures such as race, class, education, and so on. Heterosexualities and homosexualities are inevitably plural and diverse. Yet I am unable to agree with the so-called "constructionist" argument that the modern period invents the hetero/homo opposition, that individuals in earlier periods are defined by their acts, rather than by any immanent orientation towards sexual object choice; that sexual identity itself is a purely modern phenomenon.[6]

It is not my intention to suggest that the hetero/homo opposition is a stable and uncontested feature of Western culture. I wish simply to point out that a hetero/homo dialectic, similar though not identical to that which, according to many gay-affirmative writers, structures and regulates modern Western societies, manifests itself in medieval culture. For example, in one key early courtly romance—the *Enéas*—the orientation of the hero towards the correct, "courtly," sexual object choice is preceded by two virulent diatribes in which he is accused of sodomy with another man. It is implicit in these diatribes that some men have an irrevocable and immanent sexual orientation towards other men that transcends their acts. Moreover, the *Enéas* is hostile to men who have sex with men, evoking homosexuality chiefly to prove the hero's heterosexuality. As in another famous example of a hero being accused of homosexuality in medieval literature—Marie de France's Lanval in the *lai* of the same name (lines 277–86)—the immediate consequence in the narrative is resounding proof to the contrary. In other words, homophobia plays the role in medieval literature that Eve Kosofsky Sedgwick attributes to it in modern culture (1985, 3–4): it contributes to the imposition of compulsory heterosexuality.[7] Moreover, the pattern I am describing is also redolent of Judith Butler's contention that within a heterosexual matrix homosexuality precedes heterosexuality (1990, 64–65). The heterosexual matrix of courtly culture in some key texts is founded on the repudiation of homoeroticism, and the "homosexual" is consequently a crucial element in vernacular writing. In texts such as the *Enéas* and *Lanval*, homophobia is a precondition of heterosexual, masculine self-elaboration. As Butler argues:

> the repressive law effectively produces heterosexuality, and acts not merely as a negative
> or exclusionary code, but as a sanction and, most pertinently, as a law of discourse, distin-
> guishing the speakable from the unspeakable (delimiting and constructing the domain
> of the unspeakable), the legitimate from the illegitimate (65).

A dialectic between heterosexuality and homosexuality underscores many medieval texts, particularly in the central "courtly" tradition of which the *Enéas* and *Lanval* partake. If one term in this dialectic is frequently muted, this act of muting is in itself a necessary and defining moment in the production of dominant culture.

I am deliberately stressing the close fit between medieval texts and modern theory here. My point is that the rupture many modern writers perceive between the medieval and early modern periods is questionable. As many medievalists are aware, there is an ideological investment on the part of classicists, modernists, and theorists in a periodization that constructs the Middle Ages either as a thousand-year historical black hole in which nothing happened, or as a quaint prehistory to the teleology of the emergence of modern capitalist culture. It is ironic that early writers on "courtly" culture, who contended that modern notions of "love" had their origin in the twelfth century, were not far short of the mark; modern theorists of sexuality would do better to scrutinize more carefully the medieval period for continuity with the early modern period, before (re)investing in the concept of rupture. Moreover, as John Boswell has shown (1991), the Middle Ages evinced theoretical pluralism on sexuality, with writers adopting positions across the spectrum of what is now termed the "essentialist"/"constructionist" opposition (Fuss 1989; Butler 1990, 1–13).

If I am insisting on the validity of certain terms when discussing medieval culture, and on the potential importance of medieval culture in understanding our own, why then do I choose to draw hagiography into the debate? Again my motivation is strategic. I would not wish to suggest that gay and "queer" sexualities are not always *potentially* disruptive and subversive of heterosexual hegemony, for I believe they are, but if Butler and others are right that "otherness" is necessary to the identity of the dominant culture, then the "unspeakable" and the "unthinkable," the homosexuality such cultures might seek to repress, is, as Butler puts it, "fully within culture, but fully excluded from *dominant* culture" (77). To confound and subvert models of ourselves imposed by the discourses of dominant culture, we need to understand how and why homosexuality is central to cultural construction. The European Middle Ages offer excellent illustrations of this disavowed centrality, for, as John Boswell's work shows (1980), most of the evidence for homoeroticism in the period comes from within the Church, that is from within the very institution that most vociferously condemned it—Christianity. Latin hagiography is at the center of medieval ecclesiastical culture for over a thousand years; vernacular hagiography—produced from the eleventh century onwards—represents a meeting point of sacred and profane discourses, where old narratives, often borrowed from Latin sources, take on new meanings that are specific to their vernacular context while also clearly being subject to the dominant culture of the church. For most modern readers of medieval vernacular literature, hagiography has been relegated to the margins; but hagiography was at least as popular as courtly romance, if quantities of manuscripts indicate popularity.[8] As central cultural symbols, saints merit close attention from historians of sexuality. Indeed, any attempt to understand the construction of sexuality in the Middle Ages without taking account of the body of evidence offered by this socially powerful, sex-obsessed genre will inevitably be incomplete.

At first glance, hagiography would appear to be a genre dominated by male heterosexual fantasies. The sexual abstinence (or, in the case of incestuous Gregory, the sexual misbehavior) of male saints is repeatedly stressed, but men's bodies are not portrayed as desirable in vernacular hagiography: some male saints may be laconically described as good-looking, but details are rarely given, which is in stark contrast to the heroes of courtly romance, whose fair locks and lithe bodies are frequently admired. Similarly, the dismemberment of male bodies is not dwelt upon in a titillating or voyeuristic manner, and does not involve their sexual organs. Female saints, on the other hand, are always objects of desire, for pagan men, Christian men and, in different ways, for the poet, his audience and God. Whether women saints are virgins or repentant whores, their bodies are undressed and offered to men and to God as women's bodies, though they then have to be punished for the desire they stimulate, as if they were somehow responsible for it. Thus their breasts are admired and given titillating descriptions, only then to be cut off or, in the case of repentant whores, slowly withered. That the only early medieval French life of a virgin martyr known to have been written by a woman—Clemence of Barking's *Vie de Sainte Catherine*—is considerably less lascivious and sadistic, stressing the saint's intellectual and spiritual prowess rather than her physical trials (Wogan-Browne 1993, 67–68), proves the general rule that these texts inscribe the sadistic sexual fantasies of some straight men.[9]

But not all the fantasies in vernacular hagiography are as straight as they seem. Some women saints adopt a radical strategy to evade male desire: they cross-dress. Stories of cross-dressed women saints are relatively common in the early Middle Ages, but only two narratives survive in Old French and in one of these, *Euphrosine*, desires that are far from straight emerge.[10] This text tells the story of a young girl whose conception is attributed to the prayers made by an abbot on behalf of her pious parents, who have longed for a child for many years. Euphrosine grows up to be a beautiful and well-educated girl. When she is twelve, her mother dies and her father, Panutius, shortly betroths her to an eligible young bachelor. Bewitched by her "fair complexion and comely breasts" (line 132), Euphrosine's fiancé is eager to marry and above all to consummate the union as quickly as possible, but Euphrosine persuades her father to allow her for the time being to remain at home, a virgin. As is common in hagiography, she laments the threat to her virginity, and she also discusses her desire to remain a virgin with the abbot who had prayed for her conception. On one visit to the abbey, she is attracted by the singing and by the communal life of the monks, and eventually she resolves to enter holy orders. Initially she seeks to become a nun, but she soon realizes that her father will find her if she takes refuge in a convent. In a vision, Saint Sophie gives her a plan of action: she should disguise herself as a monk. Dressed as a knight and claiming to be a eunuch (a "*castré*," line 515), Euphrosine returns to the same abbey and is accepted as a monk. Euphrosine, having adopted the androgynous name Esmerade (445–46), is now a passing transvestite: she passes as a man, albeit a castrated one. But to the abbot's and her own consternation, the sight of this beautiful young man arouses the other monks to such an extent that they go out of their minds with lust, and are beset by wicked thoughts when they see him in church (569–70). In order to protect his flock from temptation, the abbot resolves to keep Esmerade/Euphrosine incarcerated in a cell, segregated from the community except for the company of an old tutor. Meanwhile Panutius, out of his mind with grief at the disappearance of his daughter and at the distress of his erstwhile son-in-law to be, soon presents himself to the abbot for comfort. Impressed by his new monk's learning and dignity, and despite the near riot which followed his first appearance, the abbot decides he is the best person to comfort Panutius, who thereupon visits his daughter regularly for thirty-eight years without suspecting who s/he really is. As the narrator comments: "who expects his daughter to be a monk?" (943). They develop an intense spiritual relationship, and Panutius's only consolation at the loss of his daughter is the acquisition of his new friend (1021–25). Esmerade spends the next thirty-eight years living in her tiny cell, praying and studying, fasting and mortifying the flesh. These years of deprivation take their toll; she eventually falls ill and, just before she dies, she reveals her identity to her father. After long laments, she is recognized as a saint.

This text has received virtually no critical attention. Edited in article form in 1919, it has recently been drawn to the attention of a wider readership by the inclusion of translated extracts in an anthology (Cazelles 1991, 172–81; see 63–66 for commentary). Only two critics, to my knowledge, comment in any depth on the text (Storey 1977; McCullough 1977); both invoke the "neglected masterpiece" *topos.* It is certainly an unusual text in the Old French corpus. As Florence McCullough suggests, it produces a depth of characterization that is unusual in hagiography (178–79). Moreover, as she also shows, it is formally different from contemporary Old French saints' lives which, like courtly romance, are written in octosyllabic rhyming couplets. *Euphrosine* is composed of dodecasyllabic lines grouped in monorhymed strophes usually ten lines in length; it is thus formally reminiscent of the *chansons de geste*. This unusual form is coupled with stylistic features (repetitions, formulae) which also clearly evoke the *chansons de geste*.[11]

Euphrosine's priority is to preserve her virginity. The symbolic value of female virginity in medieval hagiography cannot be overestimated: virgin martyrs pray not to be saved from torture, but to have their virginity preserved so that they may occupy in heaven the special place reserved for virgins, whilst Latin texts tell of women who mutilated themselves in order to make themselves unattractive enough to avoid rape (Schulenberg 1986, 44–60). But this text is unique in that nowhere else in vernacular hagiography is the attack upon lay marriage and sexual activity, implicit in much hagiographic writing, so overtly articulated; nor is the relationship between property and sexuality, a particular feature of the construction of sexuality in Old French texts, ever more clearly marked than here.

For instance, when Euphrosine's fiancé is desperate for "*delit corporal*," ("bodily pleasure"; line 174), she presents her predicament to God thus:

> "Sire, fai moi merci; si me garde de mal.
> Tu commandas, ce sai, mariage loial,
> Mais tu vassis mies naistre de ventre virginal,
> Car ja virgene et uzor ne seront d'un terral.
>
> Je sai ke loial chose at mut en mariage,
> Qui voroit netement demener sens putage,
> Ki ne s'en sorferoit ne n'i meneroit utrage,
> Cum font cil jovencel qui tot sunt plain de rage,
> Qui ne sevent lor cors atempler de folage;
> Mais assez est plus gent garder le pucelage
> Et mener sens dangier chastement son eage
> Et degerpir por toi parens et yretage.
> Ei! sire, afferme moi ver toi itel corage,
> Que toi ne puisse perdre por croistre me linage.
>
> Ei! sire, aïue moi par la toue dolzor,
> Por la vie del siecle ke ne perde t'amor.
> Contre toi n'ai ge chier ne amis ne honor.
> Petit pris l'iretage, se toi n'ai a sagnor."

Sire, have mercy upon me; save me from evil. I know that you instituted loyal marriage, but you preferred to be born of a virgin's womb, for never will the wives of mortal man remain virgins.

I know loyalty can exist in marriage if one behaves decently and without promiscuity, avoids excess and is not offensive like so many young men who behave so madly that they cannot protect their bodies from folly; but it is much more noble to remain a virgin, to live out one's life chastely, protected from the dangers of the flesh, and to renounce parents and inheritance. Ah! Lord, place this vocation in me firmly, for I do not wish to lose you for the sake of my lineage.

Ah! Lord, through your great sweetness help me, for I do not wish to lose your love because of worldly concerns. Compared to you I hold neither friends nor property dear. I care nothing for my inheritance if I cannot have you as my lord. (177–94).

The authority of Euphrosine's father to dispose of her body in marriage is overtly challenged here. Marriage is condemned as second best, a state which can lead to temptations a virgin is more likely to avoid. As the poem progresses, "*l'amors de cest vain siecle*," ("this vain world's love") is repeatedly attacked and contrasted to spiritual love (for example, lines 310–11), while one of Euphrosine's spiritual advisors cites directly Christ's words in Matthew 10:35 about His coming between the Christian and his family (lines 396–401). In other texts, saints go against their parents' wishes to marry (for examples, see Gaunt 1995, 190–95; Glasser 1981; Gouiran 1989), but the challenge to the authority of biological fathers remains a subtext. Here, the material interests of Panutius's family—bound up as they are with Euphrosine's sexuality—are directly undermined. Euphrosine disobeys her father, and disparages the value of her family and inheritance. Women, in many Old French texts, are vehicles through and with which men transmit property to each other and thereby communicate. Euphrosine, like many women saints, refuses to play this role, but her reasons for doing so are spelled out with a precision that is unusual in vernacular hagiography.

Furthermore, just as the erotic discourse of "worldly" love is combatted with an erotic discourse of spiritual love when Euphrosine acquires an alternative bridegroom, Jesus, whom she calls her "*amant*" ("lover"; 645), so an alternative notion of property emerges. The text repeatedly returns to the notion of "*iretage*" ("inheritance"), but in a variety of guises. When she enters holy orders, she is clear that she is renouncing her inheritance (which is considerable) and promises to give it, if she can, to the community. She ensures before she dies that her father's wealth will, indeed, pass to the abbey by exacting a promise to this effect from him (1112–25), but at the end of the text the value of worldly wealth is implicitly undermined, as the monks pray for a share in the inheritance ("*heredité*"; 1217) of heaven. Earlier in the text it is explained that the special advantage of virginity is that one receives a share of the celestial "*heredité*" reserved for "*saintes puceles*" ("holy maidens"; 269–70). Thus heaven becomes the "property" (and inheritance) for which one should renounce one's worldly property (and inheritance). When Euphrosine joins her "brothers" in Christ, physical kinship is replaced with spiritual kinship, corporeal sexuality with spiritual sexuality, and material property with spiritual property. The narrative combats a lay construction of (hetero)sexuality and property with a discursive spiritual counterpart, while augmenting the church's authority and—in the story—its coffers.

I dwell upon these discursive formations to give a sense of the sexuality of female saints, of the unusual explicitness of this text, and of the complex dialogue between sacred and profane models of sexuality at work in hagiography. *Euphrosine* clearly shows that the sexuality of female saints in these discursive formations is by no means effaced, nor is their sexuality divorced from secular discourses. I want now to turn to the question of cross-dressing, and to the scene where the disguised Euphrosine's spiritual brothers are driven wild with lust at the sight of her.

Although only two narratives about cross-dressed women saints survive in Old French, as a medieval narrative paradigm, cross-dressing is by no means uncommon. It is found more frequently in the early Middle Ages than in the twelfth and thirteenth centuries. There are no records of male transvestite saints; the decision of women to adopt men's clothes is attributed to a desire for the status to which only a holy man can aspire.[12] In Christian theology, man is spirit, woman is matter; in order to come close to God, a woman needs to transcend her feminine flesh.[13] One way of doing this, it is suggested, is by becoming a man.

Commenting respectively on Latin and Old English versions of the Euphrosine narrative, both of which include the scene in the church, John Anson has suggested that the story plays out a monastic fantasy of having a woman within a monastery (1974, 17), and Allen J. Frantzen speculates that it "curbs the risk" of homosexuality by revealing the monks' object of desire to be in actuality a beautiful woman (1993, 466). Frantzen further argues that the real point of the episode is to demonstrate how the monks resist temptation, and to show that Euphrosine is "above the discourse of sex" (466). The blind spots of both these critics perhaps obscure the blind spots of the material they are working on. Anson chooses to see heterosexual desire where homosexual desire is at issue. His article offers an example of the approach to transvestism against which Marjorie Garber (1992) warns throughout her recent study of cross-dressing: he looks *through* the transvestite, not *at* her. The monks' desire is not aroused simply by a woman, but by a passing transvestite, in this instance a person they believe to be a castrated man. For Frantzen, homosexuality is present in the Old English text as a "risk" (466). He acknowledges a "homosexual subtext" in the narrative, and he evokes Judith Butler's notion of performance in *Gender Trouble* to show how the text expounds an orthodox Christian message. For Aelfric, author of the Old English text, Frantzen argues that faith is the ground of true identity and everything else is "performance": "This is Butler's performativity: gender is merely the *appearance* of self that is constituted when repeated 'performance' defines the possibilities of any man or woman at any point in history" (465). But this is to misconstrue Butler's agenda, for in her work gender performance does not mask the immortal soul; if the immortal has any place in Butler's scheme it would be as an effect of performance. Furthermore, she deconstructs the foundationalism of the opposition between the essence of a "true self" and "performance." Moreover, Euphrosine is not "above the discourse of sex" (466); on the contrary, in the English and French texts she has a lover: Jesus (her *"amant"* in line 645).

Euphrosine survives in four manuscripts, and one of these (Oxford Bodleian, Canon. Misc. 74, fols. 87^r–108^v, the version edited) is an important hagiographic anthology which includes *Alexis* and *Marie l'Egyptienne*, texts in which sexuality and sanctity are closely intertwined.[14] As we have seen, in *Alexis* the hero's chastity is central; in *Marie l'Egyptienne*, a woman's body is first represented as highly desirable and then, when Marie repents of her life as a whore, the spectacle of its withering and disintegrating dominates the text. In *Euphrosine*, a woman's body is veiled by a man's clothes, and this, to a large extent, leads to its effacement. By the end of the text, Euphrosine's body is unrecognizable as the beautiful, nubile body of the opening. Now withered and wrinkled, although undoubtedly female, it is no longer dangerous as an object of desire.

Anson (1974) and Frantzen (1993) argue that the monk's desire, in the versions of the legend that they discuss, is legitimized because its object turns out to be a woman. However, it must surely be significant that in the French text, as in the English, not only does the woman's body disappear from representation at the point at which (according to this reading) it is most desirable, but also that the monks have no idea that the object of their attention is a woman. Perhaps we should look *at* the responses of the monks, rather than *through* them to any intuition they may or may not have about the sex of the new monk:

> Kant fut Eüfrosine vestie et conree[e],[15]
> Agapytus ses maistres l'at des ordenes paree.
> Az orisons l'en at en la glise menee.
> Parut sa blance cars, sa face encoleree,
> Li olh vair et riant et la boche molee.
> La congregations por pou ne fut dervee.
> Cogitasion male lor est el cuer montee.
> Li jovencel l'esgardent cum beste saëtee
> Et dient en lor cuer: "U fut ceste trovee?"[16]
> Li saive ome ont la cose a dant abé mostree.
>
> Dient il: "Fai oster cest castré d'entre nous.
> Ce n'est mie castrez, mais Sathan l'envïous
> Qui nos vuet trebuchier en ses laz a estrous.
> S'entre ces jovenciaz estat un jor u dous,
> Ja en orons tal chose dont tot serons gragnous."

> When Euphrosine was dressed and ready, Agapitun, her master, prepared her for orders. He took her to prayers in the church. Her white flesh and fair complexion, her clear and smiling eyes and soft mouth were all too apparent. The congregation was almost driven out of its mind. Wicked thoughts came into their hearts. The young men look at her as if she were a wild beast and say in their hearts: "Where was this creature found?" The wise men pointed this out to the abbot.

> They say: "remove this eunuch from amongst us. He is not a eunuch, but jealous Satan himself, who wishes to trip us up into his snares and fetters. If he remains amongst these young men for a day or two, we will hear of things which will make us all grieve."
> (564–78).

Frantzen links this episode in the English text to monastic homosexuality (466). What I find remarkable about it in both the English and the French texts is that homosexual activity is taken for granted as a danger against which monks should be vigilant. It is also noteworthy that *all* these young men are thought to be susceptible to homosexual desire. Frantzen argues that, in the English text, "the source of temptation is subordinate to their determination to resist it" (466). But in fact, in the English and French texts, the monks only resist it because it is removed and locked away. The implication of both texts is that the monks' determination to resist temptation is unlikely to last long, that if exposed to this desirable young man they will soon succumb to his charms. The impulse behind this narrative is Euphrosine's attempt to escape heterosexual desire. But in disguising herself as a man in order to escape the "normal" desire of men, she is exposed to an even more dangerous form of male desire. For Euphrosine, the alternative to being the object of heterosexual desire would appear not to be unsullied chastity, but becoming the object of homosexual desire; for the monks, the alternative to chastity would also appear to be homosexual desire. Closely behind the heterosexual in this text lurks the homosexual, and the two are locked in an inescapable dialectic that structures and impels the narrative.

The manuscript tradition indicates that this text is more central to medieval literary culture than modern scholarship has allowed. Could this in part be a result of its casual treatment of transvestism and homosexuality? There is less a homosexual subtext here than an obviously homosexual text, which needs to be recognized in order to assess the role of cross-dressing in the poem's gender politics. It may well be true that, in adopting the guise of a man, Euphrosine aspires to the spiritual status of a male ascetic, denying the troublesome femaleness of her own flesh, as the literary critics and historians who have addressed the subject of cross-dressed saints argue. And yet, as Marjorie Garber (1992) and Judith Butler (1990) have so eloquently demonstrated, cross-dressing is often a symptom of cultural anxiety, not so much a crisis of and in gender categories, but a crisis of category itself. Euphrosine's masquerade may blur gender categories, and this is amply figured in her (self-)presentation as a eunuch (perhaps, in this text, the "third" category produced by the cross-dresser that Garber suggests can be so subversive [11–12]). But a further boundary is also called into question: that erected by sexual object choice. Do the monks desire a man or a woman? Just as Panutius does not expect his daughter to be a monk, so the monks do not expect the beautiful eunuch to be a woman. Euphrosine's cross-dressing is a performance, but the point is perhaps less that she performs, than that she shows the extent to which all gender roles are performative, imitations of an absent model. Desire is elicited here less by a body than by a performance in which the body is one prop amongst others (clothes, language, gestures). Through Euphrosine's performance all kinds of "queer" wishes emerge, only to be suppressed, though not, I will suggest, effaced. The monks desire the (male) body they presume to be there, but this desire is stimulated by the transvestite act that Esmerade puts on for them.

It is thus hard to see how the monks' desire for Esmerade becomes less "risky" because s/he turns out to be a woman. On the contrary, when she wreaks havoc in the church, she is performing as a man, and consequently desired as a man, albeit a eunuch. It is less her body that is desired, than an image of masculinity that turns out to be performative. Not only is the monks' desire homosexual, but for Euphrosine's body to be desirable to them, it needs to be dressed in men's clothes.[17] The "risk" of homosexuality is not curbed here, but rather enhanced. A further risk is added, for as a passing transvestite, Euphrosine also forces us (and the monks, when they discover her sex) to question what is meant by the categories "man" and "woman." It is perhaps significant that several other instances of desire for cross-dressed women in Old French literature raise the "spectre" of homosexuality, though somewhat differently.

In the *Enéas*, a large, central section is dominated by the character Camille (taken from Virgil) who cross-dresses as a man in order to be a warrior by day, but dresses as a woman at night. Camille does not pass as a man but, as a number of critics have shown, her gendering is implicitly represented as "improper" (for example see Huchet 1985; Burgwinkle 1993, 33–35). Camille is associated in this text with a warrior ideology predicated upon unmediated male bonding, which is firmly marginalized at the end of the narrative when heterosexual desire is imposed as the norm, and homosexuality virulently chastised and repudiated (Gaunt 1995, 75–85; but compare Burgwinkle 1993, 36–43). In *Silence*, the heroine is brought up as a boy because the king has prohibited women from inheriting land: here gender as well as sexuality is bound up with property. Throughout the text Silence undergoes an identity crisis as to whether she is a man or a woman; this is enacted by an ongoing allegorical debate between Nature and Nurture. After a series of adventures as a minstrel, the appropriately named Silence becomes a successful knight; thus, although the outcome of the text seems designed to prove that women cannot be men, in that Silence's biological sex is finally revealed, several elements in the narrative suggest the opposite, and consequently hint at the idea that gender might be culturally constructed rather than biologically determined (see Gaunt 1990a). When performing as a knight at court, Silence twice has to reject the advances of the libidinous queen, and, as in *Lanval*, the rejection of a woman's sexual advances is followed by the charge of homosexuality, couched in acerbic, homophobic terms. But here the resemblance to *Lanval* ends, for there is an accumulation of confusion about sexual object choice in *Silence* that is not paralleled in the *lai*. The queen is, in fact, making sexual advances to another woman, and, although Silence is referred to with masculine pronouns throughout the passage, her female sex is stressed several times through the formulation *"li vallés qui est mescine"* ("the young man who was a girl"; for instance, in line 3785). Furthermore, at the end of the text it is revealed that the queen has had a lover at court who was cross-dressed as a nun, while the king (having had his queen and her lover executed) marries Silence, who had until recently been his favorite knight. The attempt to naturalize heterosexual desire is heavy-handed in this text: Silence cannot reciprocate the queen's kisses because *"nel consent pas sa nature"* ("her/his nature does not allow it"; 3824). Yet at the same time, the insistence on desire for cross-dressed characters is more than a little "queer." Here we have a romance in which the king ends up marrying his favorite knight and where the good woman (Silence) is preferred to the bad woman (a queen) because she was a good man!

Comparisons between *Silence* and *Euphrosine* are illuminating. There are, of course, differences between the two heroines: Silence is cross-dressed to safeguard her father's property, whereas Euphrosine cross-dresses in order to escape her father, thereby compromising his property. But with both women, it is the ability to impersonate a man that makes them good women and the objects of (male) desire; both need to cross-dress to achieve heroic status within their narratives, and cross-dressing enables narrative in both texts.[18] In *Silence*, cross-dressing is a strategy which allows a man to marry another character who has performed as a man. In *Euphrosine*, cross-dressing reveals homosexual desire more overtly. "Queer" wishes may ultimately be side-stepped in both of these texts, but the attention that is drawn to them makes them visible.

This visibility is equivocal. On one level, both *Silence* and *Euphrosine* endorse a heterosexual and patriarchal order. Silence is transformed into a beautiful woman, and her marriage to the king guarantees the transmission of her father's property; the monks who desire Euphrosine are described as having wicked thoughts (570), and she leaves them for a heterosexual marriage made in heaven. On another level, both narratives provide a forum in which we, if we choose to be "queer" readers, can locate "queer" wishes, made visible as they are repudiated by narrators who simultaneously enact and disavow them. Both texts produce an ostensibly "straight" status quo by making visible that which they apparently wish to repress. They speak the unspeakable.

If this is the case, the choice to narrate is not innocent. The poet's decision to (re)write the traditional Euphrosine narrative is significant, as is the choice of one scribe to copy it in an anthology with *Alexis* and *Marie l'Egyptienne*: whereas these texts deny (*Alexis*) or punish (*Marie*) heterosexual desire, *Euphrosine* narrates a (failed) attempt to escape from it. It is not just the monks who desire Euphrosine: the poet/narrator, and by implication the scribe, also have an erotically charged relationship with her.[19] As is very common in Old French hagiography, the poem ends with a direct address on the part of the narrator to the saint:

> Eüfrosine dame, Deu espose et amie,
> Ne te nom ne ta geste ne coniso(i)ie mie.
> En un livre d'armare vi escrite ta vie.
> Simplement astoit dite d'(el) ancïene clergie.
> Ore cant je l'ou liute, reçuie t'avou[e]rie;
> Por t'amor ai ta vie en romance recoilhie,
> Non por li amender par maior cortesie,
> Mais par ce ke je vulh qu'ele plus soit oïe.
> S'atres t'aimet o moi, je n'en ai nule envie.
> Tot le siecle en voroie avoir a compagnie.
>
> Le mien petit servise recivez par amor.
> Se je ne l'ai fait bien, je l'ai fait par dolçor.
> Apele Deu por moi, nostre chier redemptor,
> Qu'il ait de moi mercit, le chaitif pecheor;
> Ne les mie[n]s grans forfais ne mes toz a iror;

Prende droit en cest siecle d'icest sien boiseor

Et me laist parvenir, et o june et o plor

Del pechiez que j'ai fais, devant me jugeor;

Et tu, sainte pucele, franque rien, dulce flor,

En itant moi meris m'entente et me labor. Amen.

Lady Euphrosine, God's spouse and lover, I did not know your name or your story. I saw it written in a book in a chest. It was told simply in the manner of clerks of former times. Now that I have read it, I enter your service; through love of you I have translated your life into the vernacular, not to change it by making it more courtly, but because I would like it to be heard more widely. If another loves you with me, I am not jealous. I would like to have the whole world keeping me company.

Receive with love my little service. If I have not done it well, I have done it with affection. Ask God, our sweet savior, to have mercy upon me, miserable sinner that I am, and not to be too angry about my wrong-doing; may he treat this laborer of his well in this world and let me come, through fasting and weeping for my sins, before my judge; and you, saintly maiden, noble thing, sweet flower, may you reward me this much for my work and labor. Amen. (1250–79)

The poet makes the story of the saint available to the audience, so that she may intercede on his and (by implication) their behalf with God, whose will or desire is the ultimate driving force behind the narrative. The relationship between God and the saint is presented as erotic (she is God's spouse and lover), and so is that between the narrator and saint. She is described using language reminiscent of courtly texts: she is a *"franque rien"* ("noble thing") and *"dulce flor"* ("sweet flower"). Indeed the denial of "courtly" motivation on the part of the poet perhaps suggests the contrary, and the poet's hope that his "labor" in writing will pay dividends recalls the courtly lyric as well as other hagiographic texts. Furthermore, in asking for his share in the celestial *heredité* through Euphrosine, the narrator claims her as his literary property. He reveals her story from a hidden, written source (a chest rather than a closet) to which only he has access. He seeks to enclose and possess her, much as her father, fiancé and God did in the story, and he does so using erotic language. But the poet's address to his saint as a *"sainte pucele"* ("holy maiden"), despite seeming perfectly in keeping with the genre, differs in one crucial way from countless other apostrophes to holy virgins: this holy virgin was a transvestite in life. At the end of this text, the poet seems to want himself and his readers to look *through* Euphrosine's cross-dressing (to the female body), rather than *at* it, and consequently to look through her rather than at her. Now she is simply a *"sainte pucele,"* and yet this masks what made her interesting as a subject of narrative (both for the poet and for us, his readers), indeed what made her narrative possible in the first place: her cross-dressing.

When read as an address to a woman who as an adult was a lifelong passing transvestite, these strophes may hint at yet more "queer" wishes, always already repudiated by the text's orthodoxy, and yet (disturbingly for that orthodoxy) present. If the poet attributes his decision to write about Euphrosine to his finding her story particularly moving, the implication is that he finds it more interesting (one might say more enticing) than that of other women saints, and that his discovery of her story was a happy revelation. What distinguishes Euphrosine as a woman saint is that she has to pass as a man in order to accede to sanctity: the best woman saint (by the lights of this text) is then a woman who performed as a man. The apparently conventional devotion to a woman saint here becomes unorthodox when her cross-dressed career is recalled. Who is the *"dulce flor"* addressed here: the maiden Euphrosine, the young "castrated" monk Esmerade, or the combination of the two that the heroine becomes? The narrator goes to some lengths to gender the saint feminine and thereby perhaps to legitimize his interest in her in his closing address (*"dame," "espose," "amie,"* and so on), but the eroticism of the words he uses needs to be considered alongside the earlier scene in which she was the object of desire (as a man). Is it Euphrosine's ability to impersonate a man that makes her sexy? Is the object of desire here masculine or feminine? As I have said, the form of this poem recalls the *chanson de geste*. The use of the word *"geste"* (1261) to denote Euphrosine's story reinforces this, for *geste* is a word unusual outside the epic, where it is used to denote heroic deeds, lineage, and the epic text itself. The notion that the ambiguously gendered Euphrosine should be the subject of a *geste* may further the ambivalence surrounding her as an object of erotic desire, for *chansons de geste* often celebrate male bonding in spaces from which women are excluded. Does the attribution of a *geste* to Euphrosine in these closing lines in fact counteract the gendering of her as feminine, suggesting the contrary, however obliquely? In other words, is Euphrosine desirable precisely and only because she is masculinized?

The discourses emanating from the church have been extremely formative in the construction of European sexualities from the Middle Ages onwards. Those interested in premodern sexualities need to look at Christianity to understand how heterosexual hegemony was formed in and preserved by it. In the text I have examined, the mechanisms by which homosexuality is repudiated guarantee and produce a heterosexual matrix, but they fail to occlude what they seek to repress. As I have tried to show here, straight minds can harbor the queerest of wishes in the most unlikely of places.

NOTES

I would like to thank the editors of this volume and Carolyn Dinshaw for their helpful comments on earlier versions of this essay.

1. References to the editions of texts used and full references to secondary works cited are given in Works Cited; for texts about women saints, I refer for convenience to Cazelles, apart from *Euphrosine*. All translations from Old French are my own.

2. The most notable exceptions are the *Enéas*, *Lanval* and *Silence*, on which, see 157, 166–67.

3. Some of the texts I cite here have been the object of study in relation to sexuality. On *Marie l'Egyptienne*, see Karras (1990), and Gaunt (1995, 214–28); on *Catherine*, see Wogan-

Browne (1993, 67–68); on *Marguerite,* see Gravdal (1991, 38–41); on *Foi* see Gaunt (1995, 187–90); on *Grégoire,* see Guerreau-Jalabert (1988), and Gaunt (1995, 198–12). On the sexuality of female saints generally, see Heffernan (1988, 277–99), and Wogan-Browne (1994). On virginity, see also Bloch (1991, 93–112), and Gaunt (1995, 185–98).

4. *Ami* and *drut* are multivalent, and consequently ambiguous, terms in Old French and Occitan. When used of a relationship between a man and a woman, they mean "lover," but when used of a relationship between men, they mean "friend," often with overtones of close bonding within the feudal hierarchy. On competing discourses of gender and sexuality in vernacular hagiography see Gaunt (1995, 180–233).

5. On the conflict between lay and Church models of marriage see Duby (1978); Gaunt (1990b); and Goody (1983, 103–56). On the importance of consent generally, see Sheehan (1978); and in hagiography, Gaunt (1995, 192–96).

6. See for example, Halperin (1991), and Padgug (1991). I am not seeking to dispute Halperin's and Padgug's accounts of classical civilization, merely to question the historical claim that sexuality is a uniquely modern phenomenon. As Matter (1992) notes, all the medievalist contributors to the collection she introduces implicitly reject the notion that the modern period "invents" sexuality.

7. For a more extended analysis of homophobia and compulsory heterosexuality in the *Enéas,* see Gaunt (1995, 75–85); for further examples of homophobia in vernacular texts, see Gaunt (1995, 305 n. 17). Another well-known instance of homophobia contributing to the construction of the heterosexual subject is, of course, the *Roman de la Rose.* The importance of the relationship between property and sexuality in many Old French texts (including *Euphrosine,* see 161), is one important difference between medieval French and modern constructions of heterosexuality.

8. A large number of hagiographic texts remain unedited or inaccessible, while university curricula and anthologies of medieval literature rarely stray beyond the *Vie de Saint Alexis,* included as much for its early date as for its literary merits. One version of *Sainte Marguerite* (a virgin martyr narrative) survives in over 100 manuscripts (see Cazelles 1991, 217); compare Chrétien de Troyes' *Chevalier de la Charrete,* a foundational text for modern ideas of "courtly love," which survives in just six. Large numbers of manuscripts are an index of wide circulation.

9. Clemence of Barking wrote in Anglo-Norman, a dialect of Old French, rather than in Old French itself. See Gravdal (1991, 42–71) on romance as mystification of rape.

10. The other is the *Vie de Marine,* on which see Cazelles (1991, 238–57).

11. For example, see the repetition linking the opening strophes in lines 1–3 and 11–13; the repetition linking strophes XI and XII; or the *reprise* of the last line of strophe XXXI at the beginning of XXXII (311); the repeated use of the formula *"E vos."* The influence of romance on hagiography in the twelfth and thirteenth centuries is widely recognized; see Cazelles (1991, 30–38).

12. See Bullough (1974, 1383); Cazelles (1991, 66); and Garber (1992, 214–15). On transvestism in profane Old French texts, see Perret (1985), and on the early legends of transvestite saints in Byzantine texts, see Patlagean's intelligent article, (1976).

13. On the spirit/flesh dichotomy see Bynum, who shows (1991, 152) that despite the prevalence of the opposition, medieval notions of gender were in fact more complex. I cannot however agree with her conclusion that the stress medieval women place upon their humanity indicates that "humanity is genderless" (179).

14. See Hill's edition of *Euphrosine* (1919, 159–62) on the manuscripts. The Oxford MS is the work of more than one scribe, but the hands are contemporary and the compilation original. *Euphrosine* and *Marie* are in the same hand.

15. Hill edits with a full point at the end of line 564, but it is hard to see how he understood the syntax of the line with this punctuation.

16. In line 572, *"ceste"* would appear to be feminine, perhaps agreeing with "beste saëtee" in the previous line. Esmerade's grammatical femininity is then enhanced in line 573 with the reference to him as *"la cose,"* but in lines 574–75 *"cest castré"* and *"castrez"* are clearly masculine. This switching of grammatical genders here enhances Esmerade's indeterminacy, but also perhaps the danger of his/her presence. It is clear that none of the monks suspects Esmerade is a woman.

17. Thus if the monks' desire is read as heterosexual (and thereby legitimate) because Euphrosine is "really" a woman, their desire seems to entail a fairly "queer" form of heterosexuality.

18. These texts perhaps offer a mirror image of the phenomenon observed by Showalter in *Tootsie,* where a cross-dressed man—a "phallic woman"—makes a better woman than the women in the film (1987, 120–23). But the image is also asymmetrical: as Showalter shows, cross-dressing empowers the hero of *Tootsie*; it empowers Silence only temporarily, and it does not empower Euphrosine because she remains an object of desire for men, which is what she has sought to evade.

19. Although I do not find McCullough's suggestion that the author was a woman persuasive (1977, 185), were we to assume the text was written by a woman, this would have interesting implications for a "queer" reading, given the eroticism of the narrator's relationship with the saint.

WORKS CITED

Aelfric. 1990. *St Eufrosia (or Euphrosyne), Virgin. Aelfric's Lives of the Saints,* ed. Walter W. Skeat. Reprint. London: Kegan. 334–55.

Anson, John. 1974. "The Female Transvestite in Early Monasticism: The Origin and Development of a Motif." *Viator* 5: 1–32.

Bloch, R. Howard. 1991. *Medieval Misogyny and the Invention of Western Romantic Love.* Chicago and London: Chicago University Press.

Boswell, John. 1980. *Christianity, Social Tolerance and Homosexuality: Gay People in Western Europe from the Beginning of the Christian Era to the Fourteenth Century.* Chicago: University of Chicago Press.

———. 1991. "Revolutions, Universals, and Sexual Categories," in Duberman, *et al. Hidden From History.* 17–36.

Bullough, Vern L. 1974. "Transvestites in the Middle Ages." *American Journal of Sociology* 79: 1381–94.

Burgwinkle, William. 1993. "Knighting the Hero: Homo/hetero Affectivity in *Eneas.*" *Exemplaria* 5: 1–43.

Butler, Judith. 1990. *Gender Trouble: Feminism and the Subversion of Identity.* New York: Routledge.

Bynum, Caroline Walker. 1991. *Fragmentation and Redemption: Essays on Gender and the Human Body in Medieval Religion.* New York: Zone Books.

Cazelles, Brigitte. 1991. *The Lady as Saint: A Collection of French Hagiographic Romances of the Thirteenth Century.* Philadelphia: Pennsylvania University Press.

Clemence of Barking. 1964. William Macbain, ed. *The Life of St. Catherine.* Oxford: Oxford University Press.

Duberman, Martin, Martha Vicinus, and Chauncey George, eds. 1991. *Hidden From History: Reclaiming the Gay and Lesbian Past.* New York and London: Penguin.

Duby, Georges. 1978. *Medieval Marriage: Two Models from Twelfth-Century France.* Baltimore and London: Johns Hopkins University Press.

Enéas. 1929. J. J. Salverda de Grave, ed. 2 vols. Paris: Champion.

Frantzen, Allen J. 1993. "When Women Aren't Enough." *Speculum* 68: 445–71.

Fuss, Diana. 1989. *Essentially Speaking: Feminism, Nature and Difference*. New York and London: Routledge.

Garber, Marjorie. 1992. *Vested Interests: Cross-dressing and Cultural Anxiety*. New York: Routledge.

Gaunt, Simon. 1990a. "The Significance of Silence." *Paragraph* 13: 202–16.

———. 1990b. "Marginal Men, Marcabru and Orthodoxy." *Medium Aevum* 59: 55–72.

———. 1995. *Gender and Genre in Medieval French Literature*. Cambridge: Cambridge University Press.

Glasser, Marc. 1981. "Marriage in Medieval Hagiography." *Studies in Medieval and Renaissance History* NS 4: 3–34.

Goody, Jack. 1983. *The Development of the Family and Marriage in Europe*. Cambridge: Cambridge University Press.

Gouiran, Gérard. 1989. "Les saints et leurs familles dans les vies de saints occitanes." *Senefiance* 26: 469–86.

Gravdal, Kathryn. 1991. *Ravishing Maidens: Writing Rape in Medieval French Literature and Law*. Philadelphia: Pennsylvania University Press.

Guerreau-Jalabert, Anita. 1988. "Inceste et sainteté: la *Vie de Saint Grégoire* en français (XIIᵉ siècle)." *Annales* 43: 1291–1319.

Halperin, David M. 1991. "Sex Before Sexuality: Pederasty, Politics and Power in Classical Athens," in Duberman, *et al. Hidden From History.* 37–53.

Heffernan, Thomas. 1988. *Sacred Biography: Saints and their Biographies in the Middle Ages*. New York and Oxford: Oxford University Press.

Hill, Raymond T., ed. 1919. "La Vie de Sainte Euphrosine." *Romanic Review* 10: 159–69 and 191–232.

Huchet, Jean-Charles. 1985. "L'*Enéas*: un roman spéculaire" in *Relire le Roman d'Enéas*, ed. Jean Dufournet. Paris: Champion. 63–81.

Karras, Ruth Mazo. 1990. "Holy Harlots: Prostitute Saints in Medieval Legend." *Journal of the History of Sexuality* 1: 3–32.

Marie de France: Lais. 1944. Alfred Ewert, ed. Oxford: Blackwell.

Matter, E. Ann. 1992. "Introduction." *Medieval Feminist Newsletter* 13: 1–2.

McCullough, Florence. 1977. "Sainte Euphrosine, Saint Alexis and the Turtledove." *Romania* 98: 168–85.

Padgug, Robert. 1991. "Sexual Matters: Rethinking Sexuality in History," in Duberman, *et al. Hidden From History.* 54–64.

Patlagean, Evelyne. 1976. "L'histoire de la femme déguisée en moine et l'évolution de la sainteté féminine." *Studi Medievali* (3rd ser.) 17: 597–623.

Perret, Michèle. 1985. "Travesties et transsexuelles: Yde, Silence, Grisandole." *Romance Notes* 25: 328–40.

Schulenberg, Jane Tibbets. 1986. "The Heroics of Virginity: Brides of Christ and Sacrificial Mutilation," in *Women in the Middle Ages and the Renaissance: Literary and Historical Perspectives*, ed. Mary Beth Rose. Syracuse: Syracuse University Press. 29–72.

Sedgwick, Eve Kosofsky. 1985. *Between Men: English Literature and Male Homosocial Desire*. New York: Columbia University Press.

Sheehan C. B. S., Michael. 1978. "Choice of Marriage Partner in the Middle Ages: Development and Mode of Application of a Theory." *Studies in Medieval and Renaissance History* 1 (1978): 1–33.

Showalter, Elaine. 1987. "Critical Cross-Dressing: Male Feminists and the Woman of the Year," in *Men in Feminism*, ed. Alice Jardine and Paul Smith. New York and London: Methuen. 116–32.

Silence: A Thirteenth Century Romance. 1992. Sarah Roche Mahdi, ed. East Lansing: Colleagues Press.

Storey, Christopher. 1977. "*La Vie de Sainte Euphrosine*: a Reminder of a Neglected Thirteenth-Century Poem." *French Studies* 31: 385–93.

Vie de Saint Alexis. 1946. Christopher Storey, ed. Oxford: Blackwell.

Vie du Pape Saint Grégoire. 1977. Hendrik B. Sol, ed. Amsterdam: Rodopi.

Wogan-Browne, Jocelyn. 1993. "'Clerc u lai, muïne u dame': Women and Anglo-Norman Hagiography in the Twelfth and Thirteenth Centuries," in *Women and Literature in Britain 1110–1500*, ed. Carol Meale. Cambridge: Cambridge University Press. 61–85.

————. 1994. "The Virgin's Tale," in *Feminist Readings in Middle English Literature: The Wife of Bath and All Her Sect*, ed. Ruth Evans and Lesley Johnson. London: Routledge. 165–94.

Sobs and Sighs Between Women

The Homoerotics of Compassion
in *The Book of Margery Kempe*

Kathy Lavezzo

> "Don't be ashamed to weep for Jesus ... Mary Magdalene wasn't ashamed." Mary said this in a
> breathy whisper and wavered in mild pervasive distortion when Margery visited her grave; she
> cupped Margery's breasts in her hands. She viewed Margery's nipples as an opportunity to multi-
> ply flavor, skin tasting honey or sugar.... Mary was naked beneath the thin chemise of a bath-
> house attendant....
>
> —(Gluck 1994, 62)

After her arrest by the Mayor of Leicester as "a fals strumpet, a fals loller, & a fals
deceyuer of þe pepyl" ("a false strumpet, a false Lollard, and a false deceiver of the
people"; Kempe 1940, 112), Margery Kempe receives the kind of interrogation one
might expect of such a suspect—an inquiry into both her religious and her marital
propriety (115–16). But then, unexpectedly, Kempe's heretofore predictable examination takes a remarkable turn, as the mayor tells her "I trowe yow art comyn hedyr to
han a-wey owr wyuys fro us & ledyn hem wyth ye" ("I believe you have come here to
take our wives away from us and lead them with you"; 116). From querying her fidelity
to God and husband, the mayor asserts an attraction between Margery and Leicester's
wives. And the mayor is not the only man in *The Book of Margery Kempe* to express anxiety
over Margery's capacity to draw women from their husbands. Later in the *Book* the
suffragen to York's Archbishop claims that Margery—yet again apprehended as a
heretic—"cownseledyst my Lady Greystokke to forsakyn hir husbonde" ("advised my
Lady Greystoke to forsake her husband"; 133).[1] Both Leicester's mayor and York's
suffragen bespeak a masculine anxiety over female desire: the likelihood, on the one
hand, that behind this mystic's overt claim to love God "a-bouyn al thynge" ("above all

things"; 115) lies a covert attachment to women and, on the other, that women find this female mystic appealing—more appealing, according to the Mayor's charge, than their own husbands (115).[2]

The concern these men display over Margery's relation to other women is well founded; behind this medieval woman's "proper" devotion to Christ stands the desire for a far-from-proper reward. The reward Margery seeks—and, indeed, attains—constitutes a powerful and disruptive form of female homoerotic bonding. This bonding emerges in the context of Margery's primary religious practice: her affective mourning for "owyr Lordys Passyon" ("our Lord's Passion"; 39). During her weeping—an activity triggered by any image, such as a crucifix, which recalls Christ's Passion—Margery registers not only her devotion to the suffering Christ, but also her mystical figuration of the most powerful woman in Christianity, the Virgin Mary; as Christ tells Margery in a vision, "I ȝeve þe gret cryis and roryngys for to makyn ... þat my Modrys sorwe be knowyn by þe" ("I give you great cries and roarings in order that ... my mother's sorrow may be known through you"; 183). Margery performs her Mary-identified lamentation in an extravagantly emotional fashion: through the "plentyows terys & boystows sobbyngys, wyth lowde cryingys and schille schrykyngys" ("plenteous tears and boisterous sobbings, with loud cryings and shrill shriekings"; 107) that distinguish her piety. Often such extremes provoke the censure of masculine authorities (Lochrie 1991, 186–87); indeed, it is Margery's very compulsion (after seeing a crucifix) to mourn that prompts her arrest by Leicester's mayor (111).

In itself, this medieval woman's compassion is unsurprising, given mourning's long-standing designation in Western culture as "woman's work" (Schiesari 1993, 210). As Louise Fradenburg (1990) and Juliana Schiesari (1993) have demonstrated, women's mourning has typically served patriarchal ends, where the female lamenter "piously" consents to death for the sake of a compensatory masculinist "good," such as a dead soldier's eternal fame, or the sake of the nation (cf. Marcuse 1959, 74–75). For premodern Christianity, such significations often hinged upon a stoic mourning style; for example, church fathers imagined the Virgin possessing a modest grief, bolstered by her faith in the Resurrection. Margery's excessive lamentation diverges from such devotional decorum. The always-emotional Margery challenges patristic theology by portraying Mary as an inconsolable witness to the Passion. But the transgressions that obtain through Margery's mourning consist of more than her failure to signify calmly the "principle of resurrection" (Kristeva 1987, 251); they display one way in which women may have refigured mourning as an erotic and potentially empowering form of female same-sex bonding in late medieval Europe.[3]

Margery was not alone in her somatic piety, as Christian devotion underwent a markedly emotional turn in the late Middle Ages—a transformation rooted significantly in the Franciscan meditative tradition, with its Marian affective piety and literal imagining of the crucified Christ (Gibson 1989, 1–18; Kieckhefer 1984, 106; see also Duffy 1992, 260; Bennett 1982, 59). Neither was Margery unique in provoking ecclesiastical censure, which criticized compassionate excess in art as well as life: "We ... do not excuse those who portray in pictures or writings how the mother of God fainted upon the earth at the cross, overwhelmed and senseless from pain, similar to those women who, caught up in their sorrow ... proclaim loudly their misery...." (Hamburgh 1981, 47). As this sixteenth-century condemnation displays, anxiety over depictions of excessive compassion directed themselves not only at literature, but also at the visual arts, a medium epitomizing the late medieval devotional tendency toward vivid images. In speculating that the female homoeroticism represented in Margery's *Book* suggests a more general European phenomenon of the late Middle Ages, I will refer to visual representations of the Passion and Lamentation that complement the scenes of female-female bonding in Margery's text. Censure of depictions of an inconsolable Virgin and of actual female mourning practices may have been motivated by precisely the same anxiety over desire between women that lay behind the Mayor of Leicester's condemnation of Margery.[4] As Lochrie observes in her commentary on such attacks, the church criticized representations of an emotional Mary insofar as they "threatened to valorize not only female mourning practices but female mystical practices as well" (187). Even further, these depictions made available an emotional and even erotic vision of a woman, Mary, for consumption by the many women who made up a major component of the audience for Christian artifacts.

While Margery's compassion threatens to supplant the figure of Christ with that of a woman performing her figurative relation to an ever-powerful Virgin Mary, thus displaying a feminine version of the masculinist pleasures of historical identification discussed by Louise Fradenburg and Carla Freccero in this volume, this scenario is made doubly problematic by the extent to which these boisterous tears signify Margery's identification with not only Mary, but also all other Virgin-identified women. Margery's comparison with Bridget of Sweden, whose glorification of Mary bordered on the heretical (Graef 1963, 309), throughout the *Book*—in which Margery even makes a pilgrimage to the Brigittine convent at Syon—offers just one instance of how Margery's attachment to Mary also implies her identification with other holy women.[5] A metonymic relation between the suffering Virgin Mother and a community of religious women may even have figured as a trope in medieval passion discourses; in a Harley lyric from the Sequence *Stabat iuxta Christi crucem*, Mary constructs a triangulated relation between herself, her son, and "all þo þat to [her] grede, maiden, wif, ant fol wymmon" ("all who call to [her], maidens, wives and foolish women"; Brook 1956; 57, lines 47–48; Stanbury 1991, 1088).

Just as Margery—like the Harley lyric's Virgin—may include a broadly defined female community in the circuitry of suffering between herself and Christ, her boisterous sobbings (40) render Margery herself an object of both female same-sex identification and homoerotic desire. In locating the operations of both identification and desire in the scenes of female affective mourning staged within the *Book,* I follow Diana Fuss in arguing for the "the collusion and collapsibility" of these two terms (Fuss 1993, 12). Dismantling the fundamental psychoanalytic law of their independence, Fuss argues for an imbricated relation between same-sex identifications and desires—where, for example, a woman's desire to *be* like another woman may slip into the desire to *have* that woman, or where desire may even underwrite an identification, and vice versa. Thus, by aligning Margery's affective piety with her longing to be Christ's mother, I am pointing to Margery's identification with, and also her desire for, Mary and all other women who share in the Virgin's sorrows. Margery renders herself, through this display of woman-identified sorrow, an object of identification and desire in her own right, available for consumption by other Christian women.

As the triangulated organization of Passion devotion displays, the circulation of identifications and desires between women in the *Book* depends on the presence (and frequently the exchange) of a masculine icon—Christ. The *imago Christi* serves in this structure of relations as the *medium* through which Margery enables both her imaginative and her actual bonding with the Virgin Mother and other Christian women. This "traffic in Christ"—to appropriate Gayle Rubin's phrase (1975)—suggests how an inverted version of the homosocial bonding so powerfully discussed by Eve Sedgwick (1985) may have been produced in the context of medieval compassion devotion. It displays how, as Terry Castle has argued, the linkage of two female terms around a single male term effects an "alternate structure" to that of the male-female-male erotic triad—"a female-male-female triangle" that redistributes power to the two female figures, while relegating the male to the passive position of mediator (1993, 72).[6]

It is in arguing for the representation of female homoeroticism in Margery's *Book* that I most clearly depart from the *Book's* other readings since its discovery in 1934. While some of the most sensitive readers of gender and the construction of the female subject in the *Book* discuss Margery's affective identification with Mary, these critics locate only heterosexual desires at work in this text.[7] Neglecting to trace the homoerotic valences of female-female identifications in such artifacts is by no means unusual in medieval scholarship. With a few notable exceptions, scholars have left unexamined the question of desire between women, especially in the context of female affective spirituality, in the Middle Ages.[8] The lack of analyses sensitive to female same-sex desire results, in part, from the fact that the concept of a "lesbian" identity was not articulated in medieval textual culture, and even on those rare occasions when the question of sex between women was addressed, its discussion was at best obscure (Brown 1986, 17; Traub 1992; 1993). The extreme difficulty of exploring female same-sex relations is, in part, an effect of the patriarchal bias of late medieval signifying practices, which aimed explicitly at pushing the female subject outside their discursive boundaries.[9] For example, Jean Gerson's fifteenth-century reference to female sodomy as a sin that "should not be named or written" displays his intention to hide "lesbian" desires from both the eyes and ears of his culture (Brown 1986, 19).

Because medieval heterosexist cultural authorities occluded manifestations of desire between women, my essay engages with a number of modern theories of sexuality—all of which are indebted to and revise psychoanalysis—in an effort to delineate late medieval structures of female same-sex desire. While my methodology risks charges of anachronism, I contend its necessity for a politically engaged feminist inquiry;[10] and I claim that applying modern theories of the sex/gender system to premodern cultural productions does not in fact constitute the strange imposition it may seem to be.[11] If we look to late medieval devotional practices, we find that, notwithstanding attempts by ecclesiastical authorities to deny a voice to same-sex desires, imbedded within medieval religious practices is a tendency for medieval "writers and artists to fuse or interchange ... genders" that lends itself remarkably well to recent theories of sexuality (Bynum 1991, 114). The fluidity with which ostensibly male and female religious figures were imagined (where Christ could be likened to a mother and Mary to a priest), together with the prominent position cross-dressing and cross-identification played in devotion, suggest how, in the words of Caroline Walker Bynum, "the late Middle Ages found gender reversal at the heart of Christian art and Christian worship" (1991, 92).[12] The medieval Christian perception of gender as not an essential and fixed *category* but an ever-changing and contingent *role* appropriable through identificatory performance, not only stands in uneasy relation to disciplinary discourses such as Gerson's; it also bears considerable similarities to contemporary revisionary gender analyses.[13] If, as Bynum argues, religious thinkers "used gender imagery ... fluidly" and "put men and women on a continuum," what, we might ask, is there to prevent "queer" identifications and desires from emerging in the context of Christian devotional practices such as Margery's?

While the gender fluidity that generally characterized medieval Christian piety offers us an identificatory field in which a number of "queer" positions could arise in any devotional context during the Middle Ages, the particular trends produced within Margery's East Anglian culture may have especially enabled female-female identifications and desires. Christian women had received an extraordinary amount of prestige in this region of England.[14] East Anglian Osborn Bokenham, for instance, wrote the first all-female hagiographic anthology, whose lives included those of popular local saints such as Margaret, Anne, and Katherine.[15] But above all other Christian holy women, East Anglians revered the Virgin Mary. While England's identification as "the dower of the Virgin" suggests Mary's prominence in the national imaginary, in East Anglia Mariology verged upon a Mariolatry in which Christ's mother may have figured more greatly than Christ himself (Gibson 1989, 138). From the local (and international) renown accorded the Marian shrine at Walsingham, to the preponderance of Marian guilds and confraternities in towns such as Norwich, to the Marian preoccupations of the "N-town" cycle, abundant evidence points to Mary's prominence in Norfolk and Suffolk cultures. The prestige East Anglians allotted Mary would have rendered her an easily accessible object for identification by the region's women,[16] who could identify with Mary not only as Christ's mother, but as an active subject of Christian history in her own right—as, for example, the N-town "Assumption" play attests (Gibson 1989, 168).

At the same time that Mary and other women saints may have served as attractive objects for identification by East Anglian women, the very potential for identification between Christian women was imaginatively accomplished by the female groupings portrayed in East Anglian Christian art and literature—such as the "whole galaxy" of virgin martyrs depicted with such frequency upon rood screens that they outnumber all other saintly groupings on these liturgical "stage sets" (Duffy 1992, 171).[17] The predominance of Mary, together with such portrayals of religious female groups, may very well have reflected as well as produced female-female identification in East Anglia. Figuring in homologous relation to these representations of powerful women and female groups in East Anglian discourses are the two alternative communities of lay women who lived together in fifteenth-century Norwich. While we know little about these "*sorores castitate dedicate*" ("sisters dedicated to chastity"; Tanner 1984, 65) their status as the only groups of their kind known in England suggests that the climate for women gathering together in nontraditional circumstances was especially evident in Margery Kempe's native region.[18] Perhaps, indeed, it was the fear that Margery would "han a-wey" their wives for the purpose of forming such a community that lay behind the Mayor of Leicester's accusation. We can only speculate on what the women in such a community did with each other; perhaps they took their cue from the four allegorical daughters of God represented in the N-town Mary play, whose heavenly parliament, mediating the narrative movement from Mary's Betrothal to her Annunciation, culminates in an exchange of kisses between these women, in which "*osculabunt pariter omnes*" ("all kiss each other"; Merideth 1987, 72).

The rich cultural context I have sketched out, a religious environment particularly conducive to the imagining and production of female communities, suggests how the bonds between women at stake in Margery's devotional practices may have developed out of her native region's spiritual preoccupations. Of course, however prominently women figured in East Anglia, this society was finally patriarchal in character; within this world, as Hope Weissman observes, "Margery's encounters with women authorities . . . occur as decided exceptions" (1982, 202). Yet despite the marginalized position her engagements with powerful women occupy in the *Book* with respect to her many encounters with male authorities, Margery's feminine interactions—homoerotic or otherwise—occur more frequently than many readings of the *Book* indicate. Moreover, the tearful *means* by which Margery attains both her visionary and actual female homoerotic attachments constitute, in fact, *the* dominant refrain in the text. In an otherwise uneven, nonchronological, and loosely organized "lytyl tretys" ("little treatise"; 1), the spectacular sobs and sighs woven throughout Margery's *Book* hold together the text's often confusing mix of worldly adventures, domestic duties, and mystical revelations. Thus Margery's affective mourning exerts a unifying effect that is twofold, binding together both the *Book* itself and, at times, the women represented in it. The frequency of her tears suggests, moreover, that while Margery may not consistently succeed in bonding with women in her *Book*, she is always—consciously or unconsciously—trying to.

VISUAL PLEASURE AND LITURGICAL SPECTACLE

As Margery herself puts it, her lamentations take place "specialy on Sundays" (84)— that is, during the Mass, the event in which most late medieval devotional practices occurred (Duffy 1992, 91–130). On the analogous occasion of the "sermownys [which]

Duchemen & oþer men" ("sermons [which] German and other men"; 98) preach in Italy during Margery's pilgrimage to Rome and Jerusalem, a tearful outburst results from Margery's failure to comprehend these foreign men's words.[19] With a "mornyng cher for lak of vndirstondyng" ("a sorrowful expression at her lack of understanding"; 98), Margery complains to Christ, who agrees to "preche" and "teche" her personally. Not surprisingly, Christ's preaching constitutes a vision of his Passion, which leaves Margery inebriated with weeping:

> … sche turnyd hir fyrst on þe o syde & sithyn on þe oþer wyth gret sobbyng, vn-mythy to kepyn hir-selfe in stabilnes for þe vnqwenchabyl fyer of lofe whech brent ful sor in hir sowle. þan meche pepyl wonderyd up-on hir, askyng hir what sche eyled, to whom sche as a creatur al wowndyd wyth lofe & as reson had fayled, cryed wyth lowde voys, "þe passyon of Crist sleth me."

> … she turned herself first on one side and then on the other, with great sobbing, unable to keep herself stable because of the unquenchable fire of love burning in her soul. Then many people wondered at her, asking her what ailed her, to whom she, as a creature all wounded with love and as one whose reason had failed her, cried with a loud voice, "The Passion of Christ slays me" (98–99).

Significantly, while Margery may tell the onlookers that Christ's Passion lies behind her tearful gesticulations, her bodily gestures—as represented in Margery's *Book*—seem to "say" something else. For while the Passion may stir the "fire of love" in Margery, the spectacle of her pleasure deflects attention away from, not only the "Duchemen" and other male preachers, but also away from Jesus himself to the writhing figure of Margery.

Margery's sobs recall the Virgin Mary's compassion. The affective logic of this moment in the *Book* also follows that of late medieval visual representations of the Virgin during the Crucifixion—where, despite Christ's central positioning, the display of a grieving Virgin Mother vies with that of her dead son for attention (figs. 1–3).[20] Just as these distracting images of Mary's sorrow threaten to upstage Christ's Passion narrative, when Margery's copious tears and sensuous tossings and turnings arise, they break the flow of the Mass (and here, the public sermons), calling the service to a halt, and replacing the Christ-centered drama with the spectacle of a woman overcome by the "fire of love."[21] Confronted by Margery's disruptive tears, men in the *Book,* such as the Mayor of Leicester, seek to punish Margery; alternately, others seek to rescue her, while still others fetishize her into a reassuring mother figure (see Mulvey 1992, 64). The particular passage cited above, however, specifies no masculine reaction to Margery, only a feminine response. And what this feminine reaction reveals is the attraction— indeed the love—that Margery's rhythmic and autoerotic wellings stir within women: "þe good women, hauyng compassyon of hir sorwe & gretly meruelyng of hir wepyn & hir crying, meche þe mor þei louyd hir" ("The good women, having compassion for her sorrow and greatly marveling at her weeping and crying, loved her much more"; 98).

Indeed, the women love Margery so much that "þei, desiryng to make hir solas & comfort ... preyid hir and in a maner compellyd hir to comyn hom to hem, willyng þat sche xulde not gon fro hem" ("they, desiring to console and comfort her ... prayed her and in a way compelled her to come home with them, desiring that she should not go from them"; 99).

Just as Margery's affective mourning attracts feminine devotion in this episode, Mary—in the works of Van Ghent and Di Tommi—likewise draws the grieving, loving and even erotic attention of many, if not all, of the women represented in the visual works, each of which depicts the collapsed Virgin supported by two other women,[22] of whom one is grasping the Virgin's breast. The feminine display that so threatens to disrupt the ostensible Christic focus of these visual scenes thus involves not merely Mary's grief, but also the compassionate and potentially erotic attentions of the women about her. In these representations of individual women fondling Mary's breast, we might locate an emphasis on Mary's body and her sexuality akin to that which Leo Steinberg claims was placed upon Christ (1983). Of course, Mary's breasts here possess multiple iconographic significations—among them, her intercessory role, which Mary assumed by virtue of her breasts, which nursed Jesus (Lane 1984, 7). But alongside such theological meanings, I would argue, the representation of one woman caressing another's breast in these artifacts also carries with it a sexual referent—as representations of the body always at least potentially do—especially given the erotically charged source of much Marian breast iconography, the Song of Songs (Mundy 1981–1982).[23]

In the same way that her son's suffering presumably produced Mary's compassion in the Passion representations, Margery's mystical experience begins with a visionary communication with Christ. But the product of this mystical dalliance signifies a feminine self-reflexive pleasure or *jouissance* which triggers a narrative of "primary intensity"—a melodrama of sorts—between Margery and the women around her, a scene of feminine bonding akin to that which the Passion depictions dramatically visualize (Rich 1983, 192). These pleasurable sobs draw attention from the German preachers and even from Christ—the ostensible object of Margery's contemplation—to the homoerotic desires circulating between Margery herself and the women who love her.

HOLY BABIES, PHALLIC MOTHERS
While the Mass, with its emphasis upon the Passion, most frequently leads to Margery's tearful outbursts, another common stimulus for Margery's excessive weeping—any image of the baby Jesus—results from the connection medieval culture drew between Christ's passion and his infancy (Kieckhefer 1984, 106–107; Sinanoglou 1973). In the same way that the birth and death of Christ were linked, for example, by diptychs juxtaposing the Madonna with the Man of Sorrows and by spiritual writers such as St. Bridget of Sweden (Blunt 1973, 245), Margery swathes Jesus "wyth byttyr teerys of compassyon, hauyng mend of þe scharp deth þat he schuld suffer" ("with bitter tears of

Figure 1. Joos van Ghent, *Calvary* Triptych: Central Panel; Ghent, St. Bavon Cathedral *(Giraudon/Art Resource)*.

compassion, mindful of the painful death that he would suffer"; 19) during a vision in which she serves as both Mary's and her baby's handmaiden (Keickhefer 1984, 106–107; Kempe 1940, 265–66). To move Margery, the baby need not be Jesus himself: while witnessing a poor woman with "a lytel manchylde sowkyng on hir brest" ("a little baby boy sucking on her breast"; 94) Margery bursts "al in-to wepyng, as þei sche had seyn owr Lady and hir sone in tyme of hys Passyon" ("into weeping, as though she had seen our Lady and her son during the time of his Passion"; 94). Just as Margery's tears during

Figure 2. Joos van Ghent, *Calvary*: Detail Central Panel.

the Mass episode described above evoke the loving attention of her female witnesses, her sobs before the impoverished nursing mother lead to "þe powr woman hauyng compassyon of hir wepyng" ("the poor woman having compassion over her weeping"; 94). A similar trajectory obtains in the extraordinary passage below, in which Margery encounters a number of women with a "child," who share her devotion to the baby Jesus. The suggestive moment occurs during Margery's travels from Jerusalem to Rome, via Venice and Assisi, with a fellow pilgrim, a woman possessing a curious devotional doll modeled "aftyr our Lord":

> þer came too Grey Frerys & a woman þat cam wyth hem fro Ierusalem, & sche had wyth hir an asse þe whech bar a chyst & an ymage þerin mad aftyr our Lord.... And þe woman the which had þe ymage in þe chist, whan þei comyn in good cityes, sche toke owt þe ymage owt of hir chist & sett it in worshepful wyfys lappys. & þei wold puttyn schirtys þerup-on & kyssyn it as þei it had ben God hym-selfe. &, whan þe creature sey þe worshep & þe reverens þat þei dedyn to þe ymage, sche was takyn wyth swet deuocyon & swet meditacyons þat sche wept wyth gret sobbyng & lowde crying.

> there came two Grey Friars and a woman that came with them from Jerusalem, and she had with her an ass which bore a chest and an image therein fashioned in the image of our Lord.... And the woman who had the image in the chest, when they arrived in great cities, took the image out of her chest and set it upon distinguished wives' laps. And the women would put shirts upon it and kiss it as though it were God himself. And, when the creature saw the worship and the reverence that they gave to the image, she was seized with such sweet devotion and sweet meditations that she wept with great sobbing and loud crying. (77–78)

As Bynum observes, practices such as these women's attentions to the Christ-child were not uncommon among both the medieval female laity and religious, who "acted out maternal . . . roles in the liturgy, decorating life-sized statues of the Christ child for the Christmas creche" (1991, 198; Schlegel 1970). According to Bynum, such behavior signifies one way medieval women "simply" took "ordinary nurturing roles over into their most profound religious experiences" (1991, 197). If we apply Bynum's under-

Figure 3. Luca di Tommi, *Crucifixion* c. 1365 (*The Fine Arts Museums of San Francisco*).

standing of these practices to the "worshepful wyfys" in Margery's *Book*, we might call them precisely what she calls the fifteenth-century "nuns and beguines" who engaged in decorating a cradle for the liturgy: "just little girls, playing with dolls!" (198).[24]

If the wives are in fact regressing to the role of girls "playing with dolls," what is it that little girls do when they play with dolls? According to what Margaret Homans has called "the social imperative to measure all women's activities by their suitability to motherhood" (1986, 27), the "proper" cultural interpretation of this activity presumably would be that, through their doll-playing, girls playfully foreshadow what their sexual identity as women inevitably will demand of them: marriage and child-rearing.[25] The women would then be using the Christ doll for the same reason that they supposedly have a baby—as a "penis substitute," the fantastic fulfillment of their desire "to appropriate for (themselves) the genital organ that has a cultural monopoly on value" (Irigaray 1985, 87). However, Freud himself stresses an important difference between little girls playing with dolls and women having babies. In his essays on femininity and feminine sexuality, Freud contends that, while playing with dolls is often viewed as an indication of the first stirrings of femininity within a child, this activity in fact has little to do with the "proper" passive role which distinguishes the female subject from her masculine counterpart (1963, 205). According to Freud, the very active attention little girls give their dolls—much like the caressings and dressings which the wives lavish on the Christ doll—is not directed toward any masculine object, but to the original feminine object of their affection: their mothers. That is, when little girls play with their dolls, they play with their mothers, albeit indirectly. On the question of a daughter's sexual aims regarding her original maternal object, Freud argues that, although part of a girl's libido passively enjoys being suckled, fed, and cleansed by her mother, another part of the child's energies actively mimics, in play, her sexually charged passive experiences (1963, 205). Thus, identification with and desire for the mother merge in the girl's doll-play, as the girl routes through the doll (in Freud's words) "the exclusiveness of her attachment to her mother, accompanied by a total neglect of her father-object" (1963, 206; see also Freud 1973, 128; Fuss 1993).

Applied to the episode from the *Book*, Freud's scenario shows how what may seem to be a locale for "worshep & ... reverens" aimed at Christ makes a space for the representation of an attachment to a woman. The women are recalling a pre-Oedipal phallic sexuality, directing through the doll the original maternal object of their affection. But the doll here functions not solely as a conduit for the ladies' original maternal desires; it enables the condensation of a number of female same-sex fantasies. As the doll is not just any doll, but an image "mad after owyr Lord," it figures also as a means by which the wives, taking such good care of baby Jesus, perform their identification with and desire for *his* holy mother, the Virgin Mary.[26] Moreover, even as the doll enables the wives to perform their individual attachments to both their mothers and "owyr Lady," its fondling and passage from wifely lap to wifely lap additionally renders it a medium through which these women homosocially bond. In sharing the doll, the women perfom a kind of traffic in Christ; endowing this Christic commodity with a symbolic exchange value through their feminine labor, their "worshep & ... reverens," the wives refigure Christ as the bearer of feminine needs and desires.[27]

While the doll's function in the *Book* suggests how a passivized Christ could enable female homoeroticism, Margery herself speaks of no such possibility, telling the reader only that the women kiss the doll "as though it had been God himself." Registering only her identification with the ladies, she explains that:

> sche was meuyd in so mych þe mor as, while sche was in Inglond, sche had hy meditacyons in þe byrth & þe childhode of Crist, & sche thankyd God for-as-mech as sche saw þes creaturys han so gret feth in þat sche sey wyth hir bodily eye lych as sche had be-forn wyth hir gostly eye.

> she was moved so much the more since, while she was in England she had high meditations on the birth and the childhood of Christ, and she thanked God forasmuch as she saw these creatures had as much faith in what she saw with her bodily eye as she had before with her spiritual eye (78).

Yet Margery's own somatic response to the women tells us something else—that she not only identifies with the ladies' maternal devotion to Christ, but may indeed also imagine *herself* as the object of the wives' attentions. Of course, the affectionate "worshep & ... reverens" which the ladies lavish upon the Christ doll can effect no "response" from that inanimate object. But the wives' attentions do cause a proliferation of sweet tears in Margery, so that it seems that it is not the fetishized doll but the body of Margery herself that receives their caresses. Moreover, by means of her sobs, this fantasy is realized, literally, by Margery:

> Whan þes good women seyn þis creatur wepyn, sobbyn & cryen so wondirfully & mythyly þat sche was nerhand ouyrcomyn þerwyth, þan þei ordeyned a good soft bed & leyd hir þerup-on & comfortyd hir as mech as þei myth for owyr Lordys lofe, blyssed mot he ben.

> When these good women saw this creature weeping, sobbing and crying so wonderfully and mightily that she was nearly overcome by it, they prepared a good soft bed and laid her upon it and comforted her as much as they could for our Lord's love, blessed may he be (78).

Here Margery not only turns from spectator into spectacle, but also shifts from her position as an imagined recipient of feminine attention to its outright object. Through her sobs, Margery compels the women to abandon the doll, turn to her, put her to bed, and provocatively "[comfort] hir as mech as þei myth." We cannot know exactly how the ladies comfort Margery; yet the playful and affectionate prelude to this moment, as well as its bedroom setting, may suggest that the woman assuming the doll's position may have received from the wives kisses like those originally directed at the Christ-child.

While the Christ doll passage in Margery's book illustrates one site in medieval culture for the playful production of roles both pious and proper, it also illustrates the capacity for the displacement, at that very same site, of these roles. Just as the Christ-child's presence legitimates the women's gathering, conferring a pious and proper motivation upon their congregation, its position as passive and commodified object for exchange allows for a homosocial relation among the women.[28] And the intrusion of Margery's tears adds a provocative twist to this situation, whereby attending to the image of the Christ-child ends in attending to another woman.[29]

ENVISIONED COMPASSIONS

Invariably, Margery's mystical revelations prompt her affective piety: it is earlier visions of Christ's infancy that amplify Margery's somatic response to the ladies' behavior in the Christ-child episode (78), and, similarly, it is Christ's voice "sownding in her sowle" ("sounding in her soul"; 98) that produces Margery's spectacular sobs during the Mass. While Margery's contemplations always constitute the hidden spiritual referent for the visible tears and cries that enable bonds between women, the Passion-centered world of Margery's visionary experience itself also serves as a mystical locale for feminine bonding. Margery offers the most extensive account of her visions of the Passion in chapters 78 to 81 of her book, where she describes the "gostly syghtys" ("spiritual visions"; 190–91) that occur primarily during Lent. Margery's visions offer a detailed and often gory imagining of Christ's suffering that departs significantly from the Gospels, and instead realizes popular medieval meditations on the Passion, such as Nicholas Love's *Myrror of the Blessyd Lyf of Christ*, a translation of pseudo-Bonaventure's *Meditationes Vitae Christi* now ascribed to Giovanni de Caulibus (Sticca 1988, 196 n.13). Love's vernacular text, authorized by the Archbishop of Canterbury, Thomas Arundel, constituted part of the church's attempt to at once produce and control private devotion during a time of rising lay literacy. As Sarah Beckwith and Elizabeth Salter note, the "ideological function" of such vernacular works lay precisely in their capacity to mitigate the effects of Lollard heresies by textually "stage-manag[ing]" the reader to identify compassionately with a suffering Christ (Beckwith 1986, 45). To a certain extent, Margery's text seems to realize the aims of church authorities: for example, after having envisioned Christ's "betyng . . . & bofetyng" ("beating and buffeting"), Margery imagines him telling her "Dowtyr, þes sorwys & many mo suffyrd I for þi lofe, & diuers peynys . . . þu has great cawse to luyn me ryght wel" ("Daughter, these sorrows and many more I suffered for your love, and diverse pains . . . you have good reason to love me very much"; 190–91).

Yet, just as Margery's vision seems influenced by the *Myrror* in much the way authorities such as Arundel might have hoped, it also reflects and elaborates upon aspects of Love's text (and works like it) in ways that the church may not have desired. For Love "stage-manages" the spectator to identify not only with Christ, but also with other "characters in the drama" he outlines (Bennet 1982, 54). The dramatic direction which especially affects Margery is the appeal Love makes to his reader on the Sabbath following Christ's death: "And thou also by deuoute ymaginacioun, as thou were there bodily present, comfort our lady and that other felauschippe, prayenge hem to ete somwhat, for ȝit they ben fastinge" ("And also by devout imagination, as if you were physically present there, comfort our Lady and that other fellowship, imploring them to eat something, for they are still fasting"; Love 1992, 256; cf. Kempe, 335 n. 195/7). In addition to carrying out literally Love's entreaty, making "for owr Lady a good cawdel" ("for our Lady a good hot drink of gruel and spiced wine"; Kempe 1940, 195), Margery extends Love's notion of comforting and identifying with Mary throughout her vision, in which Margery serves as the Virgin's handmaiden (190). Moreover, it is Mary with whom Margery most closely identifies in her Passion visions, which consistently balance images of Christ's suffering with the exchange of tears between the Virgin and Margery.

As we have seen, Margery's desire to be with Mary, to serve and to share sorrows with her, is not confined to this passage, but surfaces throughout the *Book.* And when this desire arises in Margery's visions, it almost always coincides with Christ's legitimating presence—as it does in the book's eighty-sixth chapter, where Christ, enumerating the many things Margery has done to merit his gratitude, lists Margery's practice of keeping both him *and* his mother as bedfellows: "And also, dowtyr, I thank þe for all þe tymys þat þu hast herberwyd me & my blissyd Modyr in þi bed" ("And also, daughter, I thank you for all the times that you have harbored me and my blessed Mother in your bed"; 214).[30] Apparently, this line was a bit too provocative for one (presumably) Carthusian annotator of Margery's *Book*, who wrote beside it in the Butler Bowdon manuscript's margin the word "gostly" or spiritual (Kempe 1940, xxxvi). Significantly,

Christ consistently figures in his triadic relation with Margery and Mary as a passive presence: as a helpless baby, a grown man suffering the Passion, or a lifeless body deposed from the Cross.[31] In Margery's vision of the Passion, for example, while she and the Virgin actively exchange sorrows, both women are repeatedly beholding a Christ who is both passivized and infantilized:

> & [he] went forth ful mekely a-forn hem al modyr-nakyd as he was born to a peler of ston
> & spak no worde a-geyn hem but leet hem do & sey what þei wolde ... & than hyr thowt
> owr Lady wept wondir sor. And þerfor þe sayd creatur must nedys wepyn & cryin whan
> sche sey swech gostly sy3tys in hir sowle as freschly & as verily as 3yf it had ben don in
> dede in hir bodily syght, and hir thowt þat owr Lady & sche wer al-wey to-gedyr to se owr
> Lordys peynys.

> And he went forth very meekly before them all mother-naked as he was born to a pillar
> of stone and spoke no words against them but allowed them to do and say what they
> wished ... and then she thought our Lady wept wondrously sorely. And therefore the
> said creature had to necessarily weep and cry when she saw such spiritual sights in her
> soul as freshly and as truly as if they had actually happened before her physical sight, and
> she thought that our Lady and she were always together to see our Lord's sufferings (190).

Unrestrainedly weeping, the Mary depicted in Margery's vision conflicts with the stoic Virgin, unique to her sex, often emphasized by Marian scholarship (see Coletti 1993); rather, Mary signifies here as a woman with whom Margery identifies and homosocially shares sorrows over a suffering Christ. The women's inability to help Jesus gives rise to the exchange of grief between them: as Mary tells Margery, she "must nedys suffyr it for (her) Sonys lofe" ("must needs suffer it for [her] Son's love"; 189). Yet while the Passion ostensibly must be endured for the love of Jesus, it also—with the passivization and infantilization that accompany it in the *Book*—becomes something that "must nedys" be so that Margery and Mary can get together, sighing and sobbing over the helpless body of Jesus.

Just as the Passion of an infantilized Christ, "al modyr-naked as he was born," enables Margery to mourn with the Virgin Mother, the Lamentation of Christ's lifeless body similarly occasions the embrace of loss among women. This emotionally charged scene focuses initially upon Mary, and then broadens to the women around her, whom the Virgin gives leave to fondle Christ's limp limbs, lavish them with kisses, wash them with tears:

> ... And þan owr blisful Lady bowyd down to hir Sonys body & kyssyd hys mowth & wept
> so plentyuowsly ouyr hys blissyd face þat sche wesch a-wey þe blod of hys face wyth þe
> terys of hir eyne. An þan þe creatur thowt sche herd Mary Mawdelyn seyn to owr Lady, "I
> pray 3ow, Lady, 3yf me leue to handelyn & kyssyn hys feet, for at þes get I grace." Anon
> owr Lady 3af leue to hir & all þo þat wer þer-abowte to do what worschip & reverns þei

wold to þat precyows body. And a-non Mary Mawdelyn toke owr Lordys feet & owr Ladijs sisterys toke hys handys, þe on syster on hand & þe oþer sister an-oþer hand, & wept ful sor in kissyng of þo handys & of þo precyows feet.

... And then our blissful Lady bowed down to her Son's body and kissed his mouth and wept so plentifully over his blessed face that she washed away the blood upon his face with the tears from her eyes. And then the creature thought that she heard Mary Magdalene say to our Lady, "I pray you, Lady, give me leave to handle and kiss his feet, for I get grace from them." At once our Lady gave leave to her and all those who were there thereabout to perform what worship and reverence they desired to that precious body. And at once Mary Magdalene took our Lord's feet and our Lady's sisters took his hands, the one sister one hand and the other sister another hand, and wept very sorely in kissing those hands and those precious feet (193–94).

Margery's vision of the Lamentation reflects the influence of the *Meditationes*, as it describes both Mary supporting Christ's head in her lap and Mary Magdalen holding "the feet at which she had formerly found so much grace" (1961, 342); a striking realization and extension of this dramatic scene occurs in Giotto's famous *Lamentation* (1305–1306; fig. 4). Depicting four women surrounding, handling and grieving over Christ's body, this visual piece, like Margery's *Book*, portrays women assuming an active mourning role.[32]

Like the Christ doll, the body of Christ in the Lamentation is passivized, constituted less by anything Christ actually does than by what is done to him. That is, the power the Christic object represents is not intrinsic to itself, but is, rather, conferred upon it by the women, whose tears, caresses, and kisses invest the Christ-doll as well as the dead Christ's body with meaning. Through this investment in a passivized Christ, the women resignify his body as object for their own desiring ends, crucially resisting, at least for the duration of their performance, subordination to masculine power structures.[33] Instead of demonstrating the exalted acceptance of Christ's sacrifice prescribed by patristic theology, the women around the dead Christ spectacularly and sensuously sob, exploiting the lack embodied by Christ as well as their own gendered relation to the dead (Kempe 1940, 74–75). In opposition to a serene consent to death, which would presumably generate symbolic capital in a patriarchal economy, the feminine erotic exhibition of tears in Margery's vision produces an alternate form of symbolic capital (or, to use Kathryn Bond Stockton's term, "anti-capital") in an alternate economy of feminine desire (Stockton 1992, 348). Now appropriated as a fetishized commodity exchanged among women, the Lord's lifeless body is passed to Mary, then offered by Mary to the Magdalen, and finally extended to Mary's two sisters, uniting all four women around their communal object of desire.

As I have argued in this essay, *The Book of Margery Kempe* suggests how we might rethink Christian women's mourning, as an active and empowering practice. Whether mediated by the figure of a passivized Christ, or dispensing with that third Christic

Figure 4. Giotto, *Lamentation* 1305–1306. Detail; Arena Chapel, Padua *(Alinari/Art Resource)*.

term entirely, the female homoeroticism produced at the site of female lamentation constitutes a disruptive act in which the proper turns improper, and the pious strays into the perverse. Moreover, as a cultural artifact, Margery's *Book* offers us compelling grounds for resisting the kinds of theological hermeneutics which often dictate that medieval texts such as *The Book of Margery Kempe* must be interpreted only in terms of the extent to which the spiritual subjects they produce are heretical or holy.[34] We need instead a more flexible definition of medieval spirituality, where devout ends mingle with and possibly serve as a legitimizing cover for other, less decorous and patriarchal ends; where, to turn to one final example from *The Book of Margery Kempe*, a woman's imagining of heaven, as described by Christ, suggests a version of the afterlife that is predominantly female: "I xal take þe be þe on Hand in Hevyn & my modyr be þe oþer hand & so xalt þu dawnsyn in Hevyn wyth oþer holy maydens & virgynes. . . ." ("I shall take you by the one hand in Heaven and my mother by the other hand, and so shall you dance in Heaven with other holy maidens and virgins. . . ."; 53). Picturing the after-life as a kind of alternate female community—as a group of women dancing, united through the medium of Christ—Margery suggests, yet again, that behind her Christic devotions lies the longing for a very feminine, and very pleasurable, reward.

NOTES

Many thanks belong to Theresa Coletti, Patricia Fumerton, Carolyn Dinshaw and, especially, Jody Enders, for their generous comments on earlier drafts of this essay. I owe a special debt to Carla Freccero, whose editorial suggestions crucially improved the essay, and to the brilliant and inspiring example of Louise Fradenburg, who has overseen this project from its inception. I dedicate this essay to Harry Stecopoulos, without whom I could never have written it. Versions of this paper were given at the 1993 Early Modern conference at U.C. Santa Barbara, the 1993 CEMERS Medieval and Renaissance conference at S.U.N.Y. Binghamton, and the 1995 UC LGBA conference at U.C. Santa Barbara.

1. Elizabeth, wife of John of Greystoke, was in the process of divorcing her husband (Kempe 1940, 317 n. 133).

2. Following Valerie Traub's use of the word in her analysis of early modern "lesbian" desires, I will refer to the female same-sex desires represented in *The Book of Margery Kempe* as "homoerotic," a term which usefully falls between the modern category of the lesbian and premodern masculinist interpellations of the sodomite (Traub 1993, 69).

    Although no women in the *Book* express the desire to renounce their spouses for Margery, some wish that Margery "not gon fro hem" (99). Other women, moreover, want Margery to perform as their children's godmother (94).

3. A contemporary parallel to this enabling form of mourning may be found in Douglas Crimp's work on AIDS (1988), which promotes an "active alternative to the personal, elegiac expressions that appeared to dominate the art-world response to AIDS" (15). For a summary of readers who reject Margery's mystical practices as empowering, see Harding (1993), who argues for the subversiveness of Margery's mysticism.

4. Cf. Sedgwick (1990, 136–41); Rambuss (1994); and Stockton (1992). We may also note here the Dresden Madonna's pivotal role in Freud's famous Dora case, before which Dora "remained two hours . . . rapt in silent admiration" (Freud 1974, 116; see Fuss 1993), as well as the possession of "two photographs of the Sistine Madonna" by Olive Chancellor and Verena Tarrant in Henry James's *The Bostonians* (1945, 301). My thanks go to Harry Stecopoulos for giving me this latter citation.

5. See Kempe (47 and lxi); on Syon, Gibson (1989, 20–21).

6. Christ's "commodification" as a medium for feminine homosocial bonding displays yet another way that, as Sheila Delany (1975) first noted, the precapitalist market organization of late medieval England—in which "small scale commodity production for exchange" predominated—informs Margery's structures of feeling (Aers 1988a, 14). Here we might consider how Margery's Passion devotion fantastically resolves the problems the market posed for her (a woman whose precapitalist ventures—as a brewess and miller—always failed). For readings after Delaney on the market's influence on Margery's spiritual and secular endeavors, see Atkinson (1983); Beckwith (1986); Aers (1988a); and Ellis (1990).

7. In her fine study, Lochrie, while acknowledging that Margery "makes known the Virgin's sorrow," subordinates this Marian referent to "the text of (Mary's) sorrow"—Christ (1991, 193), and thus neglects to consider how such a reading may indeed rewrite the Passion drama in the way that I suggest. Two readers who do foreground Margery's Marian identifications in their important studies of the *Book*, David Aers and Hope Weissman, nevertheless interpret this association in terms of Margery's fantasy of at once regaining her virginal purity and playing the role of mother (Aers 1988a, 104-106; Weissman 1982, 211). While not specifically discussing identification with the Virgin in popular devotional literature, Sarah Beckwith notes that such texts encourage female readers such as Margery to play various domestic roles, including that of mother, in relation to Jesus (1986).

8. The exceptions include scholars such as Judith Brown (1986), E. Ann Matter (1986; 1989), and Bruce Holsinger (1993).

9. Just as androcentric culture forbids woman access to its figurative language, this very

discourse is grounded upon her identification with that which is not figurative, that is, the literal; see Homans (1986, 1–39).

10. The endeavor to understand the late medieval period the way its authorities intended it to be understood, risks, as Fradenburg puts it, "confusing 'the Middle Ages' with the ways in which the Middle Ages (mis)represented itself to itself" (1989, 75).

11. Traub has played a groundbreaking role in displaying how "historically distant representations of female desire *can* be correlated, though not in any simple or linear fashion, to modern systems of intelligibility and political efficacy" (1993, 62; 1992).

12. My use of Bynum here is ironic, as her assertion forms part of an overall argument about how medieval and modern readers *differ*: "For all their application of male/female contrasts to organize life symbolically, medieval thinkers used gender imagery more fluidly and less literally than we do" (1991, 108). On Bynum and sexuality see Rambuss (1994) and Biddick (1993).

13. I am thinking here of the work of Butler, Sedgwick, and Fuss. See also Goldberg, who claims a similar gender/sexual fluidity in the Renaissance (1994a, 227).

14. See Hope Emily Allen's introduction to the Butler-Bodown manuscript (Kempe 1940).

15. "The Holy Matriarch" St. Anne enjoyed a strong cult following in Norfolk (Gibson 1989, 82–84; Duffy 1992, 181–83). On Bokenham see Delany (forthcoming).

16. I refer to women such as Anne Harling, who commissioned a series of stained-glass windows depicting Mary's Joys and Sorrows for an East Harling church in the 1460s. Harling's gift asserts both her identification with Mary as well as Harling's own power in determining the devotional imagery within her parish. As Gibson suggests, many of the windows' details suggest their intended consumption by a female audience (1989, 101).

17. The virgin martyrs depicted on the screens are enlisted for their powers by Margery herself (52; cf. Duffy 1992, 176).

18. Both communities were in Norwich: an unknown number of sisters lived for roughly fifteen years in St. Swithin's parish, while another group of two or three lived from 1442 to 1472 in St. Laurence's parish (Tanner 1984, 65). As the tenement in which the latter community dwelled was owned by a Low Countries' native—the center of Beguine movement—these East Anglian communities may have been affiliated with beguinages (Tanner 1984, 65).

19. On Margery's foreign influence, see Allen's preface to the *Book* (Kempe 1940, liii–lxii).

20. Among the details that draw the viewer's eye to Mary are her eye-level placement near the bottom of each work, as well as the inclination of Christ's head, directing the viewer's gaze down and to the left of the picture, where Mary is situated. See also the *Crucifixions* of Master Hans in Vienna and the Venetian School (Meiss 1951, Plate 92; Sticca 1988).

21. My reading of Margery here reflects and revises Mulvey's analysis of woman's visual presence in Hollywood narrative film (1992). I assume a broad and flexible understanding of the terms "drama" and "performance." In referring to the Mass as a "Christ-centered drama," I recall Hardison (1965, 78). The imbrication of liturgical drama with explicitly dramatic forms—such as Corpus Christi plays—that were themselves performed within or near the very churches in which the Mass took place suggests how a late medieval Christian such as Margery may well have viewed her church as a stagelike site for spectacular impersonation. See also Honorius of Autun, quoted in Hardison (1965, 39–40), and Duffy (1992, 19–22).

22. This arrangement presumably follows the Virgin and her sisters' (the two Mary's) traditional positioning to the left of the cross.

23. Commenting on this feminine version of the emphasis on Christ's sexual organ, which Steinberg himself notes (1983, 127–30; quoted in Bynum 1991, 330), Bynum writes, *contra* Steinberg: "[t]here is reason to think that medieval viewers saw bared breasts (at least in

painting and sculpture) not primarily as sexual but as the food with which they were iconographically associated" (1991, 86). But in response to such claims I would ask, with Richard Rambuss, "why should we turn away from regarding the body as always at least potentially sexualized, as a truly polysemous surface where various significances and expressions—including a variety of erotic ones—compete and collude with each other in making the body meaningful?" (1994, 268).

24.   Bynum is here describing what she thinks "anyone who has stood before the lovely beguine cradle on display in the Metropolitan Museum in New York ... and realized that it is a liturgical object must have thought, at least for a moment" (1991, 198).

25.   For example, Bynum writes that "devotional objects ... came increasingly in the fourteenth and fifteenth centuries to reflect and sanctify women's domestic and biological experience" (1991, 198).

26.   The devotion of the fourteenth-century Dominican nuns of Toess, who constructed during Advent a "kind of a doll house ... [which] contained a bath tub in which to bathe a figure of the infant," similarly displays female identification with a woman (Mary) as mother (Berliner 1946, 268).

27.   A visual analogue to the Christ child's mediatory function in the *Book* can be found in the Master of the Passion's *Entombment* (1380–1385; Barasche 1976, 85). Behind Christ's sarcophagus, one woman (presumably Mary) puts her face near Christ's own visage while another places one hand upon his crotch. But even more suggestive for my purposes are the two women crouching before his sarcophagus: as one woman holds Christ's arm, another, huddled beside her, half covers her eyes as she looks intently over Christ's limp limb into the eyes of the smiling woman near her. The dead Christ's arm's placement between the women's heads vividly demonstrates his body's positioning as a medium for female bonding. One thousand years before the *Entombment,* in a letter from Church Father Saint Augustine to his sister, there appears an ironic gloss for the structure of desire represented in the painting: "It is not by touch alone, but also by feeling and sight, that a woman desires and is desired. Do not claim to have chaste minds if you have unchaste eyes, because the unchaste eye is the messenger of the unchaste heart; and when unchaste hearts reveal themselves to each other by a mutual glance, even though the tongue is silent, ... chastity flees from the character though the body remain untouched. ..." (1956, 5: 45). If looking can express the lust between a man and a woman, what prevents the exchange of looks between two women from being interpreted similarly? Later in the letter, Augustine implicitly refers to "lesbian" love when he warns his sister, a nun, that "the love between you [nuns], however, ought not to be earthly but spiritual," at once opening the field of desire beyond the realm of genital contact and acknowledging the possibility that an "earthly" love between women could occur there (although, of course, he frames his acknowledgment of desires between women in prohibitive terms).

28.   The role of censorship as that which both leads to and is outwitted in condensation, is displayed by the simultaneously enabling and legitimizing presence of Christ in the doll scene, as well as the other moments in the *Book* analyzed in this essay (*cf.* Freud 1960, 170–73).

29.   Both episodes from the *Book* analyzed thus far take place in Italy during Margery's pilgrimage there and in Jerusalem. Other scenes of female-female bonding in the *Book* take place in England (where Margery is accused of luring wives from their husbands). See especially ch. 53, 130–31. But as the two moments analyzed here are perhaps the most provocative, I would like to offer two reasons why this might be the case. Firstly, much of what contributed to Margery's devotional practice came from Italy—above all the enormously influential piety of the Franciscans. Secondly, pilgrimage's figuration in medieval Christianity could also explain why versions of the female homoerotics that occur in Margery's mystical visionary life are realized in the space of pilgrimage. Perceived as a

center of devotion, where both miracles and a strengthening of faith occur, pilgrimage constitutes an exteriorized version of the interior journey of the mystic. Cf. Turner (1978, 6–7). Margery indicates this parallel relation herself in the Christ doll scene, where she links her meditations on the Infancy "in Inglond" with the Italian wives' actual attentions to the image of the baby Jesus (78). As Turner also argues, pilgrimage is "the mode of liminality for the laity," offering lay Christians such as Margery a place where normal social strictures are relaxed and social orderings—such as the male homosocial triad—are inverted. Could this perhaps be the reason why so many women engaged in pilgrimage—to the condemnation of authorities such as Boniface (*Ep.* XLVIII 169, cited in Sumption 1975, 347)?

30. As Allen notes (Kempe 1940), Christ is probably recalling here Margery's role as Mary's handmaiden and Jesus's nurse, mentioned earlier in the *Book*.

31. David Aers, noting the infantilization and passivization of Christ, speculates that "It enabled Margery to identify with the 'good' mother in a way that her experience in the earthly family denied," and that it "offers an image of one sphere in which the woman obviously controls males"(1988a, 104–107). See also Beckwith (1986, 48).

32. As she spent thirteen weeks in Venice, Margery may have seen Giotto's piece in Padua's Arena Chapel (Kempe 1940, 65). Like Giotto's painting, Niccoló di Tommaso's *Lamentation* in the Congregazione de la Caritá, Parma, depicts the dead Christ surrounded solely by female mourners (Meiss, plate 123).

33. *Cf.* Butler, who asserts that the essentially historical and thus contingent nature of patriarchal cultural signifiers allows for their disfiguration into unauthorized forms (see, for example, 1992, 162).

34. Readers who assess the *Book* in theological terms include Lochrie (1991), who describes the status of Margery's tears as signifiers of Margery's devout love for Jesus (see especially 167–202), Gibson 1989, who argues for Margery's successful assertion of "her own spiritual health" (65; see also 47–49); Hirsh (1989, 9); Dickman (1980); McEntire (1987). Alternately, Weissman provocatively argues that Margery "formally accept[s] conventional (theological) images while actually coopting them" (1982, 203).

WORKS CITED

Aers, David. 1988a. *Community, Gender and Individual Identity: English Writing 1360-1430*. London and New York: Routledge.

———. 1988b. "Rewriting the Middle Ages: Some Suggestions." *Journal of Medieval and Renaissance Studies* 18: 221–40.

Atkinson, Clarissa W. 1983. *Mystic and Pilgrim: The Book and World of Margery Kempe*. Ithaca: Cornell University Press.

Augustine. 1956. Letter 211. In *Letters*, trans. Sr. Wilfrid Parsons. 5 vols. New York: Fathers of the Church.

Bailey, Derrick Sherwin. 1975. *Homosexuality and the Western Christian Tradition*. Hamden, CT: Shoestring.

Barasche, Mosche. 1976. *Gestures of Despair in Medieval and Early Renaissance Art*. New York: New York University Press.

Beckwith, Sarah. 1986. "A Very Material Mysticism: The Medieval Mysticism of Margery Kempe," in *Medieval Literature: Criticism, Ideology & History*, ed. David Aers. Sussex: Harvester. 34–57.

Bennett, J. A. W. 1982. *Poetry of the Passion: Studies in Twelve Centuries of English Verse*. Oxford: Clarendon.

Berliner, R. 1946. "The Origins of the Creche." *Gazette des Beaux–Arts* 30: 249–78.

Biddick, Kathleen. 1993. "Genders, Bodies, Borders: Technologies of the Visible." *Speculum* 68.2: 389–418.

Blunt, John Henry, ed. 1973. *The Myroure of Oure Ladye.* EETS, e. s. 19. London: Oxford University Press.

Boswell, John. 1980. *Christianity, Social Tolerance and Homosexuality: Gay People in Western Europe from the Beginning of the Christian Era to the Fourteenth Century.* Chicago: University of Chicago Press.

Brook, G. L., ed. 1956. *The Harley Lyrics: The Middle English Lyrics of Ms. Harley 2253.* Manchester: Manchester University Press.

Brown, Judith. 1986. *Immodest Acts: The Life of a Lesbian Nun in Renaissance Italy.* New York & Oxford: Oxford University Press.

Butler, Judith. 1990. *Gender Trouble: Feminism and the Subversion of Identity.* London and New York: Routledge.

———. 1992. "The Lesbian Phallus and the Morphological Imaginary." *Differences* 4: 133–71.

Bynum, Caroline Walker. 1987. "Religious Women," in *Christian Spirituality: High Middle Ages and Reformation,* ed. Jill Raitt in collaboration with Bernard McGinn and John Meyendorff. New York: Crossroad. 121–39.

———. 1991. *Fragmentation and Redemption: Essays on Gender and the Human Body in Medieval Religion.* New York: Zone.

Castle, Terry. 1993. *The Apparitional Lesbian: Female Homosexuality and Modern Culture.* New York: Columbia University Press.

Coletti, Theresa. 1993. "Purity and Danger: The Paradox of Mary's Body and the En-gendering of the Infancy Narrative in the English Mystery Cycles," in Lomperis and Stanbury, *Feminist Approaches.* 65–95.

Crimp, Douglas, ed. 1988. *AIDS: Cultural Analysis, Cultural Activism.* Cambridge and London: MIT.

Delaney, Sheila. 1975. "Sexual Economics, Chaucer's Wife of Bath, and *The Book of Margery Kempe.*" *Minnesota Review* 5: 104–15.

———. *Patronage, Politics and Augustinian Poetics in Fifteenth-Century England* (forthcoming).

Dickman, Susan. 1980. "Margery Kempe and the English Devotional Tradition," in *The Medieval Mystical Tradition in England,* ed. Marion Glasscoe. Exeter: University of Exeter Press. 156–72.

Duffy, Eamon. 1992. *The Stripping of the Altars: Traditional Religion in England, c.1400–c.1580.* New Haven and London: Yale University Press.

Ellis, Deborah. 1990. "The Merchant's Wife's Tale: Language, Sex and Commerce in Margery Kempe and in Chaucer." *Exemplaria* 2: 595–626.

Ennen, Edith. 1984. *The Medieval Woman,* trans. Edmund Jephcott. Cambridge, MA: Basil Blackwell.

Fradenburg, Louise. 1989. "Criticism, Anti-Semitism and the *Prioress's Tale.*" *Exemplaria* 1: 69–115.

———. 1990. "Voice Memorial: Loss and Reparation in Chaucer's Poetry." *Exemplaria* 2: 169–202.

Freud, Sigmund. 1960. *Jokes and Their Relation to the Unconscious* (1905). *The Standard Edition of the Complete Works of Sigmund Freud,* trans. and ed. James Strachey. Vol. 8. London: Hogarth.

———. 1963. "Feminine Sexuality," in *Sexuality and the Psychology of Love,* intro. and ed. Philip Rieff. New York: Collier. 194–211.

———. 1973. "Femininity." *The Standard Edition of the Complete Works of Sigmund Freud* (1932–1936), trans. and ed. James Strachey. Vol. 22. London: Hogarth. 112–36.

———. 1974. *Dora: An Analysis of a Case of Hysteria,* ed. Philip Rieff. New York: Collier.

Fuss, Diana. 1992. "Fashion and the Homospectatorial Look." *Critical Inquiry* 18: 713–37.

———. 1993. "Freud's Fallen Women: Identification, Desire, and 'A Case of Homosexuality in a Woman'." *The Yale Journal of Criticism* 6: 1–24.

Gibson, Gail McMurray. 1989. *The Theater of Devotion: East Anglian Drama and Society in the Late Middle Ages.* Chicago and London: University of Chicago Press.

Gluck, Robert. 1994. *Margery Kempe.* New York and London: High Risk.

Goldberg, Jonathan. 1992. *Sodometries: Renaissance Texts, Modern Sexualities.* Stanford, CA: Stanford University Press.

———. 1994a. "Romeo's and Juliet's Open Rs," in Goldberg, *Queering.* 218–35.

———, ed. 1994a. *Queering the Renaissance.* Durham, NC and London: Duke University Press.

Graef, Hilda. 1963. *Mary: A History of Doctrine and Devotion.* Vol. 1. New York: Sheed and Ward. 2 Vols.

Hamburgh, Harvey E. 1981. "The Problem of *Lo Spasimo* of the Virgin in *Cinquecento* Paintings of the Descent from the Cross." *Sixteenth Century Journal* 12: 45–76.

Harding, Wendy. 1993. "Body into Text: *The Book of Margery Kempe,*" in Lomperis and Stanbury, *Feminist Approaches.* 168–87.

Hardison, O.B. 1965. *Christian Rite and Christian Drama in the Middle Ages: Essays in the Origin and Early History of Modern Drama.* Baltimore: Johns Hopkins University Press.

Hirsch, John C. 1975. "Author and Scribe in *The Book of Margery Kempe.*" *Medium Aevum* 44: 145–50.

————. 1989. *The Revelations of Margery Kempe.* New York: Brill.

Holsinger, Bruce Wood. 1993. "The Flesh of the Voice: Embodiment and the Homoerotics of Devotion in the Music of Hildegard of Bingen (1098–1179)." *Signs* 19: 92–125.

Homans, Margaret. 1986. *Bearing the Word: Language and Female Experience in Nineteenth-Century Women's Writing.* Chicago and London: University of Chicago Press.

Irigaray, Luce. 1985. *This Sex Which is Not One,* trans. Catherine Porter. Ithaca: Cornell University Press.

James, Henry. 1945. *The Bostonians,* intro. Philip Rahv. New York: Dial.

Johnson, Lynn Staley. 1991. "The Trope of the Scribe and the Question of Literary Authority in the works of Julian of Norwich and Margery Kempe." *Speculum* 66: 820–38.

Kempe, Margery. 1940. *The Book of Margery Kempe,* ed. Sanford Brown Meech and Hope Emily Allen. EETS 212. Oxford: Oxford University Press.

Kieckhefer, Richard. 1984. *Unquiet Souls: Fourteenth-Century Saints and Their Religious Milieu.* Chicago and London: University of Chicago Press.

Klapisch-Zuber, Christiane. 1985. *Women, Family, and Ritual in Renaissance Italy.* Chicago: University of Chicago Press.

Kristeva, Julia. 1987. *Tales of Love,* trans. Leon S. Roudiez. New York: Columbia University Press.

Lane, Barbara G. 1984. *The Altar and the Altarpiece: Sacramental Themes in Early Netherlandish Painting.* New York: Harper and Row.

Lochrie, Karma. 1991. *Margery Kempe and the Translations of the Flesh.* Philadelphia: University of Pennsylvania Press.

Lomperis, Linda and Sarah Stanbury, eds. 1993. *Feminist Approaches to the Body.* Philadelphia: University of Pennsylvania Press.

Love, Nicholas. 1992. *Mirror of the Blessed Life of Jesus Christ,* ed. Michael G. Sargent. New York & London: Garland.

Marcuse, Herbert. 1959. "The Ideology of Death," in *The Meaning of Death,* ed. Herman Feifel. New York: McGraw-Hill. 64–76.

Matter, E. Ann. 1986. "My Sister My Spouse: Women-identified Women in Medieval Christianity." *Journal of Feminist Studies in Religion* 2: 81–93.

————. 1989. "Discourses of Desire: Sexuality and Christian Women's Visionary Narratives." *Homosexuality and Religion* 18: 119–31.

McEntire, Sandra. 1987. "The Doctrine of Compunction From Bede to Margery Kempe," in *The Medieval Mystical Tradition in England. Exeter Symposium IV,* ed. Marion Glasscoe. Cambridge: D. S. Brewer. 77–90.

Meditations on the Life of Christ: An Illustrated Manuscript of the Fourteenth Century. 1961. Trans. Isa Ragusa, ed. Isa Ragusa and Rosalie B. Green. Princeton: Princeton University Press.

Meiss, Millard. 1951. *Painting in Florence and Siena After the Black Death.* Princeton: Princeton University Press.

Merideth, Peter. 1987. *The Mary Play From the N-town Manuscript.* London and New York: Longman.

Mueller, Janel M. 1986. "Autobiography of a New 'Creatur': Feminine Spirituality, Selfhood, and Authorship in *The Book of Margery Kempe,*" in *Women in the Middle Ages and Renaissance: Literary and Historical Perspectives,* ed. Mary Beth Rose. Syracuse: Syracuse University Press. 155–71.

Mulvey, Laura. 1992. "Visual Pleasure and Narrative Cinema," in *Film Theory and Criticism: Introductory*

Readings, ed. Gerald Mast, Marshall Cohen, and Leo Braudy. New York and Oxford: Oxford University Press. 746–57.

Mundy, E. James. 1981–1982. "Gerard David's Rest on the Flight into Egypt: Further Additions to Grape Symbolism." *Simiolus: Netherlands Quarterly for the History of Art* 12.4 : 211–22.

Rambuss, Richard. 1994. "Pleasure and Devotion: The Body of Jesus and Seventeenth-Century Religious Lyric," in Goldberg, *Queering*. 253–79.

Rich, Adrienne. 1983. "Compulsory Heterosexuality and Lesbian Existence," in *Powers of Desire: The Politics of Sexuality*, ed. Ann Snitow, Christine Stansell and Sharon Thompson. New York: Monthly Review. 177–205.

Roof, Judith. 1992. *A Lure of Knowledge: Lesbian Sexuality and Theory*. New York: Columbia University Press.

Rubin, Gayle. 1975. "The Traffic in Women: Notes Toward a Political Economy of Sex," in *Toward an Anthropology of Women*, ed. Rayna Reiter. New York: Monthly Review Press. 157–210.

Schiesari, Juliana. 1992. *The Gendering of Melancholia: Feminism, Psychoanalysis, and the Symbolics of Loss in Renaissance Literature*. Ithaca and London: Cornell University Press.

Schlegel, Ursula. 1970. "The Christchild as Devotional Image in Medieval Italian Sculpture: A Contribution to Ambrogio Lorenzetti Studies." *Art Bulletin* 52: 1–10.

Sedgwick, Eve Kososfky. 1985. *Between Men: English Literature and Male Homosocial Desire*. New York: Columbia University Press.

————. 1990. *Epistemology of the Closet*. Berkeley: University of California Press.

Sinanoglou, Leah. 1973. "The Christ Child as Sacrifice: A Medieval Tradition and the Corpus Christi Plays." *Speculum*: 491–509.

Stanbury, Sarah. 1991. "The Virgin's Gaze: Spectacle and Transgression in Middle English Lyrics of the Passion." *PMLA* 106: 1083–93.

Steinberg, Leo. 1983. *The Sexuality of Christ in Renaissance Art and in Modern Oblivion*. New York: Pantheon.

Sticca, Sandro. 1988. *The Planctus Mariae in the Dramatic Tradition of the Middle Ages*, trans. Joseph R. Berrigan. Athens, GA and London: University of Georgia Press.

Stockton, Kathryn Bond. 1992. "God Between Their Lips: Desire Between Women in Irigaray and Eliot." *Novel* 25: 348–59.

Sumption, Jonathan. 1975. *Pilgrimage: An Image of Mediaeval Religion*. London: Faber & Faber.

Tanner, Norman P. 1984. *The Church in Late Medieval Norwich 1370–1532*. Toronto: Pontifical Institute of Mediaeval Studies.

Traub, Valerie. 1992. *Desire and Anxiety: Circulations of Sexuality in Shakespearean Drama*. London and New York: Routledge.

————. 1993. "The (In)Significance of 'Lesbian' Desire in Early Modern England," in Goldberg, *Queering*. 62–83.

Turner, Victor and Edith Turner. 1978. *Image and Pilgrimage in Christian Culture: Anthropological Perspectives*. New York: Columbia University Press.

Weissman, Hope Phyllis. 1982. "Margery Kempe in Jerusalem: *Hysterica Compassio* in the Late Middle Ages," in *Acts of Interpretation: The Text in its Contexts 700–1600*, ed. Mary J. Carruthers and Elizabeth D. Kirk. Norman, OK: Pilgrim. 201–217.

Woolf, Rosemary. 1968. *The English Religious Lyric in the Middle Ages*. Oxford: Clarendon.

Part Four

RHETORIC

AND

POETICS

Virile Style 10

Patricia Parker

In 1527, Erasmus wrote a letter in which he expressed desire for a style that would be "more genuine, more concise, more forceful, less ornate and *more masculine*" ("malim aliquod dicendi genus solidius, adstrictius, *nervosius*, minus comptum magisque *masculum*"; emphasis added).[1] "More masculine," here, might come as a surprise from the pen of a man who adopted the guise of a garrulous old woman in *The Praise of Folly*, or who was regularly accused of a "womanish" loquacity by rival humanists.[2] But desire for a style that would be "more masculine" surfaces not just in this letter, but in other texts of this influential early humanist. Just two years before, in *Lingua: On the Use and Abuse of the Tongue*, Erasmus not only speaks of the "female" tongues of men (complicating, along with a range of other sixteenth-century texts, the identification of "female" loquacity with women in particular) but also repeatedly praises a more "manly" style, appealing to the Spartans not "effeminated" ("*effoeminatus*") by indulgence in rhetoric or the arts of words. He also recites the traditional praise of a more "manly" Attic style over the effeminate "Asiatic," in that powerful mix of misogyny and orientalism conveyed from fifth-century Athens to Europe through the whole force of Roman tradition.[3]

I start with Erasmus and this early sixteenth-century expression of desire for a more "masculine" or virile style because it is precisely this influential Roman tradition that pervades early modern European praise of a stylistic (but also much more than stylistic) *virilitas*—not only on the Continent but in the articulation, in England, of a style that would have (as Ben Jonson put it) a "manly" strength and vigor, a reaction against an "effeminate" Ciceronianism that privileged words over deeds or things, and ultimately the "plain" style of a nascent early modern science described as a "*masculine* birth of time."[4] Erasmus's description of the "female" tongues of men, along with the ambiguous position of humanists themselves as men of words, also suggest the complex concerns about virility at work in the period's repeated diatribes against the "female" tongue, including, almost a century after Erasmus's *Lingua*, the English transvestite play of the same name (1607), whose "Madame Lingua," surrounded by all of the contemporary stereotypes of womens' tongues, is finally exposed as a Cambridge undergraduate in drag.[5]

In order to chart the pan-European influence of this Roman tradition of virile style—across texts whose gendering has been strikingly ignored or effaced by traditional scholarship—we might revisit, first, a famous passage from Ben Jonson's *Timber; or Discoveries*, and its description of a style that would have "bones and sinews":

> Wee say it is a fleshy style, when there is much Periphrasis, and circuit of words; and when with more then enough, it growes fat and corpulent; *Arvina orationis*, full of suet and tallow.... There be some styles, againe, that have not lesse blood, but lesse flesh, and corpulence. These are bony, and sinnewy: *Ossa habent, et nervos* (VIII: 626–27).

Apart from its contrasting of a leaner, more "sinewy" style with its "fleshy" bodily and stylistic opposite, this passage evokes the central term that links such early modern utterances to a longstanding Roman assimilation of virile style to the metaphorics of the male body. "*Ossa habent et nervos*" ("These styles have bones and *sinews*") summons the "*nervus*" or "*nervosus*," translated into English as "sinew" and "sinewy," sign of a healthy, muscular body as well as style.

"Sinewy"—as the translation of Latin *nervi* —is the watchword of English versions of this classical and continental tradition, from Sir Philip Sidney's introduction of the term into the *Defense of Poetry*, to Florio's translations of Montaigne and the articulation of an ideology of the "plain" style in Bacon, Jonson, and others.[6] In a tradition in which "*nervi*" denoted "content" or things, as distinct from words, "*nervus*" (or "*nervosus*") was a key term in the debate over the relative importance of "words" and "things"—the watchword of a style whose masculine "vigor" would have, as Jonson phrased it, "Life and Quicknesse, which is the Strength and sinnewes (as it were), of your penning" (*Discoveries* in Herford, *et al.* VIII: 632–33). The lack of *nervi*, or "sinews," produced by contrast what Richard Sherry, in the middle of the English sixteenth century, termed the "dissolute"—a style that "waveth hyther and thyther, as it were without synewes, and jointes, standing surely in no point."[7]

The *topos* of a style that would be strong, "sinewy," and "masculine"—appearing again and again across linguistic boundaries in early modern Europe—itself developed out of a massively influential Latin tradition, in which the term used by Jonson for "sinews" ("*nervi*") or the "*nervosius*" evoked by Erasmus both in the *Ciceronianus* and the letter of 1527 served as the hinge between a manly body and a manly style. When Tacitus, for example, recorded the hostility of the Atticists Brutus and Calvus to the more copious, "Asiatic" and "effeminate" style of Cicero, the word he used for "effeminate" was the charged "*enervis*" (as well as "*fractum*," "broken," "impotent").[8] "*Enervis*" ("weak, effeminate"), like the Latin "*enervo*" ("to enervate, weaken") is of course the opposite of "*nervosus*" ("sinewy, wiry, energetic"). But both also come from "*nervus*"—a term that means not only "sinew, tendon" or (by extension) "vigor, force, energy, strength," but also the male sexual member in particular. In ways important for the signal appearance of this term and tradition in Montaigne, as we shall see, "*nervus*" also appears in Latin texts preoccupied, by contrast, with a paralyzing impotence, including

Horace's *Epodes* and Ovid's often-cited *Amores* III: 7.[9] *Nervus* was thus, in Raymond Williams's as well as the philological sense, the "keyword" of an entire tradition of masculine or virile style linked to a metaphorics of the male body in its prime.[10] The term, therefore, enables us to trace the workings of this influential Latin tradition of stylistic and bodily *virilitas*—with its opposition of the virile or sinewy to the effeminate and slack—across a broad range of early modern writing.

One of the most influential examples of this linking of body and style was the passage from Quintilian's *Institutes* that introduces into its condemnation of an effeminating privileging of words over things a description of the healthy male body as emblem of a style that resists what it calls the "futile and crippling study of words," to the detriment of the "things" that are the "sinews" (*"nervi"*) of discourse:

> This does not, however, mean that we should devote ourselves to the study of words alone. For I am compelled to offer the most prompt and determined resistance to those who would at the very portals of this enquiry lay hold of the admissions I have just made and, disregarding the things [or content] that are the sinews of any speech [*omissa rerum (qui nervi sunt in causis)*], devote themselves to the futile and crippling study of words [*quodam inani circa voces studio senescunt*] in a vain desire to acquire the gift of elegance, a gift which I myself regard as the fairest of all the glories of oratory, but only when it is natural and unaffected. Healthy bodies, enjoying a good circulation and strengthened by exercise, acquire grace from the same source that gives them strength, for they have a healthy complexion, firm flesh and shapely thews [*Corpora sana et integri sanguinis et exercitatione firmata ex iisdem his speciem accipiunt ex quibus vires, namque et colorata et adstricta et lacertis expressa sunt*]. But, on the other hand, the man who attempts to enhance these physical graces by the effeminate use of depilatories and cosmetics, succeeds merely in defacing them by the very care he bestows on them [*at eadem si quis volsa atque fucata muliebriter comat, foedissima sint ipso formae labore*]. Again, a tasteful and magnificent dress, as the Greek poet tells us, lends added dignity to its wearer: but effeminate and luxurious apparel [*muliebris et luxuriosus*] fails to adorn the body and merely reveals the foulness of the mind. Similarly, a translucent and iridescent style merely serves to emasculate [*effeminat*] the subject which it arrays with such pomp of words.[11]

The passage—whose reference to a senile [*senescunt*] indulgence in words will also be important for Montaigne—is joined by others in the *Institutes* that oppose the virile to the effeminate or lax, praising the strength, for example, of Demosthenes (X: i.76: "*ita quibusdam nervis intenta sunt*") over a style like that of Aeschines with "more flesh and less muscle" ("*carnis tamen plus habet, minus lacertorum*").[12] In Quintilian's influential text, *copia* itself—though useful to the orator—is surrounded by warnings that it must always be "manly" ("*virilem*") rather than effeminate or dissolute ("*dissoluta*"). And it adds to the tradition of an "emasculate" Cicero (XII: x, 12) its own version of the Asiatic charge, reminding us, in its allusion to the "*mollitia*" ("softness") of the East, that the other keyword in this lexicon was "*mollis*" or soft.[13]

The analogy in Quintilian between body and style—with its hinge word *"nervus"* or *"nervosus"*—is exemplary of an entire tradition of Latin writing. *"Nervus"* appears in the texts of Cicero himself, in the *Orator's* disapproval of a style that "lacks the vigor and sting necessary for oratorical efforts in public life" (*Orator* XIX: 62, *"tamen horum oratio neque nervos neque aculeos oratorios ac forensis habet"*). In the *Ad Herennium*—the text (received with Ciceronian authority) from which so much of sixteenth-century critical terminology derived—it appears in the passage on the degeneration of the "middle" style from which Sherry's description of the "slack" or "dissolute" is drawn, a style "without sinews and joints" (*"sine nervis et articulis"*) that "cannot get under way with resolution and virility" (*Ad Herennium* IV: 11–16). In an influential passage of his *Dialogus*—the same text that contains the influential description of the "effeminate" (*"solutum et enervem"*) Cicero—Tacitus writes that:

> It is with eloquence as with the human frame. There can be no beauty of form where the veins are prominent, or where one can count the bones: sound healthful blood must fill out the limbs, and riot over the muscles, concealing the sinews (*nervos*) in turn under a ruddy complexion and a graceful exterior.[14]

"Nervus" is also the term that appears in the frequently translated *Ars poetica* of Horace, in its description of a style that is deficient (*"deficiunt"*) in "sinews" (*"Sectantem levia*, nervi / Deficiunt *animique*," ll. 36–37), as well as in the *"sine nervis"* of Book II of the Horatian *Satires*, in a passage charged with sexual innuendo and figures of male potency.[15] Horace, in this regard, however, is also a more complex influence, since he simultaneously alludes to the flaccidity or impotence implied by his own name— Quintus Horatius Flaccus—and his position as a man not of (military or political) action but of words. A style that is potentially impotent (*"sine nervis"*) is thus the counterpart of the political or sexual impotence pervading other Horatian texts, like the *Epodes* (8, 12) that treat of what "weakens [his] manhood" (*"viris quid* enervet") or contrast his slack and useless member (*"ad unum /* mollis *opus"*) to a "firm" (*constans*) virility (*"cuius in indomito* constantior *inguine* nervos"), a passage cited centrally in Montaigne.[16]

Perhaps most influential for the early modern iteration of this Roman tradition of more virile style, finally, are the *Epistles* of Seneca that include effeminacy of style in their general denunciation of the effeminacy of the age. *Epistle* 114 in particular, elaborating on the speech or style that shows the man (*"talis hominibus fuit oratio qualis vita"*), includes the charge of effeminacy (as well as impotence) that was a standard of Roman stylistic criticism. But it also treats of "a degenerate style of speech" (*"corrupti generis oratio"*) that is "mincing" (*"infracta"*) and "womanish" (*"effeminatus"*). And it describes such effeminacy of style as being as easily detected as the mincing gait of the *"cinaedus,"* the passive or penetrated partner in sexual relations between men (as distinct from relations with *pueri* or boys), a figure routinely described as *"muliebris"* or "like a woman":

Wantonness in speech [*orationis lascivia*] is proof of public luxury, if it is popular and fashionable, and not confined to one or two individual instances. A man's ability cannot possibly be of one sort and his soul of another. If his soul be wholesome, well-ordered, serious, and restrained, his ability also is sound and sober. Conversely, when the one degenerates, the other is also contaminated. Do you not see that if a man's soul has become sluggish, his limbs drag and his feet move indolently? If it is womanish [*effeminatus*], that one can detect the effeminacy [*mollitiam*] by his very gait? . . .[17]

Epistle 114 goes on to contrast a "manly" to an "effeminate" style: "When the soul is sound and strong (*sano ac valente*), the style too is vigorous, energetic, manly (*fortis virilis est*), but if the soul lose its balance, down comes all the rest in ruins (*ruinam sequuntur*)." The key terms here, once again, are "*nervi*" and "*enervati*" ("*mollem fuisse . . . enervati*"): the general effeminacy and decadence of the age is described as a disease that penetrates "the marrow and the sinews (*nervos*)." The *Epistle* compares the effeminate, soft, and unresisting style ("*delicati, tenera et fluxa*") to the effeminate style of Maecenas, the famously "*mollis*" man whose affect simultaneously evoked the *cinaedus*, passive or "pathic" male, and suggested excessive contact with women.[18]

This Senecan *Epistle* writes large, then, what also appears in the passage already cited from Quintilian (VIII: Pr. 18–22), comparing a virile style to a male body not touched by "the effeminate use of depilatories"—the traditional means for the passive or "pathic" man of prolonging the soft smoothness of the *puer* or boy.[19] Quintilian, indeed, discusses a whole range of such effeminate characteristics (*Inst.* 5.9.14)—"the plucked body, the broken walk, the female attire," all of them signs ("*signa*") associated with "one who is *mollis* and not a real man (*parum viri*)," indications of "*impudicitia*," a term both for unchastity and for the "womanish" nature of the passive male. Within Seneca as well as other Latin writers, words that traditionally refer to women (*patior, mollis*) also have this double valence, extending the terms of Seneca's pronouncement in *Epistle* 95—that women are *pati natae* (born to be penetrated as well as to bear)—to a passivity (from *patior*) shared by the man penetrated by other men. In *Epistle* 122—attacking men who live *contra naturam*, dressing as women ("*qui commutant cum* feminis *vestem*")—Seneca asks "*Numquam* vir *erit, ut diu* virum pati *possit*" ("Will he never be a man, so that he may *pati* (bear) a man for a longer time?").[20] And this sense of "womanish" passivity is paralleled in other Roman writing as well including Martial's epigrams, Juvenal's second *Satire*, the heckling of Pompey in Plutarch's *Life* ("Who is the degnerate general? Who is the man who seeks another man?) and Ovid's reference (in the *Ars Amatoria*) to "whatever not-man seeks to have a man." The *mollis/durus* opposition used to distinguish female from male also applied, then, to the "*molles*" as the term for penetrated or passive men.[21] And Roman expressions of desire for a "virile" style have this double aspect— that the style not be "womanish" but that it not also betray, like the "mincing gait" of the *cinaedus*, the degenerate unsoundness of the effeminate male.

These Latin passages linking body and style are reiterated again and again in early modern European writing. The passage from the *Ad Herennium* on the "dissolute" style that "without sinews and joints" ("*sine nervis et articulis*") is unable to "get under way with resolution and virility," stands behind Vives's description of the "sinews" necessary for strength of style, in the passage of the *De Ratione Dicendi* that Jonson's description of the style with "bones and sinews" so closely echoes:

> The nerves are often buried by flesh and fat, so they are weakened and are less able to perform their functions. It happens in the same way in style, that the luxuriance of words and the redundancy of flesh and that diffuse and wandering composition become responsible for a weak style, which happened to Cicero, who, while he diluted his subject matter too much with words, lost strength, as a river that flows out widely. For this reason Calvus said he was *without nerves* [*sine nervis*] and Brutus he was weak.

Vives himself then goes on to distinguish the masculine Attic that "has nothing redundant and faulty, not much flesh, just enough blood and sap, and is pure, natural, brief and clipped" ("*puri, et sani, brevis, astrictaque*") from the Asiatic "weak and *nerveless* from too great abundance of words, dilution of subject matter, and refined composition."[22]

Sixteenth-century anti-Ciceronianism generally bore a similarly gendered cast, its anxieties of virility haunted by both the female and the effeminate. The repeatedly cited complaint of the Atticists against a "feeble and emasculate" Cicero is cited by John Jewel, for example, in his *Oration Against Rhetoric*, which recalls that Cicero was "hooted from the platform as feeble and effeminate, as too relaxed, as an *enervate* Asiatic."[23] Lipsius, the anti-Ciceronian humanist whose writings heavily influenced Jonson's *Discoveries*, wrote in 1586: "I love Cicero; I even used to imitate him; but I have *become a man*, and my tastes have changed. Asiatic feasts have ceased to please me; I prefer the Attic." For Lipsius, a virile or "manly" style was the antithesis of a copious one: his *Institutio Epistolica* praises a style that is "clipped, strong, and truly *manly*" ("*oratio stricta, fortis & vere virilis*"), criticizing Pliny, for example, as "somewhat *effeminate* ... not *manly* enough." The sixteenth century generally (in ways already charted in studies that frequently, however, ignore its gendering) saw a shift from Ascham's Ciceronian view ("Ye know not what hurt ye do to learning, that care not for words, but for matter") to Bacon's Senecan reversal of the proposition, his famous lament that "Men began to hunt more after words than matter." The shift of style between sixteenth and early seventeenth-century England was also associated with the shifting of the monarch's gender. John Hoskins spoke of Elizabeth's "copious style," while Richard Flecknoe noted later that the style "of Queen Elizabeths dayes" ("flaunting and pufted like her Apparell") yielded to the "Learned and Erudite" example of King James.[24] Already in the sixteenth century, the figure of the effeminate courtier or wordy popinjay (employed in Sir Thomas Elyot's statement in *The Governour* that he "that hath nothinge but language only may be no more praised than a popiniay") appeared on the English stage in the form of effeminate men linked to an excessive indulgence in words, like Shakespeare's Osric and Parolles (or "words").[25]

Jonson's *Timber; or Discoveries*—central to the development of the plain style allied in

England with Bacon and early modern science—is filled with appeals to manliness and excoriations of the effeminate in style as in appearance. (Jonson also translated Horace's *Ars poetica*, rendering its *"nervi | Deficiunt"* as "This striving to run smooth, and flow | Hath neither soule, nor *sinnewes.*")[26] *Discoveries* opposes what it calls "Right and naturall" language to the "imbrodered" and cosmetically "painted," in a passage on "preposterous" deformations of style that directly echoes the contrast of virility to effeminacy in Seneca's *Epistle* 114: "Nothing is fashionable, till it bee deform'd; and this is to write like a Gentleman. All must bee as affected, and preposterous as our Gallants cloathes, sweet bags, and night-dressings, in which you would thinke our men lay in, *like Ladies*" (VIII: 581). To the "faint, obscure, obscene, sordid, humble, or *effeminate* Phrase" it opposes the writer whose style is "strong to shew the composition *Manly*" (588). And in one of its most frequently cited passages—"Language most shewes a man" ("speake, that I might see thee"; 625)—manliness of style is described as inseparable from manliness of body and manner:

> There cannot be one colour of the mind; an other of the wit. If the mind be staid, grave, and compos'd, the wit is so; that vitiated, the other is blowne, and deflowr'd.... Looke upon an *effeminate* person: his very *gate* confesseth him. If a man be fiery, his motion is so: if any, 'tis troubled and violent. So that wee may conclude: wheresoever, manners, and fashions are corrupted, Language is. It imitates the publicke riot. The excesse of Feasts, and apparell, are the notes of a *sick State*; and the wantonnesse of language, of a *sick mind* (592–93).

The contrast here of "manly" style to the "gate" of the "effeminate person" comes straight out of Seneca's *Epistle* 114, with its evocation of the effeminate walk of the *cinaedus* and its rhetoric of degeneration and morbidity. The term "preposterous," used by Jonson here for an effeminate deformation of style is, even more strikingly, the familiar (English as well as Latin) term in the period for homosexual coupling, understood as an inversion of the "right and natural" in the realm of sexuality as well as style.[27] "Too much pickenesse" of personal style is "not manly," Jonson writes, in a subsequent passage whose marginal Latin gloss is *"De mollibus & effoeminatis"* (607).

The section earlier cited from *Discoveries* that explicitly contrasts a slack or "fleshy" style with one that has "sinews" or *"nervos"* (VIII: 626–27)—influenced by the assimilation of body and style passed on through Vives and Continental writers—is iterated in the work of Jonson's friend, James Howell:

> Most ... among your Latin Epistolizers, go freighted with mere Bartholomew Ware, with trite and trivial Phrases, listed with pedantic Shreds of School-boy Verses. Others there are among our next transmarine Neighbours Eastward, who write in their own Language, but their Style is soft and easy, that their Letters may be said to be like Bodies of loose Flesh *without Sinews*, they have neither Joints of Art nor Arteries in them; they have a kind of simpering and lank hectic Expressions made up of a Bombast of Words, and finical affected Compliments only: I cannot well away with such sleazy Stuff, with such Cob-

web compositions, where there is *no Strength of Matter*. . . . It may be said of them, what was said of the *Echo, That she is a mere Sound and nothing else.*[28]

In addition to his comparison of such writers to the merely passive, female Echo, Howell's association of "Bodies of loose Flesh *without Sinews*" with the "soft and easy" style of "our next transmarine Neighbours *Eastward*" here translates the traditional figure of an effeminate East into a contrast between effeminate French and a more manly English writing. But its reference to "Bartholomew Ware" also nicely reminds us of a telling contradiction within the work of the famously corpulent Jonson himself, producer not only of the lean neoclassicism of the Cary-Morison Ode but of the fleshy *copia* of plays like *Bartholomew Fair.*[29]

To follow the history of this Roman tradition of sinewy, "nervous," or manly style through its subsequent English developments would be to encounter repeated appeals to manliness in early scientific writers, for example, Sprat and Boyle, or the continuing influence of this tradition's gendering in comparisons of "Eloquence" to "the fair sex" (such as John Locke's). This much longer story would trace the shift from the masculine sense of "nervous" that still persisted as late as the nineteenth century, and its coexistence with and eventual replacement by a more feminized sense of this same term. We might simply note that "nerves" in the sense of "sinews" (or what Milton called "true strength and nerve") continued to accompany praise of the "nervous" style in the Latin sense of strong, masculine, and vigorous.[30] Dryden (rendering Juvenal X. 262) could still use English "nerve" in the sense of penis ("The limber Nerve in vain provok'd to rise"), while Shelley, as late as 1818, could refer to "the nerves of manhood," Sir Walter Scott (1828) speak of the "nervous strength" of a "muscular armourer's" hands, Emerson, in 1844, allude to the "nervous rocky West" in the sense of strong and manly, and Froude, in 1870, use "nervous courage" in this older, Latin sense. While seventeenth- and eighteenth-century writers continued to draw on the Latin linking of the *nervus* with a martial and military vigor (what a text of 1726 called "the Nerve and Sinew of War"), there are also descriptions, well into the nineteenth century, of a "nervous" or masculine, as distinguished from a "nerveless," slack or enervated, style—in treatments of "nervous, close and well-composed discourse" (1637) or "strength and nervosity" of exposition (1681), in Gay's "When envy reads the nervous lines, She frets" (1727), in Sheridan's reference to a "nervous orator" (1775) in the masculinizing rather than more modern sense, in Cowper's "Whatever is short should be nervous, masculine, and compact" (1780), in Warton's praise of the "nervousness of the sentence" (1756), Seward's of "nervousness of language" (1795), or Carlyle's of the "clear, direct, and nervous" (1828). The "nerveless" in the sense of the effeminate continued in Warburton's description of an "eloquence" that "appeared nerveless and effeminate" (1763), or in the reference in Blackwood's Magazine (1822) to Lord Byron's "nerveless" verse.

In the more limited space available here, however, I want to concentrate on what happens to the Latin tradition of the *nervosus* or "virile" style in early modern France, and particularly its striking appearance in Montaigne. The Roman tradition of stylistic *virilitas*—with its celebration of muscularity, health, and a martial or military manliness—found its way into sixteenth-century French writing in part through editions of and commentaries on Quintilian such as Stigel's (c. 1550), which exhorts its readers to "convert" what is "best and most outstanding" in the "best authors" not only "into blood but also into that juice by which judgement and accomplishment in speaking can be nourished," highlighting the key terms of this classical tradition in its description of a discourse's "sinews and muscles" (*"nervi . . . et musculi"*).[31] Horace's influential *Ars poetica*, similarly, with its lines on a style that would be contrastingly "deficient" (*"nervi / Deficiunt"*), was translated by Pelletier, in the *Art poétique*, as *"efeminée sans ners,"* while Ronsard's *Art poétique* employs this terminology in its description of *"les ners et la vie du livre."* The metaphor of the *nervi* ("sinews") and *musculi* ("muscles") of a vigorous male body sounds in the *durus* (as distinct from *mollis*) of Maurice Sceve's *"durs* Epigrammes" (McFarlane 1966) and in Du Bellay's *Deffence et Illustration de la langue françoise*, which employs the metaphorics of *chair, oz, nerfs,* and *sang* ("flesh, bone, sinews, and blood") as well as of the martial or military, praising a poetry endowed with a masculine and muscular health as *"viril, non effeminé."*[32]

The *Essais* of Montaigne are filled with praise of Roman *virilitas*, as well as of a manly style and speech, in passages that explicitly summon the keyword of this entire tradition—in the *"nerveuse,* robuste, *virile"* (*"sinnowie,* sturdie, and *manly"*) of Essay I: 20; in the preference in I: 26 for a speech that would be *"succulent et* nerveux"; in the *"autant* nerveux, *puissant et pertinant"* of II: 17; and in the programmatic praise of stylistic *virilitas* as *"plus* fort *et plus* nerveux" in Essay III: 5. Essay I: 26 (*"De l'institution des enfans"*) describes an education that would "strengthen" (literally "stiffen") the "muscles" as well as the "soul" (*"Ce n'est pas assez de luy roidir l'ame;* il luy faut aussi *roidir les muscles"* "It is not sufficient to make his minde strong, his muskles must also be strengthened"), appealing to the analogy of the athlete's "sinews" (*"vigueur de nerfs"*).[33] It rehearses the traditional opposition of words to more manly deeds as well as things, citing the opposition of *res* and *verba* from Seneca and Horace's *Ars poetica*, and contrasting the less masculine "babling" of his own time (*"Le monde n'est que babil,"* "The world is nothing but babling and words") with the examples of the Lacedemonians and Spartans as men of deeds (*"accoustumer aux* faits, *non pas aux* parolles").[34] The praise in I: 26 of a speech that is "pithie," "sinnowie," and "strong" (*"succulent et nerveux, court et serré"*) rather than "delicate" and "affected" (*"delicat et peigné"*) comes in the midst of citations from Seneca's and other Latin commendations of *virilitas*. And it characterizes the speech praised as *"nerveux"* as also "not Pedanticall, nor Frier-like, nor Lawyer-like, but rather downe right, Souldier-like" (*"non pedantesque, non fratesque, non pleideresque, mais plustost soldatesque"*), calling on the comparison of the "plaine and unpollisht" (Seneca) style to the "compact body" (*"beau corps"*), with its "sinews and strength" (*"La force et les nerfs"*).[35] Essay II: 17, which treats of the growing weakness and depravity of his own age, contrasts a "virile" and even "military" speech (*"un langage masle et militaire"*) that is *"nerveux, puissant et pertinant"* with French described as *"gratieus, delicat et abondant"* ("gracious, delicate, and copious").[36] Praise of the *"soldatesque"* in I: 26 echoes the martial metaphorics of Quintilian's and other descriptions of an ideal virility; and its description of the masculine or *"nerveux"* closely resembles Erasmus's letter of 1527 expressing desire for a more "sinnewy" and more "masculine" style (nervosius ... *magisque* masculum).[37]

Montaigne's own complex relation to a Ciceronian *copia* of style similarly involves the key terms of its condemnation by the more "masculine" Atticists. Essay II: 10 ("Of bookes")—which complains of Cicero's "long-winded preparations" (*"ses longueries d'apprets"*)—comments that "He was a good Citizen, of an honest-gentle nature, as are commonly fat and burly men: for so was he: But to speake truely of him, full of ambitious vanitie and remisse nicenesse." It then proceeds to repeat the familiar passage from Tacitus's *Dialogues* ("As great Brutus said, that it was an eloquence, broken, halting, and disjoynted, *fractam et elumbem*: Incoherent and sinnowlesse"). Essay II: 11 praises the Roman Cato the Younger for his "manlike voluptuousnesse" (*"une volupté* virile") in contrast to an effeminately (*"mollement"*) pampered Epicurianism.[38] The *Essais's* championing of such virility is in part nostalgia for the martial ethos of an older, military aristocracy (against the rise of men of words like the rhetoricians, condemned for their use of figures resembling *"le babil de vostre chambriere,"* or the babbling of your chambermaid).[39] The essay entitled "Of the Parthians Armes" (II: 11) begins with the observation that "It is a vitious, fond fashion of the Nobility and Gentry of our age, and full of nice-tendernesse (*pleine de* mollesse), never to betake themselves to armes," while *virilitas* is associated with men of deeds rather than words (*OC,* 384; Florio 2: 89).[40] Montaigne praises, in Book 1 of the *Essais,* a "masculine and constant vigour" and the "true Romane proceedings" of generals who refuse to use the "Grecian policies" of substituting the arts of "parleying" for the arts of war.[41] The essay on Cicero (I: 39) contrasts figures like Cicero and Pliny, who "have gone about to draw some principall glorie from *prating* and *speaking*" (*"du caquet et de la parlerie"*) to those who "endevored to recommend unto posterity, not their sayings but their doings" (*"non leur dire, mais leur faire"*), quoting Seneca's *"Non est ornamentum virile concinnitas"* ("Finenesse is no great grace for a *man," Epistle* 115) as part of a critique of "that eloquence which leaves us with a desire of it and not of things" (*OC,* 243–45; Florio 1: 263–66). The essay "Of the Vanitie of Words" (I: 51) contrasts the art of rhetorical *copia* with the ethos of the laconic Spartans as men of deeds, where such a man would "doubtlesse" have "beene well whipped, for professing a false, couzening and deceitfull art," one even more blameworthy than the self-painting of "women" (another commonplace of the Roman tradition). This essay goes on to disparage those who "have more prevailed with words than with armes" to the "minds truly consulare" of "men borne unto warre, of high spirits, of great performance, and able to effect any thing, but rude, simple, and unarted in the combat of talking" (*"gens nays a la guerre ... au combat du babil, rude"*), while other essays speak disparagingly of a feminized "chatter" or *"caquet."*[42] Essay I. 26, similarly, heaps contempt on the educators of the day, who teach boys to be doctors and lawyers rather than defenders of the state, in a passage in which the would-be aristocrat Michel de Montaigne uses the stigma of the effeminate to distance himself from the rhetorical arts practiced by the new class of men of words.

Montaigne's *Essais*, however, are themselves marked by repeated acknowledgments of their own feminizing *mollesse* and *errance* (terms whose Latin equivalents were condemned in Seneca and the Latin tradition of virile style), a lack (*"deffaut"*) and *foiblesse* identified both with women as *le sexe foible*, and with impotence. Prominent passages are devoted to the opposition of the virile to a female chatter (*"caquet"*), "babbling" (*"babil"*), and "wordy prowess" (*"vertu parliere"*). But the *Essais* also mark their own movement away from the rigidity and emphasis on virility in the earliest versions, to passages in which a lax and feminized "parleying" characterizes the writer himself.[43] The essay "Of Vanity" in Book III is preoccupied, like "On the Vanity of Words" in Book I, with the proliferation of "empty" words, the "idle babling" (*"le babil"*), and "liberty of the tongue" (*"desnouement de la langue"*) that have "stuft the world with so horrible a multitude of volumes," words simply for the sake of words (*"Tant de paroles pour les paroles seules"*) that it also associates with a bodily looseness or laxity. It rails against the excess of "Scribling" that brought Rome to its "ruine," citing Seneca's complaints against the "wordy" (*"verbosus"*) who, like Didymus (Montaigne's "Diomedes"), wrote thousands of books. But it also classes Montaigne himself among the "weaker sort" (*"les plus foibles"*) who "imparte foolishnesse, vanity and idlenesse" (*"la sottise, la vanité, l'oisiveté"*) to the corruption of the times.[44] And the "vanity" of words or "scribbling" it complains about make it one of the very longest of his own essays, enabled by the very prowess in "words" that had been elsewhere condemned. The *Essais* repeatedly treat of Montaigne's own admiring relation to the example of ancient Rome. But when, in Essay I. 26, he evaluates his own writing in relation to Seneca, Plutarch, and the rest, he describes himself, by comparison, as *"foible"* ("impotent") and *"chetif"* ("poor"), his own defective inventions (*"defaux"*) by contrast "weak and faint" (*"foibles et basses"*). Hence the very essay that speaks the language of maleness in wishing a son or "man childe" to its addressee also treats of his own more passive yielding to the penetrating influence of stronger writers (*OC,* 145; Florio 1: 149–50).

In relation to the key terms *nervus* or *nervosus* that serve in the Latin tradition as the link between a virile body and a virile style, the most important of the *Essais* is the one from Book III whose own dual subjects are sex and style, including the embarrassing deficiency or lack (*"deficiat/deffaut"*) of a sexual *mollesse*. Essay III: 5 (*"Sur des vers de Virgile,"* "Upon some verses of Vergil") contains the famous boast of Montaigne's own virile capacity—"Never was a man more impertinently genital in his approaches" ("Jamais homme n'eust ses approches plus impertinement genitales")—in a context that recalls both the celebration of the *"virile partie"* and the concern with male impotence in Essay I: 21, an essay that includes the transformation from female to male of Ovid's Iphis and the contemporary case of Marie Germain.[45] The repeated references to Latin *"deficiat"* and French *"deffaut"* in Essay III: 5 include not only the "defect" of an impotent old age, but also problems of virility more generally, including instances in which even the young man is deprived of the use of this "virile part."

Turning from sex to writing through the *"vers de Virgile"* that give it its title, this essay praises the Latin of Virgil and others for its strength and virility, in the passage that contains Montaigne's own most explicit call for a more virile style:

> Their speech is altogether full and massie, with a naturall and constant vigor *(leur langage est tout plein et gros d'une vigueur naturelle et constante)*. They are all epigram; not only taile, but head, stomacke and feet. There is nothing forced, nothing wrested, nothing limping; all marcheth with like tenour. *Contextus totus virilis est, non sunt circa flosculos occupat.* The whole composition or text is manly, they are not bebusied about Rhetorike flowers. This is not a soft quaint eloquence *(une eloquence molle)*, and only without offence, it is sinnowie, materiall, and solid *(nerveuse et solide)*; not so much delighting, as filling and ravishing, and ravisheth most the strongest wits, the wittiest conceits. . . . *Pectus est quod disertum facit.* It is a mans owne brest, that makes him eloquent. Our people terme judgement, language; and full conceptions, fine words. . . . *Horace* is not pleased with a sleight or superficiall expressing, it would betray him; he seeth more cleere and further into matters . . . *Plutarch* saith, that he discerned the Latine tongue by things. Here likewise the sense enlightneth and produceth the words: no longer windy or spongy, but of flesh and bone *(de chair et d'os)*. . . . (*OC*, 850–51; Florio 3: 100–101).

The passage then goes on to contrast this praised Latin virility—*"nerveuse et solide"*—with the *"eloquence molle"* of "most of our moderne French writers":

> They are over-bold and scornefull, to shunne the common trodden path: but want of invention and lacke of discretion looseth them. There is nothing to be seene in them but a miserable strained affectation of strange Inke-pot termes; harsh, cold and absurd disguisements, which in stead of raising, pull downe the matter. So they may gallantize and flush it in noveltie, they care not for efficacie. To take hold of a new farre-fetcht word, they neglect the usuall, which often are more significant, forcible and sinnowy *(plus fort et plus nerveux)*.

The "natural and constant vigor" (*"vigueur naturelle et constante"*) of Latin writing is linked explicitly in this famous passage with the "virile" or manly through the *"Contextus totus virilis est"* ("The whole composition or text is manly") of Seneca's *Epistle* 33, a Senecan passage that also makes contrasting reference to the loose and "effeminate" (*"mollitiam"*) in ways that resonate here with *"une eloquence* molle." This evocation of Senecan *"virilitas"* is supplemented by citation from Quintilian (*"Pectus est quod disertum facit,"* "It is a mans owne brest, that makes him eloquent"), from a passage of the *Institutes* (X.7.15) directed against a "womanish" loquacity or flowing stream of words (*"mulierculis superfluere"*). "*Nerveux*"—the French counterpart of the Latin "*nervosus*," "virile," or (in Florio's translation) "sinnowy"—appears twice in this context in Montaigne's essay, in the opposition of "*mollesse*" to a Latinity described as "*nerveuse et solide*," and in the contrast of this Roman virility to contemporary French writing that eschews the "*plus fort et plus nerveux*."[46]

As part of the currency of a more virile style, "*nerveux*," then, serves as one of the pivotal terms of an essay devoted simultaneously to sex and style, literally a hinge or switch word between its two subjects. But the programmatic call here for a style that would be "*plus . . . nerveux*"—or fitting counterpart to Seneca's "*virilis*"—is also strikingly undermined by the different contexts the essay evokes for the "*nervus*" or "*virile partie*" itself. The discussion of style contrasts the *mollesse* of an "*eloquence molle*" with a vigor that would be "*plus fort et plus nerveux.*" But when, in this same essay, *nervosus* or *nervus* appear in their explicitly sexual sense, it is in the context not of virility, but of its failure, not of a successful penetration or ravishment, but of slackness and *mollesse*. Juvenal's witticism that not even "members of unheard-of length" ("*longi mensura incognita* nervi") will help if "destiny" is adverse, appears in the context of Vulcan's cuckolding (*OC*, 831), an ironic reminder that the very "verses of Vergil" and Lucretius praised in this essay for their virile Latinity have as their subject the unmanning of Vulcan by a Venus who stands as the classical emblem of this essay's multiple instances of the unmanning of men. Women in III: 5 are presented as anything but the passive figures its citation of Seneca's famous "*pati natae*" ("born to be passive") suggests they should be (*OC,* 863; Florio 3: 114). And the passage in which the *nervus* appears most prominently in its sexual sense (*OC*, 864–65; Florio 3: 116) begins not with a confident virility, but with a citation from Martial (VII: lvii 3–5) on the "limp" and "unwarlike" ("*imbelles*") member. Catullus's verse (LXVII: 27) on the need to replace an impotent with a "stronger" ("*nervosius*") lover is cited here in relation to the "weakness and incapacity" ("*foiblesse et incapacité*") that "may lawfully breake wedlock." And this same Catullan text (its "*languidior*" virility's slackened opposite) is cited in an earlier passage of III: 5 (*OC*, 844; Florio 3: 93) that recalls the contemporary French preoccupation with male impotence already shadowing the more straightforward celebration of the "*virile partie*" (*telos* or goal of the transformations from female to male) in Essay I: 21. The soft or "*mollis*" member is evoked by repeated quotations from Horace's *Epode* 12 ("*ad unum* / Mollis *opus*," for one encounter limp), along with the other *Epode* (8) that treats of what "unmans" his "manliness" ("vires *quid* enervet *meas*").[47] And when the debilitating impotence described by Horatius Flaccus in *Epode* 12 appears in Montaigne's essay a second time, it is in lines contrasting it to a "firmer" youth ("Cujus in indomito *constantior* inguine nervus, / Quam nova collibus arbor inhaeret," "Whose member firmer stands, in its undaunted pride, / Than a young tree upon a mountainside").[48] Quotation after Latin quotation in this essay features the "limp" and "soft" ("*mollis*") male member brought to the place where the "*virile partie*" is most required, including this text of Horace that contrasts it with the "*constans*" or "firm" (*Epodes* XII: 15, 19). The repeated citation of this slackness or *mollesse* that begins with Martial's "unwarlike" member ends (*OC*, 866; Florio 3: 117) with yet another evocation of the "*virile partie*": "Chacune de mes pieces me faict esgalement moy que toute autre. Et nulle autre ne me faict plus proprement homme que cette-cy" ("Each of my pieces are equally mine, one as another: and no other doth more properly make me a man then this"). But in the Latin fragments that lead up to this statement of what makes him "properly . . . a man," the *nervus* is cited only in its failure. And the lack of a "*constantior*" or "firmer" virility in the *Epodes* text resonates ironically against the "*vigueur naturelle et constante*" of the passage in praise of a style that would be "*plus fort et plus nerveux*," since it is cited not in its vigor but in its flaccidity, beginning with a reference to Montaigne's own "shrunken sinewes" or "*nerfs*" (*OC*, 872; Florio 3: 124).

In addition to complicating its call for a more virile style by such debilitating citations of the *nervus* itself, Essay III: 5 also ambiguously evokes the figure of the "passive" male, in ways that simultaneously echo contemporary orthodoxies of disapproval and register links between such passivity and the *Essais*'s own references to their author's passive receptiveness to the penetrating influence of stronger Roman writers (III: 5 itself contains a passage which speaks of a Latin, for example, that "caponizes" him, or "*me chapone*").[49] The figure of the *cinaedus* actually appears in III: 5 in another citation from Martial's *Epigrams* ("*Et habet tristis quoque turba cynaedos,*" "Fidlers are often had / Mongst people that are sad"), a text (VII: 57) that treats of the "effeminate" ("*mollem*") who makes a "flaccid" husband rather than a "genuine man" ("*vero ... viro*"). ("Fidler," Florio's translation of *cynaedus*, was the contemporary English term for the "preposterous" sexual inversion in which men took this passive female role).[50] But the Epigram here evoked in its scorn for the *cynaedus* also satirically exposes those (including Stoic philosophers) who pretend to a hypermasculinity and severity in the old Roman mode—calling on the Curii and Fabii as stock types of Roman *virilitas*—while they themselves are secretly "unwarlike" ("*imbellis*") pathics or *cinaedi*. The sense of the pervasiveness (albeit less than open acknowledgment) of such relations between men is made more contemporary in Montaigne's essay when, after citing another text from Martial on the male lovers (or "*concubini*") a bridegroom should (but does not necessarily) put aside at the time of marriage, Montaigne notes that, in the France of his day, "marriage which we averre should hinder [women] from burning, affords them but smal refreshing, according as our manners are. If they meet with a husband, whose force by reason of his age is yet boyling, he will take a pride to spend it else-where." Among its several references, the passage cites not only Martial, but the fact that the "Philosopher Polemon was justly called in question by his wife, for sowing in a barren fielde the fruit due to the fertile" ("*semant en un champ sterile le fruit deu au champ genital*").[51] In addition to Maecenas, familiar Roman figure of the *cinaedus* as well as of the lax or effeminated man (*OC*, 846; Florio 3: 94), Essay III: 5 rehearses instances of the opprobrium attaching to sexual relations between men, recalling Origen's refusal to "suffer himselfe to be Sodomatically abused by a filthy Egiptian slave" and citing the immodest dress of the women of Pegu as "an invention or shift devised to draw men unto them, and with-draw them from other men or boies, to which unnaturall brutish sinne that nation is wholly addicted" (*OC,* 823; Florio 3: 68). It also (more ambiguously) cites the exemplary figure of Socrates in a clearly pederastic context (Florio 3: 122), and quotes from Horace's lines (*Odes* II: v) on the ambiguous gender of a beautiful boy as an example of that "perfect beauty" that Homer extends only "untill such time as the chinne begins to bud," noting simultaneously "the cause for which the Sophister *Dion* termed youthes budding hayres; *Aristogitons* and *Harmodii*" (deliverers from tyranny), figures for the deliverance of the *puer* from the future passive status of the "womanish" man.[52]

Essay III: 5 also, however, complicates its summoning of Senecan *virilitas* and condemnations of effeminacy with its own repeated evocations of the essayist's passivity, or *mollesse*. The very passage that contrasts a virile Latinity to the "*eloquence molle*" that eschews the "*plus fort et plus nerveux*" contrasts it with the French in which the essay itself is written, in terms that recall the description in I: 26 of its writer's yielding to the influence of stronger Latin writing:

> I finde it sufficiently plenteous *(suffisament abondant)*, but not sufficiently plyable and vigorous *(maniant et vigoureux)*. It commonly faileth and shrinketh under a pithy and powerfull *(puissant)* conception. If your march therein be far extended, you often feele it droope and languish under you *(il languid soubs vous et fleschit)*, unto whose default *(deffaut)* the Latine doth now and then present his helping hand, and the Greeke to some others.

"Languid" here ("*il languid soubs vous et fleschit*") resonates with the *languidior* cited earlier in this essay from Catullus's verse on the slackened *nervus*, while "*fleschit*" shares the language of the passages from I.26 ("Quant aux facultez naturelles qui sont en moy ... je les sense fleschir sous la charge," "Concerning the natural faculties that are in me ... I perceive them to faint under their owne burthen") that treat of his own more passive reception of stronger and more virile writers. Seneca's *pati natae* is invoked in III: 5 in relation to the traditionally passive role of women. But the French that is the language of the *Essais* themselves is described as yielding and giving way, in the very section that summons the contrasting Senecan *virilis*, just as their writer admits to "running on carelessly" ("*je cours inadvertement*") in the errant style contrasted by Seneca to its virile opposite. Montaigne elsewhere in III: 5 calls himself "*un homme languager*" (a phrase that Florio translates as "a babling fellow," the term that appears in the *Essais*'s repeated contrasting of virile deeds to the "*babil*" of men of words). And the essay ends by referring to itself as "*un flux de* caquet" ("*qui m'est eschappé d'un flux de caquet*"), a "flux" or flow, once again, of a feminized "*caquet*" or babbling, in lines accompanied by a final quotation from Catullus on a girl who lets flow out something hid.[53] Whatever its appeal to a more virile Latinity—already undermined by its conflicting citations of the *nervus* and *nervosus* from Latin writing itself—Montaigne's own most extended treatment of sex and style, bodily and stylistic *virilitas* as opposed to an enervated slackness, ends by comparing its own writing to the very images (including this contrasting flowing, or "*flux*") that in this tradition are the familiar opposite of a "proper" virility.

The gendered opposition of the *Essais* contrasts feminine or effeminating "words" ("*parolles*") with more masculine "deeds" ("*faits*") as well as things, echoing the traditional early modern division of "*Fatti maschii, parole femine*" ("Women are Words, Men

Deeds"), the widely current proverb that was to become, through the Calvert Lords Baltimore, the (still-present) motto on the Great Seal of Maryland. We might, then, conclude consideration of the anxieties of virility that traversed early modern writing with the echoes both of the *"virile partie,"* and of this ubiquitous early modern proverb in the work of John Florio, the translator of Montaigne who was himself a minor humanist and language teacher. In the *"Epistle* Dedicatorie" to his *Worlde of Wordes* (1598), explicitly dedicated to words rather than deeds or things, Florio acknowledges that "Some perhaps will . . . not allowe it [*Worlde of Wordes*] for a male-broode," since, as the proverb goes, *"Le parole sono femine, & i fatti sono maschii,* Wordes they are women, and deeds they are men." But he then proceeds—in a passage that directly echoes the sex changes of Montaigne's Essay I: 21—to write that "though [words] were commonly Feminine, why might not I by strong imagination (which Phisicions give so much power unto) *alter their sexe?"* and goes on to quote the transformation of Iphis from female to male as the figure for his own text of "Wordes," assuring his patrons that his work has been successfully transformed from "she" to "he," its "strength . . . stature, and . . . masculine vigor" providing the "autenticall testimonies" that now "assure his sexe." Such stories of gender transformation in early modern writing—like the ones that Montaigne himself recounts in Essay I: 21 from both classical sources and contemporary "Phisicions"— never tire of insisting that such transformations can proceed in one direction only, from "imperfect" female to "perfect" male, never the "preposterous" reverse.[54] But Florio's invocation of Iphis and other stories that have as their *telos* the desired *"virile partie,"* in order to justify his traditionally more feminine "Wordes," itself betrays the very possibility that motivates such incessantly repeated denial and insistence. Florio himself was to characterize his own involvement in translation as an imperfect, "defective" and "female" activity ("since all translations are reputed femalls, delivered at second hand"), in a reminder of the very sense of the "imperfect" or "defective" female that subtended such desired transformations to the more "perfect" male.[55] Performing nothing less than such a sex change on his own text of *Wordes,* this "Florio" (long thought to be the model for Shakespeare's effeminate "Parolles") provides in little an example of the anxieties of *virilitas* we have traced, anxieties both about the ambiguous gender of men of words and about the activity of writing itself.

NOTES

1. Italics in subsequent quotations also indicate emphasis added; italics in original will be specified. Erasmus's *Epistle* 899 is cited in Williamson (1951, 19); see Scott (1910, 27), on the similar call for a more masculine (*nervosius*) style in Erasmus's *Ciceronianus.*

2. See, for example, Dolet's charges against Erasmus in his *Dialogus,* (1535), reprinted in Telle (1974); and Scaliger's attack on the "babbling" *(blaterans)* of Erasmus in Scaliger (1531) (MS. 1529).

3. For more detailed treatment of Erasmus's *Lingua,* see Cave (1979, esp. 164–166), with (50) (on the relation between *copia* and *loquacitas*); and Parker, (1989, 445–50).

4. See Ben Jonson, *Timber; or Discoveries,* in Herford, *et al.* (1947, VIII; 633); and, on Baconian science as a "masculine birth of time," Reiss (1985).

5. See Tomkis (1607), with the discussion in Parker (1989, 454–59).

6. See Sir Philip Sidney, *Defense of Poetry*, on "poetical sinnewes," with John Florio's *Worlde of Wordes* (1611) on *"Nervosita,"* as "sinewinesse, nervinesse" and Cotgrave's *Dictionarie* (1611), which translates French *"nervosité"* as "nervositie, sinnewie strength." The *O.E.D.*'s first citation of "nervous" in this sense is from a text of 1413 ("These armes ben nervous, that is to seyn well frett with senewes"). Shakespeare's *Coriolanus* (II: i, 177) speaks of Death's "nervie Arme" and *Measure for Measure* (I: iv, 53) of the "Nerves of State," while Agamemnon is described as the very "Nerve, and Bone of Greece" in *Troilus and Cressida* (I: iii, 55), a play that also uses *"Mistress* Thersites" for a figure famously copious in words, and "preposterous discoveries" for Achilles and his "male whore."

7. See Sherry (1555), fol. lxi, with Trimpi (1962, 105).

8. See Tacitus (1914), *Dialogus,* ch. 18. On Cicero's correspondence with Brutus and Calvus, see Hendrickson, (1926, 234–58).

9. See Adams (1982, 38, 224).

10. I am, of course, referring here to Williams's articulation of the notion of "keywords" in his influential *Keywords,* 1983.

11. *Institutio Oratoria* (*Institutes of Oratory*), VIII: Pr. 18–22, cited (with slight modifications) from the Loeb translation (1936). This passage from Quintilian ends with a reference to Eloquence as a woman who "will never think it her duty to polish her nails and tire her hair," the figure of the unadorned woman that was another familiar *topos* in this tradition.

12. Quintilian's *Institutes* are full of such masculinizing terminology, praise of a style that wears a "manly" dress (*"et nitor ille cultum virilem,"* XII: 10, 79) or that is "bold, manly and chaste" (*"virilis et fortis et sanctus"*), free from all "effeminate smoothness" (V: 3, 7). The comparison to an athlete's body in Quintilian occurs repeatedly (X: 1, 4; cf. X: 1, 33; X: 3, 7; X: 4, 4; X: 7, 1 and 23). See also VIII: 3, 11; and the praise of Demosthenes in X: 1, 60 (*"plurimum sanguinis atque nervorum"*).

13. See respectively *Institutes* XII: 10, 79, and XII: 10, 12–14, which goes on to observe that the question of virility of style is still very much alive (*"modo etiam magis virilem esse contendant"*). Quintilian also had his own detractors who, like the Atticists Brutus and Calvus, regarded a highly wrought *compositio* as a sign of effeminacy. Trimpi 1962, 6, notes that Cicero, in trying to rejoin rhetoric and dialectic after their Socratic separation, "became a partisan of an oratorically ornate or 'Asiatic' style."

14. Tacitus (1914, 73) (*Dialogus* 21).

15. See Freudenberg (1990, 187–203, esp. 192–94) on the opposition of *"acer"* (in the sexual sense of "keen" that also appears in *Hamlet*) to a style that is *"sine nervis,"* without (masculine) strength or vigor, in the context of the *topoi* of masculinity more generally in Roman writing.

16. See Oliensis (1991, 107–38); and Fitzgerald (1988, 176–91), with Freudenberg, (esp. 193–95).

17. *Epistulae morales* CXIV ("On Style as a Mirror of Character"), *Seneca* 1943, 301–302.

18. See Seneca (1943, 302–305); Richlin (1993, 523–73), Richlin (1992, 92–93), and *cinaedus* in the *Index Verborum,* with Jack Winkler's work on the Greek *kinaidos,* (1990, chapter 2). Tacitus' Dialogue 26—the one that also contains the influential description of the "effeminate" (*"solutum et enervem"*) Cicero—inveighs against a style that would be like "the coxcombry of a Maecenas" or "scarce worthy even of a man," comparing it to "the rhythms of stage-dancing," another standard figure of effeminacy. Richlin (1993, 525), comments that: "It was normal for adult male Romans to love both women and boys (*pueri*) and erotic poetry occasionally lists the advantages of boys over women. But . . . the Romans drew a sharp line between man + boy (good, at least for the man) and man + man (bad)"; *"cinaedus"* (530–531) "was a common word for a passive male . . . roughly the equivalent of the English term 'queer,' in a lexicon that also included *pathicus, exoletus, concubinus, spintria, puer* ('boy'), *pullus* ('chick'), *pusio, delicatus, mollis* ('soft'), *tener* ('dainty'), *debilis* ('weak'), *effeminatus, discinctus* ('loose-belted . . .'), *morbosus* ('sick')."

19. See Richlin (1992, 41, 93, 137, 168, 188–89).

20. See Richlin (1993, 531 (on *"impudicitia"*), 536 n. 31); Winkler (1990, 21), and Halperin (1990, 88–90). Richlin's reading of the *molles* and of what (*pace* the more Foucauldian analyses of David Halperin) might be called a Roman "homophobia" concludes with the invective of Juvenal's Second Satire.

21. See Plutarch's *Life of Pompey* 48: 7 and Ovid's *Ars Amatoria* I: 523; cited in Richlin (1993, 523); and in addition, on *"mollis"* and *"durus,"* Coleman (1977, 75).

22. Ludovico Vives, *De ratione dicendi* II: v, in Vives (1782); Trimpi (1962, 54). On Vives, see also Foster Watson's preface to his translation of *De Tradendis Disciplines* in *Vives: On Education*.

23. See Hudson (1928, 374–92, 385).

24. On the sexuality and ambiguous position of James himself in relation to public denunciations of sodomy in the period (including his own), see Smith (1991, 14, 26, 176); and Parker (1993a, 60–95, 85–86, 94). See Justus Lipsius, *Epp. Misc.* II: 10, cited in Croll (1921, 99), and his *Inst. Epist.*, (14–15); on Bacon, Trimpi (1962, 15, 251–52); for Hoskins and Flecknoe (*Miscellanea*, London 1653, 77), Williamson (1951, 99, 211).

25. Sir Thomas Elyot, *The Governour* (I: 116–17); and Shakespeare's *Hamlet* and *All's Well that Ends Well*.

26. See also *Poetaster* (III: v, 4), where Jonson translates *"sine nervis"* as "wants pith."

27. On this sense of "preposterous," see Parker (1992); with Goldberg (1992) on "preposterous venery." In his "To the Reader," appended to *Poetaster,* Jonson's "Author" says of his enemies: "Not one of them, but lives himselfe (if knowne) / *Improbior satyram scribente cinaedo"* (II: 66–67), citing explicitly the figure of the *cinaedus* from Juvenal's *Satires* 4: 106. In Jonson's *Sejanus,* a play that contrasts a more virile older Rome with contemporary degeneracy, Sejanus himself is described as having "prostituted his abused body / To that great gourmond, fat Apicius," and having been "the noted pathick of the time" (I: 214–16). See Herford, *et al.* (1932, IV: 319 and 362) respectively.

28. Howell (1892, II, 395).

29. See the discussion of this tension in Jonson in Parker (1987, ch. 2), and in Parker (1986).

30. See Locke (1961, II bk. 3, ch. 10, 105–106) and see *O.E.D.* citing Milton, 1659 Civ. Power Wks. 1851 V.336 and *Samson Agonistes* 1646, on Samson's "straining all his nerves," with the other entries under nerve(s), nervous, nerviness, and nervosity that cite the examples quoted in the remainder of this paragraph; the appeals to virility in early modern science, in, for example, the announcement by Henry Oldenburg (Secretary of the Royal Society) that the society's intention was "to raise a Masculine Philosophy ... whereby the Mind of Man may be ennobled with the knowledge of Solid Truths"; Joseph Glanvill's warning that "The *Woman* in us, still prosecutes a deceit, like that begun in the *Garden*; and our *Understandings* are wedded to an *Eve*, as fatal as the *Mother* of our miseries," together with his conclusion that the "case of *Truth* is *desparate*" when "the *Affections* wear the breeches and the *Female* rules" [italics in original]; and Thomas Sprat's advocating of a "masculine style" in his *History of the Royal Society*, which proclaims that "Eloquence" (like rhetorical ornament) should be "banished out of all civil societies" as a "cause of corruption," evokes "the primitive purity, and shortness, when men deliver'd so many things, almost in an equal number of words"), and contrasts the "Feminine Arts" of the continent to the "Masculine Arts of Knowledge" represented by English experimental science. See Easlea (1980, 70); Glanvill (1661, 1931, 117–18, 135); Keller (1985, 34–40, 52–54); Sprat (1958, 39, 111, 113, and 129); Shapin and Schaffer (1985), and Potter forthcoming.

31. Stigel's was typical of sixteenth-century forthcoming commentaries on the *Institutes*, in Aldus, Ascensius, Petrus Mosellanus, Gryphius, and Joachim Camerarius. For the citation of Stigel's commentary, from a sixteenth-century edition of Quintilian which appeared around 1550 (n.d., 149), see Coleman (1977, 73–74).

32. See Peletier (1930, 143), translating lines 25–30 of the *Ars*; Coleman (1977, 74), and (1980, 16),

cite p. 5 of Pierre Ronsard's *Art poétique* and note the same imagery from the 1587 preface to Ronsard's *Franciade*.

33. See Montaigne, *Oeuvres complètes* [henceforth *OC*] (1962, 152–53), and *The Essayes* n.d., (159–60). I have chosen to use this famous contemporary English translation of Montaigne rather than a modern one because Florio's own language participates in a contemporary lexicon of resonant English terms within this tradition, as we shall see.

34. See *OC,* 168–71, with Florio 1: 178–82.

35. See *OC,* 171–72, with Florio 1: 182–84.

36. See *OC,* 622 and Florio 3: 363. See also Florio 2: 363: "Messala complaineth in Tacitus of certaine strait garments used in his time, and discommendeth the fashion of the benches whereon the Orators were to speak, saying, they weakened their eloquence" (*"affoiblissoient leur eloquence"*). Except where noted, all translations are from Florio.

37. See Quint's discussion of Montaigne's nostalgia for a lost order of military valor, (1990, 459–89). On the links between Erasmus's letter and this passage in Montaigne, see Friedrich (1968, 421), and Compagnon (1983).

38. See respectively Florio 2: 101–102; *OC,* 395 ("une eloquence cassée et esrenée, fractam et elumbem"); I: 26 in Florio 1: 181 (on Cato's rebuke of Cicero); Florio, 110–11 with *OC* 402–403.

39. See *OC,* 294, with Florio 1: 348 (who translates *"le babil de vostre chambriere"* as "your chambermaids tittle-tattle"). 1: 26 also expresses disdain for such professionals, and contrasts them with "gentlemen." See Florio 1: 179, and *OC,* 168, the passage that also refers to the contemporary world of "babbling" (*"Le monde n'est que babil"*).

40. Florio 2: 89; *OC,* 384.

41. See I: 5 in *OC,* 27, Florio 1: 18, and I: 6 ("That the Houre of Parlies is Dangerous") with Greene 1986, 116–39.

42. *OC,* 292–95, Florio I: 345–49. See also Essay I: 40, with its *"du* caquet *et de la parlerie"* (*OC,* 243) and the *"parade de son esprit et de son caquet"* of Essay III: 8.

43. See, for example Essay II: 12 in Florio 2: 280–81. On the tension and movement between "masculine" and "feminine" in the *Essais,* see, among others, Greene (1986); Cottrell, (1981); Kritzman (1991, esp. 61–71); and, more recently, Freccero (1994, 73–83). Clark (1978) rightly challenges the notion that the shifting from masculine to feminine can be charted as a progressive development from earlier to later Montaigne, rather than remaining a tension and oscillation even in the later essays. On Montaigne's ambivalent relation to rhetoric, see, in addition to Compagnon (1983), Bowen (1975, 107–21); McGowan (1974); Cave (1979, 297ff.); and Lestringant (1985).

44. See Florio 3: 192–94; Seneca *Epistle* LXXXVIII, 1943, 372–73; and the *"lache"* of this essay (French counterpart of Latin *"laxus"*) in *OC,* 923 (*"un vieil esprit, dur tantost, tantost lache, et tousjours indigeste"*), translated by Florio (3: 183) as "the excrements of an ould spirit, sometimes hard, sometimes laxative; but ever indigested," a passage that makes clear the other bodily form of laxity in Montaigne, the opposite of the *durus* of the constipation cited elsewhere in the *Essais* (e.g. I: 21); *OC,* 923; Florio 3: 184.

45. See the discussion of I: 21 against the backdrop of contemporary impotence trials in Parker (1993b). In the medical orthodoxy represented by Ambroise Paré and others, changes of sex could be only from "imperfect" female to "perfect" male, not the reverse. Montaigne echoes Paré's story of the sex change of Marie Germain both in his unpublished travel journal (September 1580) and in Essay I: 21.

46. Cave's (1979) consideration of III: 5 treats of the sexualizing of terms such as "ravishes." III: 5 refers several times to Seneca's *Epistulae.* See, for example, Florio 3: 121 "(*Nullum intra se vitium est* (SEN. *Epi.* xcv)."

47. See respectively *OC,* 844; Florio 3: 93; and *OC,* 835; Florio 3: 82. See also Oliensis 1991 on *Epodes* 8 and 12.

48. *OC,* 872; Florio 3: 124. The Horace translation (not provided by Florio) is taken from Frame 1957, 682.

49. *OC,* 858; Florio 3: 109.

50. See Martial, *Epigrams* VII: lvii, 8; *OC,* 819–20, Florio 3: 66–67. Richlin 1992, 138–39, observes that "Martial reserves his strongest invective in this area for men who pretend to be especially old-fashioned and severe but are actually pathics. Usually this severity takes the form of a pretense of being a Stoic philosopher." She goes on to comment on this text in relation to Martial's determination to "differentiate effeminacy from virility and from the persona of the poet." For "fiddler" in the contemporary English sense, see, for example, Shakespeare's *The Taming of the Shrew* (III: i), where the effeminate Hortensio is called both "Fiddler" and a "preposterous ass."

51. See *OC,* 833, Florio 3: 79, citing Martial, *Epigrams* XII: xcix, 10–12 ("Sit tandem pudor, aut eamus in jus, / Multis mentula billibus redempta, / Non est haec tua, Basse, vendidisti"). The Montaigne passage goes on to remark that if women "match with broken (*cassez*) stuffe in ful wedlocke, they are in worse case, then either virgins or widowes." On the Martial text, see Richlin 1992, 221, 246n. 35, 258 n.5.

52. See Florio 3: 126. Frame 1957, 683 comments here that the "downy hairs of adolescence" are called "Aristogeitons and Harmodiuses" because "these hairs deliver lovers of the boys who grow them from the tyranny of love." This is an extraordinarily overdetermined passage, however, since Aristogeiton and Harmodius were also lovers.

53. See *OC,* 875, Florio 3: 127–28, Catullus LXV: 19–24, and Cave 1979. For *"un homme languager,"* see *OC,* 848, Florio 3: 97.

54. See, for example, Sandys' gloss on the story of Iphis, 1640, 184, which also refers to Montaigne's story of Marie Germain from Essay I: 21, with the discussion of the fear of this "preposterous" reverse in Parker 1993, 359–63.

55. See his "Epistle Dedicatorie" to "the Right Honorable, my best-best Benefactors, and most-most honored Ladies, Lucie Countesse of Bedford; and hir best-most loved-loving Mother, Ladie Anne Harrington," I: 1. Florio (who repeatedly plays on the links between his own name and the traditional "flowers" of language and rhetoric) refers to his earliest works of words—the language and courtesy manuals entitled *First Fruites* (1578) and *Second Frutes* (1591)—as marriageable "daughters" (offspring of the humanist's study, like Minerva born from the head of Jove), and these "female fruites" are contrasted with the "bouncing boy" represented by *A Worlde of Wordes,* the long-desired male heir ("none in th'end caries the land but he"), more "perfect" than his sisters' "sexe-imperfectnesse," in a prefatory poem to that subsequent work.

WORKS CITED

Adams, J. N. 1982. *The Latin Sexual Vocabulary.* Baltimore: The Johns Hopkins University Press.

Bowen, Barbara C. 1975. "Montaigne's Anti-*Phaedrus*: 'Sur des vers de Virgile' (*Essais* III, v)." *Journal of Medieval and Renaissance Studies* 5: 107–21.

Cave, Terence. 1979. *The Cornucopian Text.* Oxford: Clarendon.

Cicero, Marcus Tullius. 1851. *Orator,* ed. Otto Jahn. Leipzig: Weidmann.

———. 1981. *Ad C. Herennium; De ratione dicendi.* London: Heinemann.

Clark, Carol. 1978. *The Web of Metaphor: Studies of the Imagery of Montaigne's "Essais."* Lexington, KY: French Forum Monographs, no. 7.

Coleman, Dorothy Gabe. 1977. *The Gallo-Roman Muse: Aspects of Roman Literary Tradition in Sixteenth-Century France.* Cambridge: Cambridge University Press.

———. 1980. *The Chaste Muse: A Study of Joachim Du Bellay's Poetry.* Leiden: E. J. Brill.

Compagnon, Antoine. 1983. "A Long Short Story: Montaigne's Brevity." *Yale French Studies* 64: 24–50.

Cotgrave, Randle. 1611. *A Dictionarie of the French and English tongues.* Compiled by Randalle Cotgrove. London: Adam Islip.

Cottrell, Robert D. 1981. *Sexuality/Textuality: A Study of the Fabric of Montaigne's "Essais."* Columbus, Ohio: Ohio State University Press.

Croll, Morris W. 1921. "'Attic Prose' in the Seventeenth Century." *Studies in Philology* 18: 79–128.

Dolet, Etienne. 1535. *Dialogus, De Imitatione Ciceroniana adversus Desiderium Erasmum Roterodamum.* Lyon: S. Gryphius. Reprinted in Telle, *Travaux d'humanisme.*

Easlea, Brian. 1980. *Witch Hunting, Magic and the New Philosophy.* Brighton: Harvester Press.

Fitzgerald, W. 1988. "Power and Impotence in Horace's *Epodes.*" *Ramus* 17: 176–91.

Florio, John. 1598/1611. *A Worlde of Wordes, or Most Copious, and exact dictionaries in Italian and English.* Collected by John Florio. London: Arnold Hatfield for Edw. Blount and William Barret.

———, trans. n.d. *The Essayes of Michael Lord of Montaigne.* 3 vols. London: J. M. Dent & Sons.

Frame, Donald M., trans. 1957. *The Complete Essays of Montaigne.* Stanford: Stanford University Press.

Freccero, Carla. 1994. "Cannibalism, Homophobia, Women: Montaigne's 'Descannibales' and 'De l'amitié'," in Hendricks and Parker, ed. *Women, "Race" and Writing.* 73–83.

Freudenberg, Kirk. 1990. "Horace's Satiric Program and the Language of Contemporary Theory in *Satires* 2.1." *American Journal of Philology* 3: 187–203.

Friedrich, Hugo. 1968. *Montaigne.* Paris: Gallimard.

Glanvill, Joseph. 1661/1931. *The Vanity of Dogmatizing.* London. Reprint by the Facsimile Text Society, New York: Columbia University Press.

Goldberg, Jonathan. 1992. *Sodometries: Renaissance Texts, Modern Sexualities.* Stanford: Stanford University Press.

Greene, Thomas M. 1986. *The Vulnerable Text: Essays on Renaissance Literature.* New York: Columbia University Press.

Halperin, David M. 1990. *One Hundred Years of Homosexuality.* New York: Routledge.

Hendricks, Margo and Patricia Parker, eds. 1994. *Women, "Race" and Writing in the Early Modern Period.* London and New York: Routledge.

Hendrickson, G. L. 1926. "Cicero's Correspondence with Brutus and Calvus on Oratorical Style." *American Journal of Philology* 47: 234–58.

Herford, C. H. and Percy and Evelyn Simpson, eds. 1932. *Ben Jonson.* Oxford: Clarendon.

Horace. 1964. *Satires,* ed. Arthur Palmer. New York: St. Martin's Press.

Howell, James. 1892. *Epistolae Ho-Elianae; The Familiar Letters of James Howell,* ed. Joseph Jacobs. London: D. Nutt.

Hudson, Hoyt H. 1928. "Jewel's Oration Against Rhetoric: A Translation." *Quarterly Journal of Speech* 14: 374–92.

Keller, Evelyn Fox. 1985. *Reflections on Gender and Science.* New Haven: Yale University Press.

Kritzman, Lawrence. 1991. *The Rhetoric of Sexuality and the Literature of the French Renaissance.* New York: Cambridge University Press.

Lestringant, Frank, ed. 1985. "Rhétorique de Montaigne." *Bulletin de la société des amis de Montaigne.* Series 7, n. 1–2.

Locke, John. 1961. *An Essay Concerning Human Understanding,* ed. John W. Yolton. London and New York: Dent.

McFarlane, I. D. 1966. *The "Délie" of Maurice Sceve.* Cambridge: Cambridge University Press.

McGowan, Margaret M. 1974. *Montaigne's Deceits: The Art of Persuasion in the "Essais."* London: University of London Press.

Montaigne, Michelde. 1962. *Oeuvres complètes,* ed. Albert Thibaudet and Maurice Rat. Paris: Pléiade.

———. n.d. *The Essayes of Michael Lord of Montaigne,* trans. John Florio. 3 vols. London: J.M. Dent & Sons.

————. 1957. *The Complete Essays of Montaigne*, trans. Donald M. Frame. Stanford: Stanford University Press.

Oliensis, Ellen. 1991. "Canidia, Canicula, and the Decorum of Horace's *Epodes*." *Arethusa* 24: 107–38.

Parker, Patricia. 1986. "Deferral, Dilation, Différance: Shakespeare, Cervantes, Jonson," in Parker and Quint, *Literary Theory*.

————. 1987. *Literary Fat Ladies: Rhetoric, Gender, Property*. London and New York: Methuen.

————. 1989. "On the Tongue: Cross Gendering, Effeminacy, and the Art of Words." *Style* 23: 445–50.

————. 1992. "Preposterous Events." *Shakespeare Quarterly* 43: 186–213.

————. 1993a. "*Othello* and *Hamlet*: Dilation, Spying, and the 'Secret Place' of Woman." *Representations* 44: 60–95.

————. 1993b. "Gender Ideology, Gender Change: The Case of Marie Germain." *Critical Inquiry* 19: 337–64.

Parker, Patricia and David Quint, eds. 1986. *Literary Theory / Renaissance Texts*. Baltimore: Johns Hopkins University Press.

Peletier du Mans, Jacques. 1930. *L'Art poétique*, ed. A. Boulanger. Paris.

Potter, Elizabeth. Forthcoming. "Making Gender/Making Science: Gender Ideology and Boyle's Experimental Philosophy."

Quint, David. 1990. "A Reconsideration of Montaigne's 'Des cannibales'." *Modern Language Quarterly* 51: 459–89.

Quintilian. 1936. *The Institutio Oratoria of Quintilian*, trans. H. E. Butler. London: Heinemann.

Reiss, Timothy J. 1982. *The Discourse of Modernism*. Ithaca: Cornell University Press.

Richlin, Amy. 1992. *The Garden of Priapus: Sexuality and Aggression in Roman Humor*, rev. ed. New York: Oxford University Press.

————. 1993. "Not Before Homosexuality: The Materiality of the *Cinaedus* and the Roman Law against Love between Men." *Journal of the History of Sexuality* 34: 523–73.

Sandys, George. 1640. *Ovid's Metamorphosis Englished, Mythologized and Represented in Figures*. London.

Scaliger, J. C. 1531. *Oratio pro M.T. Cicero contra Desiderium Erasmum Rot*. Paris.

Scott, Izora. 1910. *Controversies over the Imitation of Cicero*. New York: Columbia University Teachers College.

Seneca. 1943. *Seneca: Ad Lucilium Epistulae Morales*, trans. Richard M. Gummere. rev. ed. London: Heinemann.

Shapin, Steven and Simon Schaffer. 1985. *Leviathan and the Air-Pump: Hobbes, Boyle, and the Experimental Life*. Princeton: Princeton University Press.

Sherry, Richard. 1555. *Figures of Grammar*. London.

Sidney, Sir Philip. 1595/1868. *An apologie for poetrie*. London: E. Arber.

Smith, Bruce R. 1991. *Homosexual Desire in Shakespeare's England*. Chicago: Chicago University Press.

Sprat, Thomas. 1958. *History of the Royal Society*, eds. Jackson I. Cope and Harold Whitmore Jones. St. Louis: Washington University Studies.

Tacitus. 1914. *Dialogus, Agricola, Germania*, trans. William Peterson. London: Heinemann.

Telle, Emile V. 1974. *Travaux d'humanisme et Renaissance*. Geneva: Droz.

Tomkis, Thomas [likely author]. 1607. *Lingua: Or the Combat of the Tongue and the Five Senses for Superiority, a Pleasant Comedie*. London.

Trimpi, Wesley. 1962. *Ben Jonson's Poems: A Study of the Plain Style*. Stanford: Stanford University Press.

Vives, Ludovico. 1782. *Joannes Ludovici Vivis Valentini Opera Omnia*. Valencia.

Williams, Raymond. 1983. *Keywords: A Vocabulary of Culture and Society*, rev. ed. London: Oxford University Press.

Williamson, George. 1951. *The Senecan Amble*. Chicago: University of Chicago Press.

Winkler, Jack. 1990. *The Constraints of Desire*. New York: Routledge.

Explicit Ink   **11**

Elizabeth Pittenger

Explicit Enchiridion magistri Alani de conquestu nature editum: this is the scribal signature in a
fifteenth-century manuscript marking off the end of the *prosimetrum* more commonly
known as *De planctu Naturae* (*The Complaint of Nature*) by Alain de Lille or Alanus ab Insulis.[1]
Among the 133 manuscripts of this twelfth-century text (1160 to 1170), at least twenty-
two designate it as *Enchiridion*, a handbook, manual, guidebook, on the subject of the
laws of Nature. The complaint targets man's deviations, explicitly the sexual perversions in, between, and among men that are sometimes grouped under the elusive
rubric of "sodomy."[2] Though generally regarded as a contribution to the "effective
campaign against sodomy," the *Complaint* has elicited surprisingly few responses to its
most controversial subject. Even so, the words *"Pereat sodomita"* ("Let the sodomite
perish") appear as early as the thirteenth century, penned as a coda to a Toledo manuscript and added to several French and Italian copies.[3] At least a handful of scribes made
their responses explicit, cheering on the campaign in which their labor was already
enlisted. These scribes are situated in a history of textual production and create the
situation of reception, for they are in a literal sense at an initial position in the chain of
dissemination. Histories of textual reception—readings, uses, influences in trajectories
that include current interpretations—are bound up with nitty-gritty histories of
production, including the ink of scribes and of the various inscriptions and imprintings
that materially "convey" what we normally like to call a text. The *Enchiridion*, manual of
the laws of Nature, becomes a weapon in the hands of scribes as well as subsequent
readers; as an arsenal for the war against so-called perversion, the text capitalizes on
the connotations of its name, in Greek, ἐγχειρίδιον, something held in the hand, especially for attacks, a dagger, a knife. The etymology makes explicit the violence implied
by the name *Enchiridion* and by the status of a text used as "an effective weapon." One
could argue that any manual implies some degree of violence, perhaps symbolic,
because it is used as a disciplinary technique that dictates rules and laws. Sometimes
the pen is mightier than the sword and sometimes it *is* one.

   The scribes who pen *"Explicit Enchiridion"* and, in the same hand, *"Pereat sodomita"* flag two positions of textual production: 1) the *explicit* as a signature marks the scribal role in reproducing the text through the labor of writing, and 2) *"Pereat sodomita"* as a response conveys the scribe's participation in the text as a reader, one with the privilege of recording his judgment for subsequent readers. The reproduction of the text in the literal sense of the labor of copying is enmeshed in the networks of transmission and circulation that elicit more explicit interpretations and uses. The scribal coda suggests an operative relationship between acts of reading and writing, which in turn has powerful effects on the campaign against perversion. This network of relations informs the two dominant concepts of the *Complaint*: writing and perversion, which at various times and in various ways stand for each other. When the scribe signs off with a curse (*"pereat sodomita"*) or even a blessing (*"Deo gratias"*), he participates in the text not simply because he reproduces it, or even comments upon it, though these are important and overlooked activities in themselves. His hand in the text takes on a further complication because his scribal function is represented in the text as a figure, most remarkably as Nature's scribe, Genius, who is pictured with pen and page as he pronounces the excommunication of those who pervert the law. The scribe literally reproducing the text by hand is reproducing the text at another level; he reproduces the "content," or perhaps it would be better to say that he reproduces his own reading of that content. On the other hand, to the extent that he takes up a role already scripted in the text, the text could be said to inscribe him, to reproduce him in its own image.

I shall argue that the text, in representing scenes of writing, figures the very dynamics that produce it as an object, not simply the act of writing but the context of scribal production, of textual dissemination, of pedagogical appropriation. The analogy of text to sex shifts into a different focus when we consider that these writing/reading scenes are also sites for the production of sexual difference and sexuality. My attempt to shift the focus is conditioned by my sense that previous interpretations often separate the issues of writing and textuality from the subject of sexuality, even when they look for the connections between them. On the one hand, the *Complaint* is regarded as an exemplary instance of the idea of the book in the middle ages (Ernst Curtius 1953) and of many corollary ideas found in metaphors of grammar, rhetoric, even script (Jan Ziolkowski 1985, Jesse Gellrich 1985, Winthrop Wetherbee 1972). On the other hand, the text is considered in its role as an "effective weapon" in the campaign against sodomy (John Boswell 1980, Michael Goodich 1979), though it must be pointed out that this side attracts fewer spokesmen. Some literary readers (Maureen Quilligan, R. Howard Bloch, Alexandre Leupin) attempt to account for both "words and sex," yet gravitate to the question of deviations in a more general sense, which is often quickly assimilated to an interest in "abused language."[4] To take one example, Quilligan denies that the *Complaint* has anything to do with "unnatural love" but is "fundamentally a tract against the abuses of language by irresponsible poets, and the way in which false poetry destroys man's natural reason" (1977, 211). Turning sodomy into perversion, perversion into language abuse, and language abuse into poetry, makes it easy to shy away from a whole range of problems and concentrate instead on the *Complaint* as yet another reflexive text about language. The problem with generalized notions of "perversion" and "language" is that they efface the specificity of the concrete registers triggered by the representations of sexuality and writing in the text, thereby making it difficult for us to conceptualize the erotic materiality of reading, writing and pedagogy.

SEMINAR

The Complaint of Nature follows the Boethian tradition of *prosimetrum* philosophical writing.[5] The nine pairs of alternating meter and prose sections begin with Alanus's lament about man's decadence (*"In lacrimas risus, in luctus gaudia verto"*), move on to extended ekphrases on the clothing of Lady Nature, then to her own complaint, her discourses on topics raised by her interlocutor, Alanus. As other personifications arrive on the scene, there are catalogues of vices and virtues, both ekphrastic and discursive. Finally Nature decides to remedy the situation by writing a letter to her secretary-priest, Genius, and the text ends with the scene of his writing the final pronouncement on man's abominations.[6]

If, as the scribes indicate, the *Complaint* is a manual, *enchiridion*, how was it used and circulated? The idea that this is a text used for education receives some support from scholars of twelfth-century curricula. In a discussion of his view of the *Complaint* as a "best selling textbook," Jan Ziolkowski explains that:

> Alan's firsthand experience with expositional methodology must have helped him orga-
> nize and compose his allegories to be suitable for classroom exposition. In dealing with
> the *De planctu Naturae*, teachers could have devoted much educational and edifying discus-
> sion to determining the metaphoric significance of all the grammatical terms (1985,
> 100–101).

To the scribes who read as they write, we can add another set of readers, those instructing and being instructed in reading and writing.[7] The network of scribal reproduction intersects with a network of educational circulation and transmission. Moreover, not only does the text function as an object of inquiry for teacher and pupil; it also represents a pedagogical scene, as a scene of instruction between Nature and Alanus.

The pedagogical frame provides a platform for Nature's missionary zeal against "nonconformist withdrawal," exemplified by the likes of "professional male prostitutes" (131). Her teaching promises results: "If you would, with well-disposed inclination of mind, collect together and store in the treasure-chest of your heart what I would say, I would unfold the labyrinth of your doubts" (Pr. 4, 130). The Latin dallies with metaphors used in a bookish realm: "si affectuoso mentis affectu colligeres et in pectoris *armario* thesaurizares que dicerem, tue dubitationis laberinthum *evolverem*" (VIII, 832). The chest of Alanus's heart, the *"armarium,"* was a common name for the book closet, library or scriptorium, which, as the saying goes, was the arsenal of arms and armor for the great monasteries; *armarium* resonates with the meanings of *enchiridion.* Inside the closet of the heart are the scrolls that Nature wishes to unroll, *"evolvere"*; the soul as a written sheet, a page, is a pervasive analogy in the text. Man's rebellious soul refuses to take the doctrine in which all of nature has been schooled. Daring to have an artificial sex change, man has abandoned "in his deviation the true script of Venus" and has become "a sophistic falsigrapher" (134; "A Veneris ergo orthographia deviando recendens sophista falsigraphus invenitur," 835).[8] "Orthography" and "falsigraphy" measure the soul's perversion in terms of script, for Nature's instructive aims draw on the technical metaphors of grammar and writing in order to delineate with precision a set of impossibly murky ethical and moral rules. The technical rules of writing provide an alternative and more euphemistic register in which sexuality and perversion can be discussed.[9] Moreover, the shift from the ethical to the technical produces the sense, more generally, that rules can be established, and mistakes isolated and corrected.

Nature's complaint and her teaching are supported by an array of grammatical analogies (*analogia, anastrophe, syneresis, tmesis*) that describe sexual aberrations in terms of textual error.[10] The effect of the shift from sexual to textual is far-reaching, for it implies that ethical problems can be handled in terms of technical rules, that there *are* rules in the first place and that they can be enforced by correct training. Yet the use of pedantic terms undercuts these aims, for Nature appears as a "somewhat pompous lecturer," in the words of translator Sheridan, who acts out in a slightly parodic form the theatrics of a twelfth-century *disputatio* (130). And this role prescribes that of her student, who responds in a "pertinacious, mock-modest" manner: "O mediatrix in all things, did I not fear that my host of questions might raise disgust in your kind nature, I would expose the haze of another doubt of mine to the light of your discernment" (138). The pleasures of unfolding are too hard for her to resist: "Nay, impart to my ears all your questions." Assured of Nature's open ears, Alanus aims his petulant point:

> I wonder why, when you consider the statements of the poets, you load the stings of the above attacks against the contagions of the human race alone, although we read that the gods, too, have limped around the same circle of aberration. For Jupiter, *translating* the Phrygian youth to the realms above, *transferred* there proportionate love for him on his *transference*. The one he had made his wine-master by day he made his subject in bed by night. Bacchus and Apollo, likewise, by inversion turned boys into women ... (138–39, emphasis added).

> Miror cur poetarum commenta retractans, solummodo in humani generis pestes predictarum invectionum armas aculeos, cure et eodem *exorbitationis* pede deos claudicasse legamus. Iupiter enim, adolescentem Frigium *transferens* a superna, relativam Venerem *transtulit* in *translatum.* Et quem in mensa per diem propinandi sibi prefecit prospositum, in thoro per noctem sibi fecit suppositum. Bachus etiam et Apollo ... verterunt in feminas pueros invertendo (836–37).

This display of classical learning, conveyed with a suspiciously ingenuous tone, makes Nature's "naturally severe countenance" twist in a grimace: she has been duped into an altercation over Ganymede. The complicated metaphors used to describe the rape of the Phrygian boy ("*transferens*," "*transtulit*," "*translatum*," awkwardly rendered as "translating," "transferred," "transference") defy translation because they depend on the complexity of the "grammatical" notion of *translatio*. The importance and range of this figure for hermeneutics is linked to its metaphysical and spiritual operations, as its many definitions, twelfth-century and modern, make clear. For instance, in *Nature, Man, and Society in the Twelfth Century,* M. D. Chenu defines *translatio* as "a transference or elevation from the visible sphere to the invisible through the mediating agency of an image borrowed from sense-perceptible reality" (138), an act that puts "the mind into secret contact with transcendent reality, not without a sense of inward exaltation" (131). Chenu supplies the most common notions of the figure, for example from Hugh of St. Victor (1096–1141), who explained in the *Celestial Hierarchy* that it is a "juxtaposition, that is, a coaptation of visible forms brought forth to demonstrate some invisible matter" (103). Snatched from the visible sphere, "metaphor was obedient to the necessities imposed by transcendent realities (Chenu 1968, 100)." The definition of the figure bears an uncanny resemblance to the rape of Ganymede. Why does this crucial trope ("*the* mental operation proper to symbolism") mirror this most improper of "transferences" between men?

As pedagogue placed in an awkward position by the teasing student, Nature must translate the Ganymede example into another, more appropriate form. To do so, she unfolds a theory of interpretation aimed at dismantling and disarming the meaning Alanus produces:

> Poetry's lyre rings with vibrant falsehood on the outward literal shell of a poem, but interiorly it communicates a hidden and profound meaning to those who listen. The man who reads with penetration, having cast away the outer shell of falsehood, finds the savory kernel of truth wrapped within.[11]

> In superficiali littere cortice falsum resonat lira poetica, interius vero auditoribus secretum intelligentie altioris eloquitor, ut exteriori falsitatis abjecto putamine dulciorem nucleum veritatis secrete intus lector inveniat (837).

The kernel-and-shell game depends on the venerable technique of stuffing the most unlikely and perhaps even oppositional writing with secret and transcendent meaning so as to render it proper. Yet this appropriative theory makes the divinely grounded operation of *translatio* even more sensual, because it requires acts of penetration that betray a desire for savory seeds. "Ganymede," as another name for perversion, reemerges as the exemplary model of male desire for and contact with the transcendent realm.[12]

Nature's application of the interpretive techniques of kernel and shell to this particular case is overdetermined, especially in light of the heated debates surrounding the figure of Ganymede. To take one instance, an anonymous twelfth-century poem,

Altercatio Ganimedis et Helene, stages a debate between two figures who represent, loosely speaking, the virtues of homosexual and heterosexual pleasures respectively.[13] Ganymede uses a strategy similar to Alanus's when he refers to divine rather than human behavior: "The game we play was invented by the gods / And is today maintained by the best and the brightest" (lines 119–20). He strengthens his case with further evidence from the treasure chest of grammar, an arsenal of analogies markedly similar to those deployed by Nature. For example, Ganymede scolds:

> Every unlike thing causes discord; like thing with like, that is what is proper. A male is joined to a male in an elegant *copula*. Perhaps you do not know your grammar, but the rule of articles must be observed: *hic* and *hic* must be joined together in grammar (lines 141–44).

Rather than question the fundamental assumptions of the analogy, Nature's seminar responds to the *Altercatio* on its own terms, for, according to Boswell, she is "directly rebutting some points scored against her" by Ganymede (310). Yet grammatical metaphors are largely up for grabs, since they can be bent to prove conflicting positions. Other proponents enlisted in the campaign argued that the rules of grammar are *not* homologous with the rules of sex.[14] Nevertheless, the analogy is dutifully maintained in the *Complaint*, so much so that the campaign depends upon the homology.[15]

The lack of inherent and stable meaning in the grammatical analogy does not seem to trouble the dogged use of the terms in these texts; on the contrary, the lines of the debate are drawn as essentially stable and irreducible. Yet the inconsistency offers the option of resisting the apparent naturalness of the analogies drawn from grammar, even if this option is most often the road not taken, for the agonistic interest in polarizing the terms spills over to readers who carry on the battle. Thus, Boswell's own account, as some have pointed out, though in the interest of defending Ganymede, leads to charged idealizations and polarizations that undermine his desired position. His narrative about the "extraordinary efflorescence of gay subculture" (1980, 265) destroyed by "an exclusively heterosexual constituency" (312) is construed in anachronistically modern and decidedly (though perhaps strategically) overstated terms.[16] We might wonder to what extent the terms of the investigation are scripted by the polemics of the text, a form of textual reproduction that supplants curses ("*Pereat sodomita*") with blessings ("*Sic homo gratias*").

Instead, we might pursue a strategic resistance to the assumptions of the texts and their cultural nexus as an alternative to the replay of the altercation. For instance, a resistance to the grammatical analogies leads to an interrogation of the shift in domain, in most cases, from charged ethical dilemmas to neutral technical difficulties regardless of the side of the debate taken. Now I want to suggest that we resist taking "grammar" as an analogy at all, for treating grammar in a metaphoric sense participates in translating it from its literal and material realm, in particular from the realm of pedagogy, reading and writing. The pedagogical realm comes into view even in the case of the Ganymede poem, for as Boswell points out, the manuscripts are bound with grammar textbooks.[17] The odd coincidence of pedagogical material and this "subculture" literature does not concern Boswell, for he cites the manuscripts only as evidence that proves the popularity of the poem, since the textbooks obviously enjoyed a wide circulation. Yet these manuscript compilations, as material that traces the circulation of the poem, do not translate inevitably into the story of the rise and fall of "the efflorescence of a gay subculture." Rather, they reveal another textual history, one that motivates the "accidental" proximity of the Ganymede poem to pedagogical texts, for the latter were used in primary instruction, perhaps largely for boys and youth. Even if we entertain the possibilities of pederasty—for pedagogy early in the Christian Latin tradition comes to be associated with the corruption of boys—the question is not that of a thriving subculture, but rather that of a dominant homosociality and normative training inscribed in power relations.[18]

The potential violence of these power relations becomes explicit in visual representations of grammar lessons, which often show the pedagogue armed with a switch, standing over boys in various states of undress. As Ziolkowski argues, the lessons of grammar, "inculcated by methods ranging from gentle persuasion through savage beating" were among the last to be forgotten (1985, 69–70). Given the proximity, in the manuscript tradition, of the Ganymede poem to the grammars, we also have to remember that in most versions of the text Ganymede does not win the altercation with Helen, and that if read in the context of primary instruction for boys, the poem could reinforce normative views, actually squelching what Boswell claims it celebrates.[19] Therefore, it cannot be treated as accidental that the Ganymede poem is bound with pedagogical material, and that grammatical metaphors convey the lessons of sexuality. Normative prescriptions find alliance in metaphors of reading and writing perhaps because the context of pedagogical instruction allows for a particularly potent linking of technical orthographics to what might be imagined as an ethical "orthopedics."

Emphasizing the success of her pedagogy at the end of the seminar, Nature says, "Now my speech has been inscribed on the tablet of your mind" (*"cartule tue mentis"*), so take precautions against "any herb from an evil seed [that] should dare to sprout in the garden of your own mind" (*"in horto tue mentis"*) (Pr. 5, 165–66). Familiar Platonic metaphors, inscription and insemination figure the transmission of knowledge in terms of active/passive roles, master and pupil; however, the inscription model does not imply writing/reading, but writing/being written on. In "this jarring displacement," as Harry Berger argues of the Platonic dialogues, "the recipient is neither an auditor nor a reader but the carrier, the servant and support, of the imprinted *logos*"(1994, 88). The boy takes up his position as page beneath his master's pen. More jarring still, the models of inscription and insemination are superimposed in a fashion that generates the specter of pederastic pedagogy. So even as Nature's seminar seeks to eliminate the bad seeds of "perversion," the metaphorics plant them afresh. In terms of the dynamics of the inscription of *doxa*, the more firmly planted, the more docile the receptacle. These grammatical metaphors of transmission are inextricably linked to sexual ones, to the mechanisms of reproduction already in play in the seminar, the seedbed of instruction. When the transmission of knowledge is likened to inscription and insemination, one has to discuss what might be called the sexual politics of writing.[20]

MECHANICAL ARTS

Jacques Le Goff reminds us that "in the *scriptoria* of the monasteries, *scribere*, to copy manuscripts, was regarded as manual labor and consequently as a form of penitence, which is the origin of the copyists' formulas at the ends of the manuscripts" (1980, 81). *Explicit Ench. Pereat sodomita.* Writing is manual and mechanical labor. And as such it is a way of working off a sinful debt. Moreover, the degrees of scribal involvement, marked by the blessings and curses following the explicit, create problems of distortion, error, lapses, and general corruption. In its capacity to go astray, writing lends itself as a metaphor for vice and sodomy. The mechanical arts in general were characterized by Alanus's predecessor Hugh of St. Victor as "adulterate," a debased and artificial art.[21] Since the association does not resonate with inevitability, editor Jerome Taylor provides a gloss: Hugh derives mechanical from the Greek μοιχός, Latin *moechus*, adulterer.[22] The various Latin forms, e.g. *moechocinaedus*, extend the meaning to all lewd and debauched behavior. Even in Greek, μοιχός can mean simply "paramour," and is at least once used of a sodomite. Hugh of St. Victor explains that he uses the term "adulterate, just as a skeleton key is called a 'mechanical' key." The skeleton key is mechanical, adulterate, just as the *moechocinaedus* is an artificial substitute; the key fits any lock, and is used illicitly and indiscriminately, in furtive acts. The negative value attached to artificial, mechanical labor is reinscribed as a condemnation of sexual misconduct. In the case of the representation of the mechanical arts in Hugh of St. Victor's text, the etymological techniques make this reinscription possible and quite easy, but the move occurs with a dogged persistence even when glosses are not readily available. Why? If we step away from the intricacies of medieval glossing and etymology, it becomes difficult to see how the mechanical arts, for instance fabric making or even writing, could be so thoroughly associated with adultery, debauchery, or sodomy that they come to stand for these and perhaps all vices.

The relation between writing and sexual perversion is maintained primarily by a metaphysical investment in the idea of a transcendent, divinely given Book. Ernst Curtius (1953) provides the most influential discussion of the Book as a symbol, a metaphysical concept organizing a scriptural culture around the idea of divinely inscribed laws. Curtius's chapter listing examples of the pervasive metaphor is perversely imitated by Jacques Derrida in *Of Grammatology*. Derrida outlines another agenda, more critical than descriptive:

> natural and universal writing, intelligible and nontemporal writing, is thus named by metaphor.... There remains to be written a history of this metaphor, a metaphor that systematically contrasts divine or natural writing and the human and laborious, finite and artificial inscription (1974, 15).

Though Derrida has another agenda that takes him away from literal writing (and from any sexual connections), he does hint at the implications of this opposition when he writes, "the good and natural is the divine inscription in the heart and the soul; the perverse and artful is technique, exiled in the exteriority of the body" (17). Writing as technique is artificial, man-made, and therefore perverse; as a material and physical production, it is tied to the body, therefore doubly perverse, perhaps even sexually perverse. This negative valence given to the materiality of writing (and to the mechanical arts) underwrites the use of graphic metaphors—in the *Complaint*, orthography and falsigraphy—to represent sexual conduct in its materiality in its "straight" and "deviant" forms.

The materiality of writing is present, yet effaced, by the representations of scribal hierarchies in *The Complaint of Nature*. Nature herself submits to divine inscription: "I carried out the administration of this office in such a way that the right hand of the supreme authority should direct my hand in its work, for my writing-reed would instantly go off course if it were not guided by the finger of the superintendent on high" (Pr. 4, 146; "quia mee scripture calamus exorbitatione subita deviaret, nisi supremi Dispensatoris digito regeretur"). His finger on her pen, his hand holds her stylus so it will not deviate from its normal orbit. Though meant in a literal etymological sense, exorbitance brings with it a range of connotations: translated differently in the passage about Ganymede, exorbitance is used to describe the "aberrant limping" of the profane and perverse gods, and limping itself is often associated with sodomy. Even so, the divine superintendent's hands-on guidance does not prevent an out-of-orbit trajectory since, for some unexplained reason, Nature becomes overwhelmed with her task, and opts for early retirement. The terms of this contract are exorbitant: she moves to the "delightful palace of the ethereal region" (146) where nothing ever happens, and she stations a skilled worker on the "outskirts of the Universe." Her replacement, Venus, must endlessly toil in the cosmic suburbs to reproduce the chain of human life.[23]

Venus is equipped with an "unusually potent writing pen" for inscribing "suitable pages" and then trained in the arts of orthography, grammar, rhetoric, dialectic, and so on (Pr. 5, 156ff.). We do not hear directly from Venus, but instead receive Nature's evaluation of her administrator's work:

> Thus for some time she discharged with a most ready diligence what was due to me from her tributary post. However, since a mind, that from birth has been disgusted by the cloying effect of sameness, grows indignant and the impact of daily toil destroys the desire to continue a task to the end, the frequent repetition of one and the same work bedeviled and disgusted the Cytherean and the effect of continuous toil removed the inclination to work (162–63).

> Sicque aliquandiu stipendiarie administrationis iura michi officiosissima curiositate persoluit. Sed quoniam ex matre sacietatis idemptitate fastiditus animus indignatur cotidianque laboris ingruentia exequendi propositum appetitus extinguitur, unitas operis

> tociens repetita Cytheream infestavit fastidiis continuateque laborationis effectus labo-
> randi seclusit affectum (848).

Though Nature's purpose is to describe the reasons for man's inclination to perversion by blaming Venus, who allowed her pen to go astray, she does not go very far toward locating the source of deviation in an intrinsic fault, but instead dwells on the adverse effects of tedious, quotidian, repetitive labor. Perversely, these are the very motives that caused Nature to hand her pen over to Venus in the first place. The emphatic disgust expressed toward repetitive manual labor bears the traces of resentment, and betrays the sense that Venus is castigated as a displaced form of Nature's desire "to live the soft life of barren ease" (162).

Venus's inclination to licentiousness is described in a parallel narrative about her kinship ties (Hymenaeus, her husband, and Desire, her son) and the deviations in lineage she introduces via an adulterous affair with Antigamus, "Antimarriage."[24] As Leupin argues, the text locates "the origin of sodomic debauchery" in an allegory of kinship relations (1989a, 68). Venus's adultery is also described in a narrative about her dereliction of duty, not merely as wife and mother, but as a skilled artisan, her repro-ductive labors paralleled to the techniques of craft: "Trapped by the deadly suggestions arising from her own adultery, she barbarously turned a noble work into a craft" (163). The association in Hugh of St. Victor between adultery and mechanical arts is present in a not-so-submerged form: mechanical arts are once again figured as sexual deviance, and are given as both the source *and* the result, in an exorbitant circle of displaced blame. In this economy, toil and labor are the signs of weakness and error. While an extremely reductive devaluation of the hand, at the same time, this notion points to the literal labor involved in the tedious repetition and copying of manuscripts.

SCRIPTORIUM

Nature has another secretary whom we encounter when she tires of trying to instruct her pupil Alanus in a seminar setting and instead takes up her pen to write "an official formula" requesting assistance in the campaign against perversion.[25] The letter, "tran-scribed" as it were in the text, is addressed to her lover and alter ego, Genius. Stamped, sealed and handed over to Venus's husband Hymen to deliver, the pages of the mystic legation arrives on the scene of Genius's own secretarial work.

The writing of Genius, though it shares many characteristics with that of Nature and her helper Venus, is more elaborately described:

> In his right hand he held a pen, close kin of the fragile papyrus, which never rested from
> its task of inscription. In his left hand he held the pelt of a dead animal, shorn clear of its
> fur of hair by the razor's bite. On this, with the help of the obedient pen, he endowed,
> with the life of their species, images of things that kept changing from the shadowy
> outline of a picture to the realism of their actual being. As these were laid to rest in the
> annihilation of death, he called others to life in a new birth and beginning. There
> Helen . . . (Pr. 9, 215–16).

Ille vero calamum papiree fragilitatis germanum numquam a sue inscriptionis ministerio feriantem, manu gerebat in dextera: in sinistra vero morticini pellem novacule demorsione pilorum cesarie denudatam, in qua stili obsequentis subsidio imagines rerum ab umbra picture ad veritatem sue essentie transmigrantes, vita sui generis munerabat. Quibus delectionis morte sopitis, nove nativitatis ortu alias revocabat in vitam. Illic Helena . . . (875–76).[26]

The life-writing incorporates details from the register of ordinary scribal production: reed pen, parchment, inscription, deletion. Not merely a blank, neutral surface, the image of the page proleptically traces its production: "the pelt of a dead animal, shorn clear of its fur of hair by the razor's bite." An animal's skin, cut, shaven, dead, its materiality remarkably figuring the life that it had to lose to become an inert vehicle.[27] Yet the skin also serves sexual and metaphysical meanings; as Kenneth Gross writes of Venus's script, her "planting of the *logoi spermatakoi* is illustrated by the image of her divine, phallic reed-pen inscribing animated shapes on the receptive animal-skin parchment of the material world, while the author moralizes about how necessary it is for the writer to obey all the rules of grammar and rhetoric" (1985, 205). Two meanings seem initially to be at work: the "*pagina*" is vagina, the only proper receptacle for semes, and it is matter, the stuff of nature, that through inscription is endowed with higher truth.

The sexualization of the text resides in sexual difference. That "*pagina*" is homologous to vagina is hardly a new or surprising equation. Yet the acts of textual production and reception that figure writing as insemination and reading as penetration, in the name of proper sexuality, carry the potential to be destabilized, because these practices are aimed at a male audience and a male pedagogy. In the Seminar section, we saw traces of such slippage when the desire of the master is to write on, to inscribe and inseminate the soul of the male student at the same time that the slippage refigures the ideal recipient and receptacle as docile and passive. Similar moves affect the figuration of the *pagina*, which tends toward a passive masculine rather than feminine alignment.[28]

The dead skin of the *pagina* is cleared of fur by the hard edge of the razor. The bite of the razor recalls other images scattered in the text: in the description of Hymenaeus, Nature's brother, his hair "had felt the scissors' bite" and his "excess of beard" was "corrected by the hard razor" (Pr. 8, 197). These descriptions serve to emphasize that "his face showed no signs of feminine softness" (196). In other words, the razor's edge cuts a figure of distinctive masculinity, one that serves the ideal marriage described just after Hymenaeus's appearance. Since the page inseminated by Genius's pen is emphatically clean-shaven, the association of masculinity with this trait would code the page as male, and reorients the obedient pen toward a passive partner of the same sex. Thus, even in right-handed orthography, the pen and page are too close for comfort. Once again we find sodomitical penetration in the textual recesses of a diatribe against sodomitical penetration.

This possible scenario never finds expression, except in virulent denunciation. In fact, just before Hymenaeus arrives on the scene, Nature complains about the perverse uses of the razor to feign feminine softness rather than hard masculinity:

> Others over-feminize themselves with womanish adornments.... Invoking the patron-
> age of the scissors, they crop the ends of their bushy eyebrows, or they pluck out by the
> roots what is superfluous in this same forest of hair. They set frequent ambushes with the
> razor for their sprouting beard with the result that it does not dare to show even a small
> growth (Pr. 7, 187).

> Alii vero sua corpora femineis comptionibus nimis effeminant.... Luxuriantis etiam
> supercilii fimbrias forpicis patrocinio metunt aut ab eiusdem silva superflua extirpando
> decerpunt. Pullulanti etiam barbe crebras novacule apponunt insidias, ut nec eadem
> paululum audeat pullulare (861).

The passage gives a double valence to the trait of clean-shavenness. Since the razor can be perverted to counterfeit femininity, cleanly shaven skin is not necessarily a sign of masculinity; in fact it could stand for excessive femininity.

What does the razor do for Genius's *pagina?* That it is shaven may, then, mean that it is appropriately endowed with female softness; *pagina* is vagina at bottom. But to be so, it has to be shaven; it has to counterfeit a womanish appearance with the razor. "Woman*ish*" because it is, in the end, a masculine receptacle masquerading as feminine. Again the domain of proper sexual practice is breached by abnormal acts of inscriptive insemination.

The masculinity of cut hair and shaved skin peeks through the blanket female/page association. At the same time, cutting and scraping the skin ensure that it is dead matter by killing it off again. Doubly dead, the *pagina* lies in ultimate passivity for the "obedient pen" to perform its death-defying feats of life-giving. Yet in this scene there is a conspicuous absence of the potent pen's usual partner, the scribal knife, held in the left hand in the two-fisted writing ubiquitous in medieval representations. The absence of the penknife eraser is made more conspicuous by the description of the death of images as obliteration, blotting out, erasure. The practical use of the razor's edge to scrape the skin is usurped by the metaphysical meaning attributed to the deletion of images.

We see the negative activities of the scribal eraser in another figure of cutting, always associated with death. In meter 8, Nature revels in the pathetic human state of toiling in life only to be cut off at the end by death, "*vites labores, mortis apocopam.*" The operative term, "*apocope,*" means a lopping off of the end, and is specifically a technical, "grammatical" term describing the shortening of words. *Apocope* serves as a figure for the swan's song in the catalogue of birds (Pr. 1, 87) and more curiously, for the beaver's habit of chewing off his own genitals (Pr. 1, 103). (The image is generated from the pun of the signifier "*castor,*" "beaver," and its proximity to castration.) Castration, *apocope,* cutting off words, erasure, the penknife, obliteration, death, the razor's edge: the complex semantic field circles from bodies to texts, always implicating the act of writing in a (meta)physical discourse. Even the signature of the text, "*Explicit Ench[iridion]*" is marked by the act of writing which favors *apocope* in the form of scribal abbreviation.

What is left in the hand that does not write is not the penknife eraser but the razor-shaven skin of dead matter. This lack of knife, or rather displacement of the function of the razor onto the dead skin and the obliteration of erasure, frees the left hand for an ambidextrous performance. In the interchange of hands, the script gives way to "falsigraphy":

> After this solemn process of inscription, his left hand, *as if it were helping a weary sister,* came to the aid of his right which *had grown tired from the toil of continuous painting* and the left took over the work of portrayal while the right took possession of the tablets and held them. The left hand, *limpingly* withdrawing from the field of orthography to falsigraphy, produced in a half-completed picture outlines of things or rather *the shadowy ghosts* of outlines. There Thersites . . . (216–17, emphasis added).[29]

> Post huius inscriptionis sollempuitem dextere manui, *continue depictionis defatigate laboribus,* sinistra manus, *tanquam sorori fesse subveniens,* picturandi officium usurpabat, manu dextera pugillaris latione potita. Que ab orthographie semita falsigraphie *claudicatione* recedens, rerum figuras immo figurarum *larvas umbratiles,* semiplena picturatione creabat. Illic Thersites . . . (876).

Yet another explanation of the origin and generation of deviant writing (falsigraphy), this scribal hierarchy between the hands enfolds elements of the others: first, the relation between Nature and Venus is recalled by the sisterly interaction of the hands and by the emphasis on toil, weariness and work. The two agencies are now compressed into one body, the secretary Genius, and then bifurcated into the agency of his scribal hands. Two opposed kinds of writing—orthography represented by Nature, and falsigraphy represented by Venus—are compressed into an image of a single body with opposing hands that produce orthography and falsigraphy and that are then represented *as if* sisters. Yet we might want to reverse this compression, and think instead of the scribal scene as the figure that gives rise to the personified writing agencies of Nature and Venus in the first place; the reading is encouraged by the brief hint and concession to personifying of the agency of the hand, "as if helping a weary sister." The weariness of *hands* at work is at the root of deviant writing; yet the labor of reproduction is figured in gendered and sexual terms, as the weakness of *women* at work, as a breach in the labor of reproduction.

Furthermore, the description of left-handed writing is programmed to trigger other suggestions of perversion: coded in the text as signs of sodomy, limping is associated with exorbitance, aberration, and deviation in the Greek gods, and shadowy figments are associated throughout the text with the sodomite, as in Narcissus *umbratiliter.*[30] The loaded terms ("shadow," "ghost," "outline") in the opposition of orthography to falsigraphy are packed with neo-Platonic resonances of the theory of "secondary forms" that mediate between the ideal, transcendent realm and the stuff of the material world. The theory is articulated alongside Genius's hand:

> While Genius was seriously devoting his attention to these ingenious paintings, Truth, like a father's reverential daughter, stood by in obedient service. She was not born of Aphrodite's promiscuous itch but entirely the offspring of the generative kiss of Nature and her son at the time when the eternal Idea greeted Hyle as she begged for the mirror of forms and imprinted a vicarious kiss on her through the medium and intervention of Image (Pr. 9, 217–28).

> Hiis igitur picture solertiis Genio sollempniter operam impedenti, Veritas, tamquam patris filia verecunda, ancillatione obsequens assistebat. Que non ex pruritu Affrodites promiscuo propagata sed ex solo Nature natique geniali osculo fuerat derivata, cum Ylem formarum speculum mendicantem eternalis salutavit Ydea, eam Iconie interpretis interventu vicario osculata (876–77).

The neo-Platonic relations—Image (icon) mediates between Idea (form) and Hyle (matter)—are figured in several networks of textual and sexual production and reproduction. The promiscuous tendencies of Aphrodite, marked in falsigraphy, are contrasted to the filial reverence of Truth, the obedient daughter born of the generative kiss between Mother Nature and boy Genius. Yet if the production of Truth is the proper offspring that stands for normative familial, sexual, and gendered relationships, the reproductive relationship between mother and son cannot stand as in its literal, material, sexual meaning. Thus, the kiss must be further glossed in neo-Platonic terms so as to remove it from sexual and material domains.

The theory of secondary forms is articulated in another text, an early sermon, in which Alanus is concerned not with cosmic generation but with human realms of existence:

> Through sense the human soul enters the world, where, examining the lower orders of existence, sense beholds as if in a sort of book the spots, the taints of corruption which are, as it were, the letters.... By imagination the human soul is borne into the abode of primordial matter, where she sees imaginatively forms which seem to weep at the disaster of their misshapen state, and beg for the support of a nobler kind of matter (d'Alverny 1965, 302–303).

Behind the shuffle of matter and form in this shell game, there is an ambivalent desire for a kinder, gentler state of matter, for matter that ceases to be matter, that avoids materiality, that avoids being steeped in sensuality, that is free from smells of corruption and taints of disfiguration. The abhorrence of matter at the core of this desire achieves only an ambivalent articulation, because its full expression would lead directly to a dualistic position, which many, including Alanus, argued was the heart of all perversion. The heretical dualism of the Cathar and Waldensian sects is described by scholars as having hinged on an abhorrence of matter (the material world, the flesh) so radical that it gave license to exorbitant behavior (bisexual orgies, extreme asceticism, scatological rites, and sodomy) in the name of submitting matter to deliberate and excessive disregard.[31] Because Alanus maintained the uncompromising position that dualism itself leads to deviant perversion, there is a rather anxious motive underpinning the investment in secondary forms.

Through the early sermon, we can read the scene of Genius's writing. Truth, not promiscuous falsigraphy, is generated by the intercourse of Form and Matter. And even more importantly, the sermon weaves in the graphic figures drawn from the scriptive domain. The tainted corruption of matter is figured as material letters, spots on a page, the misshapen blemishes reflected in a book. The transcendence of the soul begins with the world of the book. In this bookish realm, the pages of the soul need unfolding; the pages need to be read, translated from their corrupt material sense to higher forms, to the realm of the senses beyond the letter. To read is to penetrate the material density of things, to reach the transcendent world through the visible. Though in some versions the *subjecta materia* (*hyle*) is resistant to the discipline of forms, in the *Complaint*, she asks for it. Indeed even Ganymede is a willing subject for divine *raptio.*

As early as Macrobius, the techniques of reading were fashioned as a form of initiation into the mysteries. The secret to these mental operations, as Wetherbee argues, is a particular model of reality (corroborated by new interpretations of the *Timaeus*) that could be "read" allegorically (1972, 36). This model turns everything into signs, into letters, into traces of spirit. One of the most cited epigraphs of this model was penned by Alanus himself: "Omnis mundi creatura / Quasi liber et pictura / Nobis est in speculum" ("Every creature of this earth is like a picture or a book: it is a mirror of ourselves"). Yet there is an anxious hedging ("*quasi*") because the literality cannot be entirely effaced by transcendent meaning; thus in the first prose section of the *Complaint*, the moving pictures woven into Nature's robes are not merely texts but "living things" that, "although they had there a kind of figurative existence, nevertheless seemed to live there in the literal sense." To avoid a perverse position, Alanus tries to have it both ways. He wants to eat the nut without breaking the shell.

The relation between writing and sexual perversion, with which I began, is maintained by an ambivalent investment in metaphysical inscriptive mastery. On the one hand, inscribing and inseminating the proper receptacle, the soul, is natural; on the other, perverse and unnatural inscription and insemination improperly touch the body. Thus, the explicit ink of scribal labor always requires an erasure of its material and physical manifestations. Through the techniques of allegorical reading, the *Complaint* is not merely ink, not material inscription, not physical insemination, but, to paraphrase the text, a vicarious kiss mediated through the mirror of forms, archetypal words brought forth audibly in the image of material voice: "Que postquam me michi redditum intellexit, mentales intellectus materialis vocis michi depinxit imagine, et quasi verba idealiter preconcepta vocaliter produxit in actum" (VI: 825).[32] When writing is effaced, so are material practices of textual production. Hence the myth that the reproduction and transmission of texts occurs through neutral conduits—obedient pens, pliant pages, servile scribes, mechanical arts—and that its circulation produces neutral (and even neutered) effects—docile readers, passive pupils, useful techniques, liberal arts.

The laws of proper reading become metaphysical and mystical legations that bind the initiated to the secrets of fruitful translation.[33] "The graphic culture of the high and late Middle Ages tries to authenticate itself by continuing to transcendentalize authority," writes Harry Berger, Jr. in "Bodies and Texts." "But its form, its conventionality, its excesses of order or fantasy, its textual analyses of what it represents, give back to its readers an image of themselves transformed by chirographic artifice" (1987, 164). He argues that one result of this chirographic or scriptive formation is that the more its readers try to live by the book, "the more they find themselves compelled to represent their presentations of self on textual models" (164). Living by the book implies the violence of the disciplinary manual, the residual violence of the *enchiridion*, of armed hands.[34] This bookish realm is literal and material—the domain of readers and writers, of masters and pupils, of scribes and illuminators, the domain of the distribution of textbooks, of manuals, of images, of the circulation of interpretations, commentaries, techniques. These graphic regimes, in articulating theoretical positions, give material support to explicit violence, to the purging of bad seed, to the eradication of excess that characterizes not only the campaign against sodomy waged through and around Alanus's *Complaint*, but also the broader attacks launched in the name of protecting the proper way from the threat of heresy. Living by the book means dying by it as well, the implicit effects of the explicit ink.

What color ink can we imagine in Alanus's own hand, as a penned coda following his own scribal labor? Perhaps we could splice one together from what we have already seen: *Explicit Enchiridion magistri Alani. In lacrimas risus, in luctus gaudia verto. Pereat sodomita. Fiat, fiat, amen.* Here ends the handbook of the master Alanus. I turn from laughter to tears, from joy to grief. Let the sodomite perish. Or there but for the grace of God go I.

NOTES

A shortened version of this essay was presented at a Modern Language Association session entitled "Representing Sodomy" (1991). I thank Jonathan Goldberg for organizing the session, and David Hult for his many suggestions.

1. The editions used are Häring's Latin, (1978, 797–879), and Sheridan's English translation, (1980).

2. "Sodomy" is in quotation marks to flag that it is an undefined term, standing for almost anything, including heresy, idolatry, adultery. Alanus adopts the Augustinian definition: expending one's [sic] seed outside its proper receptacle (*Liber poenitentialis*, 1199). Male-centered and euphemistic, this is the broadest possible definition of acts against nature since it seems to allow only procreative (missionary) intercourse. See Goldberg's discus-

sion of the term in his introductory chapter, "'That Utterly Confused Category,'" in *Sodometries*, (1992, 1–26).

3. The curse against sodomites is from the Toledo manuscript from the thirteenth century (MS Cabildo 47–10), though it occurs in other manuscripts. See Häring's introduction, 1978, which lists the texts collated and provides a brief analysis of them (797–801).

4. Quilligan (1977, 195–216); Bloch (1983, 133–36); Leupin (1989a). Leupin's essay, published in French in 1976, is a brilliant reading of the text; I only include him here because he claims that the text has two levels (laws of reproduction, laws of cosmic order), a move that allows him to take perversion metaphorically.

5. The precursors are Boethius's *De consolatione Philosophiae*, Martianus Capella's *De nuptiis Mercurii et Philologiae*, and Bernard of Silvestris's *Cosmographia*. For a summary of these texts and of Alanus's career, see Ziolkowski's "Introduction," (1985).

6. The letter writing and final excommunication could be read in relation to the Third Lateran council, which according to Boswell, was the first to specify rules and penalties concerning homosexual acts (1980, 277). Though the Third Lateran comes after the probable date of composition, it would be relevant to the text's reception and circulation, to the scribal pronouncements and meaning invested in the text.

7. The pedagogical use of the the *Complaint* marks it as a specific kind of prescriptive text, one situated in the institutional context of pedagogical training. In an economy in the midst of shifting from "schools" to "masters," texts, and textbooks facilitate what might be called the "deroutinization" (to use a bastardized Weberian notion) and the reinstitution of charismatic figures. Textbooks would or could function as devices for entering into this competitive market, attracting students and insuring lines of affiliation; it is this problematic that structures the lines of address for Alanus's *Complaint*. Of the essays in Benson and Constable (1982), see Baldwin (1982, 138–63), and Southern (1982, 113–37).

8. The idea of "sex change" refers to Tiresias, the blind seer changed to a woman when he witnessed an unholy primal scene between snakes ("Sic homo, Venere *tiresiatus* anomala, directam predicationem per compositionem inordinate convertit" [emphasis added]).

9. The mixing Latin and Greek in "falsigraphy" (where one might expect "pseudography") is loaded since the terms are neither "natural" opposites nor are they drawn from equivalent registers. "Ortho" denotes straight, upright, vertical and thus even its connotations (correctness, moral rectitude) carry a physical sense that informs its use in reference to acts of writing; its antonym might be Greek *skolios,* our Latinate "oblique," whereas "falsi" denotes deception and lying.

10. Since the "grammatical" words in fact range from rhetorical figures to logical syllogisms, this may be confusing to some readers. The sense invoked is in keeping with the medieval *ars grammatica*, which in the twelfth century encompassed the arts of speaking and writing correctly and was the cornerstone of the seven liberal arts.

11. In the context of discussing Chenu, I have decided to cite his rather than Sheridan's translation (1968, 99), though I admit that Chenu's is more imaginative and skewed in the direction I want to go.

12. See Barkan's analysis of this nexus, (1991, especially 50–53).

13. See Boswell's chapter, "The Triumph of Ganymede: Gay Literature of the High Middle Ages," (1980, 243–66) and his translation of the poem, (381–89). I add the qualification in order to bypass entering into the debate about these terms.

14. Not exactly in favor of male-male sex, Gautier de Coincy writes, "La grammaire hic à hic acouple, / Mais nature maldit la couple. / La mort perpetuel engerne / Cil qui aimme masculin genre / Plus que le femenin ne face / Et Dieux de son livre l'efface" from "Seinte Léocade," in de Barbazan (1808, 310–11). According to Ziolkowski (1985, 68), Gilles, court physician to Philip Augustus, launched an even more violent attack against sodomy in his anticlerical poem, *Hierapigra*. Though these texts come a decade or so after the *Complaint*,

they provide evidence for the argument that the more common antisodomy tactic at this time was to challenge rather than support the analogy between sex and grammar.

15. The homology of grammatical and sociosexual gender tends to surface in scenes of language training, yet it has aftereffects beyond the classroom, which often reinscribe powerful naturalizing and misogynist "rules" of sexual difference and obedience. I detail this argument in relation to Latin training in Pittenger (1991, 389–408).

16. For the implications and problems in Boswell's position, see David Halperin, "'Homosexuality': A Cultural Construct," in Halperin (1990, 41–53, especially n. 32).

17. Three manuscripts are mentioned that combine the poem with a language textbook by John of Garland, with a primer on the Greek alphabet, and with Priscian's *Institutiones grammaticae* (Boswell 1980, 255–56 and n. 49).

18. Ziolkowski (1985) discusses the meanings of *"paedagogium"* in late Antique and early Christian Latin, (53–54).

19. Two manuscripts have the alternative reading that Boswell prefers. He claims that the "most significant [point of] the poem is not who won or lost" but the "tolerant ambience in which it must have been written"(1980, 260). While I see his point, the pedagogical context might alter it significantly.

20. For an analysis of the ways the materiality of handwriting serves various sexual and political agendas, see Jed (1989), and Goldberg (1990).

21. Eco describes the "servile arts" as compromised by physical labor and material, in contrast to the liberal arts, which are aristocratic and superior (1986, 97–98). See also Camille 1989, 35.

22. Taylor (1961, 191, n. 64). He cites a gloss of Martin of Laon: "'Moechus' means adulterer, a man who secretly pollutes the marriage bed of another. From 'moechus' we call mechanical art any object which is clever and most delicate and which, in its making or operation, is beyond detection, so that beholders find their power of vision stolen from them when they cannot penetrate the ingenuity of the thing."

23. Green locates the suburbs in the loins of the cosmic body, a place inhabited by rustics and foreigners (1956, 649–74).

24. In some manuscripts he is called Antigenius, which involves a more complex network of relations through Nature's own kinship ties.

25. The officious description of Nature's writing might well be described by Brian Stock's (1983) analysis of the increasing bureaucracy of the twelfth-century. For a critical review, see Vance (1985, 55–65).

26. What follows is a list of conventional classical examples: Helen=beauty, Turnus=courage, Hercules=strength, Ulysses=cunning, Cato=frugality, Plato=intellectual brilliance, Cicero=eloquence, Aristotle=philosophy.

27. For a similar discussion of the knife and pen, see Goldberg's "The Violence of the Letter," in Goldberg (1990, 59–107). He argues that the comparison of penknife to butcher's is not so outrageous if one considers the production of vellum as a writing surface "whose hairy backside as well as imperfections and markings remind the writer of the slaughtered animal upon whose skin he inscribes, repeating . . . an act of violence" (73).

28. In fact, the pen is "close kin of the fragile papyrus" *(papiree fragilitatis germanum),* a twin to the reed but also to the page.

29. This passage follows immediately after the description of right-handed orthography. There follows a list of bad guys: Paris=adultery, Sinon=lying, Ennius and Pacuius=bad poets.

30. Leupin makes this move (1989b, 70) in order to show the text's own flirtation with "the phantasmal seductions of narcissistic falsigraphy" (77).

31. On the legislation of perversions, see Camille (1989, 90–92). For this interpretation of the

dualistic heresies, see Russell (1972). To clarify this counterintuitive position, Russell writes that "libertinism springs naturally from the contempt in which dualism holds matter: despising matter and material pleasure, one either eschews them entirely or engages in them promiscuously and contemptuously" (128–29).

32. Sheridan's translation of the whole sentence reads: "When she realized that I had been brought back to myself, she fashioned for me, by the image of a real voice, mental concepts and brought forth audibly what one might call archetypal words that had been preconceived ideally" (Pr. 3, 116).

33. See Derrida's (1979) discussion of the hierarchies of scribes and secretaries, (116–47). "Scribble (pouvoir/écrire)" was written as an introduction to a French translation of Warburton's *The Divine Legation* (1742), reflections on the origins of writing.

34. For an interesting view of Alanus as a participant in the techniques of discipline, see Schmitt (1989, especially 140–43).

WORKS CITED

Alanus ab Insulis (Alain de Lille). 1978. *De planctu Naturae*, trans. Nikolaus Häring. *Studi Medievali,* ser. 3, 19:797–879.

———. 1980. The *Plaint of Nature,* trans James J. Sheridan. Toronto: Pontifical Institute of Mediaeval Studies.

Baldwin, John W. 1982. "Masters at Paris from 1179 to 1215: A Social Perspective," in Benson and Constable, *Renaissance and Renewal.* 138–163.

Barkan, Leonard. 1991. *Transuming Passion: Ganymede and the Erotics of Humanism.* Stanford: Stanford University Press.

Benson, Robert L. and Giles Constable, eds. 1982. *Renaissance and Renewal in the Twelfth Century.* Cambridge: Harvard University Press.

Berger, Harry, Jr. 1987. "Bodies and Texts." *Representations* 17: 144–66.

———. 1994. "Phaedrus and the Politics of Inscription," in Shankman, *Plato and Postmodernism.* 76–114.

Bloch, R. Howard. 1983. *Etymologies and Genealogies.* Chicago: University of Chicago Press.

Boswell, John. 1980. *Christianity, Social Tolerance and Homosexuality: Gay People in Western Europe from the Beginning of the Christian Era to the Fourteenth Century.* Chicago: University of Chicago Press.

Camille, Michael. 1989. The *Gothic Idol: Ideology and Image-Making in Medieval Art.* Cambridge: Cambridge University Press.

Chenu, Marie-Dominique. 1968. *Nature, Man, and Society in the Twelfth Century.* Chicago: University of Chicago Press.

Curtius, Ernst R. 1953. *European Literature and the Latin Middle Ages,* trans. Willard Trask. New York: Harper & Row.

d'Alverny, M.T. 1965. *Alain de Lille: Texts inédits avec une introduction sur sa vie et ses oeuvres.* Paris: Librairie philosophique, Vrin.

de Barbazan, Etienne. 1808. *Fabliaux et contes des poètes françois des XI, XII, XIII, XIV, et Xe siècles.* Vol. I. Paris.

Derrida, Jacques. 1974. *Of Grammatology,* trans. Gayatri Chakravorty Spivak. Chicago: University of Chicago Press.

———. 1979. "Scribble (writing-power)." *Yale French Studies* 58: 116–47.

Eco, Umberto. 1986. *Art and Beauty in the Middle Ages.* New Haven: Yale University Press.

Feher, Michel, ed. 1989. *Fragments for a History of the Human Body.* Part 2. New York: Zone Books.

Gellrich, Jesse M. 1985. *The Idea of the Book in the Middle Ages.* Ithaca: Cornell University Press.

Goldberg, Jonathan. 1990. *Writing Matter: From the Hands of the English Renaissance.* Stanford: Stanford University Press.

————. 1992. *Sodometries: Renaissance Texts, Modern Sexualities.* Stanford: Stanford University Press.

Goodich, Michael. 1979. The *Unmentionable Vice: Homosexuality in the Later Medieval Period.* Santa Barbara: ABC-Clio.

Green, Richard Hamilton. 1956. "Alan of Lille's *De planctu Naturae." Speculum* 31: 649–74.

Gross, Kenneth. 1985. *Spenserian Poetics: Idolatry, Iconoclasm, and Magic.* Ithaca: Cornell University Press.

Halperin, David M. 1990. *One Hundred Years of Homosexuality.* New York: Routledge.

Häring, Nikolaus, ed. 1978. "*De planctu naturae." Studi Medievali,* ser.3, 19: 797–879.

Jed, Stephanie. 1989. *Chaste Thinking: The Rape of Lucretia and the Birth of Humanism.* Bloomington: Indiana University Press.

Le Goff, Jacques. 1980. *Time, Work and Culture in the Middle Ages,* trans. Arthur Goldhammer. Chicago: University of Chicago Press.

Leupin, Alexandre. 1989a. "The Hermaphrodite: Alan of Lille's *De planctu Naturae,"* in Leupin, *Barbarolexis.* 59–68.

————. 1989b. *Barbarolexis: Medieval Writing and Sexuality,* trans. Kate M. Cooper. Cambridge, MA: Harvard University Press.

Pittenger, Elizabeth. 1991. "Dispatch Quickly: The Mechanical Reproduction of Pages." *Shakespeare Quarterly* 42: 389–408.

Quilligan, Maureen. 1977. "Words and Sex: The Language of Allegory in the *De planctu Naturae,* the *Roman de la Rose,* and Book III of *The Faerie Queen." Allegorica* 2: 195–216.

Russell, Jeffrey Burton. 1972. *Witchcraft in the Middle Ages.* Ithaca: Cornell University Press.

Schmitt, Jean Claude. 1989. "The Ethics of Gesture," in Feher, *Fragments.* 129–47.

Shankman, Steven, ed. 1994. *Plato and Postmodernism.* New York: Aldine Press.

Sheridan, James J., ed. and trans. 1980. *The Plaint of Nature.* Toronto: Pontifical Institute of Mediaeval Studies.

Southern, Richard W. 1982. "The Schools of Paris and the School of Chatres," in Benson and Constable, *Renaissance and Renewal.* 113–37.

Stock, Brian. 1983. *The Implications of Literacy: Written Language and Models of Interpretation in the Eleventh and Twelfth Centuries.* Princeton: Princeton University Press.

Taylor, Jerome, ed. 1961. *The* Didascalicon *of Hugh of St. Victor.* New York: Columbia University Press.

Vance, Eugene. 1985. "Medievalisms and Models of Textuality." *Diacritics* 15: 55–65.

Warburton, William. 1742. *The Divine Legation of Moses demonstrated.* London.

Wetherbee, Winthrop. 1972. *Platonism and Poetry in the Twelfth Century.* Princeton University Press.

Ziolkowski, Jan. 1985. *Alan of Lille's Grammar of Sex: The Meaning of Grammar to a Twelfth-Century Intellectual.* Cambridge, MA: The Medieval Academy of America.

Sodomy and Resurrection   **12**

The Homoerotic Subject of the *Divine Comedy*

Bruce W. Holsinger

Before departing from the sixth circle of the *Inferno*, Dante listens attentively as his *maestro* describes the sinners he will encounter on the remaining levels of Dis. The next circle down, Virgil explains, hosts the violent—the violent against others, against the self and, finally, against God:

> Puossi far forza ne la deïtade,
> col cor negando e bestemmiando quella,
> e spregiando natura e sua bontade;
>   e però lo minor giron suggella
> del segno suo e Soddoma e Caorsa
> e chi, spregiando Dio col cor, favella.

> Violence may be done against the Deity, by denying and blaspheming him in the heart, and despising Nature and her goodness; and therefore the smallest ring seals with its sign both Sodom and Cahors, and all who speak contemning God in their hearts.[1]

Their souls contained within "*lo minor giron*," the circle's "smallest ring," the sodomites the pilgrim will encounter in cantos 15 and 16 are quite literally sealed away, isolated from the remaining spaces of the *Commedia*'s fictive universe. When Dante eventually interacts with the sodomites, moreover, he will stand upon *duri margini*, or "hard margins" (*Inf.* 15, 1), an image that conflates the dikes that confine the sinners with the margins of the poem. In a certain sense, the sodomites are isolated hermeneutically as well as spatially, their very identities as infernal subjects circumscribed by the sodomitical acts they have performed.

Yet perhaps the most enabling breakthrough in the study of premodern sexualities over the last decade has been precisely the rejection of easy equations between sexual practice and individual identity. In the wake of Foucault's famous dictum—"The sodomite had been a temporary aberration; the homosexual was now a species" (1990,

43)—scholars have recently brought to light a vast array of homoerotic discourses in the premodern West that were neither filtered through nor constrained by modern sexual identity categories. In the words of David Halperin, "Before the scientific construction of 'sexuality' as a supposedly positive, distinct, and constitutive feature of individual human beings ... certain kinds of sexual *acts* could be individually evaluated and categorized" (1990, 26). While gay and lesbian history in the 1970s and early 1980s aimed primarily at either identifying gay individuals and subcultures or dating the emergence of a distinctive homosexual identity, the last decade has seen the focus shift to homoerotic acts, pleasures, and desires, to homoeroticism itself as a pervasive and diverse cultural phenomenon rather than the closeted practice of a homosexual minority (see Hunt 1994).

The study of the *Divine Comedy* has been relatively unaffected by such debates. It is still common to find interpretations of *Purgatorio* 26, for instance, that divide the company of the Lustful "between heterosexual and homosexual spirits" (Pequigney 1991, 32). Yet it would be wrong (and rather uninteresting) to attribute this unwilling-ness to reject modern categories and terms for sexual identity solely to the theoretical time lag that has often been imputed to medieval literary studies as a whole. As schol-ars have long recognized, there is a very deep sense in which the *Commedia* itself, through its careful segregations of sinners, its immense formal structures, its subtle but effective interpellations of its readers, defines and locates its inhabitants' identities—past, present, and future—through the deviant acts and desires for which they are punished. If part of this volume's purpose, then, is to scrutinize the so-called "acts versus identities" divide that predominates in the study of premodern sexualities, the *Divine Comedy* seems particularly well suited to the task.

In his introduction to *Queering the Renaissance*, Jonathan Goldberg characterizes what he sees as the anthology's underlying assumptions: "What the essays share is an acute awareness of the multiplicities of acts that can be sexualized, the ever-shifting terrains between texts, across national and generic borders ... that make available and opaque the sites upon which sexual possibilities fasten" (1994, 9). Multiplicities, acts, terrains, borders, sites, possibilities: notably absent from this enumeration of the many forms desire can take in early modern Europe are, first, the *subject* of desire, and, accordingly, any accounting for the ways in which homoerotic desires and practices, despite their multiplicity, work to constitute human beings *as* subjects at specific historical moments. As Goldberg notes, a concordant aim of the volume (and of much current work in early modern sexuality studies) is precisely "to problematize questions of iden-tity" (12), to resist reinscribing the unitary subject positions that have marked the histories of heteronormativity, patriarchy, and bourgeois humanism. The political urgency of such a project is undeniable: as several scholars have demonstrated eloquently, careful analysis of the erotic ambivalence characterizing the early modern period can challenge the lethally minoritizing notions of homosexual identity projected onto the past by (to take the most notorious example) the Supreme Court's 1986 decision in *Bowers v. Hardwick* (Goldberg 1992, 6–17; Halley 1994).

Nevertheless, it seems to me that our understanding of sexuality in the premodern West will lack an honest attention to human agency if we let our historiographical devotion to indeterminacy occlude the human subject of desire. Must we abandon the analysis of erotic subjectivity simply because the specifically gay or lesbian subject may be, as some have argued, a recent "invention"? How might we continue to reject "homogenizing definitions of identity" (Goldberg 1994, 12) while still deeming identities worthy of scrutiny?[2] In order to avoid the pitfalls of earlier gay historiography, of course, the study of homoerotic subjectivity in the premodern West—like that of homoerotic acts and desires—must be "universalizing," in Eve Kosofsky Sedgwick's sense of the term; that is, sexual definition and homoerotic desire, even if not filtered through modern categories, must be seen as "issue[s] of continuing, determinative importance in the lives of people across the spectrum of sexualities" (1990, 1). Unlike the search for homosexual individuals and subcultures, this sort of universalizing analysis will be concerned not with *sexual identities* as stable and unchanging, but rather with *homoerotic subject positions* as historically contingent, fleeting, unstable, produced at certain moments, by certain texts, and through specific cultural practices.

Historical responsibility, moreover, demands that the analysis of the homoerotic subject in the Middle Ages work with medieval categories for identity and desire. For my purposes, this will involve two somewhat antagonistic strategies. First, I think medievalists doing antihomophobic work would do well to take seriously the vast and complex array of meanings collapsed into the term "sodomy" throughout the period: to recognize, in Goldberg's concise words, "both the bankruptcy of the concept of sodomy, as well as the work that the term has been able to do—and continues to do—precisely because the term remains incapable of exact definition" (1992, 18). Here I refer to sodomy's numerous sexual connotations[3] as well as to its ubiquitous deployment in discourses seemingly outside the domain of sexual practice: the vilification of religious dissenters, diatribes against Jews and Muslims, provocations to crusading, or injunctions against blasphemy, usury, and simony, to name only a few.[4] For medieval culture, sodomy was itself a radically universalizing category—not in the simple sense that its pleasures and dangers were available to all, but in the more complicated sense in which it partially constituted the subject positions of "sodomites" but also of their detractors. Sodomy indeed could define the very borders between self and other, embodying not only sexual difference, but religious, ethnic, regional, and linguistic difference as well.[5] The medieval subject of sodomy, then, was not the "sodomite" alone, but also the anti-sodomitical polemicist, the Waldensian inquisitor, the instigator of pogroms, the Crusade *provocateur*, all of whom frequently relied upon the semiotic inexhaustibility of sodomy in articulating their own social roles and ideological agendas.

Yet this very focus on sodomy as a universalizing and multivalent category for the medieval subject risks privileging sodomy itself as the sole locus of homoerotic practice. As Caroline Walker Bynum has convincingly argued, it may be a particularly modern fetishization of genital sexuality that has caused historians of the body to focus such exclusive attention on the genitals as the privileged site of sexual definition and desire (1991, 85–88). Our particular interest in sexual practices should not keep us from examining the wide variety of ways in which human bodies came together erotically when the goal or referent of such contact was not necessarily genital (or even orificial). Among many examples of such potentially homoerotic practices in premodern Europe, those of particular relevance for this study will be, first, religious practice (see Holsinger 1993; Rambuss 1994; Freccero 1994), including mystical vision and Christian pilgrimage; literary influence, collaboration, and authorial identity (Masten 1994; Koestenbaum 1989); discourses of male friendship and companionship (Bray 1994); and familial bonds (DiGangi 1994), especially fatherhood and paternity. Again, while the pervasiveness of such practices may well invite us to "deriv[e] a methodological direction from a historical matrix of erotic indeterminacy" (Traub 1992, 16), I want to examine the particular means by which ostensibly free-floating "textual circulation[s] of erotic energy" (16) work specifically in the *Commedia* to constitute a homoerotic subject—of religious devotion, of writing, of the family.

Such an incarnational poetics of homoeroticism was not without its risks: the dense constellation of allusion, intertextuality, puns, verbal echoes, and self-referentiality that constitutes the *Commedia*'s homoerotics appeared at a historical moment in which many "practicing" sodomites were tortured, exiled, or burned at the stake (Greenberg 1988, 298). In introducing the subject into my reading of the *Commedia*, then, I also introduce subjection—discipline, coercion, pain and suffering, sexual violence; and abjection—shame, humiliation, loss, mourning—as integral to the formation and perdurance of subjectivity. More than a new name for Dante's sodomites, the "homoerotic subject" of the *Divine Comedy* crystallizes the poem's various trajectories of desire into two distinct but overlapping categories. First, the *Commedia*'s homoerotic subject is its reader, whom the poet sutures into his text with numerous direct addresses and of whom the poem itself demands a reading attuned to its pervasive intertextual resonances and multiple literary genealogies. As with any text, of course, there are as many ways to read as there are readers; yet one reading position Dante studies has scrupulously avoided delineating is that of the homoerotic reader—specifically, for my purposes, the *male* homoerotic reader, the reading subject fashioned by the same male homosocial sphere of pedagogy, poetics, and paternity that produced Dante and his writings. The *Commedia*'s homoerotics of reading is thus highly contingent: as we shall see, some of the poem's most explicitly homoerotic moments are founded upon misogynist diatribes and performances of sexual violence against women. In this sense, the homoerotic reader of this protohumanist text is implicated in what Stephanie Jed (1989) has identified as the imbrication of rape, writing, and reading that marks the birth of Renaissance humanism in the Trecento.

More importantly, this essay will situate Dante himself, the pilgrim and the poet, as a subject of homoerotic desire, an insistently "queer subject" in Elizabeth Grosz's sense of the term (1994). As he repeatedly and energetically writes himself into the desirous text of his poem, Dante's own deep-seated homoeroticism emerges *despite* his love and desire for Beatrice and his lyrical nods to the tradition of courtly love. It is precisely as a homoerotic and homoeroticized subject—of his particular pedagogical history, his poetic past and present, even his own eschatological future—that Dante assumes his highly politicized roles as vernacular author and Christian visionary. Though a canonical text in our day, the *Divine Comedy* was an exilic critique in its own, written while the poet was permanently banned from his native Florence. However tempting it might be to view the poem's homoeroticism as a loose amalgamation of acts, pleasures, and desires, we must never lose sight of Dante's own role as a subject of exile in fashioning a work as transgressive—politically, poetically, theologically, and, I hope to demonstrate, sexually—as the *Commedia* indisputably was.[6]

1.

> What? *you're* one of *those*? Huh? *you're* a *what*? This frightening
> thunder can also, however, be the sound of manna falling.
>   —Eve Kosofsky Sedgwick (1990, 78)

Dante's surprised words upon encountering Brunetto Latini, his former teacher and mentor, among the sodomites in *Inferno* 15—"*Siete voi qui, ser Brunetto?*" ("are you here, Ser Brunetto?") (30)—have eternally perplexed readers of the *Commedia*. With no "external evidence" of Brunetto's sodomy to be found—in the triumphant words of Peter Armour, "the total lack of evidence, outside the *Comedy*, that Brunetto or any of his companions indulged in homosexual or other unnatural sexual activity" (1983, 5)— the pilgrim's very question, his naming of Brunetto *as* a sodomite, effectively constitutes the only "evidence" available.[7] As Teodolinda Barolini has argued, with his unbelieving interrogative Dante "manages our scandalized reaction to encountering his beloved teacher among the sodomites by staging his own scandalized reaction … creat[ing] a complicity between reader and pilgrim that masks the artifice always present in what is, after all, a text, an artifact" (1992, 16). This staged scandal serves as well to shield both pilgrim and reader from the nature and implications of Brunetto's sin, a strategy whose effectiveness is amply demonstrated by John Freccero's reaction to the scene: "the virulence of the condemnation [of Brunetto] and the extent to which the pilgrim is dissociated from it leads us to suppose that its target is not only Brunetto, but much of what Dante learned from him as well" (1991, 63).

What exactly *did* Dante learn from Brunetto? In a certain sense, the lack of empirical evidence attesting to Brunetto's pedagogy (what Dante learned *from* him) strikingly parallels the lack of evidence regarding Brunetto's sexual practices (what Dante learned *of* him); as Armour writes in expressing the scholarly consensus, "the mode and content of Brunetto's teaching of Dante is unknown to us" (25). For Armour, the solution in linking these two enigmas is precisely to deny the specifically sexual valences of Brunetto's sin. Armour soundly rejects the notion that the poet would depict the pilgrim "accentuat[ing] his master's previously unsullied fame, the secrecy of his sin, and his pupil's cruel disclosure of his infamy to the world and to posterity" (7). Yet even in denying Brunetto's sodomy, Armour's rhetoric transparently replicates the modern ideology of the closet—the "secrecy" of sodomy, Dante's "cruel disclosure" to the "world and to posterity." The very unknowability of sodomy mediates between the private, hidden world of Brunetto's pedagogy and the public sphere within which the *Commedia* circulated.

But what if the supposed "virulence" of Brunetto's punishment were read not as condemnatory, but as defensive, as the poet's anxious attempt to distance *himself* from his master's sodomitical desires? In staging his scandalized surprise at his master's sin, Dante may also be abnegating the knowledge he alone possesses. Indeed, I would argue that the extraordinary constellation of sodomy and knowing, poetics and hermeneutics that has always surrounded Dante's encounter with Brunetto constitutes this episode as perhaps the most enduring "open secret" in Dante studies. What Leonard Barkan has aptly termed Dante's "fleetingly reconstructed schoolroom" (1991, 59) in *Inferno* 15 may be the quintessential premodern meditation on the closet, consistently preventing Dante himself from emerging as a subject of homoerotic desire in our own century.

Taking seriously Dante's own entanglement in this sodomitical web yields surprising results. In his famous speech to Brunetto, the pilgrim voices his *dimando* for his master's return to the world above as a many-layered comment on his own pedagogical memory, poetic creativity, and, indeed, his desire for everlasting life:

> "Se fosse tutto pieno il mio dimando,"
> rispuos' io lui, "voi non sareste ancora
> de l'umana natura posto in bando;
>
>   ché 'n la mente m'è fitta, e or m'accora,
> la cara e buona imagine paterna
> di voi quando nel mondo ad ora ad ora
>
>   m'insegnavate come l'uom s'etterna:
> e quant' io l'abbia in grado, mentr' io vivo
> convien che ne la mia lingua si scerna.
>
>   Ciò che narrate di mio corso scrivo,
> e serbolo a chiosar con altro testo
> a donna che saprà, s'a lei arrivo.

> "If my desire were all fulfilled," I answered him, "you would not yet be banished from human nature, for in my memory is fixed, and now saddens my heart, the dear, kind, paternal image of you, when in the world hour by hour you taught me how man makes himself eternal; and how much I hold it in gratitude it behooves me, while I live, to declare in my speech. That which you tell me of my course I write, and keep with a text to be glossed by a lady who will know how, if I reach her (*Inf.* 15, 79–90).

In these tercets, Dante images his own writing, as well as textual production in general, as a male homosocial practice founded on paternity. The pilgrim's characterization of

Brunetto's *imagine paterna* as *"fitta"* or "fixed" in his mind is a well-known allusion to Dido's affectional reaction to Aeneas ("His looks and words cling fast within her bosom [*infixi pectore*]" [*Aeneid* IV.5]), a refashioning of a classically heteroerotic image that represents the productive effects of Brunetto's paternal *imagine* on Dante's own memory and writing. The poet is moved to express his gratitude for Brunetto's pedagogy in his *lingua*—not only through the words he speaks and writes, but also in his native *lingua*, the Italian tongue. More than what Madison Sowell might term an "image of Dante working with the mother tongue to father a new text" (1994, 469), this passage casts the *lingua materna* as the very vehicle of scriptive desire between men. Dante writes what Brunetto has told him of his future, letting Brunetto's words become his ink and inscribe the pilgrim's *corso* on the text of his life. Together with the *altro testo*, Farinata's prediction of Dante's exile in *Inferno* 10, Brunetto's words literally embody the prediction of the poet's future—in the *Commedia* and in history. As Dante notes at the beginning of his speech, these relationships would still obtain *"nel mondo,"* "in the world," if his desire were answered in full.

So deeply felt is this homosocial affinity between pedagogy and poetics that Dante weaves the *memoria* of Brunetto's teaching into the very fabric of his verse. With the nostalgic image of his learning taking place *"ad ora ad ora,"* "from hour to hour," Dante constructs a subtle macaronic pun: when read *"adora adora"*—very close to the Latin *"adoro"* ("I adore"), a term signifying fervent veneration—the phrase suggests to the Latinate ear the inextricability of pedagogy and desire. Just as Brunetto recommends his *Tesoro* in parting, moreover, Dante deliberately echoes his master's texts, both the *Tesoro* itself in *Inferno* 15 (Sowell 1990), as well as portions of the *Tesoretto* throughout the *Commedia* (Delius 1887, 15–22). While Giuseppe Mazzotta would have us read this poetic identification between Dante and Brunetto as simply "another sign of Brunetto's sodomy because it implies his confusion between his own reality and the images of the text" (1979, 140), it is Dante himself who creates this supposed "confusion," intermingling fragments of Brunetto's text and his own throughout this extended meditation on the homoerotics of literary paternity.

The sensual relations between pedagogical past and poetic present characterizing this encounter must be understood within the overall context of the poet's sexualized interaction with the sodomites. More than one scholar has seen Brunetto's eager fingering of Dante's hem (*lembo*) (15, 24) as the initial step in his "cruising" of the pilgrim (see Ferrante 1984, 161n.), an eroticized progression that concludes with Brunetto's graphic description of the sodomite Andrea de' Mozzi, the noble Florentine bishop with "sinfully distended muscles" (*"protesi nervi,"* 15, 114). This palpable erotics crescendoes as Brunetto wistfully casts the pilgrim's body as an object of desire while warning him against the lusts of the Fiesolans:

> Ma quello ingrato popolo maligno
> che discese di Fiesole ab antico,
> e tiene ancor del monte e del macigno,

ti si farà, per tuo ben far, nimico;
ed è ragion, ché tra li lazzi sorbi
si disconvien fruttare al dolce fico.

But that thankless, malignant people, who of old came down from Fiesole, and still
smack of the mountain and the rock, will make themselves an enemy to you because of
your good deeds; and there is cause: for among the bitter sorb-trees it is not fitting that
the sweet fig should come to fruit (*Inf.* 15, 61–66).

Brunetto's image of Dante as a barren *fico*, a prophetic allusion to the poet's exile from
his native Florence, is generally taken to imply a threat to the poet's artistic fertility. In
a recent study of the passage, however, John Ahern has pointed to the explicit sexual
references inspiring its imagery. As he notes, "*fico*" in medieval Italian could refer to
either an individual fig or a fig tree; since a fig *tree* cannot be sweet, however, "the reader
easily takes the metaphor's concluding phrase, 'dolce fico' (a rather common phrase),
as meaning 'sweet fruit'" (1990, 81). Dante "could have avoided this small ambiguity,"
Ahern argues, by using the feminine form, "*fica*," which could connote only the fruit of
the fig. But "*fica*," as readers would have known quite well, is also Italian for "vagina," a
word, says Ahern, "a discreet sodomite, such as Brunetto, would avoid." Thus, "in his
life as in his speech, Dante's Brunetto replaces female objects of desire (*fica*) with male
ones (*fico*)" (81).

The *fico* image is so effective, argues Ahern, because the poet deploys the master-
trope of *transumptio* or transumption, a rhetorical technique in which the connotations
of a literary trope are left deliberately and self-consciously ambiguous in order to
provoke a string of metonymic associations in the mind of the reader. In classical and
medieval rhetorical tradition, transumption depended upon what might be thought of
as a collective pedagogical and literary memory between author and reader. In John
Hollander's terms, transumption is the use of a trope in which "unstated, but associated or understood figures, [are] transumed [i.e., carried from one context to another]
by the trope [and] reconstructed by interpretation" (1981, 140). Relying as it does on the
reader's erudition and interpretive self-consciousness, transumption constitutes what
Foucault termed a "technology of the self"; as Geoffrey of Vinsauf writes in a famous
passage from the *Poetria Nova*: "a transumption of words (*transumptio verbi*) is like a mirror
for you: because you see yourself in it and recognize your own sheep in a foreign
pasture (*rure alieno*)" (cited in Ahern 1990, 85).

Enabled by the hermeneutic openness of transumption, Ahern's gloss provides a
refreshing corrective to the desexualizing readings of Brunetto's sin by Armour and
other critics. Like Mazzotta and Freccero, however, Ahern takes great pains to dissoci-
ate the sodomitical implications of the *fico* from Dante: "Dante the poet made his character Brunetto hold the mirror up to Dante the Pilgrim. But the mirror reflects
Brunetto's own face, not the Pilgrim's" (86); Brunetto, not Dante, "is the barren, withered *ficus*" (84). Ahern's anxious insistence on Dante's erotic purity demonstrates the

effectiveness of the poet's cagey half-denials of his own sodomitical potential. In the passage above, Dante the poet figures *himself* through Brunetto's eyes and words as a *fico*, offering up the pilgrim's body to the eroticized delectation of other men. This reading is confirmed by a further transumption: in many classical sources, the Latin *"ficus"* signifies not only the vagina (the gloss Ahern favors), but also the anus, and even, in a few cases, a sore resulting from anal penetration (Adams 1982, 113). As Ahern notes, a close association between figs and male-male sexual practice also informs Priscian's *Grammar*, one of the most popular grammatical texts in the medieval schoolroom (84). Though ventriloquizing through Brunetto's mouth, then, Dante the poet graphically presents Dante the pilgrim as an object of male homoerotic desire, the *fico* to be desired but never tasted by the Fiesolans.

The next canto features Dante's own vocal pronouncement of desire. Here the pilgrim sees the *rota* the Florentine sodomites form, "As champions, naked and oiled, are wont to do, eyeing their grip and vantage before exchanging thrusts and blows" ("Qual sogliono i campion far nudi e unti, / avvisando lor presa e lor vantaggio, / prima che sien tra lor battuti e punti") (*Inf*. 16, 22–24). After describing the other two sodomites in his *rota*, Jacopo Rusticucci, a Florentine Guelph, reveals the reason for his own place within the wheel in the following passage, in which Dante unequivocally implicates himself in the infernal circulation of sodomitical desires:

> "E io, che posto son con loro in croce,
> Iacopo Rusticucci fui, e certo
> la fiera moglie più ch'altro mi nuoce."
>   'i' fossi stato dal foco coperto,
> gittato mi sarei tra lor di sotto,
> e credo che 'l dottor l'avria sofferto;
>   ma perch' io mi sarei brusciato e cotto,
> vinse paura la mia buona voglia
> che di loro abbracciar mi facea ghiotto.

> "And I who am placed with them in torment was Jacopo Rusticucci, and truly my fierce wife more than aught else has wrought me ill." Had I been sheltered from the fire I would have thrown myself down there among them, and I think my teacher would have permitted it; but since I should have been burned and baked, fear overcame my good will which made me greedy to embrace them (*Inf*. 16, 43–51).

For the commentator Benvenuto, writing in 1373, line 45 refers to Rusticucci's abandonment of his *fiera moglie* in favor of the sodomitical company of other men: "Indeed he had a ferocious wife (*mulierem ferocem*), with whom it was impossible to live. Thus he gave himself to this vice." When Dante states his own wish to "throw" himself "down there among" the sodomites immediately following Rusticucci's pronouncement, he both identifies his own desires with those that led the Florentine to leave his wife and, by his own admission, comes very close to abandoning his visionary quest for Beatrice in favor of the company of the sodomites. Ultimately, only the pilgrim's fear of the rain of *foco* keeps him from joining them as a *fico* in the most literal of senses; Dante himself would be *brusciato e cotto*—punished, that is, *precisely as a sodomite*—if he were to give in to his desire and leap down among them. The poet's aside, moreover ("I think my teacher would have permitted it"), may well be a bemused allusion to the homoerotic rumors surrounding Virgil, as recounted in the second-century *Vita Vergilii*, a text almost certainly known to Dante (Pequigney 1991, 37–38 and notes) but steadfastly elided in practically all modern accounts of Virgil as a character in the *Commedia* (Brownlee 1993; Hollander 1983; Barolini 1984, 201–56; Ronconi 1978).

In one of Dante's many revisionary identifications between himself and Aeneas, the pilgrim ultimately stops short of leaping down onto the burning sands, his epic poem disallowing his self-abandonment to sodomitical pleasures just as the *Aeneid* demanded its hero's abandonment of Dido. Yet Dante will ingeniously fashion other modes of subjecting himself to the forbidden pleasures these cantos embody. Indeed, as the pilgrim watches the Florentine sodomites break their *rota* and flee into the distance, the poet prefigures his future homoerotic subjection in *Purgatorio* 9 (see below) when he notes that "their swift legs seemed to be no less than wings" (16, 87), wings he too would possess if he were to join them. Dante thus projects his frustrated desires to join and embrace the sodomites into a wistful vision of their winged flight, a flight the pilgrim himself experiences in the next canto as he and his guide climb onto the back of Geryon. Here again Dante associates his fear with his desire to embrace, wishing he had the nerve to say to Virgil, "*Fa che tu m'abbracce*" ("See that you embrace me") (94). Seated behind the pilgrim on Geryon's back, Virgil calms Dante's fear of flight with the circle of his arms: "But he who at other times had succored me in other peril clasped me in his arms and steadied me as soon as I was mounted up" ("Ma esso, ch'altra volta mi sovvenne / ad altro forse, tosto ch'i' montai / con le braccia m'avvinse e mi sostenne") (94–96). The arms of Virgil ("*le braccia*") compensate for the embrace of the sodomites ("*abbracciar*") Dante denied to himself just one canto earlier. Commenting on the Geryon episode, Barolini identifies the poet's "metaphorization of desire as flight" as "one of the *Commedia*'s basic metaphorical assumptions: if we desire sufficiently, we fly" (1992, 48). If so, the pilgrim's descent to the Eighth Circle clasped in his master's arms, his first actual flight in the *Inferno*, powerfully metaphorizes a desire that is specifically and indelibly homoerotic.

2.

> Who will give me wings like those of a dove, and I will fly away and rest?
>
> —Psalm 54:7

By the opening of *Purgatorio* 9, the pilgrim's body—*quel d'Adamo* (10)—has tired, and he reclines wearily on the grasses of Ante-Purgatory. Before recounting what he remembers of his first purgatorial dream, the poet notes that his sleep took place "At that hour close to morning when the swallow begins her sad lais, perhaps in memory of her former woes" ("Ne l'ora che comincia i tristi lai / la rondinella presso a la mattina, / forse a memoria de' suo' primi guai") (13–15). Overlaying his dream's narration with the song of Procne, whose husband raped her sister Philomel, Dante suggests a paradoxical but intimate affiliation between sexual violence and artistic creativity. In Ovid's account, Tereus severs Philomel's tongue ("*linguam*") after the rape; robbed of speech and unable to communicate her pain, Philomel instead "writes" the story on her loom, "skillfully weaving purple signs on a white background" ("*purpureasque notas filis intexuit albis*"), and Procne "reads the pitiable fate of her sister" from the cloth (VI: 577–82).

Dante was well aware of the suggestive resonances in his Ovidian source between sexual violence, textuality, and authorial subjectivity. Noting the well-established tradition of endowing morning dreams with a power especially prophetic, indeed "almost divine" ("*quasi è divina*") (9, 18), Dante deploys Philomel's tuneful *memoria* of rape both to foreshadow his own impending subjection to sexual violence and to theorize his incitement to narration. Unlike *la rondinella*, however, the poet re-members his own rape by weaving into his *testo* perhaps the most enduring trope for male homoerotic desire in the Western tradition:[8]

> in sogno mi parea veder sospesa
> un'aguglia nel ciel con penne d'oro,
> con l'ali aperte e a calare intesa;
> 　　ed esser mi parea là dove fuoro
> abbandonati i suoi da Ganimede,
> quando fu ratto al sommo consistoro.
> 　　Fra me pensava, "Forse questa fiede
> pur qui per uso, e forse d'altro loco
> disdegna di portarne suso in piede."
> 　　Poi mi parea che, poi rotata un poco,
> terribil come folgor discendesse,
> e me rapisse suso infino al foco.
> 　　Ivi parea che ella e io ardesse;
> e sì lo 'ncendio imaginato cosse,
> che convenne che 'l sonno si rompesse.

> I seemed to see, in a dream, an eagle poised in the sky, with feathers of gold, its wings outspread, and prepared to swoop. And I seemed to be in the place where Ganymede abandoned his own company, when he was caught up to the supreme consistory; and I thought within myself, "Perhaps it is wont to strike only here, and perhaps disdains to carry anyone upward in its claws from any other place." Then it seemed to me that, having wheeled a while, it descended terrible as a thunderbolt and snatched me upwards as far as the fire: there it seemed that it and I burned; and the imagined fire so scorched me that perforce my sleep was broken (*Purg.* 9, 19–33).

Here Dante densely intertwines a variety of classical and medieval representations of the rape of Ganymede to crystallize his own remembered experience as an object of homoerotic desire. As Leonard Barkan argues in his study of Ganymede in the Italian Renaissance, the effectiveness of this passage, as with Brunetto's image of the *fico*, is to some degree the result of transumption, which places a self-conscious emphasis on "the activity of reading" (1991, 130 n.) and its role in assimilating tropes. For Barkan, transumption allows the sacred and the profane aspects of the Ganymede trope to coexist almost symbiotically: "The rising of Dante's theme, which is also that of his soul, is at once the narrative of Ganymede and the translation of that narrative into sacred terms, which does not, however, quite incinerate the dream of pagan culture" (65).

Yet readerly self-awareness can be only part of the story. Even the literal level of the passage—which recounts a dream, after all—seeks to evade "consciousness," whether the pilgrim's or the reader's. First, with his repeated use of the phrase *"parea che,"* "seemed that," Dante insists on the "heightened visionary reality" of his dream, its otherworldly vividness, as opposed to the "more historicized time" that follows when he awakens (see Barolini 1992, 150). Second, while Ganymede in Dante's passage is the grammatical subject of *raptus*, even if the passive subject—he "was caught up" (*"fu ratto"*)—Dante himself is subject *to* rape, the object of the eagle's action: the eagle *"me rapisse,"* "snatched me." Dante's Ganymedian *raptus*, though certainly a transumptive invitation to the reader, also invites us to consider the *un*consciousness of reading it embeds, the collective memories and personal histories it cathects and through which it interpellates the reading subject.

For this passage is not a tenuous clinging to classical erotics ultimately attenuated by Virgil's allegoresis, but rather a dense set of allusions signaling precisely the enduring presence of classical homoerotics as an integral part of medieval religious experience, Latin learning, and the subject positions these institutions and practices constructed. First, describing the eagle *sospesa* in the initial tercet before swooping down to seize him, Dante recalls two specific ekphrastic images of Ganymede, the first from Statius' *Thebaid*, in which the episode is engraved on a gold drinking cup (I, 548–51); and the second from Virgil's narration of the funeral games for Anchises in *Aeneid* V, where Aeneas presents the captain of the winning ships with an embroidered cloak depicting "the royal boy, with javelin and speedy foot, ... him Jove's swift armor-bearer has caught up *(rapuit)* aloft from Ida in his talons" (249–57). Significantly, Virgil's Ganymede appears in the games immediately following Aeneas's abandonment of Dido at the end of Book IV; the cloak's role in the games thus links the competitive bonding ritual between the *Aeneid*'s sailors to homoerotic *raptus*. This image in turn is echoed in Dante's description of the sodomites in *Inferno* 16 as *"campion far nudi e unti"* ("champions naked and oiled") exchanging *"battuti e punti"* ("thrusts and blows") (*Inf.* 16, 22–24).

Before Dante's depiction of the rape moves from ekphrastic anticipation in lines 19 to 24 to visionary experience in 28 to 33, the poet imputes to the eagle a refusal to carry "any prey found elsewhere," a gesture that privileges the pilgrim as the sole object of its desire. Here again, the two tercets directly recall a specific classical source, this time Ovid's *Metamorphoses*, in which Jove "burned (*arsit*) with love for Phrygian Ganymede, and ... did not deign to take the form of any bird save only that which could bear his thunderbolts. Without delay he cleft the air on his lying wings and stole away the Trojan boy (*abripit Iliaden*), who even now, though against the will of Juno, mingles the nectar and attends the cups of Jove" (X: 155–61). The resonances with Dante's text are obvious: Jove chooses the form of an eagle, the "only" bird that could "bear his thunderbolts," just as Dante's eagle refuses "to carry upward any prey found elsewhere"; and Jove literally "burns with love" for Ganymede, as Dante burns with the eagle in the *foco*. Here the narrative context in which the Ganymede myth appears essentially informs Dante's transumption of the legend. Near the middle of Book X, Ovid recounts the life of Orpheus during the three years following the "double death" of Eurydice, years in which the bard "shunned all love of womankind" and "set the example for the people of Thrace of giving his love to tender boys, and enjoying the springtime and first flower of their youth" (X: 79–85). Orpheus spends the remainder of his days "sing[ing] of boys beloved by gods, and maidens inflamed by unnatural love" (X: 152–54)—and the very first tale he sings is the legend of Ganymede. Jove's homoerotic violence in effect becomes a primary part of Orpheus' narrative *materia*, a reflection of the homoerotic turn his own desires have taken. Through this particular Ovidian allusion, then, Dante (himself returned from the underworld) does not simply "dream himself Ganymede" (Barkan 1991, 62), but also sings himself Orpheus, identifying his own poetic recounting of the Ganymede myth with that of Orpheus, and thus participating in the link between narrative and homoerotic desire Orpheus signifies, a link familiar to many medieval authors (Calabrese 1993; Brownlee 1982).

Ganymede himself, moreover, was not an unambiguously subjected figure in the medieval period. From the twelfth century through the fourteenth, Jove's cupbearer functioned as a vocal and articulate proponent of homosexual practice in a number of medieval debate poems—many of which survive in Italian manuscripts (Lenzen 1972)—between Ganymede and Helen. In one example, Ganymede describes a literal splitting of the desiring subject along a gendered axis of object choice: "When Jupiter divides himself in the middle of the bed, / And turns first to Juno, then to me, / He hurries past the woman and spends his time playing love games with me. / When he turns back to her, he either quarrels or snores" (Boswell 1980, 387). Though casting Jupiter as desirous of both men and women, Ganymede privileges the homoerotic in an explicit subversion of the sexual conceptions of grammar inspiring allegorists such as Alan of Lille: "For a man to be linked to a man is a more elegant coupling. / In case you had not noticed, there are certain rules of grammar / By which articles of the same gender must be coupled together" (385). Ganymede thus universalizes homoerotic desire and same-gender "coupling" as endemic to language and its embodiment in writing. In speaking and dreaming as Ganymede (and an Orphic Ganymede at that), Dante thus directly associates himself with a widely acknowledged proponent of sodomitical practice. In this respect, the dream in *Purgatorio* 9—in which Dante burns with the eagle in the *foco*—

compensates for the pilgrim's failure to jump down among the sodomites in *Inferno* 16, which would have left him "burned and cooked." What was a conscious desire in the earlier canticle here becomes a dreamed fantasy of homoerotic ravishment.

While Dante's momentary assumption of Orphic and Ganymedian homoerotics entails the spurning of women, the category of the feminine remains a persistent concern throughout the canto. Upon awakening from his dream, the poet inscribes yet another mythological allusion into his text that further instantiates the homoerotic subject:

> Non altrimenti Achille si riscosse,
> li occhi svegliati rivolgendo in giro
> e non sappiendo là dove si fosse,
> quando la madre da Chirón a Schiro
> trafuggò lui dormendo in le sue braccia,
> là onde poi li Greci il dipartiro;
> che mi scoss' io, sì come da la faccia
> mi fuggì 'l sonno, e diventa' ismorto,
> come fa l'uom che, spaventato, agghiaccia.

Even as Achilles started up, turning his awakened eyes about him and not knowing where he was, when his mother carried him off, sleeping in her arms, from Chiron to Skyros, whence later the Greeks took him away; so did I start, as soon as sleep fled from my face, and I grew pale, like one who is chilled with terror (*Purg.* 9, 34–42).

Though dreaming as Ganymede, Dante wakes as Achilles, imaging his own transformation from the victim of a transumptive homoerotic ravishment into a stunned, *non sappiendo* subject of another kind of *raptus*: while he only "seemed to be in the place where Ganymede [was]" in his dream, he wakes up "*Non altrimenti Achille si riscosse,*" "Even as Achilles started up." The line refers specifically, of course, to Statius's *Achilleid*, an uncompleted epic that, in its surviving form, traces the abduction of Achilles by his Nereid mother, Thetis, and his life on the isle of Skyros prior to his departure for the Trojan War. Dante's allusion is generally taken to refer narrowly to the moment of Achilles' awakening on the island (I: 247–50). While Statius goes to great lengths in describing Achilles' eagerness to leave Skyros and join the Greeks in war, however, Dante notes in passing that the Greeks *il dipartiro*—that they *compelled* Achilles to leave Skyros (literally, "departed him") against his will.

Dante's seemingly slight revision of the *Achilleid* significantly complicates the already charged relationship in *Purgatorio* 9 between violence and homoerotic subjection. As Dante knew very well, Thetis hid Achilles on Skyros not in the persona of a fierce warrior, but in "soft raiment and dishonourable garb" (*"molles habitus et tegmina foeda"* [142])—cross-dressed as a young woman. In order to convince her son of the propriety of cross-dressing, Thetis draws on the examples of other male heroes and gods (including Hercules, Bacchus, Jupiter, and Caenus) who donned women's clothes for various reasons. For Achilles himself, cross-gendering involves both sartorial and corporeal change: Thetis "softens his rigid neck and bows his strong shoulders, and relaxes the muscles of his arms, and tames and orders correctly his uncombed hair ... she teaches him gait and motion and modesty of speech"; in the end, Achilles "baffles beholders by the puzzle of his sex that by a narrow margin hides its secret" (I: 259–337). Like Dante's Ganymede, moreover, Statius's Achilles is *raptus*, the unknowing victim of abduction from a well-known place (and a familiar gender) to a strange one; as Calchas laments to the panicked Greek council, "Alas! he is rapt away and gone!" ("*ei mihi raptus abit*") (I: 534). Although Barkan sees this gender transformation as a "bathetic turning" from the Ganymede dream that signals the suppression of erotics (1991, 66), Dante's allusion looks very different if we consider that the *Achilleid* was actually read and learned in the medieval schoolroom as a five-book work; only Book V (a mere 167 lines) narrated the triumphant return of Achilles to the Trojan War (Statius 1968, 4). As manuscript evidence attests, the first four books for medieval readers were devoted to Achilles' gradual assumption and performance of femininity: in a sense, the crossing of gender was the whole point of the epic.

While the impetus for Achilles to take on feminine gender identity is his desire for the princess Deidamia, Dante feminizes himself as Achilles only after his fantasized homoerotic ravishment. Sodomites are very often castigated in medieval texts for taking on sexual roles proper to women; Dante thus appropriates such ubiquitous representations by deploying the transvestite *raptus* of Achilles to express the feminizing effects of his own *raptus*. Yet the momentary homoerotic life this allusion breathes into Dante's text expires in the *Achilleid* through the sudden and violent imposition of heteronormativity. Before the Greeks arrive, Achilles unequivocally resists his feminine performance and its threats to his masculinity by forcing himself upon Deidamia "in the thick darkness of the night" in what Statius describes as a "shameful rape" ("*raptumque pudorem*") (640–71). Although the *Achilleid* affords Dante a means of expressing the feminizing homoerotics of his *raptus*, then, it also allows him to escape its emasculating implications by allying himself with the misogynist violence Achilles commits before joining the Greeks.

Dante's implicit conflation of "*raptor*" and "*raptus*" by means of the *Achilleid* provides another glimpse at the text's role in medieval schoolrooms and the pedagogical subjectivities it constructed. The *Achilleid* in its entirety immediately preceded Claudian's *The Rape of Proserpina* in most versions of the *Liber Catonianus*, one of the most widely used elementary schoolbooks well into the fifteenth century (Statius 1968, 2–3). Claudian's text, a retelling of the ancient story of Pluto's abduction of Proserpina as a mythic explanation for the change of seasons, opens with a description of Pluto's "swelling anger" at his genealogical emasculation: "he alone was unmarried and had long been wasting away barren years, unable to bear his ignorance of the marriage-bed and the fact that he knew not the allurements of a bridegroom and the sweet name of father" (I: 32–36). In the middle of Book II, Pluto steals Proserpina away in his chariot as she appeals to the goddesses ("*rapitur Proserpina curru inploratque deas*") (II: 204–05), compelling her to serve him in the underworld.

Two of the six texts that formed a basic part of the elementary absorption of classical Latinity, then, revolved around sexual violence against women, violence that both texts conceive as necessary for the male subject's recuperation from emasculation—whether sartorial feminization (Achilles) or reproductive fruitlessness (Pluto). In this respect, these texts participated in what Marilyn Desmond, commenting on the medieval *Aeneid*, terms the "intensely regulated homosocial masculinity of Virgil readership [which] directs critical attention away from the female characters and their social context," an economy of reading that entails a "class-specific performance of masculinity" founded upon the forceful and reified exclusion of women (1994, 10). Throughout the *Commedia*, though perhaps in *Purgatorio* 9 more than anywhere else, this male institutional setting and the Latin idiom it employs always underlay the poem's vernacular surface. While the subject positions this institutional idiom generates come into being within the numerous homosocial and often homoerotic bonds among poet, reader, text, and *auctor,* they are maintained in part through textual and pedagogical performances of sexual violence against female bodies.

The fact that Dante's Ganymedian rape is ultimately a Christian *raptus* modelled on St. Paul's experience in 2 Corinthians 12 in no way effaces its homoerotic charge. *Pace* Barkan, I would argue that the clear connection between Dante's *raptus* and other Ganymedian allegories suggests not that "the sexual is suppressed in favor of . . . divine love" (39) in Dante's text, but rather that divine love allows for—indeed, demands—the very survival of worldly perversions. How else might we explain the extraordinary diversity characterizing medieval allegorizations of the Ganymede dream, whereby one commentator (the author of the *Ovide moralisé,* following Arnulf of Orleans) first condemns Jove's ravishment of Ganymede (as well as Orpheus' turn to pederasty) to the fate of *Gomorre et Sodome,* yet a scarce sixty lines later glosses the *raptus* as a sign of Christ's love *d'umaine nature*?[9] A particularly striking example is the *Allegorie Librorum Ovidii Metamorphoseos* of Giovanni del Virgilio (whom Dante knew and corresponded with), who wrote that the rape of Ganymede could easily be interpreted "to the good" ("*ad bonum*"), but that St. Augustine, who condemns it as perverse, must be deferred to (X: 6). Finally, considering St. Paul's *raptus* in 2 Corinthians 12, Thomas Aquinas explores in the *Summa Theologiae* the eschatological implications of the experience: "When he is said to be 'rapt up' to *(se raptum),* this means that God has shown him the life in which He will be contemplated in eternity (2a2ae: 175, 5). Citing Augustine, Thomas concludes the *quaestio* by noting that Paul "did not know whether his ecstasy had taken place in or out of his body," and that such knowledge will only be gained "when our bodies will be recovered at the resurrection of the dead, when this corruptible will have put on incorruption" (2a2ae: 175, 6). Divine *raptus* in this life thus mysteriously prefigures the resurrection of the body, the moment at which blessed souls will recover their flesh and bones. Yet even this transformation provokes a certain measure of anxiety: "the fact that the mind is lifted to God in *raptus* is not against nature *(contra naturam),* but beyond the limits of nature" (2a2ae: 175, 3). Although *natura* is of course a quite inclusive category in medieval philosophical discourse, Aquinas's anxiety that Paul's *raptus* might be "against nature" may signal his awareness of the mythographic debates surrounding the rape of Ganymede and its sodomitical resonance, for he uses the very same language in pointedly condemning "intercourse between men, which is specifically called the sin against nature" ("concubitus masculorum, quod specialiter dicitur vitium contra naturam") (1a2ae: 94, 3 ad 2). What resemblance might *raptus contra naturam* bear to the *vitium contra naturam*? Is *raptus* itself a form of "intercourse between men"? While Thomas himself would surely have been scandalized at any suggestion of the intimacy between sodomy and Christian *raptus*, we shall see that the latter half of the *Commedia* powerfully exposes how this particular perverse dynamic is inherent to the formation and salvation of Christian subjects.

3.

> Man alone turns with scorn from the modulated strains of my cithern and runs deranged to the notes of mad Orpheus's lyre ... Shunning even a resemblance traceable to the art of Dione's daughter, he falls into the defect of inverted order. While in a construction of this kind he causes my destruction, in his combination he devises a division in me.
>
> —Alan of Lille (1980, 133–34)

Readers pondering the representation of sodomy in the *Commedia* inevitably find the pilgrim's encounter with the sodomites among the Lustful in *Purgatorio* 26 as confusing as his interaction with Brunetto Latini. For critics such as Richard Kay, the canto provides explicit evidence that sodomy in the *Inferno* should not be interpreted as a specifically sexual sin (1978, 299). Pequigney, by contrast, argues that the elevation of the sodomites to just one level below the Earthly Paradise demonstrates that "Dante's thinking about homosexuality obviously and demonstrably evolved ... as composition of the *Commedia* proceeded" (1991, 39). Whatever the case, the final cantos of the *Purgatorio* point to the growing concern with the crucial links between sexual dissidence and Christian salvation; beginning with Dante's encounter with the Lustful, the *Commedia*'s homoerotic subject gradually but spectacularly comes into its own.

Dante meets the *Purgatorio*'s sodomites soon after hearing Statius's lengthy exposition in canto 25 on the nature of the shades inhabiting the *Commedia*. Although many of the spirits the pilgrim encounters react with surprise to his earthly body, the language of the Lustful in *Purgatorio* 26 is particularly striking, coming as it does immediately following the poet's self-reflexive exploration of his own poetic-visionary project and its ontological status. Indeed, the shade who first notes here that the pilgrim "does not seem to have a fictive body *(corpo fittizio)"* ties his lust for knowledge to his own punishment: *"rispondi a me che 'n sete e 'n foco ardo"* ("give me who burn in thirst and fire your answer") (26, 12–18). Once again, fire and burning are closely associated with desire, both erotic and epistemological, between men.

Before the pilgrim can slake the shades' burning thirst for knowledge by telling them why his limbs travel "together with their blood and with their bones" ("*col sangue suo e con le sue giunture*") (57), he becomes distracted by the curious movement of the sinners before him, who embrace one another "without pause." Like the eagle in the Ganymede dream, *sospesa* in the air before swooping down to ravish him *infino al foco*, the pilgrim stands in "suspense" ("*sospeso*") (30) witnessing the strange ritual:

> Tosto che parton l'accoglienza amica,
> prima che 'l primo passo lì trascorra,
> sopragridar ciascuna s'affatica:
> > la nova gente: "Soddoma e Gomorra";
> e l'altra: "Ne la vacca entra Pasife,
> perché 'l torello a sua lussuria corra."

> As soon as they end the friendly greeting and before the first step there speeds onward, each one tries to shout the loudest: the new-come people "Sodom and Gomorrah," and the other, "Pasiphaë enters into the cow, that the bull may hasten to her lust" (*Purg.* 26, 37–42).

Perplexed by this spectacular verbalization of sin, Dante asks Guido Guinizzelli to reveal his own identity and that of the "throng that is going away behind your backs" ("*e chi è quella turba / che se ne va di retro a' vostri terghi*") (65–66), so that he might "trace it on paper" (64). Guido complies, explaining the ritual as follows:

> La gente che non vien con noi, offese
> di ciò per che già Cesar, trïunfando,
> "Regina" contra sé chiamar s'intese:
> > però si parton "Soddoma" gridando,
> rimproverando a sé com' hai udito,
> e aiutan l'arsura vergognando.

> The people who do not come with us offended in that for which Caesar in his triumph once heard "Queen" cried out against him; therefore they go off crying "Sodom," reproving themselves as you have heard, and they help the burning with their shame (*Purg.* 26, 76–81).

Guido's explanation derives from Suetonius' account of a love affair between Julius Caesar and King Nicomedes of Bythinia. In his *Vitae Caesarium*, Suetonius notes that the only "stain on [Julius Caesar's] reputation for chastity" was his "intimacy (*contubernium*) with King Nicomedes": "At this time ... one Octavius, a man whose disordered mind made him somewhat free with his tongue, after saluting Pompey as 'king' in a crowded assembly, greeted Caesar as 'queen.' But Gaius Memmius makes the direct charge that

[Caesar] acted as cupbearer *(cyathum et vinum)* to Nicomedes with the rest of his wantons at a large dinner-party" (I: 49).

Dante's allusion to Suetonius further amplifies the complex intertextual relations reflected in the *Commedia* between gender difference—the feminizing language of Caesar's public detractors—and erotic difference—Caesar's supposed deviation from sexual norms. The feminization of Caesar, a classically heroic warrior, results from his passive sexual subjection to another man, a subjection that transforms him from conquering hero to "cupbearer." This erotic metamorphosis powerfully links the sodomites in *Purgatorio* 26 to Dante himself by replicating the pilgrim's transformation from the sexually vanquished Ganymede to the transvested Achilles in *Purgatorio* 9. The sodomites in *Purgatorio* 26, moreover, like Brunetto Latini in *Inferno* 15, are explicitly named as sodomites through an abjecting performative: "*Soddoma.*" And like Suetonius' Caesar, they are humiliated publically for their sexual deviance, this time with their own voices.

The clearly homoerotic counterexample of the sodomites has led modern commentators to regard Guinizzelli himself, whose "sin was hermaphrodite" (*"peccato fu ermafrodito"*) (26, 82), as a heterosexual sinner. Yet if Dante truly intended *Soddoma* and *ermafrodito* to represent a firm division among the Lustful based on a binarism of "sexual preference," why would he have chosen the one medieval term that perhaps more than any other signifies precisely an ambivalence over the gender of sexual object choice? In the *Metamorphoses*, Hermaphroditus' body joins with a woman's "as when one grafts a twig on some tree," and afterwards seems "neither [man nor woman] and yet both" (*"neutrumque et utrumque"*) (IV: 375–80). The association of hermaphroditism with both heterosexual and homosexual practice is ubiquitous in high medieval treatments of the subject. In his influential *Verbum abbreviatum*, for example, Peter the Chanter represents it as the literal embodiment of erotic ambivalence:

> If he is hotter, like a man, then he should be allowed to take the lead; if indeed he is effeminate, then he should be allowed to marry, as a bride. If, however, it should happen that the organ (*instrumentum*) is deficient, nevertheless the use of the other organ should not be allowed; it should instead be repressed forever, because alteration is the sign (*vestigia*) of the vice of sodomy (cited in Rubin 1994, 104).

The Chanter's sentiment is far from atypical; indeed, hermaphroditism in medieval medical treatises more often provokes anxiety over male sodomitical practice than it implies heterosexual practice (Cadden 1993, 223–24).

The specifically homoerotic connotations of *ermafroditi* clearly inform the poet's representation of the scriptive relationship between Guido and Dante. After describing Guido as "il padre / mio e de li altri miei miglior che mai / rime d'amor usar dolci e leggiadre" ("the father of me and of the others my betters who ever used sweet and gracious rhymes of love") (97–99), Dante echoes his unfulfilled wish to leap down and embrace the sodomites in *Inferno* 16 by stating his desire to "embrace" his poetic father;

he is prevented once again from feeling the masculine embrace he longs for, however, "because of the fire" with which Guido is punished (102). Rather than embrace physically, Guido and Dante embrace *poetically*, fashioning themselves and one another as inscribed words and writing surfaces. First, Guido says to the pilgrim, "You leave, by that which I hear, traces so deep and clear in me that Lethe cannot take them away or make them dim" ("Tu lasci tal vestigio, / per quel ch'i' odo, in me, e tanto chiaro, / che Lète nol può tòrre né far bigio") (106–108). The pilgrim's *vestigio,* which he has literally left inside of Guido (*in me*), reflect Guido's own "traces," the lines of poetry fixed to Dante's page: "Your sweet verses, which so long as modern use shall last, will make dear their very ink" ("Li dolci detti vostri, / che, quanto durerà l'uso moderno, / faranno cari ancora i loro incostri") (112–14). The pilgrim enthusiastically represents himself as Guido's writing surface just as Guido served as his: "for his name my desire was making ready a grateful place" ("suo nome il mio disire / apparecchiava grazïoso loco") (137–38). Dante's own poetic desires are indelibly inscribed with Guido's name, which joins Brunetto's *imagine* in the pilgrim's memory.

Only his passage from Purgatory proper to the Earthly Paradise, however, finally allows the pilgrim to experience the homoerotic burning he has dreamed and desired up to this point. Standing before the wall of flame in *Purgatorio* 27, Dante learns that holy souls may go no farther "if first the fire sting not" ("Più non si va, se pria non morde ... il foco") (10–11). Here the associations between homoerotic practice and burning—which we have already seen in the pilgrim's fear of becoming *brusciato e cotto* (*Inf.* 16) and his dreamed burning with the eagle (*Purg.* 9)—merge radically as Dante plunges into the fire between Statius and Virgil:

> Poi dentro al foco innanzi mi si mise,
> pregando Stazio che venisse retro,
> che pria per lunga strada ci divise.
> Sì com' fui dentro, in un bogliente vetro
> gittato mi sarei per rinfrescarmi,
> tant' era ivi lo 'ncendio sanza metro.

> Then he entered into the fire in front of me, asking Statius, who for a long way had been between us, to come behind. As soon as I was in it I would have thrown myself into molten glass to cool me, so without measure was the burning there (*Purg.* 27, 46–51).

The pilgrim's passage through the purgatorial fire has long been regarded as his final preparation for encountering Beatrice, a prefiguration of the "transhumanization" he must undergo to traverse the expanses of *Paradiso* (1, 70; see below). As the last and most frightening trial Dante endures with Virgil before Beatrice replaces him as the pilgrim's guide through Paradise, the flames themselves seem to represent a decisive move away from the homosocial and worldly sphere of poetics embodied by Virgil.

Yet even as the pilgrim's body passes through the chastening flames, the poet echoes his own most overtly homoerotic proclamation: "I would have thrown myself into molten glass to cool me," a line that unmistakably recalls *Inferno* 16, 47: "I would have thrown myself down there among [the sodomites]." In both cases, the phrase "*gittato mi sarei*" ("would have thrown myself"), which appears only twice in the entire *Commedia*, begins the middle line of a tercet, and both lines express the pilgrim's desire either to experience or to escape an explicitly homoerotic and implicitly sodomitical burning. Moreover, when Virgil urges the pilgrim to calm his fears by going "close to [the fire] and try[ing] it with your own hands on the hem of your garment" ("e fatti far credenza / con le tue mani al lembo d'i tuoi panni") (27, 30), he points to the very same *lembo* Brunetto fingered lovingly in Inferno 15. In a profound sense, Dante's passage through the fire—the *literal* burning of his body—finally gives him what he could only fear when speaking with the sodomites and only fantasize when ravished as Ganymede.

The pilgrim's burning with his guides signals the most explicit emergence of the homoerotic subject we have seen thus far. Yet this emergence is not without its costs. Finally abandoned by Virgil in the Earthly Paradise, Dante mimics Orpheus' lament upon his second loss of Eurydice in Virgil's fourth *Georgic*: "The bare voice and death-cold tongue, with fleeting breath, called Eurydice—ah, hapless Eurydice! 'Eurydice' the banks re-echoed, all down the stream" ("Eurydicen vox ipsa et frigida lingua. / a miseram Eurydicen! anima fugiente vocabat, / Eurydicen toto referebant flumine ripae") (IV: 525–27). In *Purgatorio* 30, Orpheus' loss of his wife becomes the pilgrim's loss of his male guide: "Ma *Virgilio* n'avea lasciati scemi / di sé, *Virgilio* dolcissimo patre, / *Virgilio* a cui per mia salute die'mi" ("But Virgil had left us bereft of himself, Virgil sweetest father, Virgil to whom I gave myself for my salvation") (30, 49–51; my emphasis). While John Freccero reads Dante's repetition of Virgil's name as a "merest allusion," "an effacement, further and further away from the letter of Virgil's text, as Virgil fades away in the dramatic representation to make way for Beatrice" (1986, 208), at the same time it signals the return of Orphic homoerotics just as the pilgrim feels "the great power of old love" ("*d'antico amor ... la gran potenza*") (30, 39) for Beatrice. For Dante, the object of Orphic desire is not a lost wife, but a man—the very man who would have sanctioned his leap onto the burning sands, the man whose literary production formed the core of the homosocial, Latinate pedagogy allowing the *Commedia*'s homoerotic subject to be forged. Indeed, Dante's mournful tercet evokes a second classical text: in the *Achilleid*, as the Greeks collectively bemoan the absence of their hero, Statius inscribes a triple repetition of his hero's name, perhaps inspired directly by *Georgic* IV: "the whole host burns for the absent Achilles, they love the name of Achilles, Achilles alone is called for against Hector" ("omnis in absentem belli manus ardet *Achillem*, / nomen *Achillis* amant, et in Hectora solus *Achilles* / poscitur") (I: 473–75; my emphasis). Even as he takes the final turn towards Beatrice, Dante the poet positions his own text between the texts of Virgil and Statius, just as the pilgrim's body passes between theirs through the purgatorial fire. In three short lines, Dante mourns the shattering loss of Virgil, his past guide; the imminent loss of Statius, his guide through the Earthly Paradise; and his own momentary identity as Achilles, the feminized subject of Ganymedian desire.

And it is at just this moment, as Beatrice reproves him for weeping at the loss of Virgil, that Dante's name appears for the first and only time in the entire *Commedia*: "'Dante, because Virgil leaves you, do not weep yet, do not weep yet, for you must weep for another sword!'" ("'Dante, perché Virgilio se ne vada, / non pianger anco, non piangere ancora; / ché pianger ti conven per altra spada'") (30, 55–57). "*Per altra spada*": Beatrice casts Dante's pain as the result of a penetrative sword thrust, a bodily wound that prefigures a future, more wrenching pain. The very enunciation of the pilgrim's name entails loss: the word *Dante*, despite its uniqueness within the *Commedia*, appears alongside *Virgilio* within the same line. Dante's mournful loss of Virgil is in effect the condition for his own selfhood, bound inextricably to the writing that produces it: "I turned at the sound of my name, which of necessity is registered here" ("mi volsi al suon del nome mio, / che di necessità qui si registra") (62–63). In two lines that profoundly conflate poet and pilgrim, the self-consciously performative inscription of Dante's proper name instantiates the two as one, a single subject: the pilgrim-"I" turns as the poet-"I" transcribes the appellation common to them both. Produced by the love and voice of Beatrice, "Dante" in the Earthly Paradise is a product of heterosexual desire, interpellated precisely through a naming ritual that echoes but rejects the shaming vocative—*Soddoma*—naming the sodomites just four cantos earlier, in *Purgatorio* 26. Dante's newly assumed subject position as pilgrim and poet has been enabled by the very prohibition of homoerotic desire: the wrenching pain of homoerotic loss and the poetic mourning of his *dolcissimo patre* have fashioned him into the "properly" gendered, heteroerotically desiring Dante whom Beatrice will take through the *Paradiso* (see Butler 1990, 57–65). Hereafter the homoerotic model of subjectivity the *Commedia* creates will be a utopian projection into a distant future. As I will argue in conclusion, however, for the Christian Dante this eschatological hope constitutes the very promise of everlasting life.

4.

> I desire to die, and to be dissolved in Christ.
> —Philippians 1: 23

The poet's juxtaposition at the opening of the *Paradiso* of "The glory of the One who moves all things" (1, 1) with his own artistic inadequacy—embodied by the sinking of *nostro intelletto* ("our intellect") into an abyss so profound that *la memoria* fails to follow (9)—casts Dante as both unwilling and, for all practical purposes, unable to recount in language his experiences in the final stage of the afterworld. While acknowledging here (as in the *Purgatorio*) the paradox inherent in "re-presenting what God presented" (see Barolini 1992, 122–42), however, Dante vows to try his best to mold the *materia* of his memory into the text of his third canticle: "Veramente quant' io del regno santo / ne la mia mente potei far *tesoro*, / sarà ora materia del mio canto" ("Nevertheless, so much of the holy kingdom as I could treasure up in my mind shall now be the matter of my song") (1, 10–12; my emphasis). This is a jarring image if we recall the parting words of

Brunetto Latini near the end of *Inferno* 15: "Sieti raccomandato il mio Tesoro, / nel qual io vivo ancora" ("Let my *Tesoro*, in which I yet live, be commended to you") (119–20). Although Dante will repeat *"tesoro"* as an end-rhyme five times in the course of his heavenly voyage, *Paradiso* 1, 11 is the word's first such appearance in the *Commedia* since the pilgrim watched his beloved teacher run to catch up with the other sodomites. If we take seriously Dante's almost obsessive preoccupation with the poetic possibilities inherent in such formal elements as enjambment, puns, and end-rhymes (Ferrante 1993, 159–70), the echo here on *tesoro* may imply that the poet took his master's request quite literally, figuring the *Tesoro* itself as the very stuff of poetics—the "treasure" that becomes the *materia* of his canticle—in the *Paradiso*.[10] More than a typological prefigurement for eternity in God, Brunetto's desire for everlasting *literary* life, a desire Dante himself acquired *ad ora ad ora*, is scandalously recast as the very precondition for salvation.

Dante first signals the intimacy between perversion and salvation as he records the transformation that enables his journey through the celestial world. Referring to Ovid's account of Glaucus (*Met.* XIII: 898–968), a Boeotian fisherman who became a God after eating a magic herb, the poet recounts his own miraculous metamorphosis as he gazes at Beatrice:

> Nel suo aspetto tal dentro mi fei,
> qual si fé Glauco nel gustar de l'erba
> che 'l fé consorto in mar de li altri dèi.
>
> Trasumanar significar per verba
> non si poria; però l'essemplo basti
> a cui esperïenza grazia serba.

> Gazing upon her I became within me such as Glaucus became on tasting of the grass that made him sea-fellow of the other gods. The passing beyond the human may not be set forth in words: therefore let the example suffice any for whom grace reserves that experience (*Par.* 1, 67–72).

The personal transformation signified by Dante's famous neologism, *trasumanar*, "passing beyond the human," parallels but surpasses the pilgrim's passage through the wall of flame in *Purgatorio* 27. Both involve a literal and fundamental metamorphosis of the human person, a purification that gives the subject a special nearness to God by cleansing it of the temptations and pleasures of the flesh.

Yet the poet's tendency to represent the ravishments of divine love through classical examples of sexual violence—a tendency we have already seen in the Ganymede episode and, as Rachel Jacoff has demonstrated, in Dante's representation of the rape of Europa in *Paradiso* 27 (1991b)—suggests that *trasumanar* may in fact be a resurfacing of transumption, the rhetorical mode so central to Dante's intertextual homoerotics in *Purgatorio* and *Inferno*.[11] Etymologically, of course, the two terms are related, transumption deriving from the Latin "*sumere*," "taking" or "seizing," and "*trans-*," "across"; as rhetoricians note, transumptive metonymy implies force and alienation in the transfer of a trope (and of the subject who interprets it) from one context to another. It is surely no mistake that Dante represents the process of *trasumanar* through a transumptive invitation to the reader to "live" Glaucus' experience; language alone ("*verba*") is not capable of accurately representing transhumanizing metamorphoses. For Dante indeed, "passing beyond the human" is a vicarious reliving of Ovid's text that offers a paradoxically rhetorical compensation for the inadequacy of human language and worldly existence.

If the theologized *trasumanar* enabling Dante's travel through paradise is in fact bound up with the homoerotic *transumptiones* that figure him as Ganymede in *Purgatorio* 9 and a *dolce fico* in *Inferno* 15, the "transhumanized" subject of the *Paradiso* may be a paradisiac refraction of the same homoerotic subject delineated in earlier canticles. In the *Paradiso*, however, the desired other whose absence constitutes the pilgrim as subject is not a poetic father, but God and Christ; nor are God and Christ consistently (or even primarily) masculine, but androgynous (Ferrante 1992). In a deep sense, the *Commedia*'s always ambiguous representation of gender and desire comes to a head in the *Paradiso*, where the Godhead is both female and male; where Beatrice performs the simultaneous roles of feminine object of desire and masculine voice of *auctoritas*; and where the pilgrim's desire to merge completely with God—the fantasy of the Ganymede dream—is figured as both a polymorphously erotic dissolution of self and a paradoxical affirmation of the visceral homoerotics such dissolution entails. As Joan Ferrante notes, the *Paradiso* moves away from the masculine realm of poetics in the earlier canticles, as Beatrice herself assumes an increasingly dominant devotional and exegetical role in the pilgrimage (1992). While it is certainly "a commonplace of Dante criticism that the poet's love for Beatrice" (3) allows him to complete his journey, however, the pilgrim's final approach to God entails an eroticized *triangulation* of desire, one in which the homoerotic interpenetration of his own body and desires with those of Christ are at least as crucial as his love and desire for Beatrice.

Dante explores the erotics of mystical vision and union most graphically in the *Paradiso*'s final three cantos, beginning with his vision of the Celestial Rose that opens canto 31: "In forma dunque di candida rosa / mi si mostrava la milizia santa / che nel suo sangue Cristo fece sposa" ("In form then of a pure white rose the saintly host was shown to me, which with His own blood Christ made His bride") (31, 1–3). Here the pilgrim sees the entire worldly Church, past, present, and future, contained within the Rose. Following earlier medieval commentary on the Song of Songs (especially that of Bernard of Clairvaux), the poet figures the Church as Bride or *sponsa* and Christ as Bridegroom, resulting in the matrimonial coupling of Christ and humanity and subsuming particularized human bodies within the passionate embrace of Christ. Indeed, Dante is not satisfied with the vision of the Church as collective Bride of Christ; he also yearns to discover how each individual member of the Church's body—both female and male—becomes the subjugated *sponsa*: "la luce divina è penetrante / per l'universo secondo ch'è degno / sì che nulla le puote essere ostante" ("the divine light so penetrates through the universe, in measure of its worthiness, that naught can be an obstacle to it") (31, 22–24). Such medieval notions of the penetrative force of religious rapture, which Dante himself has already explored in his dreamed ravishment as Ganymede, could often be surprisingly violent. Richard of St. Victor described the delight the subject feels when "caught up [*rapitur*] into that chamber of divine secrecy, while by that fire of divine love it is surrounded on all sides and intimately penetrated *(intime penetrature)*, it becomes so thoroughly inflamed *(usquequaque inflammatur)* that it almost puts its own self aside, takes on a certain divine inclination, and, totally remodelling itself on the beauty it has seen, crosses over into another glory" (cited in Botterill 1994, 213).

Dante signals the pilgrim's access to such devotional ravishments when St. Bernard appears at his side in the middle of *Paradiso* 31:

> e volgeami con voglia rïaccesa
> per domandar la mia donna di cose
> di che la mente mia era sospesa.
>   Uno intendëa, e altro mi rispuose:
> credea veder Beatrice e vidi un sene
> vestito con le genti glorïose.

> and I turned with rekindled will to ask my lady about things as to which my mind was in suspense. One thing I purposed, and another answered me: I thought to see Beatrice, and I saw an elder, clad like the folk in glory (31, 55–60).

As critics have long noted, the replacement of Beatrice by Bernard as the pilgrim's guide parallels Dante's loss of Virgil in the Earthly Paradise. Yet the specifically gendered nature of this oscillation is perhaps more significant than the scholarship has allowed: as Bernard reveals, Beatrice has sent him for a specific reason: "To quench your desire Beatrice urged me from my place" ("A terminar lo tuo disiro / mosse Beatrice me del loco mio") (31, 65–66). Again, it is precisely this triangulation of desire, demanding the reintroduction of a masculine guide, that will begin to allow the pilgrim to quench his burning *disiro* to be with God. This recuperation of male homosocial desire in the final stage of the *Paradiso* is emphatically embodied as well: Dante initially describes Bernard as "clothed like the folk in glory" ("*vestito* con le genti *glorïose*" [my emphasis]), recalling Solomon's image of the saved after the Resurrection: "When the flesh, glorious and sanctified, shall be clothed on us again, our persons will be more acceptable for being all complete" ("Come la carne *glorïosa* e santa / fia *rivestita*, la nostra persona / più grata fia per esser tutta quanta") (*Par.* 14, 43–44; my emphasis). Already *vestito* like those in glory, Bernard, though in reality only a ghostly body, nevertheless seems truly embodied, "dressed like" those who will be clothed in flesh when the last trumpet sounds (see Bynum 1995).

With this poetic emphasis on Bernard's corporeality, the eroticized teleology of vision and burning through the last three cantos takes on a visceral quality. Bernard tells the pilgrim that he will be able to "consummate" ("*assommi*") his journey perfectly by making himself "fly with [his] eyes throughout this garden" of the Empyrean ("vola con li occhi per questo giardino") (31, 97); "for gazing on it," Bernard asserts, "will better prepare your sight to mount through the divine ray" ("ché veder lui t'acconcerà lo sguardo / più al montar per lo raggio divino") (98–99). As Dante and Bernard gaze at the Virgin, the already eroticized dynamic of vision and flight intensifies as their two gazes burn together: "Bernard, when he saw my eyes fixed and intent on the object of his own burning glow, turned his own with such affection to her, that he made mine more ardent in their gazing" ("Bernardo, come vide li occhi miei / nel caldo suo caler fissi e attenti, / li suoi con tanto affetto volse a lei, / che 'miei di rimirar fé più ardenti") (31, 139–42). Like Virgil, who passed before the pilgrim in the wall of fire, Bernard burns with Dante, adding the ardent force of his own vision to the pilgrim's.

The consummational triangulation of desire builds through the next canto, beginning with the pilgrim's vision of Eve and the Virgin: "La piaga che Maria richiuse e unse, / quella ch'è tanto bella da' suoi piedi / è colei che l'aperse e che la punse" ("The wound which Mary closed and anointed, that one who is so beautiful at her feet is she who opened it and pierced it") (*Par.* 32, 4–6). The wound Dante sees is Eve's sinful laceration of the body of humanity, of Holy Church itself—the body of Christ on Earth. As Bernard instructs, to reach this body of Christ Dante must first gaze upon and through the Virgin, a female figure whose face "most resembles Christ, for only its brightness can prepare you to see Christ" (la faccia che a Cristo / più si somiglia, ché la sua chiarezza / sola ti può disporre a veder Cristo") (32, 85–87). As the canto concludes, the wound in the initial tercets becomes the opened and penetrable body of Christ:

> e drizzeremo li occhi al primo amore,
> sì che, guardando verso lui, penètri
> quant' è possibil per lo suo fulgore.
> Veramente, ne forse tu t'arretri
> movendo l'ali tue, credendo oltrarti,
> orando grazia conven che s'impetri
> grazia da quella che puote aiutarti

and we will turn our eyes to the Primal Love, so that, gazing toward Him, you may penetrate, as far as that can be, into His effulgence. But lest, perchance, you fall back, moving your wings and thinking to advance, grace must be advanced by prayer, grace from her who has power to aid you (32, 142–48).

The *primo amore* is now the graphically displayed object of desire, opened to an epistemological search in which the pilgrim must "move [his] wings" in order to advance along the path of salvation. Bernard concludes the canto with an image that binds him to the pilgrim through the homosocial discourse of writing we have already seen in the

Brunetto and Guinizzelli episodes: "and do you follow me with your affection so that your heart depart not from my words" ("tu mi seguirai con l'affezione, / sì che dal dicer mio lo cor non parti") (32, 149–50). Like Brunetto's perverse lessons written on Dante's *memoria* and Guido's sweet lines and dear ink, Bernard's words are inscribed on the pilgrim's heart; writing act and writing surface have become one and the same.

Paradiso 33 spectacularly assimilates these images of desire as Bernard prays to the Virgin for the pilgrim, describing him as a soul "who would have grace and has not recourse to thee," a man whose "desire seeks to fly without wings" ("qual vuol grazia e a te non ricorre, / sua disïanza vuol volar sanz' ali") (33, 14–15). Bernard's prayer once again creates an erotic triangle as he and the pilgrim burningly project their collective gaze towards the Virgin: "E io, che mai per mio veder non arsi / più ch'i' fo per lo suo, tutti miei prieghi / ti porgo" ("And I, who never for my own vision burned more than I do for his, proffer to thee all my prayers") (28–30). Bernard burns ("*arsi*") for Dante's vision as Jove burned ("*arsit*") for Ganymede, as Dante seemed to burn ("*ardesse*") with the eagle *infino al foco*. The poet next records his vision of the Circle of Christ, which signifies the incarnation and appears as a fiery ring: "one seemed reflected by the other, as rainbow by rainbow, and the third seemed fire breathed forth equally from the one and the other" ("e l'un da l'altro come iri da iri / parea reflesso, e 'l terzo parea foco / che quinci e quindi igualmente si spiri") (33, 118–20). This circle, the poet notes, is somehow "depicted with our image" ("*pinti de la nostra effige*") (131), the very body of Christ. Feasting his eyes upon this anthropomorphic spectacle, Dante articulates the *Commedia*'s final question:

> Qual è 'l geomètra che tutto s'affige
> per misurar lo cerchio, e non ritrova,
> pensando, quel principio ond' elli indige,
>   tal era io a quella vista nova:
> veder voleva come si convenne
> l'imago al cerchio e come vi s'indova;
>   ma non eran da ciò le proprie penne:
> se non che la mia mente fu percossa
> da un fulgore in che sua voglia venne.

As is the geometer who wholly applies himself to measure the circle, and finds not, in pondering, the principle of which he is in need, such was I at that new sight. I wished to see how the image conformed to the circle and how it has its place therein; but my own wings were not sufficient for that, save that my mind was smitten by a flash wherein its wish came to it (*Par.* 33, 133–141).

Dante admits to the inadequacy of his "own wings" in discerning precisely how all of humanity will merge with Christ at the resurrection, as well as the way in which he himself will become an eternal part of the burning circle. The pilgrim's need for *other* wings—wings he had previously received only momentarily while embraced by Virgil on Geryon's back and only in fantasy while ravished as Ganymede—is answered as he is *percossa*, struck violently by a flashing light, the same light that "penetrates *(penetrante)* through the universe" (31, 23–24).

Even the pilgrim's concluding vision, then, an eschatological fantasy of his own consummating dissolution in Christ, recasts the two central metaphors of desire—burning and flight—that have allowed the homoerotic subject of the *Commedia* to be articulated and discerned. The pilgrim's final assumption into the fiery circle, a circle with no beginning and no end, will entail the surrender of self in an eternal embrace with Christ. Yet it would be wrong to read such a surrender as an effacement either of homoerotic desire or of the individuated subject who experiences it; as Solomon suggestively notes, only at the Resurrection will "the organs of the body ... be strong enough for everything that can delight us" ("li organi del corpo saran forti / a tutto ciò che potrà dilettarne") (*Par.* 14, 59–60). By subsuming the burning pleasures of sodomy and *raptus* within his eschatological vision, Dante queers the very end of time, universalizing the perverse bodily practices he has explored throughout the *Commedia* and projecting them into eternity along the ring of fire that is Christ. And this particular ring, like the *minor giron* encircling the sodomites in the depths of the *Inferno*, will burn forever.

NOTES

1. *Inferno* 11, (46–51). All references to the *Commedia* are taken from Petrocchi's edition; I have relied on the translation by Charles Singleton with a few minor alterations. Latin works will be cited by section (book, chapter, paragraph, line, etc.) rather than by page.

2. A few scholars have recently begun to theorize sexual identities in the premodern west from various post-Foucauldian perspectives; see esp. Dinshaw (1994), Bredbeck (1992), and DiGangi (1994).

3. See, among others, Goodich (1979, ix); Brundage (1987, 213); Boswell (1980, 93 n).

4. See especially Boswell (1980, 210–14); Moore (1987, 91–94); Kruger (1994).

5. Dante studies have profited from a small but rich body of scholarship exploring the extra-sexual dimensions of the sins of Brunetto and the Florentine runners, revealing links between sodomy and language (Pézard 1950), governance (Kay 1978), and religious dissent (Armour 1983). At the same time, however, all three critics in some sense "defend" Brunetto—whether implicitly or explicitly—against Dante's supposed "charge" of homosexuality. A refreshing exception is Vance (1986, 230–55), which builds on Pézard's work but insists on the materiality of sodomy as a sexual category.

6. For a moving discussion of Dante and the poetics and politics of exile, see Menocal (1994, 93–106).

7. The bibliography on Brunetto is vast; for the major works see Armour (1983, 1 n).

8. See Hollander (1969, 136–49) for a brilliant allegorical reading of the three rapes that initiate this canto.

9. *Ovide moralisé* X: 3348, 3411. See also Pierre Bersuire's *Ovidius Moralizatus* (Reynolds 1971, 353).

10. Also suggestive is Ferrante's observation that Dante "speaks of 'latino' ... as the equivalent of clarity, of the highest level of discourse" at four different moments in the *Paradiso* (1993, 161).

11. Brenda Schildgen has convincingly demonstrated the relationship between neologisms in

the *Paradiso* and the Latin rhetorical tradition, arguing that, for Dante, "the rhetorical tradition allows for creating the neologism and justifies it as a legitimate poetic gesture" (1989, 102). Here I am suggesting that, at least in regard to *trasumanar* (the founding neologism in the canticle), the relationship may be self-consciously etymological as well.

WORKS CITED

Adams, J. N. 1982. *The Latin Sexual Vocabulary*. Baltimore: Johns Hopkins University Press.

Ahern, John. 1990. "Troping the Fig: *Inferno* XV 66." *Lectura Dantis* 6: 80–91.

Alan of Lille. 1980. *The Plaint of Nature*, trans. James J. Sheridan. Mediaeval Sources in Translation 26. Toronto: Pontifical Institute of Mediaeval Studies.

Aquinas, Thomas. 1964–1981. *Summa Theologiae*. 61 vols., ed. and trans. Blackfriars. New York: McGraw–Hill; London: Eyre and Spottiswoode.

Armour, Peter. 1983. "Dante's Brunetto: The Paternal Paterine?" *Italian Studies* 38: 1–38.

Barkan, Leonard. 1991. *Transuming Passion: Ganymede and the Erotics of Humanism*. Stanford: Stanford University Press.

Barolini, Teodolinda. 1984. *Dante's Poets: Textuality and Truth in the* Commedia. Princeton: Princeton University Press.

———. 1992. *The Undivine Comedy: Detheologizing Dante*. Princeton: Princeton University Press.

Bosco, Umberto, ed. 1970–1978. *Enciclopedia dantesca*. 6 vols. Rome: Istituto dell'Enciclopedia Italiana.

Boswell, John. 1980. *Christianity, Social Tolerance, and Homosexuality: Gay People in Western Europe from the Beginning of the Christian Era to the Fourteenth Century*. Chicago: University of Chicago Press.

Botterill, Stephen. 1994. *Dante and the Mystical Tradition: Bernard of Clairvaux in the* Commedia. Cambridge Studies in Medieval Literature 22. Cambridge: Cambridge University Press.

Bray, Alan. 1994. "Homosexuality and the Signs of Male Friendship in Elizabethan England," in Goldberg, *Queering the Renaissance*. 40–61.

Bredbeck, Gregory. 1992. *Sodomy and Interpretation: Marlowe to Milton*. Ithaca: Cornell University Press.

Brownlee, Kevin. 1982. "Orpheus's Song Re-sung: Jean de Meun's Reworking of *Metamorphoses*, X." *Romance Philology* 36: 201–209.

———. 1993. "Dante and the Classical Poets," in Jacoff, *The Cambridge Companion*. 100–119.

Brundage, James A. 1987. *Law, Sex, and Christian Society in Medieval Europe*. Chicago: University of Chicago Press.

Butler, Judith. 1990. *Gender Trouble: Feminism and the Subversion of Identity*. New York: Routledge.

Bynum, Caroline Walker. 1991. *Fragmentation and Redemption: Essays on Gender and the Human Body in Medieval Religion*. New York: Zone.

———. 1995. "Imagining the Self: Somatomorphic Soul and Resurrection Body in Dante's *Divine Comedy*," in *Faithful Imagining: A Festschrift for Richard Reinhold Niebuhr*, ed. Proudfoot *et al.* Atlanta: Scholars Press. 83–106.

Cadden, Joan. 1993. *Meanings of Sex Difference in the Middle Ages: Medicine, Science, and Culture*. Cambridge: Cambridge University Press.

Calabrese, Michael. 1993. "'Make a Mark that Shows': Orphean Song, Orphean Sexuality, and the Exile of Chaucer's Pardoner." *Viator* 24: 269–86.

Castle, Terry. 1993. *The Apparitional Lesbian: Female Homosexuality and Modern Culture*. New York: Columbia University Press.

Claudian. 1993. *De Raptu Proserpinae*, ed. and trans. Claire Gruzelier. Oxford: Clarendon Press.

Dante Alighieri. 1975. *La Commedia Secondo L'Antica Vulgata*, ed. Giorgio Petrocchi. Torino: Giulio Einaudi.

———. 1989–1991. *The Divine Comedy. Text and Commentary*. 3 vols in 6, ed. and trans. Charles Singleton. Princeton: Princeton University Press.

Delius, Nicolaus. 1887. "Dante's *Commedia* und Brunetto Latini's *Tesoretto.*" *Jahrbücher der deutschen Dantesgesellschaft* 4: 1–23.

Del Virgilio, Giovanni. 1931. *Allegorie Librorum Ovidii Metamorphoseos,* ed. Fausto Ghisalberti. *Giornale Dantesco* 34: 43–111.

Desmond, Marilyn. 1994. *Reading Dido: Gender, Textuality, and the Medieval* Aeneid. Medieval Cultures 8. Minneapolis: University of Minnesota Press.

DiGangi, Mario. 1994. "The Homoerotics of Early Modern Drama." New York: Ph.D. Dissertation, Columbia University.

Dinshaw, Carolyn. 1994. "Heterosexuality and its Consolations in Sir Gawain and the Green Knight." *Diacritics* 24: 205–26.

Ferrante, Joan M. 1984. *The Political Vision of the Divine Comedy.* Princeton: Princeton University Press.

———. 1992. *Dante's Beatrice: Priest of an Androgynous God.* Occasional Papers 2. Binghamton: Center for Medieval and Renaissance Studies.

———. 1993. "A Poetics of Chaos and Harmony" in Jacoff, *The Cambridge Companion.* 153–71.

Foucault, Michel. 1990. *The History of Sexuality. Volume One: An Introduction,* trans. Robert Hurley. New York: Vintage.

Fradenburg, Louise O. 1992. "'Our owen wo to drynke': Loss, Gender, and Chivalry in *Troilus and Criseyde*" in *Chaucer's* Troilus and Criseyde, *"Subgit to alle Poesye": Essays in Criticism,* ed. R. A. Shoaf. Binghamton, NY: Medieval and Renaissance Texts and Studies. 88–106.

Freccero, Carla. 1994. "Cannibalism, Homophobia, Women: Montaigne's 'Des Cannibales' and 'De L'amitié'," in *Women, Race and Writing in the Early Modern Period,* ed. Margo Hendricks and Patricia Parker. London and New York: Routledge. 73–83.

Freccero, John. 1986. *Dante: The Poetics of Conversion.* Cambridge: Harvard University Press.

———. 1991. "The Eternal Image of the Father," in Jacoff and Schnapp, *The Poetry of Allusion.* 62–76.

Goldberg, Jonathan. 1992. *Sodometries: Renaissance Texts, Modern Sexualities.* Stanford: Stanford University Press.

———. ed. 1994. *Queering the Renaissance.* Durham: Duke University Press.

Goodich, Michael. 1979. *The Unmentionable Vice: Homosexuality in the Later Medieval Period.* Santa Barbara: ABC-Clio.

Greenberg, David F. 1988. *The Construction of Homosexuality.* Chicago: University of Chicago Press.

Grosz, Elizabeth. 1994. "Experimental Desire: Rethinking Queer Subjectivity," in *Supposing the Subject,* ed. Joan Copjec. London: Verso. 133–57.

Halley, Janet E. 1994. "*Bowers v. Hardwick* in the Renaissance," in Goldberg, *Queering the Renaissance.* 15–39.

Halperin, David M. 1990. *One Hundred Years of Homosexuality and Other Essays on Greek Love.* New York: Routledge.

Hollander, John. 1969. *Allegory in Dante's "Commedia."* Princeton: Princeton University Press.

———. 1981. *The Figure of Echo: A Mode of Allusion in Milton and After.* Berkeley: University of California Press.

———. *Il Virgilio dantesco: Tragedia nella* Commedia. Florence: Olschki, 1983.

Holsinger, Bruce. 1993. "The Flesh of the Voice: Embodiment and the Homoerotics of Devotion in the Music of Hildegard of Bingen (1098–1179)." *Signs* 19: 93–125.

Hunt, Margaret. 1994. "Afterword," in Goldberg, *Queering the Renaissance.* 359–77.

Jacoff, Rachel. 1993. *The Cambridge Companion to Dante.* Cambridge: Cambridge University Press.

——— and Jeffrey T. Schnapp, eds. 1991a. *The Poetry of Allusion: Virgil and Ovid in Dante's Comedy.* Stanford: Stanford University Press.

———. 1991b. "The Rape/Rapture of Europa: *Paradiso* 27," in Jacoff and Schnapp, *The Poetry of Allusion.* 233–46.

Jed, Stephanie. 1989. *Chaste Thinking: The Rape of Lucretia and the Birth of Humanism.* Bloomington: Indiana University Press.

Kay, Richard. 1978. *Dante's Swift and Strong: Essays on Inferno XV.* Lawrence: Regents Press of Kansas.

Koestenbaum, Wayne. 1989. *Double Talk: The Erotics of Male Literary Collaboration.* New York: Routledge.

Kruger, Steven F. 1994. "Sexual, Racial, and Religious Queerness in the Late Middle Ages." Paper delivered at the 110th Convention of the Modern Language Association, San Diego, CA, December.

Lenzen, Rolf. 1972. "Altercatio Ganimedis et Helene: Kritische Edition mit Kommentar." *Mittellateinisches Jahrbuch* 7: 161–86.

Masten, Jeff. 1994. "My Two Dads: Collaboration and the Reproduction of Beaumont and Fletcher," in Goldberg, *Queering the Renaissance.* 280–309.

Mazzotta, Giuseppe. 1979. *Dante, Poet of the Desert: History and Allegory in the Divine Comedy.* Princeton: Princeton University Press.

Menocal, María Rosa. 1994. *Shards of Love: Exile and the Origins of the Lyric.* Durham: Duke University Press.

Moore, R.I. 1987. *The Formation of a Persecuting Society.* Oxford: Basil Blackwell.

Ovid. 1984. *Metamorphoses.* 2 vols. Loeb Classical Library, ed. and trans. Frank Justus Miller. Cambridge: Harvard University Press.

Ovide moralisé: Poème du commencement du quatorzième siècle, ed. C. de Boer. 1915–1938. 5 vols. Verhandelingen der Koninklijke Akademie van Wetenschappen te Amsterdam, Afdeeling Letterkunde, Nieuwe Reeks, 15 21, 30 no. 3, 37, and 43. Amsterdam: Johannes Müller.

Pequigney, Joseph. 1991. "Sodomy in Dante's Inferno and Purgatorio." *Representations* 36: 22–42.

Petrocchi, Giorgio, ed. 1975. *La Commedia Secondo L'Antica Vulgata.* Torino: Giulio Einaudi.

Pézard, André. 1950. *Dante sous la pluie du feu.* Paris: Vrin.

Rambuss, Richard. 1994. "Pleasure and Devotion: The Body of Jesus and Seventeenth–Century Religious Lyric," in Goldberg. *Queering the Renaissance.* 253–79.

Reynolds, W. D. 1971. "The *Ovidius Moralizatus* of Pierre Bersuire: An Introduction and Translation." Urbana-Champaign: Ph.D. dissertation, University of Illinois.

Ronconi, Allessandro. 1970–1978. "Virgilio," in Bosco, *Enciclopedia dantesca,* 5: 1030–49.

Rubin, Gayle. 1984. "Thinking Sex: Notes for a Radical Theory of the Politics of Sexuality," in Carole S. Vance, ed. *Pleasure and Danger: Exploring Female Sexuality.* New York: Routledge. 267–319.

Rubin, Miri. 1994. "The Person in the Form: Medieval Challenges to Bodily 'Order'," in Sarah Kay and Rubin, ed. *Framing Medieval Bodies.* Manchester: Manchester University Press. 100–122.

Schnapp, Jeffrey. 1991. "Dante's Sexual Solecisms: Gender and Genre in the *Commedia*," in *The New Medievalism,* ed. Marina S. Brownlee *et al.* Baltimore: Johns Hopkins University Press. 201–25.

Schildgen, Brenda Deen. 1989. "Dante's Neologisms in the *Paradiso* and the Latin Rhetorical Tradition." *Dante Studies* 107: 101–19.

Sedgwick, Eve Kosofsky. 1985. *Between Men: English Literature and Male Homosocial Desire.* New York: Columbia University Press.

———. 1990. *Epistemology of the Closet.* Berkeley: University of California Press.

Singleton, Charles, ed. and trans. 1989–1991. *The Divine Comedy: Text and Commentary.* 3 vols. in 6. Princeton: Princeton University Press.

Sowell, Madison U. 1990. "Brunetto's *Tesoro* in Dante's *Inferno.*" *Lectura Dantis* 7: 60–71.

———. 1994. "Dante's Poetics of Sexuality." *Exemplaria* 5: 436–69.

Statius. 1968. *The Medieval Achilleid of Statius,* ed. Paul M. Clogan. Leiden: E. J. Brill.

———. 1989. *Thebaid, Achilleid.* 2 vols. Loeb Classical Library. Trans. J.H. Mozley. Cambridge: Harvard University Press.

Suetonius. 1914. *The Lives of the Caesars*. Loeb Classical Library. Ed and trans. J. C. Rolfe. London: William Heinemann.

Traub, Valerie. 1992. *Desire and Anxiety: Circulations of Sexuality in Shakespearean Drama*. London: Routledge.

Vance, Eugene. 1986. *Mervelous Signals: Poetics and Sign Theory in the Middle Ages*. Lincoln: University of Nebraska Press.

Virgil. 1932. *Eclogues, Georgics, Aeneid*. 2 vols. Loeb Classical Library. Trans. H. Rushton Fairclough. London: Heinemann.

Contributors

DAVID LORENZO BOYD teaches Medieval Studies and Queer Theory in the English Department at the University of Pennsylvania.

MARÍA MERCEDES CARRIÓN is Assistant Professor of Spanish at Emory University. She is the author of *Arquitectura y cuerpo en la figura autorial de Teresa de Jesús* (1994) and several articles on Spanish early modern culture. She has also written on twentieth-century Caribbean poetry and drama and has published a study on *Twin Peaks* and contemporary literary theory. She is currently working on a book-length project: *Acting and Believing. Performance, Discourses and Representation in Seventeeth-Century Spanish Theater.*

RICHARD CORUM is a visiting Assistant Professor of English at the University of California at Santa Barbara. He has published on Milton and Shakespeare in *Milton and the Idea of Woman*, ed. Julia M. Walker (1988) and *Everyday Life in Early Modern Europe: Practice and Representation*, ed. Patricia Fumerton and Simon Hunt (forthcoming).

LORRAINE DASTON is Director of the Max Planck Institute for the History of Science in Berlin, and author of *Classical Probability in the Enlightenment* (1988) as well as numerous articles on the history of science from the sixteenth through nineteenth centuries. She and Katharine Park are completing a book on *Wonders and the Order of Nature.*

LOUISE O. FRADENBURG is Professor of English at the University of California at Santa Barbara. She is the author of *City, Marriage, Tournament: Arts of Rule in Late Medieval Scotland* (1991) and the editor of *Women and Sovereignty* (1992), and has written a number of articles on Chaucer and on late medieval Scottish poetry.

CARLA FRECCERO teaches Literature and Women's Studies at the University of California at Santa Cruz. She has written on early modern authors, feminism, U.S. popular culture and queer theory. At present she is writing a book, *Marguerite de Navarre and the Politics of Maternal Sovereignty*, and is working on a study of early modern masculinities.

SIMON GAUNT is a University Lecturer in French at the University of Cambridge and a Fellow of St. Catharine's College. He is the author of *Troubadours and Irony* (1989) and *Gender and Genre in Medieval French Literature* (1995).

JONATHAN GOLDBERG is Professor of English Literature at Duke University. His most recent book is *Sodometries: Renaissance Texts, Modern Sexualities* (1992). He is the editor of *Queering the Renaissance* (1994) and *Reclaiming Sodom* (1994).

BRUCE HOLSINGER is a graduate student in English and Comparative Literature at Columbia University. He has published an essay on the music of Hildegard of Bingen in *Signs* and has articles forthcoming on Bernard of Clairvaux and Edward Said. His dissertation is a study of music and the human body in medieval culture.

RUTH MAZO KARRAS is Associate Professor of History at Temple University. She is the author of *Common Women: Prostitution and Sexuality in Medieval England* (1996) and *Slavery and Society in Medieval Scandinavia* (1988).

KATHY LAVEZZO is a graduate student at the University of California, Santa Barbara. Her dissertation explores medieval literary typologies.

KARMA LOCHRIE is Associate Professor of English at Loyola University, Chicago. She is the author of *Margery Kempe and Translations of the Flesh* (1991), and is currently working on a book about medieval secrecy.

KATHARINE PARK teaches history and history of science at Wellesley College. In addition to her book project with Lorraine Daston, she is working on as series of articles on the history of anatomical dissection in medieval and Renaissance Italy.

PATRICIA PARKER, Professor of English and Comparative Literature at Stanford University, is the author of *Inescapable Romance* (1979), *Literary Fat Ladies: Rhetoric, Gender, Prosperity* (1987), and *Shakespearian Margins: Language, Culture, Context* (forthcoming). She has also co-edited various critical anthologies, most recently *Women, "Race," and Writing in the Early Modern Period* (1994), with Margo Hendricks. She is currently completing a book on Shakespeare and editing the new Arden edition of *A Midsummer Night's Dream*. The essay in this volume is from a book in progress on early modern gender ideologies.

JOSÉ PIEDRA is Associate Professor of Romance Studies at Cornell University. His latest publications on early perceptions of sexualities are "Nationalizing Sissies," in Paul Julian Smith and Emily Bergman, eds., *¿Entiendes? Queer Readings, Hispanic Writings* (1995) and "Print-Out," in *Poetics Today* 16:1 (1995).

ELIZABETH PITTENGER teaches at the University of California, Berkeley and works on the materiality of writing and bodies in late medieval and Renaissance Europe. She is currently completing a book on textual practices, pedagogy, and pederasty entitled *The Traffic in Pages*.